* * * * *

D'HOLBACH'S COTERIE

* * * *

* * * * *

D'HOLBACH'S COTERIE
An Enlightenment in Paris

* * * * *

Alan Charles Kors

PRINCETON UNIVERSITY PRESS

PRINCETON, NEW JERSEY

Library of Congress Cataloging in Publication Data will
be found on the last printed page of this book.

Publication of this book has been aided by
The Andrew W. Mellon Foundation.

This book has been composed in Linotype Janson.

Printed in the United States of America
by Princeton University Press, Princeton, New Jersey

*To the memory
of my beloved father*

SAMUEL KORS
(1903-1974)

Contents

Preface

THE subtitle of this work, "An Enlightenment in Paris," carries a double meaning. Indeed, the coterie holbachique, in its diversity, its admixture of the profound and the frivolous, its broad tolerance, and its various individual searches for ways to understand and to improve the secular world, constituted an important element, and in some ways a microcosm, of the French Enlightenment. The search *for* the coterie holbachique, however, proved to be an enlightenment of another kind.

I originally went to Paris in 1966-1967 to study the major currents of atheistic thought in the French eighteenth century. Intellectual and literary historians of the Enlightenment had assured me in their works, with an almost total unanimity, that it would be in the coterie holbachique that I would find the major movement toward atheism in the Ancien Régime. I accepted this consensus and began my research.

The first problem I faced (and which indeed gave me pause for thought) was the total absence of agreement on *who* it was, precisely, who had constituted the coterie holbachique. Thus I began the task (at first unnerving for someone anxious to commence a study of ideas) of collating memoirs, correspondences, and diverse recollections, in an attempt to discover the intimates, the regulars of the coterie holbachique. The completion of this list, and long study of the figures involved, led to several startling conclusions: (1) that almost no one had been close to establishing correctly the genuine membership of the coterie; (2) that despite the presence of individual men within the coterie who indeed were atheists, atheism was in no way the common bond or avocation of a majority of its members; and (3) that despite the traditional presentation of the coterie holbachique as somehow removed from the respectable circles of Parisian society, its members formed, on the whole, as publicly successful and contemporaneously prestigious a circle of philosophes, men of letters and scientists as almost any salon or group within the French Enlightenment.

Intrigued, I put my study of eighteenth-century atheism aside for another day and continued my exploration of the coterie. My first goal was to unravel the process by which the coterie holbachique had come to be so misrepresented. This proved to be an activity of no small interest, for there is something frankly fascinating in watching the wrong baton being passed from runner to runner. My second was to place the members of the coterie holbachique, and the coterie *qua* coterie itself, in the context of the problems, thought and structures of the Ancien Régime. This proved to open gates to historical dilemmas that I shall be exploring, I imagine, for many years to come.

The historical problems raised by my research were manifold, but the most initially surprising to me was that of the relationship between the members of the coterie and the society of the Ancien Régime. Interested in how my story would end, I had looked at the collapse of the Ancien Régime in the early years of the Revolution, and I had discovered almost all of my surviving philosophes to be at odds with the new regime almost from the first hints of disorder or fundamental change. The members of the coterie holbachique had been, in so many ways, such strident critics of their society that it seemed odd, at first, to see in them an antipathy not only toward what was most radical in the Revolution, but often toward what was most moderate in it as well. What reasons would these men have, aligned as they had been with almost all that was progressive in the Ancien Régime, for resenting, rejecting, and fearing, almost from the start, a great movement of men and ideas against so much of what they themselves had seen as harmful and anachronistic in their society? Far from being the alienated figures or outcasts that some historians had depicted as the coterie holbachique, the devotees of d'Holbach's circle, it soon became evident, with few exceptions had risen into (and in a few cases had been born into) various elites within the privileged structures of the Ancien Régime. From these heights they had served their causes. Beginning in 1789, those vantages and the roles of the men who occupied them increasingly were under assault. For the coterie holbachique the Revolution meant an end to their place in the process of enlightenment as they conceived of it.

This study, however, in no way represents any effort toward a specific theory of the interaction of society and men of letters. If by "social scientist" one means a scholar for whom data and its internal correlations constitute a set of empirical evidence useful in the construction or testing of a general model or hypothesis concerning social behavior, I am not, in that sense, a social scientist. Rather, it is precisely the data—the individuals, thought and behavior of the coterie holbachique—that I find intrinsically of interest, and it is that data I wish to explore, analyze and structure, guided in my choices less by the outstanding sociological problems of today than by the eighteenth century's sense of its own options and dilemmas. Nothing would please me more, however, than that my work should prove useful to a scholar for whom the coterie holbachique, and indeed the eighteenth century, would be but one of many references within a larger concern. I hope that this will not be deemed reactionary, and that it will not constitute a barrier between any reader and what I consider to be the findings of this book about historical myths, the coterie holbachique, and, as much by negation as by new assertion, the French Enlightenment.

One brief note concerning names is necessary. I have attempted to utilize those eighteenth-century spellings which emerged as fixed in the nineteenth century, and have placed titles in lower case (except for the abbreviated social titles M., Mme, and Mlle), but I have allowed myself the inconsistency of "Baron d'Holbach," instead of "the baron d'Holbach," or "D'Holbach," having come to know him as such, and finding it natural and useful thus to distinguish him.

* * *

I am most deeply grateful to the staffs of the Bibliothèque Nationale, the Archives Nationales, and the Bibliothèque de l'Arsenal, and to the taxpayers of France for the assistance which they rendered to me. In particular, I owe a special debt to the staff of the Bibliothèque de l'Institut for the kindness they showed me during a most inconvenient period in their schedules. To my friends, colleagues and students in the Department of History of the University of Pennsylvania, I hereby express my most profound gratitude for the support and stimulation of their concern and, above all, for their patience. To my wife Erika, I owe more than I should attempt to express in this place.

Alan Charles Kors
Philadelphia, 1975

xi

* * * * *

D'HOLBACH'S COTERIE

* * * *

Introduction

IN the shadows of every historian's distortions and inadequacies lie the partial records of actual men, relationships, and events awaiting the accident of scholarly attention and re-examination. These records may allow the scholar to touch merely the surface of men's lives, actions, and expressed thoughts, but to distinguish by touch the genuine from the unwittingly counterfeit is no small progress in our efforts to link our minds and senses to the past. For many years now I have lived with the records of the coterie holbachique, a circle of philosophes, men of letters and scientists meeting at the homes of Baron Paul Henri Thiry d'Holbach during the last half of the eighteenth century. I am offering, I hope, a contextual portrait and analysis of this coterie that should restore something of the genuine to our sense of its character and its clime.

Despite the intellectual and social prominence of d'Holbach's circle in eighteenth-century Paris, and despite the frequency with which this group has been discussed and alluded to in Enlightenment studies, the coterie holbachique has yet to receive a critical and empirically sound study. The reader exploring secondary literature concerning the coterie is faced with contradictory, incomplete and generally misleading sketches and caricatures of its nature and purposes. This present study is an effort to answer certain fundamental questions concerning the coterie holbachique's composition, its role in the Enlightenment, its place in the Ancien Régime, and its relationship to the French Revolution. In so doing, I also hope to shed additional light upon "the High Enlightenment."

As I have elaborated elsewhere, several historiographical factors have biased and clouded recent commentary on the coterie: the legacy of Rousseau's *Confessions*; the residual influence of the emigration's and Restoration's "myth" of the "club holbachique"; and the continued assumption of certain unique traits diversely and erroneously ascribed to d'Holbach's group by important historians.[1] This is not to say that error has been uniform or that no historian who has discussed the coterie holbachique has not been free of major inaccuracies. It is true, however, that accuracy, on the whole, has been the product of brevity and inadvertence, for in the absence of any systematic study of the coterie and demystification of the tradition surrounding it, the pitfalls before the incidental questioner have been manifold.

Three main themes, occasionally joined, have tended to dominate characterizations of the coterie holbachique: (1) that the coterie was a circle of uniform (or nearly uniform) materialistic atheists;[2] (2) that it was engaged in some zealous common collaboration on projects whose objectives lay beyond the confines of d'Holbach's homes;[3] and (3) that it had a special relationship to the *Encyclopédie*.[4] Throughout most of the nineteenth century, the coterie holbachique had been depicted as a uniquely fanatical salon within the Enlightenment, rabid in its antireligiosity and radical in its alienation from the Ancien Régime.[5] Sev-

[1] Alan Kors, "The Myth of the Coterie Holbachique," in *French Historical Studies*, Fall, 1976, forthcoming.

[2] See, for example, J.-P. Belin, *Le mouvement philosophique de 1748 à 1789* . . . , 266; Pierre Naville, *Paul Thiry d'Holbach et la philosophie scientifique au XVIIIe siècle*, 35-37; Carl Becker, *The Heavenly City of the Eighteenth-Century Philosophers*, 74-77; Manfred Naumann, "Holbach und das Materialismusproblem in französischen Aufklärung," in W. Krauss and M. Meyer, eds., *Grundpositionen der französischen Aufklärung*, 88-90; Paul Hazard, *La pensée Européenne au XVIIIe siècle* . . . , I, 167-171; G. R. Cragg, *The Church and the Age of Reason*, 243-244; Philippe Sagnac, *La formation de la société française moderne* (Paris, 1946), II, 99; Lester Crocker, *Jean-Jacques Rousseau*, I, 197; R. Mousnier et al., *Le XVIIIe siècle* . . . , 76; Albert Rivaud, *Histoire de la Philosophie*, Vol. IV: *Philosophie française et philosophie anglaise de 1700 à 1830* (Paris, 1962), 142-153; F. C. Green, *Jean-Jacques Rousseau* . . . (Cambridge, 1955), 115; Pierre Gaxotte, *Le siècle de Louis XV* (Paris, 1933), 362.

[3] Naville, loc. cit.; Naumann, "Holbach und das Materialismusproblem"; Frank E. Manuel, *The Eighteenth Century Confronts the Gods* (Cambridge, Mass., 1959), 228-241, where he attributes the publication of Boulanger's works to "the Holbachians"; Mousnier et al., loc. cit.; Rivaud, loc. cit., and all those listed in n. 4 below.

[4] Jean Mayer, *Diderot homme de science*, 35-36; Lester Crocker, *Diderot the Embattled Philosopher*, 294-295; Emile Callot, *La philosophie de la vie au XVIIIe siècle*, 323; Joseph R. Smiley, *Diderot's Relations with Grimm*, 11-13; Virgil Topazio, *D'Holbach's Moral Philosophy*, 18; Naville, loc. cit.

[5] See, for example, François Villemain, *Cours de littérature française* 4th edn. (Paris, 1881), III, 124-126; Alexis de Tocqueville, *Histoire philosophique*

eral significant historians have maintained this tradition in the twentieth century.[6] None of these characterizations, we shall see, is correct.

When in 1875 Charles Avezac-Lavigne attempted a fresh study of d'Holbach's circle, he discovered almost no resemblance between the accounts of d'Holbach's dinners offered by the few primary sources he consulted and the traditional views concerning the coterie. He concluded, however, most elaborately and with no documentation whatsoever (for none exists), that there was obviously a coterie within a coterie, a uniform group of "initiates" who met on Thursdays while the more diversified larger group accounted for the Sunday meetings.[7] This wholly erroneous thesis has been repeated in this century in three of the major studies of d'Holbach's thought.[8]

Among both proponents of such depictions of d'Holbach's circle and historians free of such views, however, a critical confusion over the composition of the coterie holbachique has prevailed. For many, reconstruction of the membership of the coterie has been deductive from preconceived ideas of what transpired at d'Holbach's homes. This has led some historians into overly restricted lists of participants, such as Peter Gay's handful of "indefatigable radicals."[9] Others have been drawn into creating fanciful assemblages, such as Carl Becker's "huddled little company of rationalistic enragés," among whom he placed the deceased Meslier and the exiled La Mettrie;[10] or Paul Hazard's "little band" of "monomaniacal" materialists, among whom he placed willy-nilly whomever he considered to be both monomaniacal and materialistic.[11] Emile Callot, believing that d'Holbach's home was vital in the production of the *Encyclopédie*, claimed that "it assembled all of [the *Encyclopédie*'s] collaborators"[12] (which would have been an accomplishment of no small note).

This confusion over the composition of the coterie holbachique

du règne de Louis XV (Paris, 1847), II, 73-74; N. Deschamps, *Les sociétés secrètes et la société*, II, 16-17, 33ff.

[6] Peter Gay, *The Enlightenment: An Interpretation*, I, 398-399; Hazard, loc. cit.; Becker, loc. cit.; Rivaud, loc. cit.

[7] C. Avezac-Lavigne, *Diderot et la société du Baron d'Holbach*, 44-45.

[8] Max Pierson Cushing, *Baron d'Holbach*, 14; Naville, loc. cit.; Topazio, loc. cit.

[9] Gay, loc. cit.

[10] Becker, loc. cit.

[11] Hazard, loc. cit.

[12] Callot, loc. cit.

has made it almost impossible to discuss the group from a common empirical basis. D'Holbach's biographer W. H. Wickwar refrained from characterizing the coterie, having peopled it with virtually every important philosophe who ever had been listed in accounts of visitors, however occasional, to d'Holbach's homes.[13] D'Holbach's intellectual biographer Naville, on the other hand, unable to uncover the requisite number of atheists and materialists, listed an inaccurate handful and signalled the existence of "many others still more obscure."[14] In an anthology of d'Holbach's writings, Paulette Charbonnel described the coterie in terms of the notables of French thought, including d'Alembert, Buffon and Voltaire, and changed its Sunday meeting to Saturday.[15] For Manfred Naumann great men would have been out of place at d'Holbach's coterie, for it was a center of "collective effort," in fact "a center of the revolutionary struggle of the bourgeois ideologues against the feudal-absolutist ideologues of the ancien régime."[16]

Atheists? Collaborators? Encyclopédistes? Notables? Revolutionary ideologues? Obscure materialists? Random visitors to d'Holbach's homes? Indefatigable radicals? To study the coterie holbachique and its relationship to the France around it, we first must know the cast of characters. The sources, indeed, are manifold. The letters, memoirs, published works and recorded observations of those who knew d'Holbach and who visited his coterie constitute a wealth of material which it has been possible to study, to compare and to correlate. As a general rule, historians have relied on uniquely French sources in studying the coterie. There were, however, a host of foreign visitors to d'Holbach's homes, and in their letters and memoirs there exists another set of controls, another source of valuable information. Isolated, each description or recollection offers only a partial view, and often a misleading one. Together they offer the means to identify the members of d'Holbach's circle and the nature of the coterie which they formed.

[13] W. H. Wickwar, *Baron d'Holbach*, 21-27.
[14] Naville, loc. cit.
[15] Paulette Charbonnel, ed., *D'Holbach: Textes Choisis* (Paris, 1957), 7-8.
[16] M. Naumann, "Holbach und das Materialismusproblem."

PART I

The Coterie Holbachique and the Enlightenment

* * * *

ONE · *The Members of the Coterie Holbachique*

WE owe the name "coterie holbachique" to Rousseau, for whom the term "coterie" was a pejorative. In the *Confessions* Jean-Jacques wrote of Grimm, Diderot, d'Holbach, and the social friends of these three figures as "the coterie holbachique," and he described a jealous conspiracy against his person and reputation which he believed them to have inspired and orchestrated.[1] In the course of Enlightenment studies, Rousseau's name for a limited set of friends has come to stand in general for the group of men who met regularly at the dinners of Baron d'Holbach throughout the last half of the eighteenth century, many if not most of whom, in fact, were not included by Rousseau in his own use of that expression.[2] There is little to be gained by divesting this important assembly of the name by which it now is called, but to avoid confusion we must be specific in our use of it. There was indeed a circle of men who met regularly and frequently at d'Holbach's homes, and who could identify each other as members of a unique group. It is these men whom we designate as the coterie holbachique.

The dinners and conversations of which Baron d'Holbach was the host were by no means closed affairs. Many figures—friends and critics of the philosophes alike—were occasional guests. Many foreigners and diplomats partook of his hospitality during their stays in Paris. Certain men became intimates of these dinners for a short time, but returned only infrequently, if at all, thereafter. In the course of the approximately thirty-five years during which d'Holbach held his Thursday and Sunday gatherings, a gallery of prominent Frenchmen and Europeans passed through his doors with varying degrees of individual frequency. Death robbed these meetings of several regular visitors, and before the end of d'Holbach's reign as the "maître d'Hotel de la Philosophie," as Galiani once called him, men born after the tradition of these assemblies

[1] Rousseau, *Confessions*, 439-591 passim.
[2] Alan Kors, "The Myth of the Coterie Holbachique," *loc. cit.*

had begun were being welcomed at them. Among the thinkers, men of letters and scientists who remained, in the midst of this flux, constant in their attendance and in their appreciation of these dinners, a group-identity arose, one among many such Parisian identities individuals might hold, in this case manifested in their references to themselves and other devotees as members of "the club," "the synagogue," "the bakery," "the Friends of the rue Royale."[3]

It is necessary and helpful, thus, to make a distinction between d'Holbach's salon and the coterie holbachique. The salon flourished for almost a generation, opening its doors to an ever-changing stream of guests. The coterie was composed of the figures —the men for whom d'Holbach's dinners were a regular and important part of their lives—whom this stream of guests came to visit, whose ideas they came to confront. If originally the coterie arose from the salon, it nevertheless was the coterie which provided the significance that the salon was to enjoy. From a gathering of friends in 1749 through 1751, the salon of Baron d'Holbach developed into one of the most intellectually stimulating and widely known private groups in Europe. By the mid-1760s d'Holbach made an effort to limit the growing number of guests, to restore much of the initial intimacy of his circle.[4] Guests still came, and anyone of particular prominence or interest was almost certain to be welcomed, but as always, the two groups, devotees and occasional guests, could be distinguished by the regularity of their presence and by the manner in which they spoke of the "friends of the rue Royale" or were spoken of by them. It was from the personalities and ideas of the devotees that the tone, interests, and conversations of the gatherings at d'Holbach's homes were derived. These devotees, the men who gave d'Holbach's salon its singular character, constituted the "coterie holbachique." From a study and collation of available sources—the letters, memoirs, and written works of regular and occasional visitors to d'Holbach's homes and, to be employed more circumspectly, those of their friends or families—the coterie can be identified.

First, there are those who were unquestionably members of the

---

[3] See infra, Chapter Three.

[4] Diderot, *Corr.*, v, 213-214. In this letter of December 10, 1765, Diderot informed Sophie Volland that "we no longer were having regulated dinners at the rue Royale. The Baron finally became tired of having twenty-seven to twenty-eight people, when he was expecting only twenty."

coterie, in terms both of the sufficiency of the available data and the clear nature of their association. These can be divided into two groups: (1) those who were participants throughout most of the period from 1750 to 1780—Baron d'Holbach, Denis Diderot, Friedrich-Melchior Grimm, Charles-Georges Le Roy, Jean-François Marmontel, Guillaume-Thomas-François Raynal, Augustin Roux, Jean-François de Saint-Lambert, Jean-Baptiste-Antoine Suard; and (2) those who were participants only throughout most of the period from 1760 to 1780—François-Jean de Chastellux, André Morellet, Jacques-André Naigeon. Roughly speaking, these periods are natural divisions in the life of the coterie holbachique. In the 1750s the coterie acquired its dominant characteristics, and its intimate membership became stabilized; in the 1760s and 1770s it achieved and enjoyed its brilliant international reputation.

Second, there are those to whose status certain substantive qualifications must be attached—Ferdinando Galiani and Claude-Adrien Helvétius. Finally, there are two problematic cases for discussion—that of Jean Darcet, arising from the insufficiency of the data but resolved in favor of inclusion; and that of Nicolas-Antoine Boulanger, arising from the suggestive nature of certain evidence and the tradition linking him to d'Holbach's circle, but resolved in the necessity of an exclusion.

* * *

The cast of characters is a mixture of men who require little introduction as figures of the French Enlightenment and men who have fallen into relative historical obscurity. This is not yet the place to study their lives in detail, however, but rather to make their acquaintance and to examine their status as members of the coterie holbachique.

I. PARTICIPANTS, c. 1750–c. 1780

Paul Henri Thiry, Baron d'Holbach (1723-1789). Heir to a large fortune, Baron d'Holbach began entertaining his friends lavishly in Paris during 1749-1750, shortly after his return from the University of Leyden, where he had studied from 1744 to 1748 or 1749. Alexander Carlyle, at Leyden during the same years, recalled the University as a center of remarkable coffee parties, club suppers and constant group conversations. It is perhaps to the

11

Baron's remembrances of his student milieu and its pleasures, and not to a Parisian tradition of salon life, that the coterie holbachique owed its inspiration.[5]

Originally, d'Holbach's dinners grouped his social friends, men such as Margency and Gauffecourt, to cite the two early associates recalled by Mme d'Epinay, and the young intellectuals of Paris whose acquaintance he was making, notably Diderot, Rousseau, Grimm, Marmontel, Roux, Suard and Raynal. Within a short time, his dinners had attracted the scientists Barthez (an anatomist and medical doctor) and Venel (a chemist and medical doctor), and several figures of already established reputations, such as d'Alembert, Duclos, Buffon, and the chemist Rouelle the elder. In the course of the 1750s, Rousseau, Buffon, and d'Alembert ceased to attend d'Holbach's salon; Rouelle appeared (it would seem) less and less frequently, and Barthez and Venel left Paris to accept posts at the University of Montpellier; Duclos left the coterie in 1762. To those who remained, d'Holbach added new friends, namely Le Roy and Saint-Lambert. As the dinners achieved an intellectual level increasingly esoteric and philosophical, d'Holbach's more mundane friends appeared only at rare occasions.[6]

In 1759 d'Holbach purchased the home on the rue Royale, butte Saint-Roch that has become synonymous with his coterie.[7] In addition he would entertain at his family's estate at Grandval, several miles from Paris, where, during the summer, guests often would stay for weeks on end. It is perhaps the Baron's use of Grandval that has led to a certain confusion concerning the coterie. At the rue Royale, d'Holbach entertained, in his own name, the regulars of the coterie and, by special invitation, selected guests. At Grandval, d'Holbach clearly entertained in the name of the d'Aine family, often lodging friends of the family for extended periods. In the midst of the vacation at Grandval, the coterie as well would often assemble for dinners. It was not that d'Holbach had two separate philosophical dinners throughout the

[5] See Carlyle's descriptions of student life at Leyden in *The Autobiography of Dr. Alexander Carlyle of Inveresk, 1722-1805*, J. H. Burton, ed., 172-191.

[6] On the early years of d'Holbach's salon, see Rousseau, *Confessions*, 412-415, 437, 457-458; Marmontel, *Mémoires*, I, 229-230, 482-486; *Mémoires de Madame d'Epinay*, P. Boiteau, ed., II, passim.

[7] John Lough, "Le baron d'Holbach. Quelques documents inédits ou peu connus," in *RHLF* (1957), 532. The house is now number 8, rue des Moulins.

year, one for the initiates and one for the lay public (there simply is no evidence for such a description). Rather, d'Holbach was both the head of a family which entertained often at Grandval *and* the host of a coterie which he assembled twice a week at the rue Royale while in Paris, and frequently but less punctually at Grandval during the season.[8]

D'Holbach's great wealth gave to his salon a glitter beyond its intellectual pleasures. He had, by all accounts, an excellent chef, many servants, abundant and memorable foods, and a remarkable collection of vintage wines. His home offered stimulating resources to the figures whom he entertained: he had a cabinet of natural history, a library of over 3,000 volumes and a large number of paintings by France's leading artists. In addition, he was lavish in his generosity; he supported several poor writers, painters and musicians, including Rousseau for a while, though for the latter the Baron merely was fulfilling his obligation to society in this. The initial success of his salon, therefore, may not have been due solely to the joy of its conversations.[9]

As a man of letters and philosopher, d'Holbach's name was largely unknown in his own time. He wrote voluminously, and a complete bibliography of the works in which he had a major or the single hand would comprise over fifty titles and perhaps 400 articles.[10] Yet almost every work he translated, published, edited or wrote, from the most innocuous or scientific to the most philosophically daring, was published in the strictest anonymity. His most famous work, the *Système de la nature*, published in 1770, raised a storm in eighteenth-century France second only perhaps to that occasioned by *De l'esprit*, and because of its aggressive atheism enjoyed a notoriety second to no work of his contemporaries. To have known the identity of its author, however, one would have had to hear him discuss his ideas with the coterie holbachique and believe him capable of writing or publishing them. Many of those who heard him decided that he was this

[8] On life at Grandval, see in particular Diderot, *Corr.*, II, 263-267, 279-286, 317-321; III, 86-88, 127-150, 164-182, 217-245; VII, 139-153; IX, 94-96; X, 157-164.

[9] See Rousseau, *Corr.* (Leigh), IV, 396. On the sources for d'Holbach's salon, see infra, Chapter Three.

[10] See in particular J. Vercruysse, *Bibliographie descriptive des écrits du baron d'Holbach*, which reviews and supersedes all prior work; see also John Lough, "Essai de bibliographie critique des publications du Baron d'Holbach," in *RHLF* (1939), 215-236; and Rudolf Besthorn, *Textkritische Studien zum Werk Holbachs*.

author, but they were the only ones who knew. The record reveals they kept their secret.[11] To all others the Baron was merely the wealthy host and friend of European men of letters.

Denis Diderot (1713-1784). Known to the public primarily as the editor and motive force of the *Encyclopédie*, Diderot was known to his friends and the intimates of the coterie holbachique, as he would become known to later readers of his works, as a profound philosopher, literary artist, critic and intellectual speculator par excellence. At once a scientist and poet, a cynic and dreamer, a naturalist and metaphysician, a concrete moral absolutist and abstract moral relativist, Diderot held within his own mind and imagination the diversity and dialectic of the Enlightenment. With justice his peers called him "le Philosophe."

Diderot's correspondence offers students of the Enlightenment access to the intimate details of the coterie holbachique as viewed by its most eloquent member. Above all, Diderot communicated in his letters the mood and the ambiance of the circle around d'Holbach. His correspondence is not always the most satisfying source of names and identifications, since he often assumed that its recipients knew who was there, but he made the coterie come alive, captured its tone and caught both its humor and its depth.

The evidence is contradictory as to exactly when Diderot first became involved with Baron d'Holbach. Few of Diderot's letters prior to 1759 are extant. Arthur M. Wilson, basing his opinion upon the fact that d'Holbach did not collaborate on the *Encyclopédie* until volume ii, suggested that their relations most probably began in the fall of 1751. Rousseau, on the other hand, discussing the events of 1751, wrote much later in the century that d'Holbach was already "linked for a long time with Diderot." Since d'Holbach had not established himself in Paris until 1749, however, one can say safely that at some time between then and 1751 the two men became friends, and that by 1751 the circle of Diderot, Rousseau, Grimm and d'Holbach was flourishing. Writing of the four of them as they were in 1751, Rousseau declared that "Our principal meeting place . . . was the home of Baron d'Holbach."[12]

From this time until the end of his life, Diderot remained the

---

[11] See Morellet's discussion in his *Mémoires*, i, 132-134.

[12] Arthur M. Wilson, *Diderot: The Testing Years*, 175-176; Rousseau, *Confessions*, 437-439.

intimate friend, confidant and intellectual associate of Baron d'Holbach. Extraordinarily different in temperaments and in the parameters of their speculations, the two nevertheless remained inseparable. Diderot was a constant—perhaps, with the exception of Suard, the most constant—guest at d'Holbach's dinners, both at the rue Royale and at Grandval. Once, he missed attending the gatherings of the coterie for two consecutive weeks while still in Paris and was obliged to offer explanations and apologies to the Baron.[13] Diderot disliked the social life of Paris, and rarely accepted invitations or visited salons. To one salon alone did he offer himself wholeheartedly, and only there was he truly at ease away from home. There were many "barons" in his correspondence, but d'Holbach was always "the baron" or "our baron." They often exasperated each other, but always they quickly were reconciled.[14] The conversations and the comfort that d'Holbach had to offer meant a great deal to Diderot, and the coterie holbachique became a major part of his life. Diderot contributed, in return, a major part of the vitality of the coterie. His verbal pyrotechnics made deep impressions on visitors and devotees of the coterie alike. Morellet, recalling in his memoirs the people with whom he had contact at d'Holbach's home, described the impact of "le Philosophe": "It was there that I heard . . . Diderot, treating a question of philosophy, of the arts or of literature, and, by his impromptu exuberance, his fecundity, his inspired manner, captivating our attention for so long a time."[15]

Friedrich-Melchior Grimm (1723-1807). Diplomat, Parisian literary and political correspondent for several European courts, and occasional contributor on German culture to the *Mercure*, Grimm was best known to his contemporaries as the author of a biting satire in the midst of the "music war" between partisans of French and of Italian Opera.[16] He has become best known to historians

---

[13] Diderot, *Corr.*, IV, 44.   [14] Ibid., VII, 147-149.

[15] Morellet, *Mémoires*, I, 128-130. Almost all the sources cited in this chapter document the status of Diderot as a member of the coterie holbachique and offer insight into his relationship with them. Of greatest value are Diderot's own letters describing this relationship as it developed throughout the century, especially the letters addressed to Sophie Volland. For the relevance, freshness and sensitive understanding of its view of Diderot during that period of his life when his relationship with d'Holbach's circle was being made durable, see Wilson, *Diderot*.

[16] F.-M. Grimm, *Le petit prophète de Boemischbroda, le correcteur des bouffons et la guerre de l'Opéra.*

as the author of a remarkable *Correspondance littéraire, philosophique et critique*, at once a rich journal of its time and an as yet largely unappreciated source of Grimm's own confrontation with the problems of eighteenth-century philosophy.

Grimm arrived in Paris early in 1749. At the home of the prince of Saxe-Gotha, he met Rousseau; their mutual love of music led to long discussions and an initially warm friendship. According to the *Confessions*, it was Rousseau who soon thereafter introduced Grimm into the salons of Paris, including that of Baron d'Holbach, wanting him to meet Diderot, Marmontel, Raynal and d'Alembert, with whom Jean-Jacques already was friendly.[17]

For few other figures is the documentation of participation in the coterie holbachique more rich than it is for Grimm. He was Diderot's closest friend throughout most of their lives and thus the man about whom Diderot wrote most in his letters; his presence at d'Holbach's dinners was mentioned explicitly by Diderot more than that of any other individual. Grimm himself, writing to Catherine the Great in November 1779, mentioned "Baron d'Holbach, in whose home I have lived for thirty years."[18] The word "lived," of course, was figurative, but the regularity of Grimm's attendance of the coterie and the sense of close relation which he felt towards the group made its use justifiable. In a "Philosophical Sermon," Grimm self-deprecatingly described his place within the coterie holbachique, employing the same hyperbolic Biblical flourish which had given such success to his musical satire:

> Philosophical Sermon: Pronounced New Years Day, 1770. In the Great Synagogue of the Rue Royale, butte Saint-Roch, In the presence of the arch-priests, petty marquis, and other dignitaries, as well as the simple faithful of the Philosophical Communion, Professing Reason in Paris, by Me, Native of Ratisbon, Minor Prophet, and Unworthy Missionary in the Lands and Languages Beyond China, and in the North, and one of the Least among the Faithful. . . .[19]

Given the force of his personality and the depth of his mind, however, Grimm surely was by no means "one of the least" among the coterie, but one of the most respected and stimulating. His

[17] Rousseau, *Confessions*, 437-439.
[18] *Lettres de Grimm à l'Impératrice Cathérine II*, 69-70.
[19] Grimm, *Corr. litt.*, VIII, 413-414.

regular presence at d'Holbach's gatherings is attested to abundantly for every year between 1751 and 1773, when he left for Russia. Throughout the 1770s he was often away from Paris, but when he was there, he was again at d'Holbach's home. Supremely independent in his thought and in his life, he lived comfortably for over thirty years in the circle of the coterie holbachique.[20]

Charles-Georges Le Roy (1723-1789). Charles-Georges Le Roy, Royal Lieutenant of the Hunt, is one of the forgotten men of the eighteenth century despite the fact that his alleged "confession" played so prominent a part in the formation of the myth of the coterie holbachique. He published all of his works pseudonymously, lived quietly (except for his notorious amorous escapades, well-known among his friends), and left few traces. Under his pseudonym "the Physician of Nuremberg," however, he was known to his century as an original thinker, and he was a central figure of the coterie holbachique. From his youth, Le Roy was a close friend of Helvétius. In the late 1740s or early 1750s, according to his friend and first biographer Roux-Fazillac, he began making acquaintances in the Parisian world of letters, including friendships with Diderot, d'Alembert, d'Holbach and Suard.[21] Perhaps it was at the gatherings of the coterie that Diderot discovered Le Roy to be capable of treating subjects relating to agriculture, forestry and animal behavior, and invited him to write for the *Encyclopédie*, where his first articles appeared in 1755. Apart from the coterie, Le Roy frequented primarily aristocratic circles, in which he was not likely to meet Diderot. At any rate, Diderot's cor-

[20] On Grimm as a member of the coterie holbachique, see ibid., I, 3-13 (by Meister); III, 59-71 (by Grimm); VIII, 413-439; Diderot, *Corr.*, passim; Rousseau, *Confessions*, passim; Marmontel, *Mémoires*, I, 229-230; Galiani, *Lettres de l'Abbé Galiani . . .* , E. Asse, ed., I, 216-217, 360-363; Mme d'Epinay, *Mémoires*, I, 422; P. and A. Verri, *Carteggio di Pietro e di Alessandro Verri*, I, 112-115; "Journal" of Dr. Burney, in R. A. Leigh, "Les Amitiés Françaises du Dr. Burney," *Revue de littérature comparée* (1951), 166-167; d'Holbach to Hume in *Letters of Eminent Persons Addressed to David Hume*, John Hill Burton, ed., 252-256; Wilkes, *The Correspondence of the Late John Wilkes with His Friends*, John Alman, ed., IV, 68; d'Holbach, "Lettres inédites du baron et de la baronne d'Holbach à l'abbé Galiani," 22-23; Grimm, *Lettres à Cathérine II*, 69-70.

[21] See Roux-Fazillac, "Introduction," in Le Roy, *Lettres philosophiques sur l'intelligence et la perfectabilité des animaux, avec quelques lettres sur l'homme*, v-xiv. On Le Roy during these years, see also the Hennin manuscript account of his relations with Helvétius: Bibliothèque de l'Institut, MS 1223, folios 82-87. On his "confession," see Kors, *loc. cit.*

17

respondence reveals that Le Roy was one of the most assiduous devotees throughout the 1760s. It is possible that his attendance slackened somewhat in the 1770s, for there is less mention of him, and that he was increasingly spending time in more purely aristocratic milieus. Nevertheless, members of the coterie still wrote of him familiarly, and there is further evidence in favor of continued rather than weakening ties. His response to Voltaire's attacks upon certain members of the coterie bears this out, as does his close attention to the problems of Suard at this later time. Above all, however, if we assume that his alleged "confession" was based on *something* that he told his courtier friends, he was still a close participant in the life of the coterie during the period of d'Holbach's publications of atheistic works throughout the 1770s.[22]

Le Roy almost had been forced to leave the coterie in 1762, but a reconciliation was effected. According to Diderot's letters, Le Roy became involved in a romantic intrigue at d'Holbach's home. The story allows us to see the coterie in its less intellectual pursuits. At almost the same moment of time, it seems, two betrayals occurred: Suard declared his love to the Baronne d'Holbach (the Baron's second wife); and Charles-Pineau Duclos, Grimm's rival for the affection of Mme d'Epinay, informed the latter, falsely, that Grimm had seduced the Baronne d'Holbach. Mme d'Epinay, infuriated, informed the Baron of both of these events, raising a hornets' nest, to say the least. In the end Suard apologized profusely and, encouraged by his friends, began to seek a wife; Grimm was absolved of the deed and any intention to commit the deed; Duclos was declared *persona non grata* at the coterie; and relations between d'Holbach and Mme d'Epinay were temporarily chilled. The Baronne, however, was so upset by all of this that she became depressed and ill. Her doctor, the famous Gatti (who, if we are

[22] On Le Roy as a member of the coterie holbachique, see Diderot, *Corr.*, passim, and especially volumes II-V. Georges Roth, writing of Le Roy's attack on Voltaire in 1772, termed the former "the henchman of the coterie holbachique" at this period (Diderot, *Corr.*, XII, 52), but this description assumed a putative uniformity of opinions and motives; Le Roy's role, however, does argue in favor of continued close ties with d'Holbach, Helvétius, etc. On Le Roy's continued attention to the problems of his friends at the coterie during this period, see Mme Suard, *Essais de mémoires sur M. Suard*, 84-88; D.-J. Garat, *Mémoires historiques sur le XVIII⁰ siècle et sur M. Suard*, I, 316-317; and Morellet, *Lettres de l'Abbé Morellet . . . à Lord Shelburne . . . 1772-1803*, Lord E. Fitzmaurice, ed., 18, 22-23.

to believe Diderot, was also in love with the Baronne), prescribed a milk diet and a regime of horseback riding in the fresh air. Le Roy, who was a great equestrian, was chosen to be her companion on these rides since he had access to the most beautiful woods at Vincennes and so much free time. According to Diderot, however, Le Roy was a "satyr" of no small accomplishment and had a reputation for being carried away by passion and for seduction. In short time, he too declared his love to d'Holbach's wife. The Baronne rejected him, informed her husband, and once again the coterie was thrown into a turmoil. Le Roy now joined Suard in the cycle of abject apology, depression, and repentance, and he too was forgiven before too long; to Diderot's profound relief, he was readmitted to the good graces of the coterie. Gatti recommended milk and horseback riding to Grimm and Le Roy, and Diderot attempted to make sense of it all in letters to Sophie Volland. The letters make for splendid reading, and they also bear witness to the place that Le Roy, whom Galiani called "the hunter-historian of beasts," held within the coterie.[23]

Jean-François Marmontel (1723-1799). A playwright, poet, editor, novelist, librettist and critic, Marmontel was one of the true literary lions of eighteenth-century Europe, as widely read, and in as many countries and languages, as almost any other figure of his age. He was best known for his novels *Bélisaire* (1767) and *Les Incas* (1772), his phenomenally successful *Contes moraux* (published and augmented throughout the 1750s and 1760s), his management of the *Mercure* (1758-1759, in which time he transformed and revitalized it), and his librettos for the comic-operas of Piccini. An early friend of d'Holbach, Diderot and Rousseau, Marmontel was an intimate of the coterie holbachique for as long a period as any figure. He wrote of this association proudly and informatively (if less than candidly) in his *Mémoires*, and all of the relevant sources support his claim of a close and enduring relationship.[24] In 1790, reviewing a posthumous work on morality

[23] Diderot, *Corr.*, IV, 38-148. Galiani's nickname for Le Roy can be found in a letter to Mme d'Epinay, in Galiani, *Lettres*, I, 314.

[24] Marmontel, *Mémoires*, I, 229-230, 481-489; II, 9-11. Marmontel asserted in his *Mémoires* (I, 484-486) that he *never* heard atheism discussed in his presence, which was scarcely possible. On Marmontel as a member of the coterie holbachique, see, in addition to his own *Mémoires* and other sources cited in the following paragraphs, Morellet, *Mémoires*, I, 128, 199; Garrick, *The Letters of David Garrick*, D. M. Little and G. M. Kahrl,

by d'Holbach for the *Mercure*, he offered the opinion that the book was intrinsically valuable for its ideas, and added: "But its interest is even livelier for those who, having enjoyed for forty years the intimate company of the Author, saw him put this sincere and gentle Philosophy into practice. . . ."[25]

Since d'Holbach had died in 1789, Marmontel, by his own account, would appear to have been among the first group of persons to frequent d'Holbach's home. This is supported by Rousseau's assertion that he maintained a friendship with Marmontel at d'Holbach's dinners prior to Jean-Jacques' departure from the group in the mid-1750s,[26] and by the evidence in a facsimile of a letter by Marmontel in the possession of the Bibliothèque Nationale. On the basis of internal evidence the letter must have been written in 1749 or early 1750, since Marmontel spoke of his poverty. Its recipient must have been Baron d'Holbach since it cited Gauffecourt, d'Alembert and Diderot, all of whom were close friends of d'Holbach at the time and participants in his unique group (Gauffecourt was a personal friend of the Baron with no other real ties to Parisian literary society). This letter undoubtedly signalled Marmontel's desire to continue to be present at dinners he apparently already had sampled, and it is of great interest because of the insight it offers into the carefree mood of these early gatherings: "Eh what, my dear friend! You are realizing the banquet of Plato tomorrow, and I am not a part of it! 'You are not a sage,' you will tell me. It is true. I do not have this honor; but I like sages. I like you above all. I like M. d'Alembert, Diderot, and I strongly wish to be liked by them. After all, is M. de Gauffecourt a sage, who drinks champagnes, who eats fresh oysters seven days a week? Nevertheless, you invited him. You marry Sparta and Sybaris. Do you think that you do worse when you bring together the Lyceum and Parnassus? By what measure do you weigh philosophes? I know everything that nature tells me, I take men as they are, I have no money and

eds., II, 841-842; d'Holbach, "Lettres à Galiani," 22-23; Diderot, *Corr.*, passim; Cérutti, "Lettre sur d'Holbach" in the *Journal de Paris* (1789); Galiani, *Lettres*, I, 46-48, 79, 216-217; II, 219, 308-312; Verri, *Carteggio*, I, 112-115; "Dr. Burney, 'Journal'" (Leigh), 170; Mme Geoffrin, *Correspondance inédite du Roi Stanislaus-Auguste . . . (1764-1777)*, C. de Moüy, ed., 238.

[25] *Mercure de France*, 17 July 1790, 113-121.

[26] Rousseau, *Confessions*, 592-593.

I don't give a damn. I am thus a philosophe, ergo I should be at your dinner, and I invite you to invite me [*je vous prie de m'en prier*], *bonjour*. [signed] Marmontel."[27]

All the evidence points to the fact that he was an early member of the coterie, and a constant and permanent one.

Abbé Guillaume-Thomas-François Raynal (1713-1796). Priest, editor, literary correspondent, ghost-writer for the powerful, political historian and, toward the last decades of the Ancien Régime, the Enlightenment's premier philosophical historian, Raynal, as was true of Marmontel, has fallen from contemporary eminence to relative historical obscurity. Author of a work which caused a major *affaire* in the world of letters and politics, his *Histoire philosophique et politique des établissements du commerce des Européens dans les Deux Indes* (1770), Raynal by 1789 was the most widely read and widely hailed living philosophe in France and, with Rousseau and Voltaire, one of the three most celebrated names in the world of the reading public.

Raynal's association with the coterie holbachique was a long and a fruitful one. In the late 1740s, having left the clergy and entered the world of Parisian administrative and diplomatic circles, he began to frequent the social and literary salons of Paris, meeting Rousseau, according to the *Confessions*, in 1748. By 1750 he was a close friend of Diderot, Grimm and d'Holbach as well and a regular guest at d'Holbach's home.[28] According to Morellet, who singled him out particularly in this regard, "the abbé Raynal was one of the most assiduous persons at our meetings at Baron d'Holbach's," and noted that he was "continually working on his books in the society."[29] It was undoubtedly this latter trait that has raised some suspicions that his hand in his own *Histoire philosophique* was a minor one, but a letter from Walpole to a friend, after a visit to the coterie, indicates that "working" for Raynal meant talking a great deal about his subject and soliciting whatever information he could.[30] In short, Raynal gave to the coterie his great wealth of knowledge about commerce and the international situation, and received from them, as he did from other groups of friends, whatever information and advice they had to offer. The sources reveal that, as one of the earliest members of

[27] B.N., Imprimés: Ln27. 13548.   [28] Rousseau, *Confessions*, 437-439.
[29] Morellet, *Mémoires*, I, 214-215.
[30] Walpole, *The Letters of Horace Walpole*, Paget Toynbee, ed., IX, 92.

the coterie, Raynal's intimacy with it endured until his departure from Paris in 1781.[31]

Augustin Roux (1726-1776). Medical doctor, chemist, a leading scientific editor and a philosopher, Augustin Roux was not widely known by the broad reading public in the eighteenth century, and he is virtually unmentioned today. He enjoyed the quiet respect of the French scientific and medical communities and, in Bordeaux and in Paris, of the world of letters, but as his friends complained after Roux's death, his contributions were quickly forgotten.[32] He was most famous as the editor of the *Journal de médecine, chirurgie, et pharmacie*, a post which he held from 1762 until his death.

In 1751 Roux arrived in Paris from Bordeaux. He threw himself in with a group, including Jean Darcet, of former students of the University of Bordeaux. They positioned themselves in the capital around the person and the patronage of their region's most eminent figure, Montesquieu. In this circle Roux met Darcet's friend Suard and was soon a guest at the home of Baron d'Holbach.[33] It is impossible to date precisely his entry into d'Holbach's circle, but by 1753 or 1754 at the latest, he was collaborating with d'Holbach on translations of foreign scientific works. Soon he was one of the Baron's closest friends.[34] From the early 1750s, then, until his death, he enjoyed an intimate involvement with the coterie holbachique.[35]

[31] See Rousseau, loc. cit.; Morellet, *Mémoires*, I, 128-129, 214-215; Cérutti, "Lettre au *Journal de Paris*"; Diderot, *Corr.*, v, passim, and VII, 157-160; Galiani, *Lettres*, I, 219; Ramsey, "Journal," 132-133.

[32] See Jean Darcet, *Eloge de M. Roux*; Deleyre, *Eloge de M. Roux*; and J.-A. Naigeon, "Lettre sur M. Roux," in Deleyre, op. cit., 60-72.

[33] Darcet, *Eloge de Roux*; Deleyre, *Eloge de Roux*.

[34] Darcet, *Eloge de Roux*; Deleyre, *Eloge de Roux*.

[35] In addition to the *éloges* of Roux by Darcet, Deleyre, and Naigeon on Roux as a member of the coterie holbachique, see Morellet, *Mémoires*, I, 128-134; Marmontel, *Mémoires*, I, 484-486; Mme d'Epinay, *Gli Ultimi Anni della Signora d'Epinay. Lettere Inedite All'Abate Galiani (1773-1782)*, Fausto Nicolini, ed., 31; J.-B.-A. Suard, *Lettres inédites de Suard à Wilkes*, Gabriel Bonno, ed., 51; d'Holbach, "Lettres inédites . . . à l'abbé Galiani," 24-27; Diderot, *Corr.*, VII, 157-160. Roux thought highly of d'Holbach; in one of his scientific articles, he introduced an assertion with the comment: "Here is an even more extraordinary fact, which was communicated to me by M. le Baron d'Holbach, whose testimony is more than sufficient to insure its truth." See Roux, "Observations. . . ," in *Journal de médecine* (Sept. 1762), 237.

Roux's conversation at d'Holbach's dinners impressed many listeners, and he must be seen as one of the central figures of the group. To the world he was a scientist and an unassuming public figure; to his friends at the coterie holbachique he was a philosopher of merit as well and, in their dialogues, an exciting and daring thinker. Morellet described him matching wits with Diderot at d'Holbach's gatherings, "each one trying to outdo the other"; Marmontel called him "a man of genius"; Darcet recalled that his austerity became "gaiety" in their company.[36] That his name is so wholly unfamiliar is a reflection of the minor role he played in the *causes célèbres* of his day, and not of his actual place within d'Holbach's society.

Jean-François de Saint-Lambert (1716-1803). In his own time, Saint-Lambert was best known as a soldier, poet, and, toward the end of his days, a philosopher. The author of several widely read essays and *contes*, he achieved one of the great literary successes of the eighteenth century with his *Les Saisons* (1770), a lengthy poem about nature and rural life which caught the public imagination and catapulted him to literary fame.

In 1750 Saint-Lambert arrived in Paris from the court of the King of Poland at Lunéville and quickly came to the attention of Parisian literary salons where, according to Grimm, his verse had circulated in manuscript form from the late 1740s.[37] At the home of Mlle Quinault, in 1750, he met Mme d'Epinay, and through the latter he met and became the friend of Rousseau, Grimm, Diderot and d'Holbach; it was also through Mme d'Epinay that he met her sister-in-law, Mme d'Houdetot, whose lover and companion he became in a relationship that lasted and flourished for over fifty years.[38] Leaving Paris throughout the 1750s for three- or four-month periods of military service, Saint-Lambert became, while in Paris, a regular guest at d'Holbach's dinners. Indeed, it was Saint-Lambert who published d'Holbach's first anticlerical work, *Le Christianisme dévoilé* (1756), in strictest secrecy in Nancy, while there on military affairs.[39]

[36] Morellet, *Mémoires*, I, 130-132; Marmontel, *Mémoires*, I, 484-486; Darcet, *Eloge de Roux*, 16-18.

[37] Grimm, *Corr. litt.*, II, 270-272.

[38] Mme d'Epinay, *Mémoires*, I, 215ff.

[39] A.-A. Barbier, *Dictionnaire des Ouvrages Anonymes et Pseudonymes*, I, 594-596. The testimony here was provided by Naigeon to Barbier. Cf. Vercruysse, *Bibliographie*.

The dominating presence at the salon of Mme Necker, Saint-Lambert was equally a devoted and constant member of the coterie holbachique. Although it is true his association with the coterie was broken by several extended military tours of duty, it began in the early 1750s, resumed in full in the late years of that decade, and continued unabated until the 1780s. A long relationship, this association was an intellectually rewarding one for all concerned. For Saint-Lambert it exposed a versifier to serious philosophy, a subject to which he was increasingly drawn and to which he was to devote the latter part of his life. For the coterie he added what Marmontel described as a certain non-Parisian and refreshing tone. "No one," Marmontel wrote, "conversed with a sounder reason, nor with more exquisite taste. This taste was that of the little court of Lunéville, where he had lived, and whose tone he maintained."[40] Deeply concerned with his reputation and his status, Saint-Lambert was one of those who would have dreaded most the knowledge of his future obscurity.

Jean-Baptiste-Antoine Suard (1733-1817). Suard was a ubiquitous figure in the world of eighteenth-century letters. A journalist, literary correspondent, editor, critic, polemicist and prestigious translator, he engaged in precisely the sort of work which made his name famous in his own time, without leaving an enduring monument for posterity. As a result, he is little-known today.

Suard arrived in Paris from Besançon early in 1751 and like most young men with an interest in the letters, he began frequenting the literary cafés. At one of these, most likely the Procope, he met and became the friend of the abbé Raynal, who introduced him into the literary and philosophical salons. He became the constant companion of Roux, Darcet and Helvétius, the latter remaining his closest friend, and by the mid-1750s, he was d'Holbach's comrade as well and a regular guest at the Baron's dinners. According to Suard's wife and his close friend Garat, it was d'Holbach and Helvétius who helped him through the financially difficult years of the early and mid-1750s.[41]

While the precise date of Suard's entry into the coterie cannot be fixed, he was from the mid-1750s until the mid-1780s perhaps

[40] Marmontel, *Mémoires*, I, 348. On Saint-Lambert as a member of the coterie holbachique, see also ibid., II, 128-129; Morellet, *Mémoires*, I, 128; Grimm, *Corr. litt.*, III, 59-71; Cérutti, "Lettre au *Journal de Paris*"; Diderot, *Corr.*, II-III, passim, and VII, 157-160.

[41] Mme Suard, *Suard*, 44-47; Garat, *Suard*, I, 213-215.

its most regular and consistent devotee. According to Mme Suard, "The Baron d'Holbach, more than anyone, cherished him like a brother."[42] In his own correspondence he constantly referred to his close association with the coterie, and those of his foreign friends who wrote to him, such as Hume, Garrick and Wilkes, always asked him to convey their wishes to "the society of Baron d'Holbach." It is doubtful that any man, between 1760 and 1780, attended more assemblies at the Baron's home than Suard.[43]

II. PARTICIPANTS, c. 1760–c. 1780

François-Jean, chevalier de Chastellux (1734-1788). A military officer, man of letters, historian and pamphleteer, Chastellux was the author of two works, in particular, which attracted wide attention in the eighteenth century: his *De la félicité publique* (1770), a study of the causes of and impediments to public happiness that Voltaire, in a weak moment, termed superior to Montesquieu's *Esprit des Lois*,[44] and his *Voyages dans l'Amérique Septentrionale* (1786), which caught the public fancy with its eyewitness descriptions of the new republic.

A devotee of the highest aristocratic salons during all of his adult life, Chastellux began to attend the philosophical and literary salons of Paris shortly before the Seven Years' War. According to his son, it was as a result of having read the *Encyclopédie* that he became attracted to these new milieus.[45] He appears to have known during that period many individuals who were in the circle of Baron d'Holbach, and it is possible that Chastellux visited d'Holbach's dinners prior to his lengthy service in the war. There is nevertheless no tangible evidence to that effect. Shortly after his return from duty, however, by or before the spring of 1764,

---

[42] Mme Suard, loc. cit.

[43] On Suard as a member of the coterie holbachique, see, among the wealth of documentative sources, Morellet, *Mémoires*, I, 128, 145-147; Mme Suard, loc. cit.; Garat, *Suard*, I, 207-215; Wilkes, *Corr.*, III, 174; Suard, *Lettres à Wilkes*, 10, 26-27, 34, 51, 89-91; Garrick, *Letters*, II, 444; Diderot, *Corr.*, IV-IX, passim; Galiani, *Lettres*, I, 46-48, 79, 138-139, and II, 219; d'Holbach's letter to Garrick in F. A. Hedgcock, *David Garrick and His French Friends*, 312; d'Holbach's letters to Hume, *Letters to Hume* (Burton), 253-258.

[44] Voltaire's review appeared in the *Journal de politique et de littérature* II (Paris, 15 May 1777), 85-87.

[45] Alfred Chastellux, *Notice sur le Marquis de Chastellux*, ii-iii. (This entire work is paginated in lower-case roman numerals.)

Chastellux became a regular visitor to the salon, and from then until his departure for America in 1780, he was an intimate participant in the coterie.[46]

He was in no way (contrary to a description offered by Mme de Genlis during the Restoration) an outsider among the philosophes.[47] For more than fifteen years Chastellux was a constant devotee of d'Holbach's dinners. Writing to John Wilkes, whom he met at d'Holbach's home, Chastellux, arriving in England, informed him that "I have left all your friends in good health. . . . Baron d'Holbach and all of his society were very concerned about your affairs. . . . I have a thousand compliments to send to you from them."[48] From Calais, after he had left England, Chastellux wrote to Wilkes, "In several days, I shall be reunited with all our friends and we shall drink to your health."[49] Chastellux's son himself, writing during the Restoration when there was nothing to be gained by linking his father's name to those of the philosophes, still counted among his father's closest friends d'Holbach, Grimm, Morellet, Marmontel, Helvétius, Saint-Lambert, Raynal and Suard.[50]

Abbé André Morellet (1727-1819). Master of Theology, économiste and pamphleteer, Morellet, like Marmontel (whose close friend and eulogist he was, and who had married his niece), is best known for his *Mémoires*. He was most famous in his own time for his pamphlet wars against the directors of the Compagnie des Indes, his translation of Beccaria's *Dei Delitte e delle Pene* into French, and his mordant riposte to Palissot's satirical play *Les Philosophes*, entitled *La Vision de Charles Palissot* (1760).

Morellet's reply to Palissot had offended the latter's protectress, the powerful princesse de Robecq, and had earned Morellet a month's visit to the Bastille. This injustice, he wrote, infuriated

[46] On Chastellux as a member of the coterie holbachique, see "Lettres inédites de Chastellux à Wilkes," G. Bonno, ed., in *Revue de littérature comparée* (July-Sept. 1932), 619-623; d'Holbach's letter to Hume, *Letters to Hume* (Burton), 255; Mme d'Epinay, *Lettere All'Abate Galiani*, 87-88; Garrick, *Letters*, II, 841-842; Diderot, *Corr.*, VII, 157-160, and XII, 75-148 passim; Galiani, *Lettres*, I, 155-256, and II, 39-40, 51, 61, 65, 176; Morellet, *Mémoires*, I, 128.

[47] Mme de Genlis, *Les Dîners du Baron D'Holbach*, 135-176.

[48] Chastellux, "Lettres à Wilkes," 619-620.

[49] Ibid., 620-622.

[50] Alfred Chastellux, *Notice*, xvii-xix.

the philosophes, and made a hero out of him: "I found a doubling of friendship in M. Turgot, M. Trudaine de Montigny, Diderot, d'Alembert, Clairault, and the chevalier de Chastellux; and many homes, those of the Baron d'Holbach, of Helvétius, of Mme de Boufflers, of Mme Necker, etc., opened easily for me."[51]

By his own account, Morellet began to frequent the home of Baron d'Holbach in 1760, and the evidence verifies this claim. Throughout the next two decades and into the 1780s, he remained an intimate of the coterie holbachique. Of all of the salons which he frequented, he wrote, "I must place in the first rank, for the utility, the pleasure and the instruction that I gained from it, that of the Baron d'Holbach."[52] Because of his reputation as an économiste and his influence in France, through friendships with men such as Turgot, Morellet was one of the people at d'Holbach's home whom visitors listed before their "etceteras," and the year by year documentation of his continued presence in the coterie is one of the fullest and richest to be found.[53]

Jacques-André Naigeon (1738-1810). The life of Naigeon, excepting his collaboration with Diderot and with d'Holbach, remains in almost total obscurity. His one serious biographer, Rudolf Brummer, assembled all that he could discover relating to him, including comments on him by his contemporaries; it occupied eleven and a half pages. It was an incomplete compilation, but not by very much.[54]

In his own time, Naigeon was not popular; he had the reputation of being a somewhat annoyingly combative and volatile atheist. The baron von Gleichen, who knew him at d'Holbach's

[51] Morellet, *Mémoires*, I, 119.   [52] Ibid., 127.

[53] On Morellet as a member of the coterie holbachique, see Morellet, *Mémoires*, I, 105-106, 119, 127-128; Morellet, *Lettres à Lord Shelburne*, 2-6, 16, 58-59, 122, 177-178, 184; a letter from Thieriot to Voltaire, in Voltaire, *Corr.*, XLII, 137; Garrick, *Letters*, II, 841-842; d'Holbach, "Lettres à Galiani," 23-24, 30-31; Diderot, *Corr.*, v-x and XII, passim; Diderot, *Oeuvres complètes*, J. Assézat and M. Tourneux, eds., VI, 393-396; Galiani, *Lettres*, I, 79, 216-217, and II, 204-205, 308-312; Cesare Beccaria, *Opere*, S. Romagnoli, ed., II, 864-888; a letter from Adam Smith to Morellet in W. R. Scott, *Adam Smith as Student and Professor*, 298-299; "Dr. Burney, 'Journal'" (Leigh), 170; a letter from d'Holbach to Garrick, in Hedgcock, *Garrick*, 311-312; d'Holbach's letters to Hume in *Letters to Hume* (Burton), 253-256, 311.

[54] Rudolf Brummer, *Studien zur französischen Aufklärungsliteratur im Anschlusz an J.-A. Naigeon* (Breslau, 1932).

27

home, described him as "a man of letters, a great book-collector and a little atheist. . . . He had an insupportable vanity."[55] Diderot, however, not only liked him, but toward the end of his own life counted him as one of his closest friends. He made Naigeon the executor of his will and the legatee of those of his manuscripts which he wanted published posthumously. Naigeon was thus, by Diderot's choice, the first editor of the great man's collected works.[56]

According to Diderot, Naigeon had been "a draftsman, painter and sculptor before becoming a philosophe," and Diderot often had him go to the great art exhibits, the *Salons*, to aid him in his analyses of them for Grimm's *Correspondance*. He "became a philosophe" in the mid-1760s, when he met Diderot and d'Holbach.[57] From 1766 until the mid-1770s, he collaborated with d'Holbach, in one way or another, in the editing, translating or publishing of multitudinous works, and became more or less the Baron's informal secretary, aide, agent, and serious intellectual companion.

Georges Roth, the editor of Diderot's *Correspondance*, asserted that the first mention of Naigeon by Diderot, and the probable date of their first meeting, was in July 1765.[58] There was, however, an earlier mention in the same volume: in June 1765 Diderot wrote to Damilaville that "I want to dine, next week, with Latour and Naigeon at Luxembourg or at the home of Ladel."[59] Since an article by Naigeon, "Richesse," appeared in the *Encyclopédie* in October 1765, a probable guess would be that Naigeon had been suggested as a writer to Diderot, that Naigeon undertook the article sometime before the summer of 1765, and that Diderot, in his June letter, was seeking an occasion to talk with Naigeon about its progress. Whatever the origin of their contact, however, they were soon good friends, and it probably was Diderot who introduced Naigeon into the coterie holbachique sometime during 1765. By 1766 Naigeon and d'Holbach were collaborating on a book.[60]

From this point on, Naigeon became a permanent fixture at the dinners of the coterie and remained until the end one of its most

[55] Gleichen, *Souvenirs*, Paul Grimblot, ed., 202.

[56] Diderot, *Corr.*, XII, 231.

[57] Diderot, *Oeuvres* (A-T), III, 9-14.

[58] Diderot, *Corr.*, V, 51-52.   [59] Ibid., 43.

[60] J. M. Quérard, *Les supercheries littéraires dévoilées*, I, 565.

zealous members. Shortly after the Baron's death, Naigeon wrote a letter to the *Journal de Paris* in praise of his deceased friend. He termed d'Holbach's death "an irreparable loss" and added: "I have lived with him for twenty-four years in the confidence and intimacy of the most tender and constant friendship. I loved him, I respected him, and I weep for him as for a father."[61]

It was at d'Holbach's home with the coterie that Naigeon felt most useful, most stimulated, and most at ease. Commenting, in his edition of Diderot's works, on a particularly glowing description of the coterie by Diderot himself, Naigeon added in a footnote, "*Et in Arcadia ego.*"[62]

III. PARTICIPANTS (WITHIN CERTAIN RESTRICTIONS OF TIME)

Abbé Ferdinando Galiani (1728-1787). Priest, diplomat, literary historian and economic theorist, Galiani was best known in France as the author of a remarkably forceful treatise against free trade in general and the free circulation of grain in particular, his *Dialogues sur le commerce des blés* (1770), and as the author of a scholarly *Commentaire sur Horace*, the fruit of a life-long interest.[63] In 1759 Galiani was sent to Paris by Ferdinand IV, the king of Naples, as secretary to his ambassador, to seek an alliance among all the Houses of Bourbon and a diminution of the power of the Jesuits, vigorous opponents of the Bourbons in Naples. In 1769 he committed the diplomatic indiscretion of confiding to the Danish ambassador his doubts about the loyalty of Bernardo Tanucci, one of Ferdinand IV's most important ministers. Gleichen, the Danish ambassador, informed Choiseul of this, and the latter, who did not appreciate Galiani, used it to obtain his recall from the Court of Naples. Thus on May 16, 1769, Galiani received orders from Ferdinand IV to return and to resume a less important charge as a commercial magistrate.[64]

[61] *Journal de Paris* (9 Feb. 1789), no. 40, 175-177. On Naigeon as a member of the coterie holbachique, see also Gleichen, *Souvenirs*, 202; Morellet, *Mémoires*, I, 398; Diderot, *Corr.*, VII, 157-160, IX and XI, passim; Galiani, *Lettres*, II, 206-207.

[62] Diderot, *Oeuvres* (N), XIII, 266n.

[63] See L. Magnotti, *L'Abbé Ferdinand Galiani, sa philanthropie et ses rapports avec la France*, 7-11. An excellent critical anthology of Galiani's work has been compiled by F. Nicolini, *Il Pensiero dell'Abate Galiani*.

[64] See Magnotti, *Galiani*, 7-34; J. Rossi, *The Abbé Galiani in France*, passim; Galiani, *Amici e Corrispondenti Francesi Dell'Abate Galiani*, 7-54.

While in Paris, Galiani, like so many foreign diplomats, participated in the social and intellectual salons. At Mme Geoffrin's, one of the first he visited, he met many of the members of the coterie holbachique, and by September 1760 Diderot was writing of him as someone already associated with the Baron's circle. For the next nine years, approximately, there existed between Galiani and the coterie a mutual admiration and mutual love. He appeared to be always there, and he impressed them as strongly as they impressed him.[65]

Galiani was apparently a remarkable raconteur, with a sense of humor and a streak of cynicism that beguiled his newly acquired friends. Morellet recalled him at d'Holbach's dinners "telling us long stories, in the Italian style, kinds of dramatic presentations that one listened to right to the end."[66] Marmontel, discussing d'Holbach's dinners, related, "It was there that Galiani was at times astonishing in the originality of his ideas and the adroit, singular and unexpected path along which he developed them."[67]

His departure from Paris and the coterie left him saddened. "My mother is dead, my sisters are nuns, my nieces are stupid; the only company I have is a cat," he lamented in 1771.[68] To d'Holbach in April 1770 he wrote, "Does Philosophy, whose *maître d'hôtel* you are, still eat with such good appetite?"[69] By March 1771, when he received from Mme d'Epinay a copy of the sermon Grimm had pronounced at the coterie holbachique, Galiani waxed wryly sentimental in reply.[70] Indeed, ten years later he wrote to Mme d'Epinay that he was working full time on a serious book, and he added: "Ah! If only I could work on it in Paris, and communicate pieces of it in the corner of your hearth, or at the dinners of Baron d'Holbach! But that cannot be!"[71]

The regret was shared by the coterie, as d'Holbach never failed to remind him in his own letters to Naples. Often d'Holbach used

[65] Diderot, *Corr.*, III-IX, passim. Galiani made such a striking impression upon his listeners that, as was the case with Diderot, most of the sources cited in this chapter make mention of his presence at d'Holbach's dinners throughout most of the 1760s. Galiani was not in Paris that whole decade; from May 1765 until November 1766 he was once more in Naples. Those eighteen months, however, constituted the only hiatus in his relationship with the coterie holbachique during that time.

[66] Morellet, *Mémoires*, I, 129-130.

[67] Marmontel, *Mémoires*, I, 353, 484-486.

[68] Galiani, *Lettres*, I, 230-231.   [69] Ibid., 46-48.

[70] Ibid., 216-219.   [71] Ibid., II, 363.

the plural "we" to send him wishes from the entire circle, and he employed the familiar terms peculiar to them; thus in December 1771: "Adieu, very dear abbé. Receive the best wishes of the entire *boulangerie.* . . ."[72] And Diderot, writing to Galiani in June 1770 on behalf of the coterie, assured him that he was irreplaceable.[73]

Galiani, thus, for most of the 1760s enjoyed the status of an important and a valued participant in the life of the coterie and flourished in it during the period of its own *flouraison*. Whatever he was the coterie accepted and approved of, in its determination of what constituted its philosophical parameters and the style and substance of its inner life. Whatever he contributed, the coterie absorbed as a component of its diversity. Nevertheless, he was a temporary visitor to Paris, enmeshed in the social and professional cadres of another kingdom. In that sense, Galiani should be excluded from considerations of the interaction of the members of the coterie holbachique and the society of the Ancien Régime in France. In discussions of the thought of the coterie, Galiani will be considered as a participant; in discussions of the coterie's social and professional place in France, where he lived for so short a time, he will not.

Claude-Adrien Helvétius (1715-1772). Tax-farmer, then philosophe, Helvétius is a figure known in the twentieth century—as in the eighteenth—as the author of *the* dramatic *cause célèbre* of the 1750s, the philosophical treatise *De l'esprit* (1758). D. W. Smith, in his remarkable study of the publication and persecution of *De l'esprit*, asserted that it was as a result of this *affaire* that Helvétius became associated with the coterie holbachique. Helvétius, he claimed, had enjoyed no relationship with Diderot before 1758 or 1759 and, indeed, "he had probably not met Diderot before the condemnation of *De l'esprit*." Before 1759, he argued, Helvétius, during the months that he was in Paris, frequented the salons of the "older generation," above all that of Mme Geoffrin.[74]

There is reason to question Smith's thesis. In 1749, during his imprisonment, Diderot, in a letter to the *lieutenant-général de police*, listed Helvétius among several people "of whom I have

---

[72] D'Holbach, "Lettres à Galiani," 37-39.

[73] Diderot, *Corr.*, x, 66-69.

[74] D. W. Smith, *Helvétius: A Study in Persecution*, 158-159.

merited the protection, close acquaintance, esteem or friendship."[75] Smith's argument also ignored the interconnections of
Parisian society; among Helvétius' closest friends *before* 1758
were Charles-Georges Le Roy and Suard, both early friends of
d'Holbach and participants in the coterie. Indeed, Mme Suard
recalled that d'Holbach and Helvétius were the men who aided
her husband in the early and mid-1750s.[76] Smith misunderstood
the nature of Mme Geoffrin's Wednesday salon, at which Helvétius was a frequent guest in the early 1750s; it was "conservative"
in its conversation, but not in its composition. In addition to Helvétius, its regular frequenters before 1758 included, for example,
Grimm, Marmontel, Saint-Lambert and Raynal; indeed, Baron
d'Holbach himself was occasionally there. Before *De l'esprit*
Helvétius was in direct contact with Diderot, with d'Holbach,
and with many members of the coterie holbachique, two of whom,
at least, were among his dearest friends. It is difficult to imagine
that these associations and friendships did not lead to invitations
to the Baron's dinners, if not to close ties with the coterie as a
whole. Marmontel, describing his own association with the coterie in about 1752, recalled, "It was there that I came to know
Diderot, Helvétius, Grimm and Jean-Jacques Rousseau. . . ."[77]
The passage does not prove, of course, that he met Helvétius *at
that time*, but the presumption is plausible; this was not the part
of Marmontel's *Mémoires* devoted to d'Holbach's coterie and the
men he met there, but rather to the period from 1749 to 1752. It
is more reasonable, therefore, to assume that Helvétius was introduced into the coterie holbachique early in the 1750s by one or
more of his close friends, or by d'Holbach himself, to whom he
would have been introduced at Mme Geoffrin's. After the scandal
of 1758-1759 he was perhaps less welcome at the latter's home, and
his ties with the coterie holbachique may have intensified.

What *does* necessitate a qualification of Helvétius' status as a
member of the coterie holbachique is the fact that he was in
Paris only four months out of the year, spending the rest of his
time at his estate at Voré. He frequently invited individual members of the coterie to Voré, and also entertained many of them
at his own weekly salon while in Paris, but these were his own
private affairs. Because of his prolonged absences from the capital, his participation in the life of the coterie was much less than

[75] Diderot, *Corr.*, I, 87.   [76] Mme Suard, *Suard*, 43-47.
[77] Marmontel, *Mémoires*, I, 229-230.

that of all the other figures of the group. It is perhaps ironic that his membership must be stringently qualified, for it has been generally assumed that, because of his ideas, he was one of the most central figures of the coterie. Such an assumption, of course, wholly begs the question of the nature of d'Holbach's circle.[78]

D. W. Smith, in fact, qualified that membership yet further and saw the relationship between Helvétius and the coterie as close only during 1759 through 1764. After that, in Smith's view, his meetings with them were less frequent, and they gradually lost contact.[79] The evidence which Smith submits for this, however— an obituary of Helvétius in Grimm's *Correspondance littéraire*— does not support his assertion. Helvétius did leave on a tour of Europe in 1764-1765, but he re-established his links with the coterie when he returned. He did develop a particularly painful case of the gout, but only in the very last years of his life, as his condition worsened, may this have prevented him from spending four months in Paris annually. Thus Grimm wrote explicitly, in his obituary of 1772, that Helvétius spent four months in Paris "every year," which would have been an odd comment if true only of the period from 1751 to 1763.[80] And in 1766 d'Holbach wrote of Helvétius as a member of "our little society."[81] In 1767 Helvétius wrote to Hume, whom he had met at d'Holbach's home, and asked him to send Walpole "to us" in Paris, which accounted for the latter's visit to d'Holbach's salon when he came to France.[82] In 1767 Diderot still wrote of Helvétius as one of "the society" of d'Holbach's dinners.[83] In 1771 Galiani, who had spent only the 1760s in Paris, imagined, on reading Grimm's sermon to the coterie, that he could see "the Senator Pococurante Helvétius" during its performance.[84] In that very sermon on January 1, 1770, Grimm had asked for prayers for "our dear and venerable brothers Claude Helvétius and Paul, Baron d'Holbach," not for their health

[78] Morellet in his *Mémoires*, I, 136, claimed that the salon at Helvétius' home drew "about the same people as that of Baron d'Holbach," despite the more social (and less philosophical) tone of the former's dinners. For a fuller discussion of the difference between the two salons, see infra, Chapter Three.

[79] Smith, *Helvétius*, 187-188.   [80] Grimm, *Corr. litt.*, IX, 417-424.

[81] D'Holbach's letter to Servan, in Paul Vernière, "Deux cas de prosélytisme philosophique au XVIIIe siècle à propos de deux lettres inédites du Baron d'Holbach," *RHLF* (1955), 496-497.

[82] *Letters to Hume* (Burton), 14-15.

[83] Diderot, *Corr.*, VII, 157-160.   [84] Galiani, *Lettres*, I, 216-217.

but "to the effect of preserving in their cuisine this spirit of choice and discernment which makes the fare exquisite, and in their wine-cellar the purity of dogma concerning vintages and choice-years."[85] An odd prayer for a man allegedly dying in pain and isolation at Voré and allegedly out of touch with the coterie for some six years!

Thus for at least twelve or, more likely, eighteen to twenty years, Helvétius was a recognized intimate and consistent devotee of d'Holbach's coterie during the four months of the year that he was in Paris. In terms of that recognition, no qualification need be made; in terms of time, his participation was a partial one.

IV. Problematic Cases

Jean Darcet (1724-1801). Chemist and medical doctor, Darcet was best known in the eighteenth century for his work in applied chemistry, above all in reference to the arts and the manufacture of porcelain and soap, and for his analyses of various sources of drinking water. It was less widely known, or at least less discussed, that he also had aided Montesquieu in the classification of materials to be used in the latter's *Esprit des Lois*. Impressed with the young Darcet in Bordeaux, Montesquieu had brought him to Paris in 1742 to direct the education of his son there.[86]

The evidence concerning Darcet's participation in the coterie holbachique is highly suggestive, but unfortunately scant. Given Darcet's friendships and the nature of what evidence does exist, it appears at first highly probable that he was a devotee of d'Holbach's dinners; the unimpressive quantity and often circumstantial nature of such evidence, however, necessitates a certain caution.

Darcet, in the period of the formation of the coterie holbachique (1749-1751), was a central part of the circle of young provincial intellectuals—Roux and Suard among them by the end of 1751—gathered around the person of Montesquieu. Roux in particular, whom he appears to have known as a student in Bor-

[85] Grimm, *Corr. litt.*, VIII, 436. On Helvétius as a member of the coterie holbachique, see, in addition to the sources cited in this chapter (notes 77-85), Morellet, *Mémoires*, I, 128; Diderot, *Corr.*, III, passim; Suard, *Lettres à Wilkes*, 26-30; a letter from Adam Smith to Morellet, in W. R. Scott, *Adam Smith*, 298-299.

[86] On Darcet's early life and career, see Michel Dizé, *Précis historique sur la vie et les travaux de Jean D'Arcet*; and René Cuzacq, *Un savant chalossais: le chimiste Jean Darcet (1724-1801) et sa famille*.

deaux, became his closest friend, a relationship which endured for most of their lives, and the two were disciples of the chemist Rouelle, whose daughter Darcet later married.[87] By the early 1750s, Roux, Suard, and Rouelle were frequent visitors to d'Holbach's dinners, the first two being among the people to whom the Baron was most attentive. It is reasonable to assume, on the basis of these facts alone, that Darcet was a part of the important scientific contingent among d'Holbach's early guests. This would appear to be borne out by Morellet's description of the early days of d'Holbach's dinners: "As a consequence [of his 'noble' use of his fortune 'for the good of the sciences and letters'], his house assembled the most striking men of French letters, Diderot, J.-J. Rousseau, Helvétius, Barthez, Venelle, *Rouelle and his disciples, Roux and Darcet*, Duclos, Saurin, Raynal, Suard, Boullanger [sic], Marmontel, La Condamine, le chevalier de Chastellux, etc."[88]

This list, however, is potentially misleading for several reasons. First, written decades after the events, it was not intended to aid historians to establish who attended d'Holbach's gatherings frequently and regularly, but rather to inform readers of "the most striking men of French letters" whom d'Holbach entertained, in order to establish the importance of Morellet's having been admitted there. Second, and following from this, the list clearly is based upon the men whom d'Holbach entertained in the 1750s, regardless of whether their association endured until 1760, when Morellet, by his own account, saw the home of Baron d'Holbach opened to him because of his imprisonment. In this manner, Morellet can include Rousseau on the list despite the latter's break with d'Holbach in the 1750s; and Boulanger, despite his death in 1759; and Barthez and Venel, despite their departures for Montpellier in 1758-1759. The value of Morellet's citation of Darcet, therefore, is moot.

More to the point, perhaps, is a letter from Diderot to Sophie Volland in October 1767, describing his efforts to convince "almost the whole society, which you know almost as well as I [from his letters?]" to visit d'Holbach at Grandval, where the Baron was driving his family to "despair" because of his loneliness. Darcet was listed as one of those contacted, but described as "perhaps hidden away under lock and key by the comte de Lauraguais, until he [Darcet] makes a [scientific] discovery for

[87] Dizé, op. cit., 1-18; Garat, *Suard*, I, 100-106.
[88] Morellet, *Mémoires*, I, 128 (emphasis added).

him."[89] The description hints at the caution with which this source as well must be employed. It is a lengthy, charming and extremely amusing letter written to Diderot's mistress, and filled with hyperbole. Diderot sarcastically catalogued the seemingly endless efforts he had made to provide company for d'Holbach at Grandval, and it was in his stylistic interest to expand the list of men contacted to as large a number as imaginable. It included social friends of d'Holbach's family, temporary visitors to Paris, and people who could not possibly have gone to Grandval, as they were at that time far from Paris. Indeed the "society" mentioned by Diderot might well have been the whole of Parisian or French "society" known to Sophie Volland or, at least, anyone whom the d'Holbach or the d'Aine family ever entertained. It establishes Darcet as someone known in d'Holbach's circle, and a visitor to the coterie perhaps, but it does not inform us of the frequency or intimacy of that tie.

The heart of the problem, then, is that there is no contemporary consequential documentation of a frequent and self-conscious participation of Darcet in the assemblies of the coterie holbachique. There well may have been letters and comments to that effect, but they are not extant or recorded. We know that Roux and Darcet were close, and that both attended d'Holbach's salon in its early days. We know, from Diderot and from others, that Darcet continued at the least to make appearances there throughout the 1760s and 1770s.[90] We know of no break between Darcet and any members of the coterie. We know that he collaborated with d'Holbach and Diderot on various works requiring scientific advice up to the 1780s and, from Naigeon, that Darcet and Diderot were friends.[91] From all of these factors, it seems highly probable that Darcet was a regular figure at d'Holbach's dinners. Yet how can we explain the almost total silence toward him in the letters and descriptions of contemporary visitors to the coterie? Darcet appears to have been a quiet and unprepossessing figure, and it is possible, quite simply, that he rarely behaved at d'Holbach's home in a manner that would have produced comments upon his presence there. Unknown outside of Parisian and scientific circles, he

[89] Diderot, *Corr.*, VII, 157-160.

[90] See also d'Epinay, *Lettere (Gli Ultimi Anni)*, 31.

[91] See Mme de Vandeul's recollections in Diderot, *Oeuvres* (A-T), I, liv; Naigeon's "Avertissement" to Diderot's *Histoire de la peinture en cire*, in Diderot, *Oeuvres* (N), xv, 295-297; see also infra, Chapter Six.

would not have been a likely candidate for mention in accounts of the coterie by foreign visitors writing to impress their friends about their time in France. Even so, such hypotheses, however plausible, fall short of desirable proof.

There are two testimonies, however, both given somewhat in passing, that tip the scales in favor of treating Darcet as a member of the coterie holbachique. The first and lesser of the two appeared in an *éloge* of Darcet written by a lifelong friend and protégé, the scientist Dizé. Describing Darcet's contributions of scientific notes and clarifications to various men of letters, Dizé noted that his friend saw these men and "was intimately linked" with them "at the home of Baron d'Holbach, whose friend he was." The use of the phrase "intimately linked," the use of the imperfect tense [*"le baron d'Holbach, dont l'ami il était"*], and above all, the fact that the contributions offered by Darcet at d'Holbach's home ranged from advice for the *Encyclopédie* to scientific notes in works published throughout the period from 1779 to 1782 all implied a close and enduring relationship.[92]

The second testimony, in Morellet's *Mémoires*, appears to be conclusive however. Discussing a secret of Baron d'Holbach's that was kept for twenty years by d'Holbach's intimate "society," men who "lived constantly together," Morellet listed, in particular, "Marmontel, Saint-Lambert, Suard, Chastellux, Roux, Darcet, Raynal, Helvétius and I."[93] With this added to Dizé's observation and to the more immediately contemporary evidence discussed above, it appears highly probable that despite the infrequency with which his presence was noted, in Darcet's case we are dealing with an unassuming but nevertheless constant participant in the coterie holbachique.

Nicolas-Antoine Boulanger (1722-1759). Engineer, scientist, linguist, and philosophical historian, Boulanger was one of the most creative and influential thinkers of the eighteenth century. His fame, however, was wholly posthumous, for all of his important works were published from manuscript copies of his books after his death, most prominently by Helvétius with help, it would appear, from d'Holbach and Diderot.[94] Among these were his *Recherches sur l'origine du despotisme oriental* (1761) and *L'An-*

---

[92] Dizé, op. cit., 30-31.   [93] Morellet, *Mémoires*, I, 133-134.

[94] See the information provided to Barbier by Naigeon and others in Barbier, *Dictionnaire des anonymes*, IV, 30, and Quérard, *Supercheries*, I, 565.

tiquité dévoilée par ses usages (1766), in both of which he developed the theory that the origins of religion and despotism could be found in the response of early civilizations to the cataclysms of nature, in particular to the universal flood so prominent in the mythologies of the many cultures whose sacred and historical literature he traced. This hypothesis concerning the traumatic etiology of organized supernatural cults and political authoritarianism made him, in France, one of the most widely discussed writers, and focused many of the issues in the debate over the causes of man's institution of structures that so many of the philosophes saw as violating the natural self-interest of the species.

Having established, at least tentatively, the little-known Darcet as a participant in the coterie holbachique, however, the available sources argue strongly for the exclusion of Boulanger from such a list, despite his prominence in so many historical accounts of the thought and activities of d'Holbach's group. This is not simply because of the fact that he arrived in Paris in 1751 and died in 1759, so that, at best, his association with the coterie would have been of only eight years' duration, but because there is presumptive proof that he never was truly an active participant.

At first glance at the evidence this claim appears improbable. As is often remarked, the coterie holbachique indeed referred to itself at times as "la boulangerie," and it is more than possible, as is often argued, that this was a pun on Nicolas-Antoine Boulanger's name. Diderot wrote a biographical sketch of his life and referred to him as "serious in society, gay with his friends, and [someone who] took great pleasure in conversations on philosophy, history and erudition," traits that it is assumed Diderot had the chance to observe during frequent contacts at d'Holbach's home.[95] Morellet, we have seen, although he did not become associated with the coterie until the year following Boulanger's death, listed him among the men whom the Baron assembled. Indeed, as the term "la boulangerie" implies, there is evidence, if one were inclined to count it as such, that Boulanger left an indelible im-

[95] Diderot, *Oeuvres* (A-T), VI, 339ff. This "Lettre sur Boulanger" was written in 1766 to d'Holbach as a preface to the 1766 edition of Boulanger's *l'Antiquité dévoilée*, published by the Baron, and was reprinted as an introduction to an edition of Boulanger's works, the anonymously published *Oeuvres de Boullanger* [sic], I, ix-xx. See also Naigeon's comments on Boulanger and on this letter in Diderot, *Oeuvres* (N), III, 409-410, and in Naigeon, *Mémoires sur Diderot*, 191-193.

pression on d'Holbach's circle. Horace Walpole, writing in a dour vein from Paris in 1765, remarked: "I forgot to tell you that I sometimes go to the Baron d'Holbach's; but I have left off his dinners, as there was no bearing the authors, the philosophers, and savants, of which he has a pigeon-house full. They soon turned my head with a new system of antediluvian deluges. . . . The Baron is persuaded that Pall Mall is paved with lava or deluge stones. In short, nonsense for nonsense, I like the Jesuits better than the philosophes."[96]

For all this evidence, however, there is not a shred of proof that Boulanger was the friend of any other members of the coterie apart from Diderot, Helvétius (whose own status within the coterie during this period is unclear) and d'Holbach, or, despite references such as Morellet's to his having been present in d'Holbach's home, that he was there frequently. These indications have nevertheless sufficed to give Boulanger a firm place in the coterie holbachique as traditionally described. At d'Holbach's home, it is believed, he met and talked frequently with the intimates of the coterie holbachique. Yet in September 1759 Diderot wrote to Grimm from Grandval, where he was on an extended vacation, about the death of a man named Millot, and added: "I do not know if you know a young man named Boulanger, who had begun by making holes in the ground as an engineer in [the department of] *ponts et chaussées*, and finished by becoming a Greek, Hebrew, Syrian, Arab, etc., naturalist. He also died. He had genius, and his progress marks it well."[97]

This letter simply cannot be reconciled with a claim that would place Boulanger in the midst of the coterie holbachique between 1751 and 1759. That Boulanger met d'Holbach and Diderot, that he was invited to dine at d'Holbach's home at least once, that his ideas were widely admired—all of this is seemingly certain. If Diderot was obliged to inform Grimm in 1759 of who the "young man" was, however, uncertain if Grimm knew him or even knew of him, clearly Boulanger was neither an intimate nor a frequent guest at d'Holbach's circle. Whatever Boulanger's legacy, he was not, in his lifetime, a member of the coterie.

[96] Walpole, *Letters*, vi, 370.

[97] Diderot, *Corr.*, ii, 257-258. This letter provided Grimm with the basic information he then utilized in a notice on Boulanger's death in the *Corr. litt.*, iv, 151.

Our list thus contains fifteen names: Chastellux, Darcet, Diderot, Galiani, Grimm, Helvétius, d'Holbach, Le Roy, Marmontel, Morellet, Naigeon, Raynal, Roux, Saint-Lambert, and Suard. It should not be considered a closed or definitive compilation. It is possible that new sources might reveal that men who now appear to have been but infrequent guests, in particular Bernard-Joseph Saurin, Charles-Marie de La Condamine and Voltaire's friends Damilaville and d'Alainville, were in fact more regular in their status at d'Holbach's home than the available evidence would indicate. It is very doubtful that any of these figures played any but the most infrequent role in the life of the coterie, but this is always open to revision. No one among these four, it should be pointed out, fits the mold of the "myth" concerning the coterie, and their exclusion is based solely on the absence of anything but one or two mentions of their having been at a given dinner at the rue Royale or, apart from the d'Aine family's more social entertainments, at Grandval—the absence, in short, of anything suggesting a close relationship to the coterie as a group. The list is static, not taking into consideration brief disputes or temporary absences from Paris, and thus it obviously does not constitute, in terms of any particular person except the Baron, a necessarily rigorous indication of the combination present at a given dinner at any given time. Nevertheless, it allows the historian for the first time to discuss the coterie holbachique with the knowledge of to whom his discussion applies and to know where, in whose lives and thought, to seek verification or invalidation of historical propositions concerning the coterie and its place in the Enlightenment and Ancien Régime.

TWO · *Various Theses*

IN attempting to account for the uniqueness of the coterie hol-bachique, most nineteenth and twentieth-century observers have presented its singularity in terms of one or more of three puta-tive traits: that the coterie was a salon of atheists and/or a center of collaboration and common efforts and/or a headquarters of some sort for the direction of the *Encyclopédie*. Let us evaluate these theses in the light of the actual membership of the coterie.

Was the coterie holbachique a salon of atheists?

Once it became accepted in scholarly circles that d'Holbach's group was a coterie of atheists, anecdotal evidence that otherwise might have been treated with more skepticism or with more cau-tion as to its application, simply became additional cement in the tradition surrounding the holbachians. The most frequently cited anecdote is one found in Diderot's letters to Sophie Volland, de-scribing a visit by David Hume to d'Holbach's home: "The En-glish philosopher took it upon himself to say to the Baron that he did not believe in the existence of atheists, that he never had seen any. The Baron said to him: 'Monsieur, count how many of us there are here.' There were eighteen of us. The Baron added: 'I am lucky enough to be able to show you fifteen atheists at one glance. The other three have not yet made up their minds.' "[1]

Let us assume that the anecdote is substantially true, for it is one which Diderot repeated some sixteen years later to Samuel Romilly.[2] Nevertheless, in the absence of other corroborative documentation, there is no reason why it is more valid to see d'Holbach's riposte as a factual account of things than, for exam-ple, to see it as a hyperbolic attempt to startle Hume or as a sarcasm directed to his friends at the table. Following Diderot's account, Hume had informed the coterie that in England atheists did not exist, and that the appellation was synonymous with

[1] Diderot, *Corr.*, v, 133-134.
[2] Sir Samuel Romilly, *The Life of Sir Samuel Romilly, Written by Him-self*, I, 131-133.

"scoundrel." In this context, d'Holbach made his famous reply. True or false, it surely was the most effective answer he could have made. To assume that it is literally true, however, is to beg the question entirely. Unsubstantiated, the story may reveal more about d'Holbach's sense of humor and timing than it does about his coterie. The reply was not necessarily serious, and the anecdote should not serve as anything more than a stimulus to further research.

For eight and a half years, the abbé Galiani was a regular participant in the Thursday and Sunday dinners of Baron d'Holbach. Although one of the abbé's biographers has depicted him as a believing Christian,[3] Galiani emerges from his and his friends' writings and letters as a somewhat cynical deist who often argued against atheism at d'Holbach's assemblies. He believed he knew what atheism meant to those who espoused it, and what it required to hold such a view of the universe. In a letter to Mme d'Epinay he described the unbeliever as a man who deprived himself of all wonder and substantial knowledge. The atheist, he continued, was "impoverished of all ideas," remaining in "a horrible void," "a nothingness." He compared the unbeliever to a tightrope walker: "He fills all of the spectators with fear and astonishment, and no one is tempted to follow him."[4] Galiani knew well the members of the coterie holbachique. Is it possible that he was talking about them all?

Marmontel, in his *Mémoires*, chose to indicate that the abbé would have been talking about none of them, at least not in their capacity as guests in d'Holbach's home. "There," Marmontel assured his readers, "God, virtue, the holy laws of natural morality, were never placed in doubt, at least in my presence; to that I can attest."[5] This need not be taken seriously, however, and it was contradicted by his own account of events. Atheism was discussed constantly; the question is, by how many was it espoused?

When Morellet penned his own *Mémoires*, he too felt obliged to justify his long involvement with a coterie which, by the early

---

[3] Magnotti, *Galiani*, 129-131, wrote: "Galiani is a Christian philosopher. He ardently defends the Christian religion, above all during his sojourn in France." Magnotti probably has confused Galiani's defense of the argument from design, discussed below, with a defense of Christianity. There is no evidence of his having defended Christianity either in Paris or in Naples, and Magnotti has presented none.

[4] Galiani, *Lettres*, ii, 245-246.   [5] Marmontel, *Mémoires*, i, 484-486.

nineteenth century, already was considered to have been a den of virulent atheism. The philosophy of atheism, he admitted, often was elaborated at the coterie holbachique, presented by its adherents with "an edifying probity, even for those among us who, like myself, did not believe in their teaching. . . . For it must not be believed that in this society . . . these overly free opinions were those of us all. There were a good number of us theists there, and not shamefully, for we defended ourselves vigorously, yet always loving the atheists of such good company."[6]

Morellet described an extended discussion which he alleged to have occurred between Diderot and Galiani at two separate dinners of the coterie. At the first Diderot expounded his atheistic materialism. At the second Galiani replied. Following Morellet's recollections, Galiani asserted that if Diderot were playing a game of dice, and the same regular combination continued to appear to his disadvantage until he had lost a fair bit of his money, the philosophe would be the first to scream that the dice were loaded. He allegedly continued: "Ah, philosophe! How about that? Because ten or twelve rolls of the dice have been thrown in such a way that you lose six francs, you believe firmly that it is in consequence of an adroit maneuver, an artful combination, a well-hidden trick; and in seeing in this universe so prodigious a number of combinations thousands upon thousands of times more difficult and more complicated and more sustained and more useful, etc., you do not suspect that the dice of nature are also loaded, and that there is on high a great trickster who plays a game to get the better of you!"[7]

Morellet alleged as well that he himself participated actively in these intellectual disputes among friends. He claimed that once, after he had defended the deistic position against a certain atheist in the group, the two of them agreed to put their arguments in writing. "Twelve days later," he continued, "I sent him a small paper, which will be found among my belongings, which began with these words: Sir and dear atheist, etc."[8] Was Morellet, like Marmontel, disingenuously discussing the atheism of the coterie in order to preserve his own reputation? Is there indeed any reason to believe that Galiani's rather original restatement of the argument from design actually was uttered at d'Holbach's

---

[6] Morellet, *Mémoires*, I, 130-131.   [7] Ibid., 131-134.
[8] Ibid.

home, or that Morellet's defense of the belief in God actually was written?

In fact, it appears that Morellet was relating the truth in both accounts. In December 1769 Galiani, recently returned from Paris, wrote to Mme d'Epinay from Naples: "Let the Baron come to tell me at present that 'the dice are not loaded'; he babbles."[9] To d'Holbach himself, in July 1770, Galiani observed: "There is nothing better than to persuade oneself that the dice are loaded. This idea gives birth to a thousand others, and a new world appears."[10] As for Morellet's "small paper . . . among my belongings," the evidence seems equally clear. In a catalogue detailing a sale of manuscripts to be held in 1832, the following entry appeared:

> Item . . . Autograph letter of twelve pages, small, in-quarto, from the abbé Morellet to the Baron d'Holbach, on the existence of God.—Answer in the name of Baron d'Holbach, by Naigeon and Diderot, in forty-three pages, in-quarto, in the handwriting of Naigeon, and the marginal notes in the handwriting of Diderot. These two particulars in-quarto are unedited . . . [and are] in a very cramped handwriting.[11]

For some reason, this seems always to occur: we begin with "the atheists of the coterie holbachique," and we arrive at "d'Holbach, Naigeon and Diderot." Why is this the case? Is there any substance whatever beneath the traditional "etcetera"?

* * *

The general use of the term "the atheists of the coterie holbachique" is one which attributes to the intimates of d'Holbach's circle the goal of proselytizing for atheism and the authorship of the many books to that effect which appeared in France during the 1760s and 1770s. This view is without foundation in fact. There were only three men within the coterie holbachique who wrote explicitly atheistic works for the reading public at large—d'Holbach, Naigeon and Diderot. There were only two men for whom the publication of such works was a major priority of their concern and time—d'Holbach and Naigeon. Within the

---

[9] Galiani, *Lettres*, I, 21.   [10] Ibid., 113-114.

[11] *Notice de livres précieux . . . des manuscrits . . . de lettres manuscrites . . . dont la vente aura lieu les 18, 19, 20 et 21 mars . . . par le ministère de M. Bonnefonds . . .* (Paris, 1832). This *Notice* is part of the Q-100 collection (of booksellers' catalogues) of the B.N.

limits of this precise sense of "the atheists of the coterie," only three, in broad terms, and only two, in more circumscribed terms, are qualified for the cast of characters.

D'Holbach's *Système de la nature* (1770), his *Le Bon-sens* (1772), and his *La morale universelle* (1776) were prolonged and vigorous statements and variations of the same three basic themes: (1) that the only coherent deduction from a sensationalistic epistemology was a rigorous materialism, (2) that the only coherent conception of matter was of an uncreated substance containing motion as an essential property, obviating the need for a First or Immaterial Cause, and (3) that the only humane and beneficial morality was one deduced from the imperatives for the happiness and survival of mankind, empirical imperatives established by the interaction of an amoral material universe—the whole—with one of its unfavored and unprotected parts, the human animal. *Système de la nature* urged these views in detailed argumentation for that reading public which could hold its own in philosophical analysis. *Bon-sens* sought to popularize such views for a somewhat broader audience in less detailed and more accessible prose. *La morale universelle* attempted to reassure both reading publics that an atheistic morality, for all its alterations of the moral code both in terms of what it approved and what it disapproved, was compatible with order, decency and familial devotion. D'Holbach was an atheist, and he proselytized.

This last characterization applies equally to Jacques-André Naigeon. Naigeon admitted freely that he worked with d'Holbach "to atheize" the works which they edited or revised.[12] He himself edited, in the *Recueil philosophique* (1770), treatises of an antideistic, atheistic nature.[13] In his own *Philosophie ancienne et moderne* (1791-1794), he braved the religiosity of both the constitutional monarchy and the Jacobins in his frank support of atheistic philosophies. In some directions Naigeon developed his mentor's atheism along paths that the Baron himself had not

[12] Barbier, *Dictionnaire des anonymes*, I, xlii, xlii n.; II, 182, 262-263, 1,190, 1,217, 1,284-1,285; III, 300, 694; IV, 717; Quérard, *Supercheries*, II, 1(b), 97-102. As Barbier indicated throughout his comments on d'Holbach and Naigeon, it was Naigeon who provided him with bibliographical information and assistance, carefully distinguishing among often thematically indistinguishable works in terms of the presence or absence of his own hand.

[13] Naigeon, *Recueil philosophique, ou mélange de pièces sur la religion et la morale, par différens auteurs*. The *Recueil* also contained pieces of a deistic outlook.

traveled. While both men established the *need* for atheism in terms of its intellectual, social, and moral benefits, d'Holbach's formal system of materialism relied heavily upon the assumed value of the Hobbesian goal of a language wholly bound to sensitive conceptions. Naigeon, on the other hand, presented a systematic atheism that he conceived of as primarily an empirical induction from the data of the modern life-sciences and medicine. In this he was more in the school of those materialists dealing with the intellectual legacies of eighteenth-century Cartesians and of La Mettrie than was d'Holbach, whose problems were those bequeathed by Hobbes and by the John Toland of the *Letters to Serena*. Thus, although d'Holbach and Naigeon generally are discussed as interchangeable philosophers, Naigeon was in fact closer to Diderot's more biological definitions of the problem of matter-in-motion than to d'Holbach's more English and hence more physical and cosmological definitions of the problem. Nevertheless, both d'Holbach and Naigeon, whatever their formal differences, denounced with equal fervor the abuses of theistic morality, and asserted as a central metaphor their view that the belief in God was a Pandora's box from which had issued a host of social and psychological confusions and traumas. They wrote in the same aggressive language and surely were, for the majority of their reading public, thematically indistinguishable. They collaborated often and, as Diderot once wrote to Sophie Volland, they made their task one of seeing to it that "Bombs are falling in the House of the Lord."[14] It was far from all they did or published between the mid-1760s and the mid-1770s, the period of almost all of d'Holbach's atheistic publications and of his collaboration with Naigeon, but it was a significant part of their lives.

Diderot's atheism, in his *Additions aux pensées philosophiques* and his *Rêve de d'Alembert*, was as explicit, as philosophically earnest and, at times, as angry as that of d'Holbach and Naigeon. In the *Additions*, Diderot told of a misanthropic hermit who brooded many years in search of the one act he could perform from which the maximum of human suffering would follow; he emerged, at last, announcing the existence of God.[15] In the *Rêve de d'Alembert*, Diderot likewise suggested a "solution" to the

[14] Diderot, *Corr.*, VIII, 234-235.
[15] Diderot, *Oeuvres* (A-T), I, 169-170.

problem of matter's acquisition of motion by denying the need for acquisition, and denying, by means of the hypothesis of *sensibilité universelle*, the need for a distinction between living and inert matter. He suggested that the implications of determinism for men were self-acceptance within the limits of possible change and self-improvement within the limits offered by knowledge of causes; and he suggested, in the concept of adaptation to a changing environment, an ultimate natural source of normative values. Such themes focused on the very heart of the broadest problems raised by d'Holbach and Naigeon.

Diderot was not, however—and it obscures his singularity to see him as such—a polemicist for atheism in the style of the latter two. He did not choose to publish his works through the same efficient channels they utilized, but preferred to circulate certain of his efforts among his friends and to bequeath his more materialist manuscripts to Naigeon for posthumous publication. In his letter authorizing Naigeon to so act for him, he specifically informed his friend that he was counting on him to publish only those works "that would harm neither my memory, nor anyone's peace."[16] Where d'Holbach and Naigeon were active and ingenious proselytizers for their systematic atheism, Diderot had chosen a quieter and less impatient route. He was speculating freely (at times, if we are to believe him, unsure of his own intellectual ballast),[17] pursuing his own internal dialogue on the nature of the material and the conceptual world. He was pleased to discuss and to show to his friends his atheistic speculations, and pleased indeed to offer them to posterity, but it was not for him to assume pseudonyms, devise methods of foreign publication, and carefully oversee the process of getting such speculations before the reading public in order to lead the eighteenth century into the realms of his own advanced thought. Atheism mattered to Diderot, but it was not the social issue of the moment as it was for d'Holbach and Naigeon. When Naigeon, for example, turned bitterly against Voltaire for the Patriarch's sustained polemic against atheism, Diderot wrote him a stinging letter, reminding him that Voltaire had "all of his life held his whip raised against tyrants, fanatics and the other great evildoers of this world. . . .

[16] Diderot, *Corr.*, XII, 231.

[17] On his *Rêve de d'Alembert* he wrote Sophie Volland in September 1769: "It is not possible to be more profound and more insane." Diderot, *Corr.*, IX, 140.

We think differently," Diderot concluded, "but let us not like each other any the less for it."[18]

In the publication of the *Encyclopédie*, Diderot was constantly active, constantly aware of the social goal. The *Encyclopédie*, however, did not reflect the materialist views of Diderot in its articles on "God," "Atheism," or "Soul," but rather those of the more theistically orthodox pastor Formey and the abbé Yvon.[19] Diderot was not about to jeopardize what enlightenment of his century he believed to be possible for the pyrrhic victory of expressing views for which he believed but a handful of his contemporaries to be prepared. In a letter of 1769 urging Hume to abandon philosophy and concentrate on history, Diderot wrote, "We preach wisdom to the deaf, and we are far from the century of reason."[20] It is not surprising then, as Herbert Dieckmann reminded us in his study of the *fonds Vandeul*, that Diderot was so insouciant about the propagation of his own philosophical views: "It is a well-known and often repeated fact that Diderot, after a certain point, no longer worried about publishing what he had written. He seems to have made no effort to have his true masterpieces published, the *Neveu de Rameau*, *Jacques le Fataliste*, the *Religieuse*, the *Rêve de d'Alembert*, the *Supplément au Voyage de Bougainville*, the *Réfutation d'Helvétius*."[21]

"Far from the century of reason," Diderot had time to wait for the world to know him as the author of his works. For d'Holbach and Naigeon the task was to preach atheism then and there, to

[18] Ibid., XII, 52-55.

[19] The abbé Yvon, whose signature in the *Encyclopédie* was X, was forced to leave France for exile in Holland, following the persecution of ecclesiastical authors of the *Encyclopédie* in the wake of the de Prades affair. His articles, however, were wholly orthodox, and his rational theology much in keeping with the theological tenor of his age. Upon his return to France in 1762 he quickly resumed the advance of his ecclesiastical career, ultimately becoming canon of the cathedral of Coutances and historiographer of the comte d'Artois. On the ecclesiastical writers for the *Encyclopédie* and the orthodoxy of so many of the critical theological articles, see Jacques Proust, *Diderot et l'Encyclopédie*, 18-22, 119-127, 153-162, 255-340. See also Franco Venturi, *Le origini dell'Enciclopedia*, passim; and Paul Vernière, "Le Spinozisme et l'Encyclopédie," *RHLF* (1951), 347-358. On Formey and his theological contributions to the *Encyclopédie*, see Eva Marcu, "Un encyclopédiste oublié: Formey," *RHLF* (1953), 296-305.

[20] Diderot, *Corr.*, IX, 40.

[21] Herbert Dieckmann, *Inventaire du Fonds Vandeul et Inédits de Diderot*, xii.

preach it in as many styles, on as many literate levels, with as many assumed pseudonyms as the traffic of the more advanced reading public would bear, and not to wait upon that age of wisdom. Having offered his civilization the *Encyclopédie*, a step toward that wisdom, Diderot could accept a slower pace. In this he must be distinguished from d'Holbach and Naigeon, for all the intellectual and stylistic help he may have given them. The latter two, and they alone, correspond to the traditional stereotype of the proselytizing atheists of the coterie holbachique.

If we expand the implications of the phrase "the atheists of the coterie holbachique" to include men identified as such by contemporaries who knew them and could distinguish between atheism and deism or anticlericalism, there are only three additional members of the coterie who, on circumstantial evidence alone, possibly should be placed beneath this rubric: Roux, Saint-Lambert and Helvétius. All three, however (assuming for the moment that such an identification would be correct), chose to refrain from explicitly communicating this side of their thought to the reading public, even through the medium of posthumous publication.

Both Morellet and Naigeon identified Roux as an atheistic materialist. In his *Mémoires*, Morellet, describing the diversity of conversations at d'Holbach's dinners, recalled three men's atheism in particular: "It is there also, since it must be said, that Diderot, doctor Roux and the good Baron himself established dogmatically the atheism of the *Système de la nature*. . . ."[22] Even though Naigeon made no secret of his own atheism, Morellet could not have added his name since Naigeon was still living when Morellet wrote his *Mémoires*, and it would have been a violation of a certain social code to have so described him. Naigeon himself, in his *Philosophie ancienne et moderne*, listed only six men as comprising the list of those of "our modern atheists" whose names could be made public, four of whom had been members of the coterie: d'Holbach, Diderot, Roux, and Helvétius.[23]

Roux did not publish his atheistic views nor leave such to be published by his friends. Quite to the contrary, in his one serious published philosophical work, his *Nouvelle encyclopédie portative* (1766), he took great pains to establish his own theism. In

[22] Morellet, *Mémoires*, I, 130-132.
[23] Naigeon, *Philosophie ancienne et moderne*, III, 351-352.

his introduction he explicitly announced and sought to justify his belief in God, arguing in addition that knowledge of and obedience to God's laws were necessary for happiness in the next world.[24] In his analysis of the paths to knowledge, he secured theology in certainty rather than in empirical probability by making it a science whose truths were discernible by pure reflection, as were those of mathematics.[25] Although he borrowed heavily from other sources, including Diderot's *Encyclopédie*, for his articles, and thus could have relied upon an orthodox theologian's article on God (thereby avoiding the appearance that yet another philosopher was raising his voice in support of deistic theses), Roux, in his detailed admission of his debts to other books or thinkers, specifically claimed credit for his theological chapters, listing them among the handful emanating from his own work.[26] In his formal treatment of theology he added to the rational proofs of God's existence a classical statement of the argument from design, concluding: "We are thus assured that there exists a necessary and eternal Being, the cause of everything which exists in this universe . . . even of matter."[27]

It is possible, of course, that simple caution dictated Roux's inclusion of such passages. Indeed his attempt at anonymous publication of his *Nouvelle encyclopédie*, an unorthodox work on many subjects, was not very successful. In February 1766 the work became the subject of an investigation by the police, who concluded that the abbé de la Porte was its author; one week later, however, inspector d'Hémery's journal recorded: "It is not M. l'abbé de la Porte who is the author of the *Nouvelle encyclopédie*, but in fact, M. Roux, author of the *Journal de médecine*."[28] Nevertheless, there appears to have been more to his deistic arguments than this.

As his phrase "everything which exists in this universe . . . even

---

[24] Augustin Roux, *Nouvelle encyclopédie portative, ou Tableau générale des connaissances humaines*, I, v-vii.

[25] Ibid., xxxvi-xli.

[26] Ibid., lxxi-lxxxiii. This is a most interesting section of Roux's work, constituting a *Who's Who* of respectable mid-eighteenth-century authorities: the *Encyclopédie* on "arts et métiers"; Blaise on geometry; Trabault on mechanics; Condillac on epistemology; Marmontel on literature; Laugier on architecture; Boerhaave, Newton, Helsham and Haller (among others) on the natural sciences; Benjamin Franklin on electricity, etc.

[27] Ibid., I, 397-400.

[28] B.N., MS *Coll. Anisson-Duperron*, CIV, folios 7-8.

of matter" indicates, Roux was explicit in his formal rejection of materialist hypotheses. In fact, he went a good deal farther than simple caution would have indicated. In his chapter on movement he specifically attempted to weaken the heart of the materialist argument by denying the validity of describing motion as an essential property of matter. Movement, he wrote, was not a thing that matter contained, but rather "an action by which masses . . . augment or diminish the distance which separates them." However clear or confused in his own mind Roux may have been in urging the conceptual distinctions which he articulated in this chapter, he was attempting to establish a point that he was to exploit to great advantage in his chapter on God; specifically, that in all our conceptions of motion, it is understood not as something inherent in matter but as a relationship which we observe to exist between or among material bodies. It was axiomatic for d'Holbach's materialism that the concept of motion could not be separated from the concept of matter, and it was precisely this contention that Roux was challenging.[29]

Elsewhere he went yet farther. For d'Holbach, Naigeon, and Diderot, the ability to reduce the behavior of matter to "inviolable laws" of mechanics constituted a major proof of the conceptual necessity of uniting the idea of matter and the idea of motion into one ontological entity, matter-in-motion. Roux, in his review of Haller's *Elémens de la physiologie*, a work of great importance to Diderot's, Naigeon's and (to a lesser extent) d'Holbach's materialism, as it had been to La Mettrie's, specifically warned against such a use of Haller's science: "[I]t is necessary to be careful not to fall into the error of the mechanists of the last century [the Cartesians], who believed that they could submit everything to their calculations. There are, in the animal machine, an infinity of movements that it is impossible to bring under the known laws of Mechanics. M. de Haller certainly felt all of these difficulties, and he avoided them with much care."[30]

From these considerations Roux deduced the antimaterialist arguments that were to occupy a major portion of his defense of theism in the *Nouvelle encyclopédie*. From experience, Roux asserted, man learns that matter is constantly in a state of flux; the substance remains, but assumes an almost endless variety of forms. Observation, he continued, teaches us that such change is

[29] Roux, *Nouvelle encyclopédie*, I, 320-385.
[30] *Journal de médecine* XVIII (Jan.-June 1763), 105-106.

always "a result of some motion." Since, conceptually, the concepts of matter and motion are distinguishable, and motion can be identified as the cause of all change, and, hence, of all phenomena, the critical question in the debate over the ultimate cause of the universe as we know it can be reduced to the following empirical question: do we learn from experience that bodies are capable of "putting themselves into motion" spontaneously or, rather, that there must exist "some cause outside of [material bodies], which is foreign to them." Since experience teaches that no body at rest "puts itself into motion," Roux answered, it is proven that: "There exists, thus, outside of material substance, a cause capable of putting it into motion . . . the principal of all of the changes which occur in this universe . . . a first cause . . . a necessary and eternal Being . . . the prime mover [and] also the author of Matter . . . eternal, infinite . . . all-powerful, supremely free, supremely good, supremely just."[31]

Roux's arguments joined issue so directly with "the atheism of the *Système de la nature*" that if Morellet had been the only figure to identify "doctor Roux" as an atheist, it would be tempting to hypothesize that he simply misunderstood a series of philosophical disputations pitting Roux *against* the materialists. Naigeon's identification of Roux as a materialist, however, cannot be so dismissed. Several possible explanations present themselves. It is plausible that Roux was a deist as late as 1766, but was "converted" by d'Holbach, Diderot and Naigeon before his death in 1776. If that were the case, then it should be noted that he was a deist for over half the duration of his participation in the coterie. It is equally plausible that Roux, understanding so well the nature of the issues at hand, was capable of arguing both sides of the materialist-deist controversy and was many things to many men. The context in which Naigeon counted Roux among "our modern atheists" was one in which he was naming the individuals whom he thought capable of carefully refuting the most talented philosophical spiritualists of the past. A third possibility, raised by certain passages in the *Nouvelle encyclopédie*, is that Roux was privately a consistent atheist and materialist, but one who did not believe such doctrines useful to society.

For d'Holbach and Naigeon, the "utility" of atheism was an almost overriding concern: a morality and a social code, however

---

[31] Roux, *Nouvelle encyclopédie*, I, 397-400.

beneficial, that were founded upon a metaphysical system demonstrably false, rested upon an insecure base. This is an aspect of their thought that often is overlooked, the argument that many of the *traditional* norms would be *better preserved* and *more respected* if made independent of the truth or falsity of theological propositions. In addition, for d'Holbach and Naigeon, so long as man believed in any entity, sphere of reality, or source of values above or apart from the material world of nature, he was free to ignore (or to appeal beyond) the realm of human consequences in his normative codes and self-justifications. For d'Holbach and Naigeon, precisely this aspect of theism had borne the most pernicious fruit, and nothing mattered more than the elimination of all theistic doctrines from moral philosophy. Roux, however, established the same humanistic outlook—that the desire for "the conservation of the species," joined to "a sentiment of general benevolence," was at the origin of human moral impulses—by basing it upon the deistic natural-law argument that self-preservation and benevolence were self-justifying norms because they were "found written in the depth of [man's] heart . . . engraved there [by] the Creator." It would be, therefore, a violation of *God's* law to harm or destroy human life. What "prevented" man from acting upon this, he continued, was that "the passions, by blinding his mind," had caused man to deduce often incorrect personal and social codes from the principle which God had instilled in nature. To correct this God had given to man a Revelation, with its message of the punishments and rewards in the afterlife. In so discussing Revelation, Roux, at least in this one maneuver, not only went beyond the frontier of atheism and deism, but beyond the frontier of deism and traditional Christianity as well.[32]

The myth of the coterie, thus, has planed down some of the more interesting distinguishable characteristics of even those men who were identified as unbelievers by their contemporaries. Why would Roux, an atheist to his friends, publish a work so distinctly antimaterialist or at least, since we do not know at what point he could be identified as an atheist, allow such a work to stand unrevised? Given his foundation of benevolent moral principles upon God's natural law and revelation, and assuming that he himself did not at the time believe this, perhaps Roux quite simply

[32] Ibid., II, 123-134.

would have agreed with a sentiment that Voltaire later expressed, namely, that atheism was fine for the quiet philosopher but woe to the society whose powerful men felt free of a divinely supported moral code.[33] Darcet, in his *éloge* of Roux, claimed that his friend's *Nouvelle encyclopédie* was conceived of while Roux was the tutor of the prominent d'Héricourt family whose son, his charge, was destined for a brilliant career in the parlement de Paris. The *Nouvelle encyclopédie*, according to Darcet, was intended to serve as a model for the private education of young noblemen, equipping them to make their public mark in the world.[34] While d'Holbach and Naigeon wanted their audience to understand the moral implications of an atheistic cosmology, it is more than possible that Roux thought it most unwise to tell his young noblemen that the duty to respect life and act benevolently was not divine. In an earlier scientific work, Roux had written that the fact that men unqualified to be scientists believed themselves capable of understanding physics had retarded rather than advanced the accomplishments of that discipline. "Everyone believes that he has eyes, and wants to see," he wrote, but most dilettantes were not prepared to see in the same phenomenon what a scientist could see.[35] This view would not be incompatible with the fear that in the realm of metaphysics and moral philosophy, the dilettantes were even less prepared to understand the implications of the systematic truth of things.

In the case of Saint-Lambert we have only the testimony of Mme d'Epinay, who knew him well, to the effect that he was an avowed atheist. Her *Mémoires* were written long after the events she described, almost as an autobiographical novel, but her portraits were not too consciously distorted. In this work she recalled her first meetings with Saint-Lambert and described a discussion of religion which had shocked her. Rousseau, Saint-Lambert and several other men were discussing the world's religions, and Saint-Lambert was denouncing them all with great bitterness. Mme d'Epinay recalled that when she asked him "to spare natural religion," Saint-Lambert had replied, "No more than the others." The notion of God, he continued in her account, "is, like many

[33] Voltaire, *Corr.*, LXXVI-LXXVIII, passim. This aspect of atheism worried him terribly in the period following the publication of d'Holbach's *Système*.

[34] Darcet, *Eloge de Roux*, 11.

[35] Roux, *Recherches historiques et critiques, sur les différens moyens qu'on a employés jusqu'à présent pour refroidir les liqueurs*, 2.

others, very useful in several great minds, such as Trajan, Marcus-Aurelius, and Socrates, where it can produce only heroism; but it is the seed of all folly."[36]

This remembered snippet of conversation offers very little from which to re-create Saint-Lambert's metaphysics or cosmology. When we turn to his published philosophical works written, he claimed, in the 1780s, but not presented to the public until 1798, there is nothing that either belies or confirms an assumption of his atheism. Quite simply, Saint-Lambert discussed moral philosophy, the focus of his *Catéchisme universel*, without reference to a Supreme Being. This omission constituted atheism for the critic Nisard,[37] writing in the mid-nineteenth century, but for Saint-Lambert's Directorial and Napoleonic contemporaries, who had no tolerance for atheism, it in no way could be taken as such. In April 1799, the minister of the Interior decreed that "precepts extracted from the *Catéchisme universel de morale*, by Saint-Lambert, would be placed on bulletin boards in all of the primary schools of the Republic."[38] They were not teaching atheism in those schools.

What Saint-Lambert had done in the *Catéchisme universel*, as he carefully explained in a "discours préliminaire," was to define morality as a systematic regulation of human *moeurs*, based upon an empirically determined "knowledge of men," toward the ends of human happiness, self-preservation and order.[39] The view that a "science" of morality was possible was a view shared by atheists and deists, not to mention many Christians as well, in the eighteenth century. In a brief history of the formulation of ethical codes, Saint-Lambert observed that almost all had been linked to religion, and added in one context: "It is even certain that this idea that our fathers are images of this creator-being who wants the good of men and imposes virtue upon them, must have added to respect, to filial love and to the power of education. . . ."[40]

The problem, as Saint-Lambert defined it, was simply that such

[36] Mme d'Epinay, *Mémoires*, I, 371-383.

[37] Suard, *Mémoires et correspondances historiques et littéraires*, Charles Nisard, ed., 67-68. Nisard, discussing Suard's role in attempting to influence Saint-Lambert's publisher to reissue the *Catéchisme universel*, commented, "It's the pure doctrine of materialism."

[38] *Moniteur universel* (12 April 1799).

[39] Saint-Lambert, *Principes des moeurs chez toutes les nations, ou Catéchisme universel*, I, 1-51.

[40] Ibid., 4-6.

codes were not "knowledge" of morality, "knowledge" being defined as learning gained from observation and experience. If one appreciates that for Saint-Lambert "morality" was a science analogous in terms of its development to astronomy and physics, one can see that his thesis merely stated that its laws were to be *discovered* in empirical knowledge of the natural world. This is in no way incompatible with a deistic explanation of why this should be the case. D'Holbach and Naigeon argued that true moral knowledge would be wholly inconsistent with the implications of any theistic metaphysics or cosmology whatever, and sought to identify and root out any residue of theistic philosophy in Western ethics. Saint-Lambert made no such claim and no such effort. He attacked "superstition" as a major cause of immoral behavior, but he followed Plutarch in identifying superstition as that which "fears air, earth, seas, stars, lights, shadows, noise, silence, sleep and dreams," to which he added the fear of pleasure.[41] In that same context, Saint-Lambert explicitly employed the familiar deistic critique of superstition as that which absurdly assigned human emotions to God. Discussing the tradition of seeing in comets the anger of God, he asserted, "God does not become angry."[42] For d'Holbach and Naigeon, such an assertion would have been as much an invitation to supernaturalism as an assertion that God favored the collection of tithes. Such a phrase was inconceivable in their atheistic works.

Naigeon, in his list of "our modern atheists," could not have been expected to mention Saint-Lambert, who was still alive at the time of that writing, so his omission adds nothing to the evidence at hand. He did, however, specifically identify Helvétius in that context. This could not have surprised too many of his contemporaries, since one of the primary charges against *De l'esprit* had been that it favored a system of materialism.

In fact, *De l'esprit*'s discussion of "matter," occurring in a chapter on "the abuse of words," was above all an assertion of a fundamental skepticism concerning the possibility of resolving the spiritualist-materialist debate. Since at the time of its writing the loudest dogmatism appeared in the spiritualists' camp, Helvétius directed most of his analytic critique to *their* positive assertions; nevertheless, his argument was hostile to a dogmatic materialism as well. For Helvétius the spiritualist concept of matter depended

[41] Ibid., II, 307-330.   [42] Ibid., 316-317.

upon the dogmatic assertion that extension, solidity, and impenetrability were the sole properties of material bodies, necessitating a recourse to an immaterial substance to account for their acquisition of *sensibilité*. What Helvétius argued in reply was that from experience alone, it was impossible to prove that "all bodies are absolutely *insensible*."[43] This was nothing but a restatement, substituting "sensibilité" as the phenomenon to be accounted for, of Locke's argument (repeated by Voltaire) that there was no way to *prove* that matter could not be inherently endowed with thought.[44] Helvétius was in decidedly unatheistic company. The essential thesis of his discussion was that such questions could not be decided empirically, and there is no reason to assume that d'Holbach's *Système de la nature* would not have struck him as equally philosophically unfruitful. As he wrote: ". . . it was thus not necessary to construct different systems of the world, to lose oneself in the combination of possibilities, and to make those prodigious efforts of the mind that have led to, and really had to have led to, more or less ingenious errors."[45]

Upon textual analysis alone, the other two aspects of Helvétius' *De l'esprit* that raised the cry of atheism from his contemporaries —his determinism and his moral naturalism—reveal themselves equally susceptible of deistic interpretation. Helvétius was as strictly deterministic in his concept of the laws of nature as d'Holbach or Naigeon, but so were many deists. When Helvétius discussed the issue of determinism, he mentioned the Turks "who, in their religion, admit the dogma of necessity, a principle destructive of all religion, and who can, as a consequence, be regarded as deists." In that same discussion, arguing that temporal pains and pleasures sufficed to preserve moral and punish immoral behavior, he cited the examples of both virtuous deists and atheists.[46]

In *De l'esprit* and in his posthumously published *De l'homme*, Helvétius was concerned primarily with the delineation of a strict sensationalistic epistemology and its moral and social consequences. There was almost no attention paid in either work to cosmology or systematic metaphysics, and it is not surprising that Morel-

[43] Helvétius, *Oeuvres complètes*, I, 43-45.

[44] See John Locke, *Essay Concerning Human Understanding* (London, 1690), Book IV, Chap. III, Sec. 6; Voltaire, *Lettres philosophiques* (Paris, 1734), Letter 13.

[45] Helvétius, *Oeuvres Complètes*, I, 43-45.

[46] Ibid., 305-306.

let did not list Helvétius among those who argued the materialist hypothesis within the coterie. Where for d'Holbach the clear implication of sensationalism was the inconceivability and hence the nonexistence of a God, for Helvétius the unavoidable implication of his epistemology was that such an issue simply was not worth discussing. As he wrote in his posthumously published work: "In fact, what does the word God signify? The still unknown cause of order and movement. Now what can one say about an unknown cause?"[47] Helvétius did remove the muzzle of caution in the work which he intended to be published after his death; he presented bitter and rhetorically violent attacks against the Roman Catholic Church and its priesthood with an explicitness and frankness that he had in no way allowed himself in *De l'esprit*. All things must be judged as they appear to our senses, Helvétius now urged, and by this criterion he condemned the Roman Catholic Church as hypocritical, avaricious and cruel. Going further, he added that as opposed to the true religion, the Roman Catholic Church was of human institution: "Intolerance and persecution," he asserted, "are not of divine commandment."[48] So once again a philosophe identified as an atheist employed theistic language to add weight and force to his social arguments. Describing the true "universal religion" as one based upon empirically determined natural truths and promoting life, liberty and the security of property, Helvétius elaborated that man did not have this religion in a direct Revelation from God because "heaven . . . wanted man to cooperate in [the achievement of] his happiness by [the use of] his reason.

"There is the only cult to which I want man to aspire," he continued, "the only which could become universal, the only worthy of a God and bearing His seal and that of the truth. Any other cult bears the imprint of man, of deceit and falsehood. The will of a just and good God is that the children of the earth be happy and that they enjoy all the pleasures compatible with the public good."[49]

Thus, in a work in which he was free to proselytize for whatever mattered most to him, Helvétius, like Roux and Saint-Lam-

[47] Ibid., III, 119.

[48] Ibid., 412-417. For examples of Helvétius' ardent discussion of the evils of the Roman Catholic Church, see ibid., III, 58-62, 67-81, 255-265, 392-401, 408-423; IV, 173-237.

[49] Ibid., III, 63-65.

bert, focused upon issues he considered of a higher priority than the question of atheism. All three may well have agreed with d'Holbach and Naigeon that there could be no higher court of appeal in ethical, social and political thought than the demonstration of natural human consequences, but if that jurisdiction could be established firmly by enlisting divine support for its authority, all three, unlike the two unremitting atheists, appeared willing to pay the price of philosophical silence or duplicity. After all, what counted, by their own ethical systems, were the consequences of their actions; they would not have been the only philosophes who would have agreed with d'Alembert's warning that to expose men who had been for so long in the dark to too much light too quickly was not to enlighten them, but to blind them.[50] Plato had said much the same millennia before and had termed it the "noble lie." If Morellet, Mme d'Epinay and Naigeon were correct in their descriptions of Roux, Saint-Lambert and Helvétius, there were noble liars among even some of the atheists within the coterie. This is a far cry from the concept of a "school of atheism" preaching from d'Holbach's home. There appears to have been little agreement on the need to atheize the reading public of their time.

The coterie contained a one-man school of philosophical skepticism as well, in the person of Friedrich-Melchior Grimm, a would-be pyrrhonist who appeared to play the role of Hume's Philo in the dialogues of d'Holbach's group. Frank to the point of bravado in his *Correspondance littéraire*, or perhaps feeling that his small but select circle of royal and princely subscribers were entitled to receive from Paris something strong and heady, a vicarious participation in the philosophical lustiness of France, Grimm hid almost nothing from his audience. He shared with them his knowledge of the philosophes' quarrels and debates. He also shared with them his own consistent view that in matters of philosophy and theology, almost no one in France, neither priest nor philosophe, was uttering an intelligible word. This negative judgment held true for him in the debate between deistic and atheistic cosmologies. The limits of reason's ability to structure the chaos of experience were so manifest to Grimm that it appears to have shocked, but not surprised, him every time someone presumed to speak about the nature of the world. The closest he ever came to the deists was in once admitting that he thought

[50] D'Alembert, *Oeuvres et correspondances inédites*, C. Henry, ed. (Paris, 1887), 8.

there was more of what we call good in an evil man than there was of what we call evil in a good man, which on the whole gave the nature of things a somewhat orderly balance. He never repeated that one retreat from the ramparts of the New Academy. In the same passage, discussing a recent deistic work, he made it clear that his own philosophy began and ended with what he was unable to know by reason and what he was unable to deny by personal experience: "I conceive nothing of the existence or essence of God; I understand nothing of the principles and first causes of this universe; I do not know what matter is, nor space, movement and time: all of these things are incomprehensible for me. I know that the idea of my existence and the desire for my well-being are inseparable; I know that nature has attached me to these two things by invincible chains; I know that reason often tells me to hate, to despise life, and that nature always forces me to hold on to it. I know that nature has impressed within my heart the love of order and of justice, which makes me prefer constantly the tranquillity of conscience to the most useful crime."[51] There were not many philosophes in Paris who would link together God and matter as things equally incomprehensible, and set at variance with each other nature and reason, the just and the useful.

In his skepticism Grimm at times made common cause with the atheism of d'Holbach, Naigeon and Diderot, when such atheism was analytic and critical of theism, although never when it was itself synthetic and constructive. He could follow none of them into a speculative or systematic materialism, but he could join with them in posing the difficulties of rational theology. He related with relish, for example, the story of a walk in the countryside with a friend of his with whom he was discussing the argument from design, of which his companion was an enthusiastic advocate. Pausing at an ant mound, his friend grew more and more rhapsodic as he drew the arguments for providence from the manifest order, purposefulness, design and constitutional harmony of the ant colony. In his excitement, Grimm noted, the deist stepped on the mound, and "with one kick, he exterminated the entire population with its laws and its government."[52]

For d'Holbach and for Naigeon, however, the elimination of theistic metaphysics was only the first step toward the construction of a materialist world-view. They drew from philosophy, cosmology and natural science, theories and data with which they

[51] Grimm, *Corr. litt.*, III, 509-510.   [52] Ibid., IV, 136-139.

systematically established an alternative to the history and nature
of the theistic cosmos. Its basic formal features were a thorough-
going epistemological materialism, mechanism and determinism
from which it was concluded that the movements of matter according to fixed and invariable laws accounted for all of the
known, and would account for all of the as yet unknown, phenomena of the universe. When they argued that immaterial substance, spiritual causality, and a free human will were concepts
devoid of meaning, Grimm would be at their side. "So long as
we do not know this universe," he once wrote in support of Diderot, "then, as they say in the schools, *a priori* everything is necessity. Liberty is a word void of sense."[53] But as he himself approvingly quoted Diderot in another context, "You can establish and
destroy anything by some reasoning, but nothing proves like the
facts."[54] And when it came to facts, it was not only that man had
so few at his disposal, but that, Grimm asserted, there were those
which man never could acquire. Thus, as Hume later was to write
in the *Dialogues*, man would have to have observed the beginnings
of his or other universes to know what was necessary in the origins
of things and what was not. Nature was indeed in "fermentation,"
Grimm agreed with the materialists, and it added nothing to hypothesize an immaterial cause. It also added nothing, for Grimm,
to deduce from this that one knew the materiality of the universe's
origins: "In what manner did this fermentation begin? There is
a question that will remain forever without an answer."[55]

In the face of these considerations theology was for Grimm the
most presumptuous of all areas of human thought, and he termed
it "the absurd science."[56] He called, however, not for a systemati-
zation of natural philosophy without God, but for a pure "admission of ignorance" by all philosophers of all schools.[57]

D'Holbach might write a "Système" of nature, but he did so
against the implicit advice of his friend Grimm, who asserted that
"the facts are everywhere missing, and everywhere the philosophers have substituted their false systems for them."[58] Grimm
warned that the problem lay not simply in the absence of data,

---

[53] Ibid., III, 249. [54] Ibid., V, 135.

[55] Ibid., IV, 132-134. [56] Ibid., VII, 292-293.

[57] Grimm, *Corr. litt.*, IV, 136-137.

[58] Ibid., VI, 23-24. See also ibid., V, 55-59, where Grimm warned students
of nature: ". . . do not make systems in that area. . . . Above all, never
make yourselves interpreters of nature, and be persuaded that an infant
who knows only to babble is not made to penetrate into her mysteries."

but precisely in the disproportion between subject and object, concluding that "nature will remain eternally impenetrable for us."[59] To assume a deterministic mechanism and wait for patient research to fill in its laws, thus, would be illusory: "All our competence consists in generalizing our ideas, in imagining relationships which exist only in our heads, and which, as much as they do honor to our imagination or sagacity, are none the less chimerical; in forming, finally, from several particular facts, inductions upon which we establish allegedly eternal and invariable laws which nature has never known."[60] It was not a state of affairs that for Grimm could be remedied by the substitution of one formal philosophy for another: "Thus, the source of the errors is in ourselves, and as a result irremovable."[61]

Grimm did not conceal in the pages of his *Correspondance littéraire* that he was not himself a theist, but he did not stress the fact, and he allowed his protégé Meister, who edited the *Correspondance* frequently during Grimm's absence, to express distinctly theistic views.[62] In reviewing Voltaire's deistic critique of the *Système de la nature*, Grimm declared that the problems involved in the controversy were "a sea of difficulties," but in the end he supported d'Holbach on the grounds of fewer such difficulties. That movement alone, without intelligence and design, could produce the phenomena of the universe was indeed "inexplicable," Grimm admitted, but it was "also a fact," he continued, that in supposing a God in command of movement, "you explain nothing, and you add to one inexplicable thing a thousand difficulties which make it absurd over and above the going rate. . . ." It was not that d'Holbach had known what he was talking about, but that he had asserted merely one inexplicable hypothesis instead of several. In the end, in Grimm's closest accord with the atheists, he declared that given Voltaire's admitted concept of necessity, "[It is] better to believe that intelligence can be the effect of the movement of matter than to attribute it to an all-powerful worker who does nothing, and whose will can prevent nothing whatsoever nor change anything's manner of being."[63]

[59] Ibid., VI, 23-24.   [60] Ibid., 26-27.   [61] Ibid.

[62] See, for example, Meister's disobliging reviews of d'Holbach's works and their influence, in Grimm, *Corr. litt.*, XI, 495-496; XII, 205-206. See Meister's own support of theistic writers critical of atheism in ibid., XV, 229-235.

[63] Ibid., IX, 111-121.

This conclusion, however, no more made Grimm an atheist and materialist than the final passages of Hume's *Dialogues* made the Scottish skeptic a deist and believer in Providence. Grimm's one concession to the critical dogma of deterministic necessity made his own position abundantly clear: "If there is anything constant in the world, it is the incomprehensibility of the things that we observe."[64]

* * *

Apart from the manifest atheism of d'Holbach, Diderot, and Naigeon, the perhaps temporary, perhaps enduring private atheism of Roux, Saint-Lambert, and Helvétius, and the skepticism of Grimm, there is no record of any other critique of the belief in God emanating from members of the coterie holbachique in their published works or in reported conversations. In 1804 Sylvain Maréchal, an atheist and a friend of Naigeon, published a quickly notorious *Dictionnaire des athées*, proudly listing all philosophers and men of letters whom he possibly could term atheists (by almost any criteria), including, for example, Bayle, Spinoza, and d'Alembert, and living men as well, such as Naigeon, Cabanis, and Volney. If there were a single passage of poetry or prose, or a single anecdote concerning a conversation that established someone ever so tenuously as an atheist, above all someone from the eighteenth-century world of letters in France, such evidence was employed to add a name to Maréchal's compendium. His 500-page book included only five names from among the members of the coterie holbachique: Diderot, Helvétius, d'Holbach, Naigeon, and Roux.[65]

* * *

Two additional thinkers of the coterie holbachique, Chastellux and Le Roy, discussed questions which usually impinged upon the

[64] Ibid., IV, 136-137.

[65] Sylvain Maréchal, *Dictionnaire des athées anciens et modernes*. Maréchal's ultimate criterion for a man's being an atheist, he explained in his preliminary discourse, was that a person believe that "I can be wise without a God" (Maréchal, *Dictionnaire*, x). See the following pages for his particular comments on members of the coterie holbachique: Diderot, 108-109; Helvétius, 182; d'Holbach (listed under "Mirabeaud," a pseudonym), 286-287, 295 (under "*Morale universelle*, l'auteur de"), 312-313 (under "Olback"); Naigeon, 299-301; Roux, 403 (Maréchal's identification of Roux as an atheist was, he indicated frankly, based wholly upon Naigeon's opinion to that effect).

debate between atheism and theism in its eighteenth-century terms, and both might be read by the unwary or predisposed as offering support to important materialist theses. Chastellux dealt with the question of motion and its relationship to matter, and Le Roy dealt with the division between human and animal life and with the question of whether or not the implications of Helvétius' *De l'esprit* were materialist. An analysis of the relevant works, however, reveals that neither man was addressing himself to the question of atheism, and that both authors granted at least one fundamental theistic or spiritualist hypothesis.

In 1784 Chastellux published a brief essay entitled "Pensées sur le mouvement." It began with the assertion that man did not know by direct experience the essences of things, but rather formed concepts by virtue of "existence and privation." By this Chastellux meant that we could only form ideas of things whose presence *and* absence we experienced. Because there is day and its absence (night), we form ideas of both the existent entity and its privation; were there only a continually present entity or experience, "we would have no conscious perception of it, we would not give it a name." Because we have seen things both in motion and at rest we have the idea of motion. From this we have concluded that motion is something "which does not always exist." This conclusion, however, has placed us, Chastellux continued, in a great conceptual difficulty, for given our experience and scientific understanding of motion, "It is nevertheless impossible to imagine how movement is destroyed." What we must assume then is that "rest," considered as the absence of any *force* of motion, is an appearance, a fortuitous one in that it makes us aware of motion as a separate entity, but an appearance nonetheless. Should we conceive of matter as ever *truly* at rest, in the sense of devoid of a force of motion, the universe and its operations would become incomprehensible. Chastellux thus urged that the distinction between "inert" and "animate" matter is a false one, causing us to rely on an "incomprehensible process" or an "occult quality" to account for the behavior of matter. All observed matter possesses its own force of motion, and thus of activity.[66]

At first glance this would seem to be reasoning directly aimed at a fundamental point of contention between materialists and spiritualists in the French eighteenth-century's odd philosophical

[66] Chastellux, "Pensées sur le mouvement," in Bergasse, *Considérations sur le magnétisme animal*, 143-145.

grapplings with the concept of matter and the cause of its behavior. The materialists were arguing, to put the case simply, that we needed no recourse to theistic or spiritualist hypotheses concerning the causes of the behavior of "inert" matter, because matter was not "inert." Did one need a God or a spiritual force to set an inert material body into spontaneous motion? No, wrote Diderot, in the *Rêve de d'Alembert*, and to prove it he turned a marble statue into moving human flesh by soaking it in rich mud, planting seeds in it, and feeding the crop to a man.[67] The terms of the debate, if you will, were set by the theists and spiritualists: given what we know of matter, its possession of the power to move and to act is incomprehensible in terms of its own properties; matter being inert, the presence of an "immaterial" substance is a necessary inference from the existence and maintenance of motion and activity.[68] What is inconceivable and counter-em-

[67] Diderot, *Oeuvres* (A-T), II, 105-110.

[68] See, for example, abbé Nicolas-Sylvestre Bergier, *Examen du matérialisme, ou Réfutation du Système de la nature*, I, 154-155, 174-176, where the Assemblée du Clergé's official apologist asserted that the dispute between spiritualists and materialists depended for its resolution upon empirical and logical factors, urging his readers to decide which position had "fewer difficulties"; if the doctrine of the materialists were "less cloudy" or rested on "clearer proofs and more solid foundations," he continued, "we must not hesitate to prefer it." Bergier stated the matter explicitly in this context: "As soon as it is evidently proven that movement is not essential to matter, that the latter is purely passive by its nature and without any activity, we are forced to believe that there is in the universe a substance of a different nature, an active being to which movement must be attributed as it is to the first cause, a Motor that is not itself matter." On Bergier's appointment as pensioned apologist, specifically for the purpose of refuting d'Holbach's work for the Assemblée du Clergé, see *Collection des procès-verbaux des Assemblées générales du Clergé de France*, VII, Part Two, 1817-1819 (4 May 1770).

The Benedictine monk Louis-Mayeul Chaudon, in his *Anti-Dictionnaire philosophique*, I, 66-70, and II, 125-129, also addressed himself to d'Holbach's materialism, agreeing with Bergier (explicitly) that the debate must be resolved in the study of nature and concluding: "The study of Physics is quite properly the cure of the two extremes, Atheism and Superstition. . . . It proves that there is an intelligent first cause, and it makes known the particular mechanical causes of this and that effect. Physics augments admiration and diminishes astonishment." Johann von Castillon, professor of philosophy at the University of Utrecht, concluded in his *Observations sur le livre intitulé Système de la nature*, 528, that "One must not forget that the *Système de la nature* hazards only this proposition in entirety—*there is no God*. In order to accord the nonexistence of God with the actual state of things, these are necessary: (1) that matter exists by itself, (2) that move-

pirical, d'Holbach, Diderot, and Naigeon urged, is that matter should be viewed as inert. In this context, was not Chastellux's argument clearly that of a materialist?

It was not, because he did not address himself to the origins of his "force of motion," but only to its presence. He did not urge that this "force" arose from the fundamental properties of matter or was itself a fundamental property, but only that all matter now possessed this force. In the final analysis, the debate in France was not over the "forces" that material nature possessed, but over the question of whether such forces were essential or acquired. There could be empirical questions involved at times, such as the use of Tremblay's polyp to demonstrate the *divisibility* of the power of generation (divisibility being incompatible, according to the spiritualists' own definitions, with the concept of spiritual or immaterial substance). In the end, however, the debate was truly conceptual: could one conceive of such forces and powers, whatever they be, as arising from the properties of matter considered abstractly? On this question, Chastellux was silent; he did not argue that his "force of motion" was essential or acquired. By implication he seemed to assert its acquired nature, for he spoke of it as "spread throughout matter" ("répandu dans la matière"), seemingly separating it conceptually from its host.[69] The reason for this is that Chastellux's "Pensées" were not intended to be a discourse on the nature of matter, but a discourse on the nature of the force of motion. They were not intended to establish atheism, but to establish mesmerism.

Chastellux, having established the existence of this "force of motion spread throughout matter," believed that he knew the nature of that force: currents of "electricity and magnetism" which were the motor of nature.[70] To understand the substance and purpose of Chastellux's discussion, we must enter his sense of physics, dynamics and science.

"It is slightly repugnant to reason to imagine an absolute void," Chastellux wrote; so to rescue Newtonian physics from its doc-

---

ment is essential to it, (3) that all that exists is either matter or a mode of matter." The central argument which he urged against d'Holbach, in ibid., 97-145, was that since observation demonstrates that all movement by or in matter is contingent upon prior movement, there must be a First Cause which is itself not material.

[69] Chastellux, "Pensées sur le mouvement," 144.

[70] Ibid., 147-148.

trine of action-at-a-distance, Chastellux proposed that electrical and magnetic forces are communicated from one body to another across space, providing for the motion necessary to their observed gravitational behavior. This would not be Descartes' *plenum*, which Newton, it was believed, had demonstrated to be incompatible with observed phenomena (since the plenum would have to exert some friction which did not appear in physical calculations applied to celestial bodies), but it would not be Newton's "inconceivable" effects-without-physical-contact either: ". . . we would be very relieved by an hypothesis which would see the very causes of motion in fluids which should [according to Newtonian hypotheses concerning the effects of friction upon motion] retard it, and this difference would be entirely attributable to this single principle, that instead of considering space as filled with a dead and inert matter [as Descartes had considered it], we suppose it ceaselessly crossed by currents which support and conserve motion."[71]

A disciple of Mesmer, Chastellux concluded that the most manifest evidence for the existence of such forces was to be found in human and animal magnetism and electricity (which Chastellux believed Mesmer's experiments to have established). In man, Chastellux urged, such forces take the form of "emanations . . . which appear to leave the body in a state of perfection."[72]

By "perfection" Chastellux meant equilibrium, for this was the central concept of his thesis: movement can generate either equal motion per se or the production of additional force of motion. In Newtonian physics and dynamics, the motion of any body closer to or further away from another body, or the introduction of a new mass, all ought to affect in some great or small way the motion of that other body. But, Chastellux argued, if that were the case, the universe and the earth ought to be constantly complicated by new and irregular movements, for not only inanimate but, increasingly, animate bodies were generating new motions and new mass continually. "What becomes of these motions," Chastellux asked, "in the systems adopted in our days, in these systems which consider matter as if dead or, if you will, passive?" The births, deaths, walks, movements and emanations of living beings all ought to count for something, following Chastellux's bizarre sense of Newton, in the gravitation of the earth, in the solar system. But where are "the irregular movements," "the

71 Ibid., 149.   72 Ibid., 147-148.

anomalies"? To "rescue" basic physics and the coherence of our conceptions, Chastellux proposed the following hypothesis: the earth receives from animate motions not additional movement, but additional force; it converts the motion of living beings into magnetic and electrical forces, which it releases from its storehouse of such forces in the forms of currents, in order to restore equilibrium when necessary. Thus, nature "modifies, alters [and] distributes" as electrical and magnetic emanations the force communicated to it by living beings. "The interior of the globe," then, "is a great receiver of movement and thus a great center of activity," and "electricity and magnetism are the products of this interior elaboration, of the particular secretions of the globe, of the principles of the life of this vast individual entity, of its correspondences with the entire world."[73]

To prevent his reader from questioning piece by piece this safety-valve theory of magnetic forces preventing cosmic disorder, Chastellux settled the question of what became of missing motion once and for all in an argument which preceded, chronologically, the above considerations. We know, Chastellux urged, that at the moment of creation God stamped the earth with living things. This must have given a dramatic new movement to the earth, but such a movement has not appeared in the calculations of the physicists. What became of that motion, of that force? Clearly, he concluded, "inanimate" matter must have been able to transform it into additional force; all matter must respond to disequilibrium not by moving irregularly, for the universe is orderly, but by creating additional force which it releases in ways beneficial to the order and coherence of things: ". . . if animated matter can produce irregular movements, must it not be necessary that the center [of the earth] is itself animated in order to proportion itself to these anomalies and thus to restore the equilibrium or the forces of the conservation of the world?"[74]

The same hypothesis which for Chastellux preserves Newtonian physics and Cartesian clarity thus finds its strongest support from (and itself preserves) the concept of an ordered creation. Who could question the necessity of a creation? Only an atheist, of course, a d'Holbach, a Diderot, or a Naigeon. As d'Holbach had written, if one could accept the "miracle" of a creation, one could accept any and all chimerical miracles.[75]

---

[73] Ibid., 145-149.   [74] Ibid., 145.
[75] D'Holbach, *Système de la nature*, II, 386-387.

This interpretation of Chastellux's "Pensées sur le mouvement" is supported by the context of its publication. Chastellux was an early and vociferous supporter of Mesmer and one of the founders of the society devoted to furthering his theories of animal magnetism in France. Chastellux's "Pensées," although they never mentioned Mesmer specifically by name, were published as an appendix to Bergasse's *Considérations sur le magnétisme animal*, an important defense of Mesmer's hypotheses, to be read and understood in the context of *that* debate. And in that debate Chastellux and his friends within the coterie were on diametrically opposite sides. D'Holbach had invited Mesmer to demonstrate his theories experimentally before the coterie, and he had not impressed the Baron or his guests at all. Indeed, according to Meister, he had impressed no one within the coterie; no one, that is, except Chastellux, who by April 1784 was chairman of a committee formed to purchase Mesmer's secret for 100,000 *écus* and to pay him to teach them his mysteries. Chastellux must be counted not as an example of the uniformity of the coterie holbachique, let alone of its atheism, but rather of its diversity.[76]

Le Roy as well must be counted as an example of the diversity of the coterie, for he truly wished to discuss matters of natural philosophy and natural history without having to deal with the various metaphysical implications which his peer group, both theological and philosophical, insisted that a thinker confront. He was a man with much leisure time, in charge of royal hunts at Versailles, who spent many years observing and following game animals through the royal woods, noting their behavior, habits and responses to adversity, and speculating on the mental life that underlay their ways. He argued that animal behavior was inexplicable solely in terms of instincts and automatic mechanisms and that animals reasoned, learned, adapted, felt, remembered, and communicated—in short, that they possessed the same psychological and intellectual qualities as man. What interested him, above all, were the concrete details of animal life that necessitated such conclusions, and not the philosophical implications that others saw in these. His work was remarkable for its observations, not for its metaphysics.

Yet his subject matter was such that it placed him in a tradition associated with eighteenth-century materialism. As Le Roy himself noted with some irony, there once had been a time when Des-

[76] Grimm, *Corr. litt.*, XIII, 248.

cartes' view of the automatism of beasts was considered philosophically dangerous; now, those who ascribed cognitive and sensitive faculties to animals were considered dangerous. The debate, Le Roy urged, was an empirical one, without fundamental philosophical overtones. Descartes' automatism, he wrote in 1768, entailed uniform operations among members of the same species, but observation had proven that individual animals responded and adapted to their environment in ways that required memory and learning, cognitive and emotional change. Theologians who saw a metaphysical stake in such a debate "have not understood that the animal kingdom, although provided with faculties common to it and to man, still can be at an infinite distance from man."[77] Theologians, he had written in 1760, actually were worried about the implications of natural history and natural philosophy for the doctrine of the immortality of the soul. But natural history and philosophy, he urged, limiting themselves as they did to study of the natural world by systematic observation, could not impinge upon such matters beyond their ken.[78]

In the face of the arguments of the materialists, theologians in the eighteenth century had retreated to two not wholly complementary theses—one, that matter of itself was brute and inert, requiring spirit or divine force to acquire activity and motion (it was from the appearance of debating that point that we sought to remove Chastellux); two, that while the mechanisms of matter in motion according to fixed laws accounted for many phenomena of the natural world (however such motion and such mechanisms were acquired), the case of man's soul, its powers, thought and immortality, proved the reality of the spiritual and hence of the divine. Combating this second thesis, the materialists sought to reduce man's mental and emotional life to material and mechanistic models, to blur the line between man and beast. Le Roy, however, was attempting something far removed from that, namely, to raise the mental and emotional life of animals to terms the equivalent of those necessary to describe human psychical processes, without attempting to "reduce" such processes to any material model. When a critic in 1765 accused "the doctor of Nuremberg" (Le Roy's pseudonym) of "a suspicion of materialism," Le Roy responded directly to the issue at hand: "It is true,

[77] Le Roy, *Lettres sur les animaux*, 131-173; the concluding quotation is from pp. 148-149.

[78] Le Roy, *Examen des critiques du livre intitulé De l'esprit*, 159-168.

Monsieur, that I recognize in animals the faculty of sensation, that of recollection, and all of the products following from these two faculties. But far from wanting to insinuate materialism by means of this, I declare that it is impossible for me to conceive that matter is capable of the slightest degree of sensation. The faculty of sensation is inconsistent with all of the ideas that I have of the material substance: I adopt all of the reasonable proofs that have been made of the necessity of a simple and indivisible being in order to receive different sensations and compare them among themselves."[79]

This of course was more than a simple denial of the charges, for it granted fully and unreservedly the central and most fundamental argument of the antimaterialists, that matter capable of sensation was inconceivable and self-contradictory. This went farther than any caution dictated. Going beyond the nonmaterialists Locke and Voltaire, Le Roy, his identity protected by a pseudonym, not only denied the materialist hypothesis, but denied its theoretical conceivability. In this he supported the view that not even God could contradict Himself by making matter capable of thought, since the two concepts were mutually exclusive. As La Harpe had urged against d'Holbach, matter capable of thought was no longer matter.[80] Perhaps it was more than pique that had led Le Roy once to assert that Pascal was a greater philosopher than Voltaire.[81]

What Le Roy was saying most forcefully was that such questions were properly metaphysical questions, that they could not be influenced by our observations of animals and had no bearing upon such observations. In a similar manner he had anonymously defended Helvétius from his theological critics after the publication of *De l'esprit*. Helvétius had claimed that from the standpoint of natural philosophy "the immateriality of the soul" was an hypothesis that could not be confirmed or disconfirmed, and the function of the student of natural man was to describe natural processes in natural terms. The Jesuit *Journal de Trévoux* had condemned this as an "insinuation" of materialism. Is it now, Le Roy asked, an article of faith that natural evidence exists for the

[79] Le Roy, *Lettres* (1768), 127-128. The criticism appeared in January 1765, according to Le Roy.

[80] J.-F. La Harpe, *Lycée, ou Cours de littérature ancienne et moderne*, III, 327-329.

[81] Le Roy, *Réflexions sur la jalousie, pour servir de commentaire aux derniers ouvrages de M. de Voltaire*, 24.

immateriality of the soul? By its very nature, he continued, no such evidence could exist, for the question is not an empirical one, and natural philosophy should be free simply to examine natural processes in natural terms. Metaphysical truths, Le Roy urged, are always "abstract," and being such are always open to diverse interpretations. The natural philosopher must look for natural laws that are concrete, in that they are grounded in precise evidence and in observations to which all men can look in common. It is the theologian and not the natural philosopher, he concluded, who creates conflict between metaphysical abstractions and natural inquiry.[82]

Le Roy indeed was frightened of the peculiarly Christian theses that his view of animals and man might threaten, and on many questions he was often ironic and covert in his fundamental arguments. On the question of materialism, however, he unabashedly announced its incompatibility with his own concepts and its irrelevance to natural philosophy. Following his death, manuscripts that he had determined to be too dangerous to offer to the public in the face of Christian intolerance were published by the atheist Naigeon in his *Philosophie ancienne et moderne* and by Roux-Fazillac, the former revolutionary legislator, in an edition of 1802. Both editors stressed in prefaces that Le Roy, despite his pseudonymity, had hesitated to publish his thoughts with full candor during his lifetime.[83] Naigeon was willing to publish both his own and others' atheistic works in his history of philosophy, yet neither in the "Instinct des animaux" by Le Roy that he printed nor in Roux-Fazillac's edition of additional "Lettres sur les animaux" and "Lettres sur l'homme," did any arguments whatever concerning materialism appear. Le Roy simply dropped all pretense of distinguishing qualitatively between man and animals, and argued for strict parallels in both psychic and social behavior. He had denied materialism during his lifetime and he avoided all discussion of it in the "dangerous" works which he left to be published posthumously. He was a student of the species, human and animal; he was not a metaphysician.

* * *

The thinker of the coterie who appeared to limit most narrowly (perhaps most rigorously) the scope of his concern to the area

[82] Le Roy, *Examen des critiques*, 101-116.

[83] Naigeon, *Philosophie ancienne et moderne*, III, 47; Roux-Fazillac, in Le Roy, *Lettres philosophiques*, v-viii.

of his recognized intellectual competence was Jean Darcet, chemist and disciple of the great teacher and pre-Lavoisierian chemist Rouelle the elder. Darcet devoted his publications to reports of pyrolytic analyses of metals and minerals, reports of water-source residue analyses and the records of various precise scientific studies made for various royal committees of investigation. Although his most recent biographer has claimed that Darcet was a "believing Christian" during all of his life, the evidence is social rather than intellectual, and such evidence misleadingly could establish the Christianity of a d'Holbach as well.[84] There simply is no record of Darcet's philosophical and religious views, and no suspicion of atheistic incredulity or materialism was ever associated with his name.

Darcet's attitude toward the scientific use of the mind may well have precluded even his serious consideration of abstract conceptual and cosmological problems. He was committed to a strict inductionist sense of his field of metallurgical and mineralogical chemistry. Close to the most idealized Baconian model, he believed that the scientist must be a collector of "facts and observations," and from this dutiful labor, generalizations would after a great deal of time begin to emerge. In 1776 he published a study of the Pyrenees, a compendium of variegated and often unrelated "facts and observations" gathered by "following Nature in these far-off places," ranging from descriptions and analyses of its stones to barometric readings on its peaks.[85] There appeared to be no place in his work for speculative system-building or considerations of the implications of his findings. Indeed he often seemed annoyed at those who did so, and his complaint would appear to apply to his materialist friends as well as to formal systematizers within his own field. As he observed in 1771: "We live in a time when the taste for experience and the knowledge of facts is winning over all minds. Woe to the authors who devoid of these resources affect today to hazard opinions [instead of facts] and to erect them into a system of any branch whatsoever of the science of nature. A hundred-thousand mouths would open to say to them: 'But you, who claim here to dominate our understanding, tell us what is your mission? Where is that series of experiments to come to the aid of your doctrine? Show us that very well-ordered se-

[84] Cuzacq, *Darcet*, 28.
[85] Darcet, *Discours en forme de dissertation sur l'état actuel des montagnes des Pyrénées.* . . . See especially pp. 3-7.

quence of experiments which masters prejudices and condemns even doubt to silence.' "[86]

The problems facing natural history, for Darcet, were a result of its prior concern for generalities and abstractions before it began what must be its arduous scientific *sine qua non*, the gaining of familiarity with the particulars and concrete elements of nature. There was a need to eliminate abstract thought and to restrict inquiry to the collection of data: "Let us say it thus: there is no other route than experience and observation to reach the goal of forming precise and clear ideas, and of dissipating the chaos of what is called 'Natural History'; this science has its elements; and its elements, as with all of the branches of physics, are facts."[87]

Men of science, Darcet wrote, worked in the hope that a great intellectual edifice one day might be constructed as a result of their labors. The scientist would be overjoyed to live to see "the first foundations laid." His task, however, was to see that such first foundations would be solid; "posterity will do the rest."[88] D'Holbach and Darcet had several intellectual interests in common; both had studied mineralogy, and both were interested in the translation of leading German works in this field into French. Darcet thanked d'Holbach in print for his assistance in experiments and for his clarifications of the work of the German Henckel.[89] What they did not share, from all evidence, was d'Holbach's concern for the speculative implications of science and of its "observations and facts," nor d'Holbach's desire to systematize, at that point in man's history, his view of nature and the universe.

* * *

Besides overt and covert atheists, skeptics, antispeculative specialists and scientists, and a mesmerist, the coterie holbachique consisted of men who formally and, to all appearances, sincerely expressed and allied themselves with the deistic attitudes that so permeated the enlightened community in France. In addition to Morellet and Galiani (and perhaps to Chastellux and Le Roy), three thinkers—Marmontel, Raynal, and Suard—gave strong indications of formal deistic beliefs.

It is a disappointment that there remains no trace of Morellet's manuscript reply to d'Holbach, Diderot, and Naigeon, for it would

---

[86] Darcet, *Second mémoire sur l'action d'un feu égal, violent, et continué* . . . , iii-iv.

[87] Ibid., iv. [88] Ibid., iv-vi. [89] Ibid., 87-91.

aid immeasurably in reconstructing the terms of debate within the coterie. As we shall see in his discussion of toleration in a later chapter, Morellet was an astute religious polemicist, well-grounded in formal doctrine, who had evolved intellectually from a Catholic doctor of theology to a bitterly anti-Catholic critic of the Church's teachings. He had the ability to summarize succinctly the issue of contention, and his statement of the issues which separated him from "the atheists of such good company" would have given us entry into not only his own mind, but into the actual discussions of the coterie. Galiani's "loaded-dice" argument from design offered an entertaining view of such discussions, without truly clarifying the more serious statements of his and his interlocutors' positions. Like Morellet, the Neapolitan abbé left no formal treatise on theology, and we could only speculate unprofitably on the fuller substance of his views.[90] Fortunately, however, Marmontel did publish his own theological principles (to his own discomfort) in his controversial work *Bélisaire*.

During the storm of protest and persecution raised by the appearance of *Bélisaire* in 1767, Marmontel was to claim that his work was historical and moral rather than philosophical, and that that philosophy which did intrude in it was wholly consistent with Christianity. However, his theological critics, who were multitudinous, saw all too clearly that the work was intended to establish the principles of deistic natural religion. As Riballier, the syndic of the Faculté de Théologie, wrote to Marmontel in 1767, the fifteenth chapter of *Bélisaire* (which discussed religion) "has no other goal but to establish Deism and to cause Christianity to

---

[90] Galiani did write a dialogue among "Mirabeau, Voltaire, and the curé de Venise" on the origin of slippers, which paraphrased the d'Holbach-Voltaire debate on the origin of the belief in God; see Fausto Nicolini, *Il Pensiero dell'Abate Galiani*, 252-258. Nicolini correctly identified the "curé de Venise" as the curé de Deuil, an occasional visitor to many of the salons which Galiani frequented, but he identified Mirabeau as the marquis de Mirabeau rather than as the personage whom Galiani intended, "Mirabaud," d'Holbach's pseudonym when he wrote the *Système de la nature*. The dialogue parodies Voltaire's criticism of the materialists, but in the end does not decide among the interlocutors. Ultimately it is a clever parody of the entire debate, and in it Galiani seems most to want to prove that, given the complete absence of any concrete evidence, no one can convince anyone of anything in terms of the origins of religious belief. The constant refrain of the dialogue, "That proves nothing," is perhaps the author's point of view here, but he seems much less intent to prove any points than simply to paraphrase it all.

75

be regarded as an odious or at least most indifferent Religion." All of his opponents made the same charge, and none of them accused him of atheism or materialism, despite the looseness with which the latter charges usually were made.[91]

In 1759 Marmontel had written that "Religion and honor are the supports of innocence, the restraints upon vice, the motives of virtue, and the counterpoises to human passions: to deprive man of these aids is to abandon him to himself."[92] This view was anathema to the materialists within the coterie. The crime of religion was for them its separation of man from the realm of the natural. No aspect of this alienation was more to be detested than the influence of religion in persuading man that the evil he did, he did of his own nature, while the good he did, he did of divine aid. Innocence, self-control, virtue and calm were as fundamentally human as their opposites for d'Holbach, Diderot, and Naigeon; religion, by causing self-contempt in man, undermined the inner peace most likely to produce such positive attributes. As Naigeon also complained, the real bases for benevolence, decency and self-control were the benefits of survival and happiness which these virtues conferred upon the individual and the species, but religion removed these conceptually for man from such certain foundations (in which man's self-interest would see to their prevalence) and tied them to chimerical theological speculations on divine morality.[93] Marmontel here was in fundamental conflict with the atheists among d'Holbach's circle.

In *Bélisaire*, eight years later, Marmontel added another dimension to his view of religion. True religion, he wrote, is the counterpoise to despair, because it is the feeling of the good man that God is with him. This was the triumph of such religious devotion: "to console man in misfortune is to mix a celestial sweetness with the bitterness of life."[94]

To console man (Marmontel's Bélisaire informed the Emperor Justinian), and hence to fulfill its divine purpose, religion must present to humanity a kind, merciful and "exemplary" God;

[91] "Lettre de M. Riballier à M. Marmontel," in Marmontel et al., *Pièces relatives à Bélisaire*, 4-6.

[92] Marmontel, *Réponse . . . à la lettre adressée par M. J.-J. Rousseau à M. d'Alembert*, 155.

[93] Naigeon, "Discours préliminaire," in d'Holbach, *Système de la nature* (1770), I, 1-16.

[94] Marmontel, *Bélisaire* (1767), 231-233.

the greatest theological error was to depict God as "a gloomy and ferocious tyrant."[95] For the atheists, however, any "divine intelligence" which man would see as omnipotent in the universe would immediately become accountable for the sufferings and unrequited tragedy of man's history and present state. The universe was uncaring and amoral; in the midst of its flux man must make his way as best he could, unaided and unguided except for his own and his fellow man's knowledge and concern.[96]

D'Holbach, in his *Système de la nature*, condemned the impulse to personify nature, to believe that nature cared for man, to call "natural" the things man deemed good and "unnatural" the things man deemed evil. This has been the error of the deists and their "God of Nature," and it stemmed from an inability to face the amoral necessity of the world realistically.[97] Man, he urged, learns of no God of Nature from a study of the universe, but only of that "vast chain of causes and effects" upon which—and upon our interaction with which—our relative happiness and unhappiness are based.[98]

Marmontel argued to the contrary that such knowledge of God was possible. To know Him, Bélisaire urged, God has given man two guides, "the light of faith and the light of feeling." It was thus not reason or experience that established deism for Marmontel, but faith (which he made synonymous with what is true in Revelation) and feeling (which he made synonymous with the "natural sentiments" of the heart). These two could be made coequal, and the more accessible heart made the arbiter of religious truth. Since two sources of divine knowledge could not be in discord: "It is the same voice which speaks in Heaven and in the depths of my soul." Within the human heart then, God had placed the light of divine truth.[99]

Bélisaire's interlocutor, the Emperor Justinian, is disturbed by this assertion, and asks Marmontel's hero how he knew that this "inner voice" was truly a secret revelation from God. Bélisaire replies that religion itself depends on accepting that it is: "If it is not, God is deceiving me . . . and everything is lost. It is this voice which announces a God to me, which prescribes his cult to me, which dictates his law. . . ." Further questioned, Bélisaire

[95] Ibid., 238-239.
[96] See, for example, Naigeon, "Discours préliminaire," I, 3-4.
[97] D'Holbach, *Système de la nature*, II, 25-28.
[98] Ibid., I, 27-33.   [99] Marmontel, *Bélisaire*, 231-233.

makes this inner voice, as Rousseau had done in *Emile*, synonymous with conscience: ". . . leave me my conscience; it is my guide and my support. Without it I no longer know the true, the just nor the honest; . . . it is then that I am blind."[100] Conscience, then, was for Marmontel, as much as for d'Holbach's deistic rival Rousseau, the faculty by which man truly knew divine truth and divine law.

Christian critics of Marmontel saw this as leading to a theological anarchy, and questioned if that were not his goal. One of them, de Legge, described Bélisaire's doctrines as leaving religion "abandoned to the caprice of each individual."[101] For Marmontel, however, the dependence of religion upon each individual's conscience carried no danger of theological solipsism. Like most eighteenth-century deists, he saw the truths revealed by conscience as being obvious and accessible to all men, once understood without prejudice. His own personal revelation contained no "mysteries," he claimed; it was, in effect, that the Golden Rule was divine and hence applied to both God and man. Conscience informed him "That a religion which presents to me a propitious and benevolent God is the true one . . . and that everything that is repugnant to the idea and the sentiment that I have conceived of is not part of that religion. . . . What attaches me to it is that it makes me better and more humane. . . . To love God and to love one's fellow-men; what could be simpler and more natural!"[102]

For d'Holbach such conclusions were as "mysterious" as those of the Church: "The God of the deists is neither less contradictory nor less chimerical than the God of the theologians . . . everything in this world refutes the beautiful qualities that you give to your God. In the numerous family of this so tender Father, I perceive only the afflicted."[103]

Suard, however, ought to have approved of *Bélisaire*, for it embodied themes that appear to have been his own as well: loyalty to the monarchy, religious toleration, and a fundamental deistic outlook upon the world. In another context Suard would write: "How can one not admire one who employs his genius to defend the oppressed; to speak of God as the common father of all men; of tolerance as the most sacred of the rights and the dearest of

100 Ibid.
101 De Legge, *Pièces relatives à l'examen de Bélisaire*, 113-114.
102 Marmontel, *Bélisaire*, 239-241.   103 D'Holbach, *Bon-sens*, 141.

their duties?"[104] He did not approve of d'Holbach's *Système de la nature*, criticizing it quite strongly in his own "Correspondance littéraire" and terming it "wholly gratuitous in its reasoning."[105] According to both Mme Suard and Garat, Suard, utilizing "the principles of Clarke and Newton, which were his own," argued frequently with d'Holbach and Helvétius about their views.[106]

Such an adherence to a rational theology consistent with natural philosophy would help to explain why Suard chose the conflict between philosophical progress and atheism as one of the basic themes of his inaugural discourse to the Académie Française in 1774. Suard was by no means obliged to address such a topic. Elected as a man of letters, he easily could have confined his remarks to literary matters. He chose, however, to argue that true philosophy was no enemy of religion. Descartes once was accused of atheism, he noted, but now his arguments for the existence of God are taught everywhere, even at the facultés of theology that once despised him. Suard reminded his audience that even Pascal and Malebranche had been denounced as atheists by their enemies, and he observed that at last men were beginning to understand that the great Montaigne was a "very religious" man as well. It is not philosophy which leads to atheism, he continued, but ignorance. Atheism flourishes, he argued, only when philosophy is impeded or silenced. As befitted someone imbued with admiration for the theology of Samuel Clarke and the deistic Newtonians, Suard asked his audience to compare the situation in France, which had both philosophical censorship and atheistic thinkers, to that in England, where there was "extreme" liberty of the press and the most philosophical progress, but where "atheism fears even more [than in France] to present itself in the light of day." Where philosophy is freest and most advanced, Suard concluded, religion is the least under assault.[107] It was not a theme to please the atheists.

Nor was there much in Raynal's celebrated *Histoire philosophique des Deux Indes* to please the atheists either. He attacked organized religion and the political role of the priesthood, but he

---

[104] Suard, *Mélanges de littérature*, ii, 2.
[105] Suard, "Correspondance littéraire avec le margrave de Bayreuth," 146-147.
[106] Mme Suard, *Suard*, 43-47; Garat, *Suard*, i, 208-209.
[107] Suard, *Mélanges*, iii, 390-393.

did so without ever blaspheming the Deity by whom he claimed the laws of justice were ordained. It is the role of the philosophe, Raynal urged, to teach men "that liberty comes from God, authority from men."[108] His historical analyses revealed a certain distrust of all metaphysics and often focused upon those religious doctrines whose consequences led to intolerance and violence, but such a characterization would apply to a Voltaire as well. Indeed, like Voltaire, Raynal distinguished categorically between natural religion and supernatural theology, and he even went so far as to claim in a discussion of natural religion that "The best of all governments, if it were possible to maintain it in its purity, would be theocracy. . . ."[109] Fanaticism, superstition and metaphysical theology all drew his ire, but he identified these precisely in their contrast to a natural belief in a Supreme Being, the "simple and sublime idea" of that "theism to which the human mind will be elevated from idolatry."[110]

In a discussion of China (in which an atheist subtly could have advanced his beliefs by identifying them, as others had done, with the code of Confucius, which the eighteenth century admired and saw as responsible for so much of the greatness of Chinese civilization), Raynal instead chose to engage in an analysis of precisely the *theistic* basis of Confucian thought. The reason that there was "no superstition" in China, he asserted, was because the Confucian code "is nothing but the natural law, which should be the foundation of all the religions of the earth, the foundation of every society, the rule of all governments. Reason, Confucius says, is an emanation of the Divinity; the supreme law is only the accord of nature and reason. Every religion which contradicts these two guides does not come from heaven."[111]

Raynal was aware that there were those who identified the "nature" of that divine guide with material nature alone, but he specifically rejected that interpretation, asserting the spiritualism of the Chinese cult.[112]

Atheism, Raynal concluded, is not the official creed of China: "It is simply tolerated there like superstition." Such an official Chinese view of what could be tolerated would not please the ecclesiastical authorities of France, but it was a far cry from an

---

[108] Raynal, *Histoire philosophique des Deux Indes* (3rd edn.), I, 103.
[109] Ibid., IV, 241.
[110] Ibid., I, 13, 294-295; II, 79-80, 105-106; III, 351-352; IV, 337-338; X, 1-14.
[111] Ibid., I, 178-179.   [112] Ibid.

avowal of atheism. The same could be said of Raynal's view of religion. Indeed the same could be said of the diversity of the coterie holbachique.

Was the coterie holbachique a center of collaboration?

The opinion that the coterie holbachique linked its members together to pursue a common goal requiring joint planning and effort, thus setting them apart from the rest of Parisian enlightened society, has been a prevalent assumption. The durability of this opinion demonstrates well the power of an historical myth; for in all the extant memoirs and letters of the members of the coterie, in all their published works and in the record of their actions, there is no evidence to justify the claim that a collaboration whose object or audience lay beyond the walls of d'Holbach's home was the basis for, or even an element of, the life of the coterie.

This does not mean, of course, that agreement on specific goals never united the members of the coterie. When there was such agreement, however, it was a part of the larger consensus of opinion prevailing throughout the "philosophic community" of Paris. Like all members of that community, the members of the coterie were willing to use what individual talent and influence they possessed to support those causes almost unanimously seconded by liberal opinion, for example, the efforts of Voltaire to rehabilitate Calas, or the struggle to legalize inoculation, or the campaign in favor of the right to publish the *Encyclopédie*. There is no evidence that the coterie holbachique was a center where such common causes were initiated, or where any movement, overt or conspiratorial, was elaborated or developed by a group of men coming together for that purpose. When a campaign for a particular reform was being formed in Paris, the coterie holbachique, like any other circle in which philosophes were present, became a center for communication; those of its members who wished to participate in the endeavor could be enlisted in d'Holbach's home, or at another salon, or even at a café in the Palais Royal. Thus, for brief periods of time the coterie holbachique might become one of many nuclei pursuing a goal adopted informally by certain broad sectors of opinion. No cause was unique to the coterie holbachique, however, nor, for that matter, was pursued by individual intimates of the coterie specifically in their capacity as members of that group. Indeed there was no truly *sustained* common effort uniting the coterie, even in terms of its devotees' participation in the campaigns of the broader community. Given the diversity of professions, intellectual interests and formal philosophies represented at d'Holbach's home, this should not be surprising. For almost all its members, the coterie holbachique constituted but one among many of the focal points of their social, public and intellectual lives; there were at least five other days in the week.

The belief that d'Holbach's circle was the center for the diffusion of the Baron's atheistic works already has been made untenable by the manifest differences of opinion that existed there over both the substance of atheism and the wisdom of its propagation. Who in fact worked with d'Holbach in his efforts? So far as a genuine collaboration was concerned, there was only Naigeon, who helped d'Holbach in the editing and publishing of some of the Baron's own manuscripts, and who worked with him in the rewriting of several anti-Christian texts by other thinkers. Diderot helped d'Holbach infuse a certain style and rhetorical flourish into some of his works, but his contribution, aside from the question of his general intellectual influence, was limited to that extent. Only three other names can be introduced in any other context involving the writing or publication of any of d'Holbach's antireligious texts. Saint-Lambert, it will be recalled, had published in Nancy an early version of d'Holbach's *Le christianisme dévoilé* in 1756, a work devoid of any explicit atheism. Grimm included at least one antireligious satire by d'Holbach in his *Correspondance littéraire*. In September 1762, according to Diderot, d'Holbach traveled to Voré to read Helvétius a book he had written. This was at a time when the Baron was writing and translating anti-Christian literature, before he turned his attention to the propagation of atheism in the later years of that decade. Less specifically, Mme Suard, in her memoirs on her husband's life, claimed that Suard corrected d'Holbach's style on occasion. She did not reveal, however, on which works this assistance was provided and, given Suard's reputation primarily as a translator from English, it more likely than not related to d'Holbach's translations of the English deists.[113]

---

[113] On Naigeon, see Barbier, *Dictionnaire des anonymes*, I, xli-xlii, and Barbier's n. 1, xlii *ff*; on Diderot, see Diderot, *Corr.*, VII, 139-140; on Helvétius, see Diderot, *Corr.*, IV, 154; on Saint-Lambert, see Naigeon's comments in Barbier, op. cit., I, 595-596; on Suard, see Mme Suard, *Suard*, 44-48; cf. Vercruysse, *Bibliographie descriptive des écrits du baron d'Holbach*.

Jacques-André Naigeon provided A.-A. Barbier with much of the information about d'Holbach's publications that the great bibliophile incorporated into his *Dictionnaire des anonymes* during the First Empire. After Naigeon's death, Barbier obtained a copy of the *Système de la nature* that had been owned by Jacques-André's brother, identified only as "Naigeon le jeune," which contained a long handwritten marginal note providing additional information on the method used to insure the safe entry of such atheistic works into print. The two brothers' accounts coincided and offered a view of how restricted a collaboration these maneuvers entailed.

According to this account, the publication of d'Holbach's atheistic and "atheized" works followed a regular pattern. After the Baron presented his manuscripts to Naigeon, the latter would pass them on to his brother, either directly in Paris where his brother often visited, or in Sedan through the private mail of Naigeon's (and d'Holbach's) friend Bron, a tax-farmer and the *inspecteur-général* of the *bureau du départ*. In Sedan the younger Naigeon would copy d'Holbach's manuscripts and destroy the originals, sending the new manuscripts "in a package covered with two layers of wax-sealed cloth" to one Mme Loncin in Liège, a correspondent of d'Holbach's publisher Marc-Michel Rey of Amsterdam. According to Barbier, writing in 1806, the notes of Naigeon le jeune, jotted down on the flyleaf of d'Holbach's work in the 1770s, "are in perfect accord with the information that his brother gave me verbally fifteen years later."[114] If we accept these accounts, only Naigeon, of all the members of the coterie, was involved in an endeavor in which d'Holbach limited the participation as strictly as possible.

This corresponds well with Morellet's assertion in his *Mémoires* that d'Holbach's role as an author never was discussed in the coterie and never was a matter of overt advice or concern. Having heard the Baron elaborate his ideas, many or most of his frequent guests must have suspected his authorship, but Morellet's account makes it clear that they did not think it proper even to raise this topic. No works were more scandalous than d'Holbach's in his time, and his status as a published philosophe was a remarkably well-kept secret. Not a trace of suspicion was associated with d'Holbach's name outside the coterie, neither in police records dealing with the book trade nor in the correspondences of men such as Voltaire and d'Alembert, all of whom were indeed curi-

---

[114] Barbier, op. cit., i, xli-xlii, and n. i, xlii *ff.*

ous about the author's identity. In fact, in no extant letter of any member of the coterie holbachique was d'Holbach's name given (before 1789) as that of the author of his own works, a situation which strongly supports Morellet's claim of silence on this issue. Galiani might write to d'Holbach and Mme d'Epinay to describe his response to the thought of "the author of the *Système de la nature*," and Diderot might write to Sophie Volland about the "bombs raining in the house of the Lord" and list titles all by d'Holbach in fact, going on to add that "I am always terrified that a certain one of those bold cannoneers will find himself in trouble over these," but that is as close as anyone came to alluding to his role. Morellet described this *passive* complicity for his readers: "A good many of us knew, beyond any doubt, that these works were the Baron's, whose principles and conversation we found in this book. I can say that at least, as we later admitted, we were deeply convinced of it, Marmontel, Saint-Lambert, Suard, Chastellux, Roux, Darcet, Raynal, Helvétius and I. We lived constantly together, and, before the Baron's death, not one of us confided to the other our knowledge of this point, although each certainly thought that the other knew as well."[115]

There is no evidence to suggest that the writing and publication of d'Holbach's books occurred in any other manner. Diderot, Grimm, Galiani, Le Roy, and of course Naigeon, none of whom was mentioned by Morellet in his list, undoubtedly knew d'Holbach as the author of his books, but they avoided public indiscretion as well during the Baron's life. This did not mean, as we have seen, that they necessarily approved of the Baron's endeavors. The deists and skeptics, of course, had substantive criticisms, but negative judgments on the Baron's products often could go far beyond these. Grimm, for example, who approved of d'Holbach's *Théologie portative* in terms of its desire to ridicule theological pretentions, nevertheless found it "very badly executed . . . bilious . . . without taste"; he advised "the author" that he found it ". . . insane to risk one's peace and one's happiness for the pleasure of throwing stones at an old hovel [the Church] guarded by mastiffs who rip apart all those who do not pass without raising their eyes."[116]

Diderot, writing to Naigeon and demonstrating that he could

[115] Morellet, *Mémoires*, I, 132-134; Galiani, *Lettres*, I, 94-96, 110-114; Diderot, *Corr.*, VIII, 234-235.

[116] Grimm, *Corr. litt.*, VII, 425-426.

not have aided d'Holbach stylistically on all his works, described the Baron's prose as "too lengthy, flat and diffuse," and complained that "it is fatiguing, it is boring, and it makes a book fall from one's hands."[117] Naigeon himself, demonstrating that his own collaboration with d'Holbach, however extensive, had clear boundaries, discussed d'Holbach's translation of Toland's *Letters to Serena* in his own *Philosophie ancienne et moderne* and offered a remarkably harsh criticism of the Baron's own work.[118]

Naigeon's stern critique of d'Holbach's style was neither hypocritical nor deceptive on his part. He collaborated with d'Holbach on a number of important works, but these constituted a decided minority of the Baron's efforts; in addition, he independently took the major responsibility for a small number of works in which the Baron may or may not have taken any active part. It is an odd fate that has befallen Naigeon; despite repeated verifications of his claims, he apparently is never believed at his word. It was assumed that he had falsified Diderot's manuscripts, but modern research has proven him to have been a faithful editor. He appears to have been a meticulous and honest man. He had a reputation for being a "virulent" atheist, but this was undoubtedly because he was such an open and candid one. He was a scholarly bibliophile who, near the end of his life, had a reputation in the world of letters as being something of a pedant. It was precisely at this period that he confided to Barbier the extent of his own role in the production of d'Holbach's books. There is no hypothesis of any ulterior motive that could explain so frank and so precise an accounting as the one he gave to Barbier. Indeed, modern bibliographical scholarship, however much it has debated the question of the original authorship or the original sources of the works which d'Holbach and Naigeon translated or re-issued, has not found Naigeon's estimation of his own role suspect or incorrect. Many of these works were selectively edited and selectively rewritten, but it was Naigeon who first revealed that fact to Barbier by admitting freely that he and/or the Baron "touched up," "atheized," and "augmented" many of these works. According to his own statements to Barbier, he provided the introduction and the notes to the *Lettres à Eugénie* (1768); he reviewed, corrected and substantively altered the *Lettre de Thrasibule à Leucippe* (1768); he had the major hand in editing *Le Militaire philosophe* (1768),

---

[117] Diderot, *Corr.*, XII, 45-47.
[118] Naigeon, *Philosophie ancienne et moderne*, III, 665.

to which d'Holbach appended a final, more atheistic chapter; he "touched up and rectified in an infinity of places" the original French translation of Crellius' seventeenth-century treatise on toleration, issued as *De la tolérance dans la religion* (1769); and he provided the notes to the *Essai sur les préjugés* (1770). In addition, according to Naigeon's own statements, he provided two notes to that edition of the *Letters to Serena* (1768) of which he so disapproved, and wrote an introduction to d'Holbach's *Système de la nature* (1770). He also admitted to Barbier the works that were largely his own.[119] With the exception of Diderot, whose contribution of intellectual and stylistic advice constitutes an unresolved and perhaps unresolvable problem, there is no other intimate of the coterie whose name can be brought into discussion of the publication of these works during the period of d'Holbach's and Naigeon's collaboration. Once again, we are dealing only with d'Holbach, Naigeon and, tangentially, Diderot.

It is in no manner surprising that individual figures within the coterie should have collaborated on various endeavors. D'Holbach and Naigeon collaborated on certain books; D'Holbach and Roux published scientific translations; Roux and Darcet published chemical analyses of underground springs; Diderot (along with Mme d'Epinay and Meister) worked on Grimm's *Correspondance* at times; D'Holbach and Diderot helped publish Galiani's critique of the *économistes* in France; Raynal called upon Diderot and d'Holbach (among a host of others) for assistance on certain sections of his *Histoire philosophique*. All of these cases represented two or three men in collaboration and were typical of relationships in the eighteenth-century world of letters. None of these cases tells us anything about the collectivity of the coterie. Each of the figures who assembled at d'Holbach's home traveled in many different circles, and individual collaborations were established by them in most of these various milieus. The associations of Marmontel and Piccini, of Suard and Arnaud, of Morellet and Turgot, of Raynal and Pechméja, for example, represented joint efforts far more important to the figures involved than any collaboration established with other members of the coterie holbachique.

The one time that Grimm mentioned to his readers a rumor of

[119] Barbier, op. cit., I, xli *ff*, 633, 1,090-1,091; II, 182, 1,217, 1,284-1,285, 1,354; III, 262-263, 300, 694, 717; IV, 114, 717; Quérard, *Supercheries*, II, 1(b), 97-102, 1,156-1,157.

a common effort by the coterie holbachique, d'Holbach's circle was implicated precisely because it stood for some people as a symbol of the Parisian intellectual community as a whole. The tutor of d'Holbach's children, one M. de la Grange, had published a translation of Lucretius during the summer of 1768; Grimm commented: "Since M. de la Grange lives in the home of Baron d'Holbach, *and consequently in the center of the philosophes of Paris*, people have not failed to say that his translation was their work and that he only gave his name. . . . It is not true that other hands other than those of M. de la Grange participated in this translation, [although] M. Diderot, in truth, reviewed it with the author before publication."[120]

Naigeon informed Barbier that he also had taken a hand in the reviewing of La Grange's translation, and Brière, a Parisian man of letters who edited Diderot's works in 1831, asserted that he had it on good authority that La Grange had undertaken the translation at d'Holbach's request, which does not seem unreasonable. Thus at the most we find only three members of the coterie publicly identified with La Grange's work.[121]

The publication of this translation led to an interest in the didactic possibilities of the classics on the part of d'Holbach, Diderot and Naigeon, and led to a similar collaboration a decade later. In 1778-1779 Naigeon edited a collection of the works of Seneca and published it with Diderot's *Essai sur la vie de Sénèque le philosophe . . . et sur les règnes de Claude et de Néron*. In 1782 he published both a translation of excerpts from Seneca's moral philosophy (to which he appended an original preliminary discourse) and a translation of Epictetus. As Grimm had described in the case of La Grange's work, there were those who again saw the work of a circle of philosophes at d'Holbach's home behind these publications. This suspicion must have been widespread in some quarters, for in his notes to Diderot's *Oeuvres* in 1800, Naigeon mentioned the *Oeuvres de Sénèque*, "of which a formerly celebrated *society* is generally accused of being the author."[122] Diderot, in his *Apologue* defending his *Essai sur les règnes de Claude et de Néron*, quoted an article by Marmontel in the *Mercure* which had denied a charge by the abbé Grossier "That there exists in

120 Ibid., VIII, 151-154 (emphasis added).
121 Barbier, op. cit., II, 1,354; *Oeuvres de Denis Diderot*, J.-L.-J. Brière, ed., XII, 1-3.
122 Diderot, *Oeuvres* (N), VIII, 11n.

our time a philosophical confederation," a charge which both Diderot and Naigeon identified as directed toward the Baron's circle. Marmontel and Diderot both replied that it was absurd to think of such a work being written secretly and conspiratorially.[123] When Barbier later asked Naigeon to clarify this, Naigeon informed him that five men had been involved in the preparation and editing of this edition of Seneca's works: La Grange, who began the translation; Naigeon, who completed and corrected the translation, and who provided many of the critical notes; Darcet and the scientist Desmarets, who furnished the scientific notes clarifying some of Seneca's references; and Baron d'Holbach, who supplied almost all of the notes for the volumes of Seneca's letters.[124] Barbier did not have to pose the question, however. If he had consulted the second instead of the first edition of Diderot's *Essai*, he would have discovered that Diderot, apparently disliking the whole charge of covert anonymity surrounding this work, had included an introductory letter dedicating that second edition to Naigeon: "If men had in their graves some notion of what occurs on earth, with what sentiments of gratitude would not that premature victim of Epicurus and Zeno, the honest and laborious La Grange, be filled for you, for the Baron d'Holbach, and for your worthy colleagues MM. Desmarets and Darcet?"[125] If these men formed a "philosophical confederation," it was one that was quite distinct from the coterie holbachique.

Was the coterie holbachique a center for the production of the Encyclopédie?

René Hubert has demonstrated by simple chronological reconstruction that the coterie holbachique had no hand in the initiation of the *Encyclopédie*.[126] In a sense, however, this missed the point of the traditional linking of these phenomena. What has gained currency in historical circles is not the view that the coterie planned the *Encyclopédie*, but that it itself grew and flourished around that vast enterprise. The question, thus, merits to be posed

[123] Ibid., IX, 172-173. Brière, in Diderot, *Oeuvres* (B), XII, 112-115, added his own note, praising d'Holbach and observing that since the Baron's identity as the atheistic author had become known, his reputation had been "the object of calumnies without end." Assézat, in Diderot, *Oeuvres* (A-T), III, 385-387, reprinted both Naigeon's and Brière's notes.

[124] Barbier, op. cit., III, 694.

[125] Diderot, *Oeuvres* (A-T), III, 11-12.

[126] René Hubert, *D'Holbach et ses amis*, 9-23.

less narrowly: did the coterie holbachique enjoy a special relationship with Diderot's *Encyclopédie*?

Two concrete questions suggest themselves immediately. Were the men most involved in the production of the *Encyclopédie* members of the coterie holbachique? Were all the members of the coterie holbachique contributors to the *Encyclopédie*?

In 1756 the editors of the *Encyclopédie* included in the preface to the sixth volume a list of the twenty-six regular contributors to the encyclopedic undertaking who merited a mark of identification. Of these, only three among the fifteen men with whom we are dealing in this study are listed: Diderot, d'Holbach, and Morellet (by his own account, Morellet was not to join the group meeting at d'Holbach's home for another four years). They listed as well some forty irregular contributors who had furnished articles for this volume, of whom two were members of the Baron's circle, Marmontel and Charles-Georges Le Roy, and of whom four were occasionally guests at d'Holbach's home, Duclos, Rouelle, Barthez, and Margency. The editors' closest collaborators during this period were the chevalier de Jaucourt, Boucher d'Argis and de Cahusac. These three, along with the original and the constant contributors such as Daubenton, Mallet, Dumarsais, Yvon, Toussaint, de La Chapelle, Goussier, d'Argenville, Tarin, Malouin, Vandenesse, Blondel, Le Blond, Landois, Jean-Baptiste Le Roy, Eidous, Louis, and Bellin—in short, the genuine encyclopédistes— were not and never became involved with d'Holbach's circle.[127]

Following both the identifications of authors in the *Encyclopédie* itself and the revisions and augmentations of these identifications by modern scholars, the important personnel of the encyclopedic enterprise emerge as a group quite distinct from the personnel of the coterie. The 1957 study of "The Collaborators of the *Encyclopédie*" by Kuwabara, Turimi and Higuti distinguished among those involved in that effort a group of thirty-five men who could be classified as permanent collaborators and editors; of these, only four—Diderot, d'Holbach, Marmontel and Morellet—were members of the coterie holbachique.[128] They

[127] *Encyclopédie, ou Dictionnaire raisonné des sciences, des arts, et des métiers*, VI, vi-viii. See also ibid., I, xli-xlvi; II, i-ii; III, iii, xiv-xvi.

[128] Takeo Kuwabara, Syunsuke Turimi and Kiniti Higuti, "Les collaborateurs de l'Encyclopédie," in *Zinbun, Memoir of the Research Institute for Humanistic Studies, Kyoto University* (1957), 1-22. See also Frank A. Kafker, "A List of Contributors to Diderot's Encyclopédie," *French Historical Studies* (1963), 106-117. Kafker lists some thirty fewer writers of the *Ency-*

perhaps should have added Saint-Lambert, as Dieckmann's study of his contributions has indicated.[129] Of the 142 contributors listed by the prefaces to the *Encyclopédie*, only six were members of d'Holbach's circle—Diderot, d'Holbach, Charles-Georges Le Roy, Marmontel, Morellet, and Roux; of the forty-nine names added to these by the research of Jacques Proust, only three were members—Grimm, Naigeon and Saint-Lambert.[130] This leaves six members who did not write articles for the *Encyclopédie*, men who constituted an important element of the coterie—Chastellux (who did contribute to the later *Supplément*), Darcet (who, according to Dizé, contributed scientific notes), Galiani, Helvétius, Raynal, and Suard.

The coterie holbachique thus neither constituted the core of the most significant encyclopédistes nor contributed an important number of persons to that core. Jaucourt, Boucher d'Argis and de Cahusac either did not choose or were not invited to participate in d'Holbach's dinners. Most of the coterie's members did indeed become involved in that great work of their century, but most did so only sporadically and infrequently. The production of the *Encyclopédie* did not particularly occupy the coterie holbachique.

The following list indicates the probable date of association of the various members of the coterie with the *Encyclopédie* (based upon the probable date of the writing of their first articles) and the first volume in which their articles appeared: Diderot (c. 1746, I), d'Holbach (c. 1751, II), Marmontel (c. 1753, III), Le Roy (c. 1755, V), Morellet (c. 1756, VI), Saint-Lambert (c. 1756, VI), Grimm (after 1758, X), Roux (c. 1764, XIII), and Naigeon (c. 1765, XIV).[131] The chronology of association does not lend itself too well to the assertion of an organic, or even a symbiotic,

---

clopédie than did the Japanese scholars, but he includes a second list of men "who volunteered information for the *Encyclopédie*," which adds over thirty-five names to the number of "collaborators." See also Henri Zeiler, *Les collaborateurs médicaux de l'Encyclopédie de Diderot et d'Alembert*.

[129] H. Dieckmann, "The Sixth Volume of Saint-Lambert's Works," *The Romanic Review* (1951), 109-121. See also H. Dieckmann, "L'*Encyclopédie* et le Fonds Vandeul," *RHLF* (1951), 318-332.

[130] Proust, *Diderot et l'Encyclopédie*, 511-531.

[131] On d'Holbach, Marmontel, Le Roy and Morellet, see above, n. 127, this chapter; on Saint-Lambert, see above, n. 129, this chapter; on Grimm, see *Encyclopédie*, X, 768; on Roux, see *Encyclopédie*, XIII, 906; on Naigeon, see *Encyclopédie*, XIV, 281.

relationship between Diderot's role as an editor and the members of the coterie. He did not recruit his friends at d'Holbach's home directly into the encyclopedic enterprise and, with the apparent exception of Naigeon, did not introduce writers for the *Encyclopédie* directly into the coterie. It has recently been demonstrated that d'Holbach's contribution to Diderot's efforts were vaster than first suspected, and Diderot himself singled out the Baron's efforts as having been particularly useful in terms of financial aid and influence.[132] That d'Holbach played such an active role in this endeavor, however, clearly did not oblige his guests to follow his lead. In addition to the six devotees of the coterie who did not contribute articles, Grimm, Roux, and Naigeon made only minimal offerings.

This does not mean that Diderot did not recruit articles actively at the Baron's dinners; he well may have done so. He met many potential and actual contributors among the Baron's less frequent or less constant guests, men such as Buffon, Barthez, Boulanger, Damilaville, La Condamine, Margency, Montamy, Rouelle, Tressan, Turgot, and Venel. However, judging from his correspondence, it seems more likely that Diderot appreciated d'Holbach's dinners because they offered him a chance to escape from the work and pressures of the *Encyclopédie*. He would indeed write at d'Holbach's estate at Grandval, but the gathering of the circle there would be alternately an impediment to or a release from such work. At the most then, the coterie holbachique served the great collective effort of the *Encyclopédie* by providing Diderot with access to yet another group of men whom he could cajole for an occasional article. It was not for this insignificant role that the coterie holbachique maintained itself for a generation.

[132] Dieckmann, "L'*Encyclopédie* et le Fonds Vandeul," 330-332; Diderot, *Corr.*, II, 119-122; IX, 29-31; cf. Vercruysse, *Bibliographie*. On the possibility that d'Holbach's *personal* contribution was yet larger, see the persuasive study by John Lough, *The Contributors to the Encyclopédie* (London, 1973).

THREE · *The Coterie Holbachique Dévoilée*

THE nature of d'Holbach's circle never was kept a secret. The portrait of the dinners at d'Holbach's home was drawn and re-drawn by his guests, and the testimony of his devotees was abundant. The coterie holbachique was a group of men who came together to talk freely among themselves and among invited guests. It was nothing more, and it was nothing less. Nothing less, because that already was something remarkable and unique in Paris in the eighteenth century.

In most cultures there exist social barriers to spontaneous conversation and fundamental tensions between the world of private thought and the world of public expression. We often think of the eighteenth century in France as a time when the free play of ideas proceeded unimpeded, but there were great impediments to that freedom. The assemblies of the world of letters in Paris during the Enlightenment were linked inextricably to the mores of polite society, and the rules of that society posed definite limits to the liberty of saying what one thought. It was impolite to challenge the vague religiosity of the ladies; it was impolite to be pessimistic; it was impolite to offer in the midst of a pleasant afternoon or evening a view of man and the universe that was without inherent charm, inherent warmth, inherent light. In addition, there were limits to the *forms* of expression tolerated at these gatherings; it was impolite to quarrel and, above all, to quarrel sincerely and doggedly. Pervading the society of these assemblies was the need to say things well—not in the sense of saying them as rigorously and as thoughtfully as one might, but in the sense of saying them wittily, of delighting one's listeners, of making the discussion pleasurable less by its content than its mood. The hosts and hostesses who fêted the philosophes of Paris brought them together not for an intellectual feast, but for a social feast; the intellectualizing therefore had to serve the end at hand. Men who could not accept these norms, such as Naigeon, were not accepted in that society; men who did not find it worth the effort, such as Diderot, rarely sought entrance there.

92

One mechanism by which these values governing discussion so pervaded Parisian society can be isolated in the institution of the female hostess, for the great salons, the great centers of sociability above all, were presided over by women who accepted the "respectability" they had been so dutifully taught: Mme Geoffrin, Mme du Deffand, Mlle de Lespinasse and Mme Necker. Polite society from Versailles to the homes of the upper-bourgeoisie allowed remarkable women to have their lovers, but it dictated rather strictly the limits to the earnestness and honesty of their talk. These hostesses insisted upon the rules of polite conversation, and the philosophes adapted as best they could. The women repaid them by intriguing for them to obtain places in the Académies, taking their sides in various feuds, and flattering their vanities.

Even at the salons presided over by men—indeed by philosophes, such as those of Suard, Saurin, and Morellet—the same rules of sociable behavior applied, for their wives (in the cases of the first two) were considered co-hosts, and the wives of their guests were invited. It was not with Mme Suard or Mme Saurin that the mortality of the soul would be discussed; it was not their fault, but it was the way things were. At the aristocratic salons, these rules, of course, were inviolable, as they were at the dinners of the financiers despite the heralded freedom to be "licentious." Most other salons—those of the academic scientists, for example, or those of the économistes—were limited to special concerns.

The philosophes delighted in these assemblies, delighted in the good company, the good food, the dazzling conversation, and the chance to display themselves as men of manners, taste, wit and sentiment. Finding a great place in their lives for these constant gatherings, they welcomed the pleasures that were offered, and they abided by the rules of discussion that were imposed.

Drawing from the letters and recorded anecdotes dealing with these salons, the historian can draw the celebrated picture of the philosophes' great sociability, their humor and *bons mots*, their gallantry, their talent for playing the courtier or even, at times, the fool. It was one side of their lives. Yet for all their renown in such circles, for all their response to the appeal to be charming and available men of the world, the philosophes inhabited another more private and more subjective world as well. The elegant ladies, wealthy bankers and engaging fops might at times laugh at the philosophes' sarcastic jibes against the literal Bible and the Roman Church, but they did not truly understand the ferment

93

that lay beneath such iconoclasm. The philosophes, wherever they might live their public lives, saw themselves as standing between eras in the history of a civilization and its thought. They were men who examined in their minds the whole fabric of the traditions and givens of the culture that had been passed on to their age. They were men whose minds were increasingly unfettered, for whom the term "free thought" indicated not only a rejection of certain dogmas, but a description of how the mind of man could behave. They consciously saw themselves as men whose ideas represented a major period of transition for the West in the realms of philosophy, science, art and morality. Some held theories that threatened not only the structure of Catholic or Christian thought, but the structure of a more modern deism as well. For those to whom that deism was the religion of a free and learned man, there was in the very consideration of atheistic or skeptical alternatives a certain heady sense of intellectual liberty and daring to be had. Many held their ideas with a conviction whose spontaneous expression, especially in the face of facile disagreement, would have overstepped the limits which "sociability" set to that expression. For many of the philosophes, therefore, to be in social accord with the rules of the salons was to a very great extent to be alienated from their own private thoughts, their own convictions, their own enthusiasms.

The contribution of the coterie holbachique as an institution to the world of eighteenth-century letters and thought was that it offered to those philosophes who gravitated to it a haven from that conflict. It was the one place where the philosophes were *chez eux*, the one place where they were not merely visitors, but at home. D'Holbach had the wealth to entertain and feed his friends, and he could do it as a philosophe. It was there that diversity, candor, intellectual enthusiasm and free speculation could flourish. That is why it became "our" coterie to its members; that is why d'Holbach became not a host, but "the *maître d'Hôtel* of Philosophy." It was not the mores of that Paris in which they spent the rest of their social lives which dominated the assemblies of the rue Royale; what set the tone there was the need of the philosophes themselves to find a social outlet for their most private and their most extravagant beliefs and speculations. It was not that there were not atheists at the other salons, or skeptics, or men by whom the universe was conceived of as a cold and uncaring abode; it was that only at d'Holbach's home could the atheists and skeptics *be* the atheists and skeptics that they were, and speak their minds. It was only at d'Holbach's that the deists, the scientists and the literary figures could meet such men in earnest and engage them in open discussion. The sharing of that free exploration and open communication created the exhilaration, community and singular nature of the coterie holbachique. Those who thrived on the spontaneity and candid dialogue of the coterie became its devotees; those who, like Rousseau, felt threatened by the presence of the free-speaking atheists or by the constant questioning of opinions simply left. Frequenting the coterie holbachique, Rousseau had written in his *Confessions*, "far from weakening my faith, had strengthened it, *because of my natural aversion to disputation, to division.*"[1] To Mme de Créqui he had written: "I have never thought much of philosophy, and I have detached myself absolutely from the party of the philosophes; I don't like them to preach impiety; . . ."[2] Mme d'Epinay recalled a scene consistent with these opinions, in which Rousseau grew bitter hearing deism attacked. The group chided him for his unwillingness to listen. "If it is cowardice to allow people to speak evil of one's absent friend," she recorded Rousseau as replying, "it is a crime to allow evil be spoken about God, who is present; and I, gentlemen, I believe in God."[3] So did many members of the coterie holbachique. What delighted *them* was to engage in open dialogue with those who did not—with d'Holbach, Diderot, Naigeon and the skeptical Grimm; in fact, what delighted them was to engage in open dialogue per se.

It need not be assumed that d'Holbach's salon began with the intention of filling this need. The coterie developed gradually out of the more social gatherings of d'Holbach's personal friends and bright young acquaintances. The composition of the salon was quite different in its early years, we have seen, from what it became by the end of the 1750s. For various reasons, people came and went as devotees of this salon, and some of those reasons must have had something to do with the freedom to speak, the audacity of the conversations there. Describing Buffon's decision to leave the group, Marmontel recalled that "Buffon, surrounded in his own circles by servile men and flatterers, and accustomed

[1] Rousseau, *Confessions*, 463-465 (emphasis added).
[2] Rousseau, *Correspondance générale de Jean Jacques Rousseau*, T. Dufour, ed., v, 358-359.
[3] Mme d'Epinay, *Mémoires*, I, 379-381.

95

to an obsequious deference to his systematic ideas, was sometimes disagreeably surprised to find among us less reverence and docility. . . ." Spoiled by adulation, Marmontel continued, Buffon could not tolerate the arguments and the disagreements he encountered at d'Holbach's home, being "ill at ease among his peers." For this reason, he claimed, Buffon left the group.[4]

For those who remained, the coterie holbachique was a special phenomenon. It was there, for over thirty years, that one could say what was on one's mind, and its guests and devotees took full advantage of this opportunity. Writing once of Galiani's views on early Christianity, Grimm lamented, "What a shame that so many rare, fecund and original ideas are confided only to a small number of philosophes. . . ."[5] There one could confide one's most private speculations, there the fetters were removed, and it was for these reasons that the coterie was so important to its members and so unique. There was good food, good wine, good company and, above all, the freedom for a philosophe to be himself.

* * *

Marmontel, in his *Mémoires*, distinguished among the salons of Paris. There were, he wrote, the salons of the financiers, literary and licentious, and the salons of the ladies, where everyone was ingenious, gay, animated and amusing. "Nevertheless," he remarked, ". . . however interesting in *esprit* I found the society of these kind ladies, it did not make me neglect to go and fortify my soul, to elevate, to broaden, to enlarge my thought, and to make it fertile, in a society of men whose spirit penetrated mine with warmth and with light. The home of Baron d'Holbach, and for a while that of Helvétius, were the meeting-places of this society, composed in part of the flower of Mme Geoffrin's guests, and, in part, of some minds that Mme Geoffrin had found too bold and too rash to be admitted to her dinners."[6]

Morellet agreed that the same people met at d'Holbach's home and at Helvétius', but in addition to Marmontel's emphasis on the more permanent nature of d'Holbach's coterie, he made another important distinction, one that was central to the singularity of the Baron's dinners. To assemble the same people, he observed, did not mean necessarily to establish the same ambiance: "The home of Helvétius drew together about the same people as that

[4] Marmontel, *Mémoires*, I, 484-485.   [5] Grimm, *Corr. litt.*, VI, 116.
[6] Marmontel, *Mémoires*, I, 481.

of Baron d'Holbach, on different days; but the conversation was less *good* there, and less well-developed. The mistress of the house, attracting to her side the men who pleased her the most, and not choosing the worst, disrupted the society a bit. She did not like philosophy any more than did Mme d'Holbach; but the latter, keeping herself apart without saying anything, or conversing in a low voice with some of her friends, prevented nothing, whereas Mme Helvétius, beautiful, with an original mind, a lively, natural disposition, greatly disturbed the philosophical discussions."[7]

The coterie holbachique, wrote Marmontel, "found in itself the sweetest pleasures that liberty of thought and the commerce of minds can procure." This was a welcome change from the inhibition of free exchange effected elsewhere: "We were no longer led about and restrained on a leash, as at Mme Geoffrin's. . . ." At d'Holbach's home, he continued, "Our friends . . . were at their ease, and so much more likable; for the mind, in its movements, cannot deploy its strength and its grace well, except when nothing hinders it; and there [at d'Holbach's] it resembled Virgil's steed: *Quabis ubi, abruptus, fugit preosepia, vinclis, Tandem liber equus: campoque potitus aperto . . . Emicat, arrectisque fremit cervicibus alte, Luxurians.*"[8]

Morellet distinguished the coterie holbachique from all other salons in the same manner: "Now it was there that one could not fail to hear the freest, the most animated and the most instructive conversation that ever was; when I say free, I mean in terms of philosophy, of religion, of government. . . . Cicero said somewhere that there is no opinion so extravagant that it has not been advanced by some philosopher. I shall say equally that there was no bold thought in politics and religion that was not brought forward there, *and discussed pro and con*, almost always with much subtlety and profundity."[9]

For Morellet, this atmosphere made the coterie holbachique the most valuable of the Parisian salons: "But among the societies that zeal for the cause of philosophy opened up to me, I must place in the first rank that of the Baron d'Holbach, for the utility, the pleasure and the instruction that I gained from it."[10]

In the *Salon de 1765*, Diderot remarked on the emotional impact of certain pictorial representations of familiar scenes; were

---

[7] Morellet, *Mémoires*, I, 386.   [8] Marmontel, *Mémoires*, I, 467-468.
[9] Morellet, *Mémoires*, I, 128-130 (emphasis added).
[10] Ibid., 127.

he in Moscow, he mused, what memories and pleasures a picture of Paris would conjure for him. He listed as among such pleasures the coterie holbachique and its free discussion: "There is the rue Royale-Saint Roch! It is there that assemble all that the capital contains of decent and clever people. To find the door opened to you, it is not enough to be titled or to be a savant; one must also be good. It is there that exchange is secure. It is there that history, politics, finance, belles-lettres and philosophy are discussed. *It is there that men esteem each other enough to contradict each other.* It is there that the true cosmopolitan is found. . . ."[11] It was this passage which led Naigeon in his edition of Diderot's *Oeuvres* to note: "A true and charming portrait of Baron d'Holbach's Society.—*Et in Arcadia ego.*"[12]

In Diderot's letters there are a series of portraits of the discussions at d'Holbach's home, and the subjects were as diverse as the interests of the people involved, encompassing metaphysics, history, morality, literature, science, music, theater and politics. Only among the company of d'Holbach's circle did Diderot feel truly at ease in a group, and when d'Holbach's second wife fell temporarily ill in 1765, it never occurred to him that the meetings at d'Holbach's should cease for a while. Rather, he thought of another expedient. Writing to Sophie Volland, he explained: ". . . you will agree that the habitual company of about twenty men who dizzy her from morning until evening with politics and philosophy is not the proper remedy for her illness. I have decided, therefore, on the first walk that the Baron and I take alone, gently to convince him to establish his academic society in his study, and to leave his wife in her apartment with De Cothe [Kohaut, her music tutor], her lute, and a small number of her close friends, who will keep her company and converse with her of sweeter and gayer things than our eternal moralities."[13]

The charm of the coterie for Diderot was that all ideas could be entertained in such company, that the mind could turn itself loose and speculate as deeply or as absurdly as it saw fit. Describing a dinner at d'Holbach's home to Mme de Maux in 1769, Diderot wrote that they began with d'Holbach defending Boullainvillier's *Traité de l'astrologie judiciaire* (a work whose metaphorical title covered one of the earliest French doctrines of

[11] Diderot, *Oeuvres* (A-T), x, 378-379 (emphasis added).
[12] Diderot, *Oeuvres* (N), xiii, 226, n. 1.
[13] Diderot, *Corr.*, v, 220-221.

materialism, linking the movements of every piece of matter in the universe with the movements of every other such particle, and explaining all phenomena by this means). Diderot debated the point, "and I asserted that Saturn had about as much effect on us as the effect that an atom of dust has on the face of a great clock." From this, the conversation (with the help of champagne, wrote Diderot) moved to the subject of pre-existent germs, "and, as one insanity leads to another, the thought came to me that just as there are bad years for apples, pears, peaches and grapes, perhaps there are also bad vintage years for men." The company took up the idea, "and there we were, embarked on the multitude of experiments one would have to do," from which they conceived of a plan to found "a great college of monks uniquely devoted to the study of nature." Suddenly the conversation took a more serious turn. A question was raised concerning the extinction of species. Diderot declared that not only did species become extinct, but stars, or suns, also became extinguished: "I added, 'Ours can thus undergo the same fate.'" Asked what would become of life on the planet, Diderot suggested that it would disappear, but that if one could imagine the sun reigniting, one could see the whole cycle of life beginning anew. Would man also reappear? he was asked. "Yes," he answered, "man, but not as he is. At first, I don't know what; and then at the end of several hundreds of millions of years and of I-don't-know-whats, the biped animal who carries the name man." The conversation, in the light of the *Rêve de d'Alembert*, was a remarkable one, and those intellectual historians who have wondered at the proto-evolutionary thought that appeared in the work of Diderot, of d'Holbach, and, one might add, of Grimm, might smile to see such theories developed at d'Holbach's home at the end of a consideration of judicial astrology, pre-existent germs, bad years for men, colleges of monks, and suns that die. For Diderot it was all a part of the speculation that was the pattern of life at d'Holbach's home: "All these ideas, true or false, make the hours go by in a delicious way. They amuse the friend with whom one talks."[14]

Grimm also appreciated the unique freedom of expression at d'Holbach's dinners. During his "Philosophical Sermon" to the coterie on New Year's Day, 1770, he announced that he had a message for the group from Mme Geoffrin, to the effect that they were welcome at her home, but that she "renews the bans of the

[14] Ibid., IX, 94-96.

preceding years." One will not be permitted to discuss the following subjects, Grimm wryly declared: religion, philosophy, science, literature, politics, finances, art, natural history, etc., etc., etc., "nor, in general, any matter whatsoever." He also announced the answer of the coterie: "The 'Eglise,' judging that silence—and notably on the matters in question—is not its strong point, promises to obey as long as it will be forced to do so by means of violence."[15]

Yet for all the humor of his discourse, Grimm was also able to criticize his fellow members of the coterie in a blunt and candid manner: "I can say to several among you: you are superficial on all important matters; who asks you to deal with them? You know only how to exhaust the ideas of your masters . . . in this very place where I reproach you; who asks you to steal from them? You are often dry, heavy, prolix reasoners without perspective. . . . You speak occasionally by pure chance, without knowing what is involved."[16]

It was not clear whom Grimm was criticizing: Roux and Naigeon for repeating the atheism of d'Holbach and Diderot? Raynal and Chastellux for working on books on trade and international relations, where Grimm saw himself as expert? Morellet for his work as an économiste? The correct identification of the target(s) of this critique matters less than the fact that it was said, for in no other salon of Paris could he have used such language in addressing his fellow guests. To speak freely, to be criticized freely, and to remain associates—this was a rare phenomenon in eighteenth-century Paris.

Garat, in his biography of his friend Suard, prefaced his discussion of Suard's relationship with the coterie holbachique with a cogent observation, especially in the light of Suard's role as censor of Beaumarchais and as counterrevolutionary journalist. For Suard, he wrote, there was a great difference between the act of discussing politics and, above all, religion, and the act of writing about it, of communicating his thoughts to the public. Suard, he remarked, would not write beyond those bounds of measure and prudence he thought vital to preserve order; to do otherwise was the mistake he believed that many of his friends were committing. He loved, however, to speculate on all of these questions and to

---

[15] Grimm, *Corr. litt.*, XIII, 438.
[16] Ibid., 414-418. The entire sermon is found in pp. 414-439.

discuss his thoughts with his friends at d'Holbach's home.[17] This distinction between discussion and the written word was a very real one for many members of the coterie, as we have seen in the discussion of the atheists within the group; it explains to a large degree both the appeal of d'Holbach's assemblies to their devotees, and the confusion that has existed concerning the nature of these meetings. It was not to spread a gospel of the "holbachians" that the coterie existed, although there were individuals in the coterie who indeed had individual messages they wished to spread; it was in order to discuss and exchange ideas, to communicate their latest thoughts and hear them criticized that the coterie assembled. Attributing the philosophies of those who actually published bold ideas to those members of the coterie who came to hear them, to discuss them, and to present their own opinions on a host of subjects has been one of the great errors of interpretation that have so distorted our view of d'Holbach's circle.

Garat noted how close Suard was to the Baron despite their profound differences of opinion. They argued theology constantly, he wrote, but always remained the closest of friends. The same was true, Garat added, of Suard's relationship with Helvétius; they debated the principles of *De l'esprit* at d'Holbach's dinners, often without ever a harsh personal note. Admitting there were atheists among Suard's acquaintances there, Garat nevertheless did not find that aspect of d'Holbach's circle to be its distinguishing feature. Although his information was probably all secondhand (since there is no evidence that he ever visited d'Holbach's home), Garat was one of Suard's closest friends and had full access to the latter's memoirs, personal papers, and letters, from which the biography was written. "The pro and the con were listened to there," he wrote of d'Holbach's group, "and they thus were not very 'intolerant in preaching tolerance.' " (There are, it would appear, some timeless clichés!) D'Holbach's home, Garat continued, "resembled an INSTITUTE, at a time when there were only academies. The most distinguished members of all the academies of the capital composed his society and the guests of his table."[18] If one adds the flow of visitors to the regular frequenters of the dinners, Garat's description was very close to the truth.

Suard himself identified very closely with the coterie holbachique. In his letters to the Baron's friend John Wilkes, whose

---

[17] Garat, *Suard*, I, 171-207.   [18] Ibid., 207-242.

friend he also had become during the latter's stay in Paris, he demonstrated the familiar habit of the members of the coterie of speaking in the name of the group. Characteristically advising Wilkes to moderate his attacks on Parliament so as not to jeopardize his maintenance of his seat, Suard added: "All of your friends of the rue Royale are anxious to learn the sequel of your adventures." In December 1768 he wrote, "All of the rue Royale toast Wilkes and Liberty." He sent Wilkes the wishes of Roux, d'Holbach, Marmontel, Helvétius, Morellet and Chastellux, and kept him informed of their activities. As late as 1777, long after Wilkes' visit to Paris, he wrote to him, "All of our friends are rather well. I am going to dine *chez le Baron*, where I will talk of you. Raise a toast sometimes to the club of the rue Royale."[19]

Given such interest, such advice, and the fact that Suard communicated often to Wilkes in the name of the coterie, historians accepting the mythical model of the coterie might choose to see in all of this a demonstration that the coterie holbachique was seeking to further the cause of Wilkes in England, perhaps as a part of some broader plan of incitement to radical change. Nothing, however, could be farther from the truth. In the spring of 1768 Wilkes' election as an M.P. from Middlesex had led to tumultuous demonstrations in the streets of London, during which some of his partisans had forced foreign ambassadors to descend from their carriages to drink a toast to Wilkes, and had forced people on the street to don a blue cockade. In the same letter in which he informed Wilkes that Grimm now considered him a political hero, Suard also added his own response to these events: "I like the esteem of the few to justify the enthusiasm of the multitude. I would ask only that your laurels not be tainted by blood, and I would forgive that glass gets broken, if no heads get broken as well. I also would ask that ambassadors who are not thirsty not be made to drink against their wishes."[20] Wilkes had become the friend of d'Holbach's circle, and Suard was free to greet him as a member of that group and to criticize him as a Jean-Baptiste-Antoine Suard. No one submerged himself in the coterie holbachique.

There were those who visited the coterie and flourished in its atmosphere of spontaneous conversation and speculation. David Hume and Lawrence Sterne, both of whom visited the coterie in

[19] Suard, *Lettres à Wilkes*, passim.   [20] Ibid., 26-27.

the 1760s, were taken aback by the tone there, but delighted in it, and were constant guests while they stayed in Paris. Hume called them "the sheiks of the rue Royale," and Sterne labeled them (in the original spelling) "the joyous sett."[21]

Not all the visitors to the rue Royale, however, found the intellectual freedom so exhilarating. Horace Walpole was singularly unimpressed, as we already have noted. Walpole, however, was an entity unto himself, and his dislike of d'Holbach's circle must be put into proper perspective. He indeed denounced them as atheists, but Walpole denounced all Paris as atheists in his letters to England. To appreciate the coterie holbachique a visitor had to be open to new ideas, from the most reasonable theses to the most extravagant. Walpole's general attitude toward speculation and toward views which differed radically from his own, as well as his appreciation of who properly could be termed an "atheist," best can be seen in a letter he wrote to George Montague from Paris in November 1765: "I have yet seen or heard anything serious, that was not ridiculous. Jesuits, Methodists, philosophers, politicians, the hypocrite Rousseau, the scoffer Voltaire, the encyclopédistes, the Humes, the Lytteltons, the Grenvilles, the atheist tyrant of Prussia, and the mountebank of history, Mr. Pitt, are all to me but imposters in their various ways."[22]

Walpole's attitude was *not*, one may safely assert, one conducive to favoring what the Baron's circle had to offer. All this aside, however, Walpole himself belied his claim that he had left the coterie holbachique during his stay in Paris because he found their particular irreligious philosophy absurd. When Raynal's *Histoire philosophique* had made the abbé's name a familiar one in Europe, Walpole recalled in a letter to a friend his experience with Raynal in Paris. It shed some light on why Walpole had left the coterie of his own accord: "The first time I met him was at the dull Baron d'Olbach's [*sic*]: we were twelve at table: I dreaded opening my mouth in French, before so many people and so many servants: he began questioning me, 'cross the table, about our colonies, which I understand as I do Coptic. I made him signs that I was deaf. After dinner he found I was not, and never forgave me."[23]

---

[21] *The Letters of David Hume*, J.Y.T. Grieg, ed., II, 195-196; Sterne's phrase is quoted in Alice Green Fredman, *Diderot and Sterne*, 7-8.

[22] Walpole, *Letters*, VI, 358-359.   [23] Ibid., IX, 92.

Gibbon was another foreign visitor who had some unkind things to say about the coterie holbachique, but the record of his comments is confusing. There were four manuscript copies of his autobiography found among his papers; in two of these he told one story about the coterie, and in the two others he offered a quite different account. In Memoirs B and C, as they are known, he denounced "the friends of d'Olbach [*sic*] and Helvétius" as dogmatic atheists whose "intolerant zeal" he could not bear. Describing d'Holbach's dinners in Memoir D, however, he recalled them as being "frequented by the first literary characters of France, and enlivened by the free conflict of wit, learning and philosophy." In Memoir E, he called them "elegant Symposia, to which I was welcome without invitation," and recalled that "I saw and heard the most eminent of the wits, scholars and philosophers of France."[24]

Gibbon's letters to friends and family in England during his stay in Paris (January-May 1763) offer few clues to the conflicting statements of his autobiographical memoirs. Describing the dinners in Paris to Dorothea Gibbon two weeks after his arrival, he wrote nothing critical of any salon, but simply, "We may say what we please of the frivolity of the French, but I do assure that in a fortnight passed in Paris I have heard more conversation worth remembering and seen more men of letters amongst the people of fashion, than I had done in two or three winters in London."[25] Of Helvétius he wrote, "Besides being a sensible man, an agreeable companion and the worthiest creature in the world, he has a very pretty wife. . . ."[26] Two weeks later he mentioned that he had been dining for some time both at Helvétius' home and at d'Holbach's. For the former he had only additional praise, describing him as one "who from his heart, his head and his fortune is a most valuable man." On d'Holbach he commented only that he "is a man of parts and fortune and has two dinners every week."[27]

A possible explanation of this discrepancy is that Gibbon may have had an unpleasant experience with several members of the coterie, and recalled this most vividly at the moments he was writing Memoirs B and C. Reflecting on this, he may have altered his

[24] *The Autobiographies of Edward Gibbon*, J. Murray, ed., 203-204 (Memoir B), 262 (Memoir C), 301 (Memoir E), 404 (Memoir D).
[25] *The Letters of Edward Gibbon*, J. E. Norton, ed., I, 132.
[26] Ibid., 133.   [27] Ibid., 136.

prose more objectively in the later memoirs. The two sides are interesting, however, because they *both* reflect the truth of the situation. There were in fact dogmatic atheists, intellectually intolerant of religious beliefs, at the coterie; there was also "the free conflict of wit, learning and philosophy." Precisely in that combination was the value of the coterie to be found.

Despite all the assumptions that d'Holbach's assemblies were somehow a secretive affair, the truth is they had a high reputation not only among important Frenchmen, but among European men of letters, diplomats, and luminaries in general. They offered the opportunity to meet the free-thinkers of Paris on their own home ground, and it was an opportunity many sought. No complete list of the important figures who visited d'Holbach's Thursday and Sunday dinners ever could be compiled, but the available sources reveal a diverse and striking company. The diplomatic corps in Paris was well-represented at the rue Royale. Among the guests who often mingled with the coterie were many ambassadors: the baron of Gleichen (Denmark), Dr. James (England), the marquis of Carracciolo (Naples), the baron of Studnitz (Saxe-Gotha), the baron of Schweidnitz (Saxe-Coburg-Gotha), the baron of Thun (Würtemberg), and the count of Creutz (Sweden).[28]

For Englishmen who came to Paris, reception at d'Holbach's home appeared to become an almost standard part of a respectable itinerary. Among those whom the Baron entertained during their stays in Paris were David Garrick, Allan Ramsey, Samuel Romilly, Adam Smith, Dr. Burney, Dr. Gem, John Wilkes, General Clerck, Lawrence Sterne, David Hume, Horace Walpole, Edward Gibbon, Andrew Stuart, Lord Shelburne, Isaac Barré, and Joseph Priestley.[29] German guests included the hereditary-prince of Brunswick, the margrave of Bayreuth, baron Dieskau, and the baron d'Alberg, who later became the elector of Mainz. Italian guests included Beccaria, Dr. Gatti, and the thinkers Frisi and Allesandro Verri. The Swiss philosophe Georges-Louis Schmid visited the coterie, as did Williem van Hogendorp, son of the burgomeister

[28] Gleichen, *Souvenirs*, 169; Diderot, *Corr.*, II-X, passim; Morellet, *Mémoires*, I, 128-130.

[29] Diderot, loc. cit.; Morellet, loc. cit.; *Letters to Hume* (Burton), 136-138; Gibbon, *Letters*, I, 132; Walpole, *Letters*, VI, 358-359; Hume, *Letters* (Grieg), II, 275; Carlyle, *Autobiography*, 292; "Adam Smith's Correspondence," in Scott, *Adam Smith*, 298-299; Wilkes, *Correspondence*, II, 35-36; Garrick, *Letters*, II, 444; Verri, *Carteggio*, I, 112-114.

of Rotterdam. The notable American visitor was, of course, Benjamin Franklin.[30]

The Frenchmen who were welcomed as occasional guests at the rue Royale and at Grandval are too numerous to mention, but a partial list is indicative of the broad spectrum of French society that was pleased to dine with the coterie holbachique. They included two ministers, Turgot and Sartine; the marquis de Pézay, who was Louis XVI's military tutor when the latter was still dauphin; and the comte de Schomberg, who rose to the rank of *lieutenant-général* in the French army.[31] Other guests included the chevalier de Valori; Trudaine de Montigny, *intendant des finances*; Rodier, one of the six *intendants de la marine*, who had married d'Holbach's cousin; Montamy, *premier-maître d'hôtel* of the duc d'Orléans; and Servan, *avocat-général* of the parlement de Grenoble.[32] From the world of letters came Dumarsais, La Condamine, Saurin, Coyer, d'Alainville, Colardeau, Damilaville, and in the late 1770s Condorcet, Cabanis and Volney.[33] The painter Delormes and the musician Schistre were also received by the group.[34] Perhaps most startling of all, the most dedicated Catholic apologist of the eighteenth century, the abbé Bergier, was also an occasional visitor, as was the Benedictine Dom Lefèbvre, the originally devout Catholic who gradually became Helvétius' friend and who served as a curé of the civil church during the Revolution.[35] While women were not generally welcome at the gatherings of d'Holbach's circle, they frequently were invited to

[30] On the German visitors, see Diderot, *Corr.*, ii-x, passim; Morellet, *Mémoires*, i, 128-130. On the Italians, see Verri, op. cit., 23-29, 43-44, 112-115; "Lettres à Galiani," 24-27; Morellet, loc. cit.; Diderot, *Corr.*, v-vi, passim; Beccaria, *Opere*, ii, 882-883. On Schmid, see Voltaire, *Corr.*, lxxviii, 155; on Hogendorp, see Diderot, *Corr.*, xi, 58; on Franklin, see Morellet, loc. cit.

[31] On Turgot, see *Letters to Hume* (Burton), 136-137; on Sartine, see Marmontel, *Mémoires*, i, 385; on Pézay, see Mme d'Epinay, *Lettere (Gli Ultimi Anni)*, 87-88; on Schomberg, see Gleichen, *Souvenirs*, 169; and Galiani, *Lettres*, 8, n. 1.

[32] Diderot, *Corr.*, vii, 157-160; Mme d'Epinay, *Mémoires*, passim; J. Lough, "Le baron d'Holbach," 524-543; P. Vernière, "Deux cas de prosélytisme philosophique au XVIIIᵉ siècle à propos de deux lettres inédites du baron d'Holbach," *RHLF* (1955), 495-499.

[33] Morellet, *Mémoires*, i, 128-130; Diderot, *Corr.*, passim; Jean Gaulmier, *L'Idéologue Volney (1757-1820)*, 34-40 and passim.

[34] Diderot, *Corr.*, xii, 146.

[35] On Bergier, see ibid., vii, 157-160, and also below, this chapter, n. 63-67; on Dom Lefèbvre, see Vernière, ed., "Deux lettres de d'Holbach," 495-499.

spend time at Grandval, where d'Holbach's dinners were held during the summer months, and thus occasionally they found themselves at full assemblies of the coterie. At one time or another, Mme Geoffrin, Mme de Maux, Mme de Saint-Aubin, Mme Riccoboni, Mme d'Houdetot, Mme d'Epinay, and Mlle d'Ette all dined with the thinkers of d'Holbach's group.[36]

As the letters of Walpole and the memoirs of Gibbon have revealed, the candor and openness of the coterie holbachique did not alter in the presence of guests. Samuel Romilly, who visited them in 1781, was horrified to hear atheism openly espoused; writing to a friend about his conversations with Diderot there, he exclaimed, "Diderot . . . talked to me as if I had been long and intimately acquainted with him. . . . On the subject of religion he had no disguise; or rather he was ostentatious of a total disbelief in the existence of a God."[37] Carlyle in his *Autobiography* recalled an anecdote relating to Andrew Stuart, the Scottish lawyer and Keeper of the Signet of Scotland, when the latter had met "the club in Paris—Baron d'Holbach's." According to this account, "they laughed at Andrew Stuart for making a battle in favour of a future state, and called him 'L'âme Immortelle.'" Stuart must have taken it all well, for he became a good friend of the Baron's and continued to make appearances.[38] Dom Lefèbvre, who visited the coterie in 1769, before he had moderated his devout views, apparently wrote a letter to d'Holbach, thanking him for his hospitality in Paris. D'Holbach replied and assured him of the affection he had gained among "my friends, during your brief stay in Paris." Inviting the monk to visit with them again when he returned to Paris, d'Holbach alluded to their differences of opinion with humor and sincerity: "Complete philosophes that we try to be, that is to say, completely damned as we are, we render justice to merit, and we interest ourselves in people who reveal it."[39] Naigeon apparently did not even temper his great zest in discussing atheism at the coterie. The baron of Gleichen described him as demonstrating "an unbearable vanity" when they talked, and added that "M. d'Holbach used to say of [Naigeon] that he displeased him [d'Holbach] because he was so

---

[36] Diderot, *Corr.*, II-IV, passim; Mme d'Epinay, *Mémoires*, passim; Garrick, *Letters*, II, 444.

[37] Romilly, *Life of Romilly*, I, 46; see also 131-133, 145-146, 166.

[38] Carlyle, *Autobiography*, 292.

[39] Vernière, ed., "Deux lettres de d'Holbach," 498-499.

proud of not believing in God."[40] These views were not hidden from ambassadors, monks, or visiting Englishmen at the coterie, for these men were the visitors and, as such, it was they who observed the rules of the *boulangerie* at d'Holbach's home. Given the continual popularity of the coterie and the flow of visitors it received, many must have found something of value in its atmosphere.

Indeed the visitors became so many that in 1765 Diderot wrote to Sophie Volland that "The Baron at last has become annoyed at having twenty-seven to twenty-eight people [at dinner], when he was expecting only twenty," and was going to institute a reform. The occasional guests kept coming, but it appears they now needed a formal invitation. Distinguished visitors, however, continued to be welcome throughout their visits to Paris.[41]

The esteem in which d'Holbach's coterie was held can be gauged by this steady flow of visitors, but it should not be surprising given the composition of the coterie, the reputation of its members, and the free intellectual air that prevailed there. In 1766 the Italian philosophe Beccaria, whose *Dei Delitti e delle Pene* had made him one of the most honored men in Europe, wrote to his French translator, the abbé Morellet, for an additional service. He had received many congratulatory letters from leading Frenchmen, he wrote, from d'Alembert, Diderot, Helvétius and Buffon, and he wanted Morellet to thank them for him. He also had heard from d'Holbach, who had extended an invitation to visit the coterie in Paris. Telling Morellet whom to thank, Beccaria merely mentioned their names, then added, "Above all, tell M. le Baron d'Holbach that I am filled with veneration for him, and that I desire above all that he find me worthy of his friendship."[42] David Hume, writing to Suard in 1773, announced that a friend of his was going to Paris, whom he and the historian Robertson were recommending to Suard's attention. Hume wrote that his friend, a Mr. Jardine, already knew d'Alembert, "but as I know that M. d'Alembert never goes to our friend Baron d'Holbach's, where my countryman would have access to see the best company; I would further request, that, if you find him worthy of that society, which I make no doubt of, you would, in my name as well as your own, present him to the Baron. I suppose that the

40 Gleichen, *Souvenirs*, 202.   41 Diderot, *Corr.*, v, 213-214.
42 Beccaria, *Opere*, ii, 864.

Baron's house is on the same footing as formerly, a common receptacle for all men of letters and ingenuity."[43]

When the economist Adam Smith visited d'Holbach's home in 1766, the Baron invited Turgot to meet with him there; Turgot wrote of this encounter to Hume, recalling the latter's "liaisons with the society of Baron d'Holbach."[44] Smith and Morellet became good friends at d'Holbach's dinners and maintained a long correspondence in later years. In 1786 Smith wrote to Morellet, "I have not heard of Baron d'Holbach these two or three years past. I hope he is happy and in good health. Be so good as to assure him of my most affectionate and respectful remembrance, and that I shall never forget the very great kindness he did me the honor to show me during my residence at Paris."[45]

Not only did the coterie allow visiting foreigners to meet French thinkers in a free atmosphere; in some cases, it brought together fellow-countrymen who never would have met to talk in their home countries. Thus Wilkes wrote to a friend from Paris that he had met David Hume "at baron d'Holbach's where we laughed much."[46] It is not probable that the radical and the sober Scotsman would have met socially in the United Kingdom, and still less likely that they would have laughed.

Wilkes' stay with the coterie holbachique was a profitable one for him. He began a long correspondence with both Chastellux and Suard as a result of it, and was visited by Chastellux, Roux, and Morellet in London. When his daughter went to Paris to study, he committed her to the care of the d'Holbachs, the Suards and, for her summer vacation, to Helvétius and his wife. Again, the relationship was expressed as one that existed socially between Wilkes and the coterie as a whole. "The baron d'Holbach and his entire society were strongly concerned with your affairs," Chastellux wrote to him in 1768, and "I have a thousand compliments to give to you on their behalf."[47]

When Joseph-Michel-Antoine Servan, *avocat-général* of the parlement de Grenoble, came to Paris in the winter of 1765-1766,

[43] Hume, *Letters* (Grieg), II, 275.
[44] *Letters to Hume* (Burton), 136-138.
[45] "Adam Smith's Correspondence," in Scott, *Adam Smith*, 298-299.
[46] Wilkes, *Correspondence*, II, 35-36.
[47] The final quotation is from Chastellux, "Lettres à Wilkes," 619-620. See also ibid., 620-623; Suard, *Lettres à Wilkes*, passim; and Wilkes, *Correspondence*, II, 188-189; III, 174, 177; IV, 27-28, 39-40, 43, 68, 75.

he too visited the coterie. In February he sent a note of praise and thanks to d'Holbach, along with a gift of truffles. D'Holbach's reply is of special interest. On one hand, it revealed he was not above flattering a man as important as Servan: "If our little society merits your esteem," he wrote in acknowledgment, "it is because of the justice which it rendered to you." He compared the "speculators" of his group to "active sages such as yourself," and declared the latter to be "much more capable of serving and enlightening society than several thinkers, perpetually obliged to cover themselves with their cloaks." He asked Servan to "Receive the sincere praise and compliments of my society. . . . We shall count ourselves most fortunate if we can fortify our epicurianism with a friend such as you." On the other hand, the letter revealed that d'Holbach felt perfectly free to preach a sermon on duty to the recently appointed *avocat-général*. He wrote that he expected an attempt to be made to persecute Diderot when the last volumes of the *Encyclopédie* were published. Nevertheless, d'Holbach urged, no one had the right to disengage himself from the efforts at enlightenment being made: "One must choose one's side on these questions, and keep before one's mind that if falsehood has immolated so many victims, truth has much more right than it to create enthusiasts and martyrs." In November 1766, as Paul Vernière, who unearthed this letter, has noted, Servan startled France with a discourse to the opening session of his parlement calling for drastic reforms in the administration of justice. Since he had visited Voltaire in that year, Servan has been considered a convert to the cause of the philosophes through the medium of the Patriarch at Ferney. Yet d'Holbach's letter to Servan indicated that the official had been in contact with the coterie before his visit to Voltaire, and in Vernière's words, "it offers an estimate of the intellectual influence of the cenacle of the rue Royale."[48]

The letters of Lawrence Sterne help us estimate d'Holbach's standing in Paris as well. When Sterne arrived in France, during a time of war, he carried no passport, and he had to secure the sponsorship of leading Frenchmen who could vouch to the government for his comportment. Sterne fictionalized an account of his travails in this pursuit in his *A Sentimental Journey Through France and Italy*. In his chapter "The Passport (Paris)," he recounted how his hotel-keeper, discovering his lack of a passport,

---

[48] Vernière, ed., "Deux lettres de d'Holbach," 495-497.

switched from "Mon Seigneur" to "monsieur" and assured him he would rot in the Bastille. After a nightmare about his imprisonment, he claimed, he at last succeeded in obtaining one in the name of "Mr Yorick, the King's Jester," from an anglophobic count in Versailles.[49] In truth, however, he received it once he secured the proper sponsors; Sterne asked d'Holbach to so stand for him, and the Baron accepted. As the author of *Tristram Shandy* wrote to David Garrick from Paris in January 1762, "The Baron d'Holbach has offered any security for the inoffensiveness of my behavior in France. . . . This baron is one of the most learned noblemen here, the great protector of wits, and the savants who are no wits . . . [He] keeps open house . . . [and] his house is now, as yours was to me, my own—he lives at great expense."[50]

Sterne appeared to love his stay in Paris, but he assured his readers in the *Sentimental Journey* that the demands which the diverse opinions of Paris made upon his hypocrisy were almost too great to bear: "For three weeks together, I was of every man's opinion I met—*Pardi! le Monsieur Yorik a autant d'esprit que nous autres.—Il raisonne bien*, said another.—*C'est un bon enfant*, said a third. And at this price I could have eaten and drank and been merry all the days of my life at Paris . . .—the higher I got, the more I was forced upon my beggarly system—the better the coterie—the more children of Art—I languished for those of nature: and one night, after a most vile prostitution of myself to half a dozen different people, I grew sick—went to bed—ordered La Fleur to get me horses in the morning to set out for Italy."[51] Assuming a basis of truth in his account, perhaps that was why Sterne, who had been fêted by all of literary Paris, sent only one greeting to that city, in a letter from Toulouse while en route to Italy to his banker Foley, who attended many of the salons, "My best respects to my worthy Baron d'Holbach and all that society."[52]

Indeed it was Sterne who was the recipient of a certain intellectual compromise on the part of his sponsor. Sterne was a clergyman as well as a novelist, and when he returned to Paris in 1764

---

[49] *The Works of Lawrence Sterne*, VII, 81-109. The count, as revealed in Sterne's letter to Garrick (see below, n. 50), was the comte de Bissie.

[50] *Letters of Lawrence Sterne*, 44-45.

[51] Sterne, *Works*, VII, 134.   [52] Sterne, *Letters*, 69-71.

and renewed his ties with the coterie, he was invited to preach a Sunday sermon in the chapel of the English embassy. Among those who attended were the atheists Diderot and d'Holbach.[53]

When the celebrated Shakespearean actor David Garrick visited Paris, he too was entertained by the coterie holbachique. Frank Hedgcock's *David Garrick and His French Friends*, written in 1911, paid little attention to the actor's relationship with d'Holbach's circle, and it is the work most often cited on the subject of Garrick's stay in Paris. The recent publication of Garrick's letters, however, revealed that he was close to d'Holbach's group. He wrote from Paris to his friend George Colman in February 1765, "We had a fine laugh at Baron d'Holbach's (where you din'd once) about the *wicked company* I keep [Garrick's emphasis]: I am always with that set."[54] It was there he met the novelist Mme Riccoboni, with whom he became infatuated. In the spring of 1765, back in England, he wrote to Suard, "My best wishes and services will always wait upon my best friends in the rue Royale, to whom my wife begs her most grateful respects." In June he wrote to Suard that he and his wife were never happy "by the Thames' side, without wishing that some of our friends of the rue Royale were partaking with us. . . ." Writing in November, again to Suard, he spoke of "all I would say to you, the Baron d'Holbach (to whom I beg my best Affections), and to all friends in ye rue Royale." In 1770 his letters to Suard closed with the same refrain, "My best love and faith to rue Royale."[55] Writing to Morellet in 1773, he sent his greetings "to you and all our dear and worthy friends in and about Paris, such as the Chastellux, the Diderots, the Marmontels, Suards and that most worthy of all worthy Mortals my dear Baron d'Holbach."[56] The "wicked company" of "that set" seemed to stay in his mind as a pleasure quite distinct, and to no other group in Paris did he express such sentiments as these.

Another visitor who was struck by the tone of d'Holbach's circle was the Italian thinker Alessandro Verri. Visiting the coterie on October 19, 1766, he wrote his brother Pietro that he had witnessed heated and vigorous arguments there, on many subjects, but that all of the discussion was "with the best good faith in the world." "The Baron d'Holbach," he noted, "is an admirable man,"

[53] Diderot, *Corr.*, IV, 295.   [54] Garrick, *Letters*, II, 444.
[55] Ibid., 458-459, 463-464, 479-480, 706-707.
[56] Ibid., 841-842; see also 862-863.

and the dinners superb.[57] A week later he returned to d'Holbach's, and he wrote to his brother in amazement over the passion of the attacks against orthodoxy which he heard there. For d'Holbach he had increasing flattery; it is, he wrote, "impossible to praise him enough," he is learned in all fields, and "his knowledge, goodness and wit are grandiose."[58] His most informative letter to his brother was written on November 26, and he described in it the sequence of an entire evening with the coterie. They began by debating the stature of Voltaire, whom d'Holbach denounced as "jealous and nasty." From there the conversation moved to the quarrel between Hume and Rousseau. Wilkes was present, and he moved the discussion to the English political situation. Following this, Marmontel recited a poem about Venus which he recently had composed. From literary topics the coterie turned to an exploration of the implications of so great a scientist as Newton having commented on the Apocalypse. He was very impressed, Verri wrote, with Grimm's observations. What most astounded Verri, however, was a talk with d'Holbach in which the Baron argued before the coterie that religion was the principal source of man's suffering, and that the idea of God, being the source of all religion, had to be eliminated from moral concerns. Verri asked his brother to keep all of this a strict secret.[59]

Alessandro Verri's letter of November 26 is a valuable one, for it shows how varied the conversation was at d'Holbach's home and how struck by this could be an unsuspecting visitor. Verri's earlier comment about heated arguments "in the best good faith" illustrates most clearly the essence of the coterie. His letters also demonstrate how the coterie maintained its spontaneity before strangers and refused to worry, in its own abode, about the shock their candor might cause.

Nowhere is this openness more dramatically revealed than in the association of the abbé Bergier with the coterie holbachique. Nicolas-Sylvain Bergier (1713-1790) was one of the few Catholic apologists of the eighteenth century to write with a depth, grace and cogency capable of keeping his name above the ridicule so often directed to these apologists by "enlightened" public opinion. His letters reveal him to have been a man of deep conviction, zeal and faith, coupled with a warm sense of humor and a necessary and gentle cynicism about the intellectual qualities of many

---

[57] Verri, *Carteggio*, I, Part II, 23-24.   [58] Ibid., 43-44.
[59] Ibid., 112-115.

of his ecclesiastical peers. A scholar, church historian and some-what of a classicist, he gained great fame in France and engen-dered great enthusiasm in ecclesiastical circles with his *Le déisme réfuté par lui-même* (1765), an attack upon the intellectual in-consistencies of Rousseau's thought. In 1767 Bergier published an equally well-received attack upon the new antisupernaturalist phi-losophies in his *Certitude des preuves du Christianisme*. At about the same time, he engaged in an exchange of published pamphlets with Voltaire, which further added to his luster in Catholic eyes. Even Grimm felt obliged to comment that "as a defender of the Christian Religion, the abbé Bergier is certainly very superior to his brothers. . . ."[60] In 1768 Bergier published a refutation of d'Holbach's anonymous *Le Christianisme dévoilé*, entitled *Apolo-gie de la religion chrétienne*. By now Bergier, whose books were enjoying numerous editions, had established himself as the fore-most thinker of the French clergy. In 1770, when d'Holbach's *Système de la nature* had captured the attention of the reading public, the Assemblée du Clergé in solemn session voted a pension of 2,000 *livres* to Bergier, charging him to devote himself "entirely to the defense of Religion" and, above all, to the refutation of the *Système de la nature*.[61] The result of this devotion was the pub-lication in 1771 of Bergier's monumental work, his two-volume *Examen du matérialisme, ou Réfutation du Système de la nature*, a closely reasoned analysis of the assumptions of d'Holbach's thought, and an attempt to demonstrate the "fallacies" in the epis-temological and scientific presuppositions of the materialists. He was the one Catholic apologist of his time who dramatically (and consistently) agreed to argue the case for theism and Christianity solely on the plane of reference accepted by the unbelievers.

Bergier, before his refutation of Rousseau in 1765 brought him to the attention of Christophe de Beaumont, archbishop of Paris, had led a quiet and modest clerical life. Educated at the Seminary and University of Besançon, where he received a doctorate in theology in 1744, he continued his education at the Sorbonne, where he also was received as a doctor of theology in 1748, and was appointed by the archbishop of Besançon as a parish priest in Flangebouche. He reorganized the educational and medical facili-

---

[60] Grimm, *Corr. litt.*, VIII, 94.

[61] *Collection des procès-verbaux des Assemblées générales du Clergé de France*, VII, Part Two, 1817-1820. The *Procès-verbaux* of the Assemblée of 1770 was published in 1776.

ties of his parish, began teaching at the collège de Besançon, whose principal he became, and devoted himself to academic and clerical affairs. After 1765 the archbishop of Paris attempted continually to gain Bergier as a member of his own diocese, while the local archbishop struggled to keep him in Besançon. Bergier made many trips to Paris between 1767 and 1769, some for extended periods. In 1769 he at last agreed to remain in Paris and was appointed a canon of Notre Dame. In Paris he collected many pensions, sinecures and favors, including the duties and privileges of being named a royal confessor, and he occupied an honored place in his Church. He was, in short, the leading Catholic apologist of his time and a favored associate of the archbishop of Paris.[62]

He was also a frequent visitor to the coterie holbachique! It seems that during his first stay in Paris in 1767, Bergier established himself as a guest at d'Holbach's dinners. The first indication of this was offered in a letter from Diderot to Sophie Volland on October 4, 1767, in which he listed the usual guests at d'Holbach's dinners whom he was seeking to convince to go to Grandval, where a family feud apparently had left the d'Holbachs in need of their friends to cheer them up. Among them he listed "the fat Bergier," but added that he wasn't certain the abbé should be included since he was "of a suspect commerce."[63]

Suspect or not, the abbé continued to frequent the coterie, although the suspicions apparently remained. When Bergier published his first attack on d'Holbach's work, in which the abbé's treatment of the philosophes was harsh and personal, Grimm exclaimed in his *Correspondance*, June 1768: "What displeased me about his book is that he had sought out the company of the philosophes here, that he covered them with marks of esteem, while he treats them in his refutations as men fit to be hanged, and that he had undertaken to establish himself in homes in which, unless he was playing the role of a spy, the men of the cloth and of his party would have been very annoyed to find him."[64]

Nevertheless, about a month after Grimm wrote these words, a visit by Bergier to the coterie was again recorded by Diderot. The scene which he described in a letter to Mme de Maux was a singularly ironic one. The discussion in which Bergier was taking part centered upon whether or not a philosophe should retract

[62] On Bergier's life, see Alfred J. Bingham, "The Abbé Bergier," *Modern Language Review* (1959), 337-350.
[63] Diderot, *Corr.*, VII, 157-160.   [64] Grimm, *Corr. litt.*, VIII, 94.

his thoughts when faced by punishment by a tribunal if he did not. Diderot (whose own behavior in 1749 strikingly contradicted the principles he espoused here) suggested that under no circumstances should the thinker submit. The group chided him, Diderot wrote, "because I wanted to be burned at any price." "Never," he continued, "was so important a question treated more gaily, and with less pedantry, for we laughed like children." Nevertheless, the account went on, Diderot continued to debate the issue, reconstructing what the life of Socrates would have been like had he followed their opinions, and declaring that a philosopher must be willing to die for the truth. Given the company, the moment suddenly became grave: "Naigeon, Suard, the Baron and this great pumpkin Bergier turned their eyes away from each other on this question of sacrificing one's life in witness of the truth."[65] Where else but at the coterie holbachique could the most outspoken atheists of the Enlightenment, their foremost ecclesiastical critic, and a cautious philosophe like Suard have come together, in the presence of Diderot, to debate both lightly and seriously a question such as this?

This liaison continued after Bergier's permanent move to Paris and after the Assemblée du Clergé (who would have given infinite *dons gratuits* to know the identity of the author of the *Système de la nature*) had appointed Bergier as the apologist to refute that book. There can be no doubt that Bergier discussed materialism with the members of the coterie holbachique, and it appears that he well may have known d'Holbach to be the author whom he was refuting. Nothing could demonstrate more compellingly the candor of the coterie, nor, for that matter, the ultimate discretion of their friends. On June 6, 1770, Bergier wrote to his friend the abbé Trouillet: "I will ask permission to dedicate the refutation of the *Système de la nature* to the Clergé; I am two-thirds finished with it. Diderot and d'Holbach have seen the first, and the most essential, section; they answered that this work would be considered victorious in my camp, but that I did not understand their language, and that there were not fifty people in Paris who were capable of understanding it. So much the better; it is a proof that their language is not that of common sense."[66]

Diderot, in a letter to his brother in May 1770, referred to this

[65] Diderot, *Corr.*, IX, 113-116.
[66] "Lettres inédites de Bergier," L. Pingaud, ed., *Mémoires de l'Académie de Besançon* (1891), 231.

liaison with Bergier and went to the heart of what the coterie holbachique represented to its devotees. Diderot's brother was an intolerant cleric who continually criticized him for his views and for the company he kept in Paris. In reply the philosophe wrote: "You apparently know the abbé Bergier, the great refuter of the modern Celsus. Well, I live in friendship with him. . . . If I don't write [publish] about religion, I discuss it still less, unless I am led into such discussions by doctors of the Sorbonne, or *by learned people with whom I can express myself without fear of the consequences*; and when that happens, it is always . . . without bitterness, without insult, and with the decent tone that is fitting among honest men who are not of the same opinion."[67]

Discussions at the coterie holbachique did not always draw men into discussions about religion and its alternatives; such were its most striking occasions, but the evidence has demonstrated the wide scope of interests that could feed the conversations of d'Holbach and his guests. When Allan Ramsey visited the coterie, he discussed literature and the criminal law with them.[68] When Dr. Burney, the English musicologist, came to Paris and visited with the coterie in 1770, he recorded in his journal that "I supped and stayed until midnight when various subjects were discussed relative to my History [of music] and the age of the world. . . ." The latter subject led into discussions of "Chemistry, Minerals, Fossils and other parts of Natural History." He was struck by the diversity and learning of the group, and by the amount of good conversation that transpired. Indeed Burney arrived in the late afternoon to dine with the coterie, left at seven to visit Rousseau, and returned for supper, with the conversation still alive. His descriptions of the dinner, in retrospect, ended on an unintentionally ironic note. He wrote that he was seated at a table "where there were above 20 persons, and we had a most frank and open conference. Mme la Baronne and her two sons and two daughters were there, the celebrated Mr. Grimm, to whom I was introduced, and all the rest were men of letters and merit of the first order in Paris—the dinner and conversation were charming and I was sorry to quit them, even to go to Rousseau."[69]

The three adjectives Burney employed to describe the conver-

[67] Diderot, *Corr.*, x, 61-63 (emphasis added).
[68] On Ramsey's visit, see his letter to Diderot, and Naigeon's commentary, in Diderot, *Oeuvres* (N), IX, 429-431.
[69] "Dr. Burney, 'Journal'" (Leigh), 167-170.

117

sation at d'Holbach's—"frank," "open," and "charming"—taken together offer an important insight into the mood and tone of the coterie. Most historians have assumed they were frank; the list of visitors and the reports of such guests have demonstrated that they were open. They also were indeed charming, in the sense that for all of their earnestness they remained speculative, usually without immediate implications for struggle or sacrifice in the social lives of the interlocutors. Morellet re-created this ambiance faithfully in his *Mémoires*, an ambiance much a part of the pre-Revolutionary world of the Ancien Régime, before the thinkers of Paris understood that men at times live or die for speculations such as theirs. Discussing "the spirit of tolerance which reigned in our group," Morellet recalled "a truly good scene that I shall never forget." One evening, he wrote, Diderot and Roux had presented lengthy arguments to the coterie in favor of materialism. When the two men finished, one of the deists among them, Galiani, spoke up: "I begin by saying that if I were the pope, I would send you to the Inquisition, and if I were the King of France, to the Bastille; but as I have the pleasure of being neither one nor the other, I shall return to dine with you next Thursday, and you will hear me as I had the pleasure of hearing you." They were all delighted with this, wrote Morellet, "and the atheists among us first of all."[70] For Morellet the most significant aspect of this mutual good will and toleration was the perfect discretion maintained by the deists and guests at d'Holbach's dinners in the face of obvious similarities between certain discussions at the coterie and certain anonymous works whose authors would have suffered if their identities had come to light. Justifying this attitude for his Restoration readers, after the experience of the Revolution, Morellet recalled for them the atmosphere of the Ancien Régime, and how "innocent" then seemed "philosophy that remains in limits of speculation, and does not imply greater boldness than in a calm exercise of the mind." He continued: "Such was manifestly the nature of the philosophy of the baron and of those of his friends, like Diderot, who went the farthest. . . . Certainly none of them were capable of entering into a conspiracy, nor into the least project of troubling the government and the public peace; not one of them would have incited a religious persecution, nor insulted a monk or a curé."[71]

[70] Morellet, *Mémoires*, I, 130-131.   [71] Ibid., 131-134.

The only visitor to the coterie holbachique who ever put *into print* accusations of atheism against members of the coterie, during the lifetimes of those involved, was Jean-Jacques Rousseau in his attacks upon d'Holbach, Diderot, and Grimm. By the time he wrote his final works, he was distinguishing, in general, between his own theism and the atheism of his former friends, in the process tarring d'Holbach's whole circle with such a dangerous charge. For this, Marmontel, writing after the myth of the coterie had begun, could never forgive him: "D'Holbach's home was the rendezvous of those who were called philosophes; and in the full security that the inviolable sanctity of the haven where they assembled inspired in honest souls, d'Holbach and his friends had admitted Rousseau into their most intimate commerce. Now, one can see in his *Emile* how he had described them. Certainly, even if the sobriquet of atheism that he attached to their society had been only a revelation of the truth, it would have been odious. But, with regard to the majority, it was a calumnious accusation, and Rousseau knew it well; he knew perfectly well that the theism of his vicar had its proselytes and zealous defenders among them. The Baron had thus, at his expense, come to know him."[72]

The "inviolable sanctity of the haven where they assembled"— that was what d'Holbach offered at his home, and that was what attracted the diversity of thought that flourished there. Writers, philosophers, scientists and historians; nobles and commoners; atheists and deists; cautious men and flamboyant men—all of these found something that attracted them to d'Holbach's gatherings, and all of them coalesced into the coterie holbachique. They created an ambiance which made the coterie a familiar place to a host of visitors, and a place of distinction for celebrated foreigners who found their way to Paris. There one was free to speculate, on anything, in the company of exciting minds. If this has not been the coterie holbachique of most historians, it was, nevertheless, the coterie holbachique of history.

[72] Marmontel, *Mémoires*, II, 9-10.

FOUR · *A Diversity of Philosophes*

TRADITIONALLY the thought of the coterie holbachique has been understood in terms of the atheism of d'Holbach, Naigeon and Diderot. As we have observed, however, there was no single metaphysic or attitude toward philosophy which dominated that assemblage of thinkers. D'Holbach's circle embodied a diversity of interests and outlooks which made it a meeting-place of idiosyncratic intellectual goals and expressions. Its devotees came to the rue Royale and to Grandval with their own individual contributions to offer, from their own individual perspectives and experiences.

Many members of the coterie, of course, may have been influenced (in any of several directions) by ideas expressed there. Boulanger's thesis of the traumatic etiology of supernaturalism, for example, and, more particularly, its emphasis upon the effects of a universal deluge on the consciousness of prehistoric man, which d'Holbach had adopted in his own work and which he expressed at the coterie, appear to have entered the work of many of d'Holbach's regular guests. The same ideas, however, were widespread in other circles where the same men might meet, and Boulanger enjoyed something of a posthumous vogue in enlightened Paris as a whole.

The central concerns of some members of the coterie were often merely the peripheral interests of others there. Most members of d'Holbach's group appeared to define their range of interests as universally as possible, as was the case with so many thinkers of the eighteenth century, but the scientists rarely took literary criticism as seriously as a Marmontel, and the versifiers rarely took chemistry as seriously as a Darcet or a Roux.

Given these observations, it is clear that the individual thinkers of the coterie most profitably would be studied in the contexts of their particular intellectual and professional milieus. It is nonetheless essential to the broad thesis of this work to establish the diversity of such thought, to demonstrate that those who met to share their ideas were men of differing concerns and involve-

120

ments. Some of the currents of thought which manifested themselves at d'Holbach's dinners have been (or are being) more or less well studied in their proper contexts: the literary criticism of Marmontel and Grimm, the scientific contributions of Darcet and Roux, the historical polemics of Raynal, the economic doctrines of Morellet and Galiani, the literary journalism of Suard, the poetry of Saint-Lambert, and of course the materialism of Diderot and d'Holbach, to mention several among many. Some of these currents, but by no means all, touched upon the central concerns of these thinkers as philosophes.

It is, however, precisely the "philosophic" diversity of the coterie that must be established. The term "philosophe" was a vital one for most of the thinkers of the coterie holbachique, embodying as it did their self-image as men whose work at one point or another touched upon the most profound problems of human experience. Three such concerns were vital to almost all men who designated themselves as philosophes: the cause of tolerance, the implications of history, and the fruits of wisdom. To help us lay to rest forever the myth of a single-minded and single-purposed circle of philosophes, let us examine aspects of the intellectual life of the coterie holbachique which rarely have been associated with that group's place in the Enlightenment.

The Cause of Tolerance

The members of the coterie holbachique most actively involved in the campaign against civil intolerance were two former students of theology, Morellet and Marmontel. The former, for all his deep conviction, was ultimately simply a gadfly for the cause of tolerance; the latter, and his character, Bélisaire, became symbols of that very cause itself.

In the early 1750s the Protestants of Languedoc were accused of agitating in favor of religious freedom for their cult and civic equality for themselves and their children. Morellet was still a student at the Sorbonne during this period, and he recalled later in his *Mémoires* that he and a handful of students braved their superiors to defend civil toleration for heretics (while maintaining ecclesiastical intolerance, the belief that Catholicism was the one true faith and only path to salvation). In 1755, when Morellet was working closely with Diderot and d'Alembert on the *Encyclopédie*, the issue was again brought to his immediate attention. A friend introduced him to a Protestant lawyer who described to him the persecutions in the Midi. Sensitized to the issue, Morellet responded bitterly to a series of ecclesiastical brochures which had demanded severe repression of the remonstrating heretics. He decided that the best weapon against intolerance would be to reduce to absurdity its logical conclusions. The result, published in 1756, was his *Petit écrit sur une matière intéressante*, printed (its sardonic title-page informed the reader) in "Inquisition Road, under the sign of Saint Dominick."[1]

The narrative voice created by Morellet for this satire was that of an inquisitorial cleric who was shocked by the suggestion of an acquaintance that the king should grant toleration to the Protestants of North America after the "impending victory" of French armies there. The program of the *Petit écrit* envisaged the creation of the Inquisition in North America, and its suggestions ranged from the absurd (send all Quakers, Baptists, Lutherans, Calvinists and Anglicans a copy of the Catholic catechism, and *order* them to believe) to the sanguinary (burn all Protestant ministers in North America at the stake, but do it clandestinely, lest they address the crowds). Its essential thesis, however, was that France had to choose between "trivial" interests, such as commercial and agricultural prosperity, and "important" interests, such as the happiness of the king's subjects in the next world, or attendance at mass. Its point, in this regard, was simple: these were mutually exclusive choices for a temporal government, not only in North America, but, above all, in France.[2]

Significantly, the *Petit écrit* emphatically asserted the existence of a Catholic position other than its inquisitor's on the question of toleration. The "author" objected continually to those "suspect ecclesiastics" who persisted in citing "Christ, Scripture and the Church Fathers" against intolerance. In refuting such use of Catholic tradition, the priest betrayed what Morellet saw as the illogic and specious analysis of intolerance.[3] The *Petit écrit* satirized not the Church, but the inquisitorial element within the Church.

In 1762 Morellet, deeply involved in the philosophic community in Paris, published his *Manuel des inquisiteurs*, an abridgment of the *Directorium inquisitorium* of Nicolas Eymeric, a four-

---

[1] Morellet, *Mémoires*, I, 31-39; Morellet, *Petit écrit sur une matière intéressante*.

[2] *Petit écrit*. The entire brochure was 38 pages long.

[3] Morellet was simply a better student of theology than his created priest; it was not a subtle work.

teenth-century inquisitor. The text caused a brief sensation, and Voltaire could not contain his joy at its publication and success.[4] The text of the *Manuel* was dramatic precisely because its language was so calm, so matter-of-fact. It described, in a formal and academic manner, the ruses, deceits, false promises, tortures and punishments to be employed by the inquisitor, and its flights of casuistry, to the eighteenth-century mind, must have appeared as ludicrous as its procedural narrative appeared inhuman. Yet it was not only the text itself which Voltaire found important; as he wrote to Thieriot: "The abbé *Mords-les* never has taken a better bite, and the preface is one of the best mouthfuls. . . ."[5]

In his preface Morellet now rejected the possibility of a Catholic option for tolerance. Historically, the abbé noted, those who are burned reject the inquisitorial premise, but those who do the burning have in fact the better precedents. The jurisprudence developed by Eymeric, Morellet argued, was wholly licit and orthodox: "Councils and Sovereign Pontiffs dictated the laws of these Tribunals, and Bishops and Inquisitors delegated by the Holy See put them into execution."[6]

In his discussion of the fate of Eymeric's work, Morellet stressed the continuous endorsement of the *Directorium* by the Church and the continuity of inquisitorial theory. This manual, he informed his readers, was no mere apology of the Inquisition by an isolated individual or age; it was the embodiment of the Catholic spirit and the textbook of ecclesiastical authorities throughout its existence. It had received high praise throughout the sixteenth and seventeenth centuries in works published with the approval of the Pope. What the work truly revealed, Morellet concluded, were the very *few* basic procedural changes in the Inquisition since the fourteenth century; if the Inquisition in Italy in present times has softened in practice, it never has done so in theory, while the Inquisitions of Spain and Portugal "have preserved all of their former severity." The principles of Eymeric, he observed, are still official doctrines.[7]

In the *Petit écrit*, Morellet had cited Tertullian, Athanasius and Saint Ambrose, among others, in an effort to distinguish between

---

[4] On the effect of the book, see Grimm, *Corr. litt.*, v, 21-22; Voltaire, *Corr.*, XLVIII, 43-46, 50-52, 69, 81, 89, 111.

[5] Voltaire, *Corr.*, XLVIII, 43-46.

[6] Morellet, *Manuel des inquisiteurs*, 5-10.

[7] Ibid., 11-26.

inquisitorial dogma and Catholic dogma per se. In the *Manuel des inquisiteurs*, however, he deliberately linked Eymeric's doctrines to the Papacy, to Church Councils, and to 400 years of Catholic tradition. He did not state a thesis explicitly, but the implication was there; one had to choose between the Church and toleration, between the Church and reason, between the Church and civilization. It was a far cry from d'Holbach's position, in the *Système de la nature*, that one had to choose between belief in God and these secular values, but it signalled, nevertheless, a major battle that had to be waged. Precisely the same choice and the same struggle Voltaire had delineated as his own, and his enthusiasm for Morellet's *Manuel* was appropriate.

Voltaire opposed the atheists of the coterie holbachique quite bitterly when the works of d'Holbach and Naigeon appeared,[8] but he offered encouragement to Morellet, and active, enthusiastic aid when the storm broke around *Bélisaire*. In chapter fifteen of that work, Marmontel's hero preached a sermon to the emperor Justinian on toleration both ecclesiastic and civil that became a *cause célèbre*.

At the end of his deistic creed, Bélisaire had expressed his belief that God would not punish men for their theological errors. This view rested upon two premises—God's comprehension of man's limited understanding, which necessitated His indulgence of error, and God's goodness, which necessitated His use of penalties only insofar as He was unable to pardon. It followed, for Marmontel, that no one logically could assert the necessity of Catholic, or even Christian, belief to the means of salvation. Asked by Justinian what men he expected to find in "the Court of God," Bélisaire spoke of the virtuous pagans and "all the good men of all the nations and of all the ages. . . ."[9]

Marmontel's Justinian was prepared to accept such arguments in theory, but he emphasized the special position of sovereigns. Agents of God's will on earth, the sovereigns were obliged to demand the unity of dogma and religious practice in their state, not only to serve divine truth as they saw it, but to insure domestic

[8] See, for example, Voltaire, *Corr.*, LXXVI, 58, 65-67, 122-126, 203-204; LXXVII, 3, 16, 35, 60-62, 81; Voltaire, *Les Cabales* (s.l., 1772); Grimm, *Corr. litt.*, IX, 117-120; Bachaumont, *Mémoires secrets pour servir à l'histoire de la République des lettres en France*, XXIV, 173-174.

[9] Marmontel, *Bélisaire*, 239-254, which comprises the discussion of toleration upon which the following four paragraphs also are based.

order. In Bélisaire's replies Marmontel attacked the entire concept of civil intolerance, both from a religious and a political point of view.

The duty of the sovereign, wrote Marmontel, is not to judge of truth or error, but to secure the happiness and tranquillity of his domains. Revelation is irrelevant to this, as are all religious dogmas, because moral precepts are freely available to all men in nature and can be enacted into secular law. Men are made no more or less moral by the acceptance or the rejection of any dogmas embodied in mysterious truths, since God in his wisdom has made morality independent of mystery. Duties, being natural and known, are simple, and kings should enforce them. Truths are not simple, however, and the sovereign should be wary of assuming the contrary. Political power as easily would place the sword in the hands of error as in those of truth.

It would be delusory, Marmontel urged, for the sovereign to imagine that God required his assistance in His cause; God's omnipotence is independent of man's active consent. The only theoretical justification for civil intolerance would be a secular and utilitarian one, the view that coerced unity of belief was beneficial to a realm. History, in Marmontel's view, argued against such a view, intolerance engendering at all times the martyrdom of the brave citizen, the dishonesty of the average citizen, and the violence of the fanatical citizen. Indeed Marmontel rejected an assumption common to many deists, that natural truth would lead peacefully to common doctrines, and that such uniformity, as exemplified by Rousseau's civil code, was a good to be pursued. Asked by Justinian whether peace in society did not require a union of the minds within it, Bélisaire replied, "Minds are never more united than when each man is free to think as he sees fit. . . ."

In short, Bélisaire informed Justinian, the sovereign must be absolutely indifferent to the thoughts and religious beliefs of his subjects. A king's authority extends over behavior, and the more he limits his attention to maintaining obedience to secular laws, the easier it will be for him to maintain peace and order. If he attempts to determine which men are infallible and which are not, his natural authority becomes involved in matters which can only harm it. If there are loud and angry religious disputes in his kingdom, he should allow them to continue undisturbed, taking no sides, so long as obedience to civil laws is maintained. In the end boredom, "the boredom of disputing on that which one does not

125

understand, without being listened to by anyone," will put an end to violent disputation. Zeal, wrote Marmontel, is "perhaps only the pride of ruling over other minds"; remove the question of political power from religious disputes, and the zealous will have to seek other, more constructive means of becoming famous and powerful men. Toleration and freedom of thought and expression, he urged, are the allies, not the enemies, of authority, peace, and order.

Within a few weeks after the publication of *Bélisaire* early in 1767, Marmontel found himself in the center of a controversy that would rage for over a year.[10] In the face of the initial outrage of the Sorbonne over the doctrines of *Bélisaire*, and under pressure from the archbishop of Paris to avoid a scandal, Marmontel weakened and, in the hope of averting a formal censure, agreed to all *theological* modifications demanded by the syndic of the Sorbonne, Riballier. Thus, in the second edition of his work (the first having been exhausted within two weeks), he inserted a footnote asserting that pagans could be in heaven only by means of a supernatural miracle of God, and reassuring his readers of his "Christian" intentions. For this effort to avert a censure on purely theological matters, if we are to believe Grimm, he was chided sardonically by many at the coterie.[11]

[10] John Renwick, in "Reconstruction and interpretation of the genesis of the *Bélisaire* affair, with an unpublished letter from Marmontel to Voltaire," *Studies on Voltaire and the Eighteenth Century* (1967), 171-222, argued that the Sorbonne misunderstood Marmontel's theology. For Renwick, Marmontel was sincere in asserting his Christian belief and was proposing to the Church "its basic and pure antecedents in the New Testament." The syndic Riballier's denunciations of Marmontel's deism were for Renwick "malicious accusations" emanating from the theologian's "dogmatic stand." Renwick repeated these arguments in his "L'affaire de *Bélisaire*: une phrase de manuel" (in the anthology *Jean-François Marmontel (1723-1799)*, J. Ehrard, ed., 249-272), and asserted that Riballier's charge that Marmontel's profession of faith in *Bélisaire* was deistic was "without a doubt erroneous and certainly stubborn." For Renwick, Marmontel acted "in good faith" when he attempted to reassure the theologians of his sound Christian belief. As I have indicated in Chapter Two, Marmontel's deism was manifest in the fifteenth chapter of *Bélisaire*; his alleged commitment to primitive Christianity is nowhere apparent in his work or life. For a fuller discussion of the context, particulars and politics of the affair, see Kors, "Storm Over *Bélisaire*," in *The Coterie Holbachique* (Doctoral Dissertation, Department of History, Harvard University, 1968).

[11] Grimm, *Corr. litt.*, VII, 292-293; see also *Nouvelles ecclésiastiques* (1768), 33, 42-43; Marmontel, *Mémoires*, II, 27-31; Bachaumont, *Mémoires secrets*,

When the Sorbonne further demanded that he retract his views on civil intolerance, Marmontel stiffened. The book was achieving an enthusiastic audience, the rivalries among the Jansenists, the Sorbonne and the archbishop were making it impossible for the Church to unify its action or public posture vis-à-vis the author or the issues, and the philosophes were beginning to rally around their beleaguered colleague. Whatever the weight of diverse reasons, Marmontel published in the late winter a brochure entitled, "Exposé of the motives which prevent me from subscribing to Civil Intolerance." Such a doctrine, he wrote, was not a dogma of the faith (and hence separate from the issue of ecclesiastical intolerance); it was contrary to the spirit of Christianity, to the interests of true religion (which were spiritual), and to the welfare of mankind. "In subscribing to it," he concluded, "I believe that I would be dipping my pen in blood. My voice is nothing, I know, but my conscience is something; it forbids me to approve of a system which I believe injurious to Religion and fatal to humanity."[12]

Throughout the spring and summer of 1767, an intense polemic whirled around the figure of Bélisaire. While theologians rushed to refute the deism and, above all, the thesis on toleration of the work, Voltaire, Turgot, and Marmontel himself orchestrated the ripostes of the philosophic camp.[13] By ignoring Grimm's and others' desire for him to confront the Church on the theological issues, Marmontel had maneuvered himself into a favorable position. Agreeing to sign any profession of faith involving dogma but refusing to recognize civil intolerance as a point of dogma, Marmontel had forced the Church to choose between either let-

---

III, 145; C. Collé, *Journal et mémoires . . . sur les hommes de lettres*, H. Bonhomme, ed., III, 127-128. The added note concerning the pagans is found in Marmontel, *Bélisaire*, 2nd edn., 237, n. 1.

[12] Marmontel, *Pièces relatives à Bélisaire*, Cahier III, 2-52, and Cahier V, 412. See also *Nouvelles écclésiastiques* (1768), 44; and de Legge, *Pièces relatives à l'examen de Bélisaire*.

[13] Among the theologians, see in particular abbé Coger, *Examen de Bélisaire*; de Legge, op. cit.; Reynaud, *Lettre à Marmontel par un déiste converti* (s.l., 1767). Reynaud was in fact the abbé de Vaux. Among the philosophes, see Marmontel, *Pièces relatives à Bélisaire*; A. R. Turgot, *Les XXXVII vérités opposées aux XXXVII impiétés de Bélisaire*; and the following works published in 1767 by Voltaire: *Anecdote sur Bélisaire; La défense de mon oncle* (Chapter XXII); *Seconde anecdote sur Bélisaire; La prophétie de la Sorbonne de l'An 1530*.

ting his public statement against intolerance stand, or fighting him in precisely the area where the government could be expected to be the most sensitive. Bélisaire had preached that both the laity and the Church owed full obedience to a king acting to secure the peace and order of his realms. For the king himself to declare his religious duties to the Church was one thing; for the Sorbonne or the archbishop, in a censure of *Bélisaire*, to publicly lecture the king on them was delicate and dangerous. Theses advanced by diverse theologians and by elements within the Sorbonne seemed to imply that a king could not, as a matter of policy, allow toleration, even if it were in his sovereign interest. Marmontel succeeded by asserting that the king had a *sovereign right*, as well as a moral duty (in Bélisaire's view), to establish toleration. By the fall, when the Sorbonne at last had effected a compromise response to such a view, the royal ministry found the entire affair compromising. A royal committee rejected the chapter of a projected censure which attempted to specify royal obligations of intolerance, and imposed in its place a brief general statement against religious indifference. When several members of the Sorbonne refused to yield, the king himself intervened and sent a letter ordering them to accept the revised document.[14]

By the time *Bélisaire* was formally censured, almost a year had passed, in the course of which Marmontel had become a celebrity in France, publicly defended by Voltaire, Catherine the Great, the king of Poland, Frederick the Great, and the prince of Sweden. Voltaire had published works which had made *Bélisaire*'s enemies the laughingstock of Paris, and Turgot pseudonymously had made the doctrine of Marmontel appear as the only possible propositions to which a reasonable man could subscribe.[15] Marmontel suffered no penalties and continued his literary and philosophical campaign against intolerance.[16] D'Holbach and Naigeon never would win enlightened Paris to their cause of atheistic materialism. Marmontel, by stressing political over theological points of

[14] A.N., MS *Faculté de Théologie*, MM 258, and in particular, folios 192-195.

[15] See above, n. 13, for Marmontel, Voltaire and Turgot. In addition, see Bachaumont, *Mémoires secrets*, III, 278; F. Baldensperger, ed., "Deux lettres inédites de Marmontel à un correspondant suédois," *Revue du dix-huitième siècle* (1917), 197-199; Grimm, *Lettres à Cathérine II*, passim; Voltaire, *Corr.*, LXV, passim.

[16] See Marmontel, *Les Incas, ou La Destruction de l'Empire de Pérou*.

contention, succeeded in making the issue of tolerance a safe and popular cause for the philosophic community as a whole.

The Implications of History

There was no single school of historical thought among the thinkers of the coterie holbachique. The most celebrated historian at d'Holbach's dinners, Raynal, had sought in his *Histoire philosophique des Deux Indes* to create in his reader an informed moral aversion to the historical operations of error, tyranny, superstition and avarice in man's affairs, to make him feel the suffering which these caused, and to impel him to seek safeguards against their continuing manifestations. The work of Raynal, however important the wealth of statistical data on commerce and the accounts of the details of European colonization which he bequeathed to his readers, was most directly related to the current of didactic history prevalent in the eighteenth century. Roux, in the article devoted to "History" in his *Nouvelle encyclopédie*, had stated the credo of this approach to man's past in clear terms: the goal of the historian was to inspire his fellow men with a love of virtue and the benefactors of humanity, and with an abhorrence of vice and the scoundrels who had deceived, oppressed or afflicted mankind. Roux's own history of the world, which followed these remarks, was nothing more than a generally depressing chronicle of wars, regicides and rebellions, interspersed with the presence of an edifying hero or two.[17]

Such graphic didactic chronicles, however, by no means exhausted the possibilities of historical inquiry as conceived by other members of the coterie holbachique. Two thinkers whose historical writings are less well known than Raynal's today, Charles-Georges Le Roy and François-Jean de Chastellux, both attempted, from different perspectives and toward different ends, to discover the underlying causes of the malaise of human history and to confront the question of whether or not such a cause need continue to operate in man's affairs.

For Chastellux the subject of the historian must be man in organized society, and the ultimate question which historical analysis must answer is if "society, in the final analysis, [is] susceptible, if not of perfection, at least of amelioration."[18] To examine

---

[17] Roux, *Nouvelle encyclopédie*, ii, 343-529.
[18] Chastellux, *De la félicité publique*, i, viii-xviii, 1.

the question of social amelioration, one required a normative standard, and Chastellux attempted early in his work to define his own, that of "public happiness."

For Chastellux most students of "happiness" erred by projecting their subjective idea of happiness upon a society or, indeed, the species. Happiness, in his view, was a private experience or standard, and could not be measured. What *could* be measured, he believed, was the *precondition* of every individual's private happiness, and it was this factor he labeled "félicité publique." It was the amount of time and energy preserved by the individuals of a given society to pursue their own idiosyncratic visions of happiness, and it could be understood as what remained of *a* after subtracting *b* and *c*—*a* being the amount of work a man can do without becoming miserable, *b* being the amount of work a man is required to do in order to secure the necessities and basic amenities of his life, and *c* being the amount of work demanded of a man by his sovereign authorities. While these components would vary from individual to individual, "public happiness" existed when "the greatest [private] happiness of the greatest number of individuals" was secured by the relationships among those three components.[19]

The task of historical analysis, Chastellux believed, was to determine whether a society enjoyed (or enjoys) public happiness and to isolate the particular causes of its presence or absence. In his reviews and analyses of the major civilizations of the West, he presented what he saw to be the permanent record of continual public unhappiness, and almost invariably this state arose from the depradations of sovereign authorities, the "expropriation" of the work of the many by the sovereign few.

The two primary supports of such expropriations for Chastellux were superstition and the practice of warfare. These were the greatest "scourges" of mankind, for rulers and subjects both accepted them, the former justifying the confiscation of the work of others in their name, the latter generally acquiescing to such demands in respect of them as well. In Egypt the priests and pharaohs could claim the work of their subjects almost at will in the name of superstition; in Sparta the sovereign military commanders could do the same in the name of war. In Rome the pagan political superstitions and the myth of war's glory gave the

[19] Ibid., 8-14.

despots, the patricians and the military leaders the right to effect such seizures. For Chastellux, Christianity emerged as a desperate, inchoate attempt of the people of Rome to overthrow the superstition and thus the political system of the patricians, but, he theorized, the new religion degenerated into a new superstition that soon became the support of expropriation by the emperors and the new priesthood.[20]

Chastellux's linking of superstition and unhappiness was in fact tautological, and his two "scourges" were one, the myth of war's glory being simply a critical superstition. He saw man, species and individual, as a creature who inevitably sought pleasure and fled pain. The problem was that one could seek pleasure and err. In the final analysis, superstition for Chastellux was any set of beliefs which led the majority of men to err in the pursuit of pleasure, or, perhaps, which *systematically* and *ineluctably* led to such error. Superstitions were simply those beliefs which successfully justified to men the expropriation of work in quantities that made it impossible for the greatest number of citizens to pursue their private pleasures. His implicit thesis was that the two most pernicious superstitions have been *supernatural religion* and *the myth of martial glory*.

The history of Christian and feudal Europe was for Chastellux the history of a perpetual struggle among three groups of expropriators for a proportionally larger share of the work of others; kings, nobles, and the Church fought amongst themselves while "the people" were "the spoils over which they fought, the prey in whose hunt they shared." Taught by "superstition" to expect their rewards in a world to come, the majority of men acquiesced in their misery. The Renaissance diverted the minds of the educated from social problems to those of erudition, while the Reformation plunged mankind back into a fanaticism and civil bloodshed equal to the Dark Ages. By the seventeenth century, as the kings of Europe began to emerge as dominant among the expropriators, the situation in Europe remained fundamentally as it had been; the few prospered parasitically, while the people could not pursue their own happiness.[21]

However, in the course of the seventeenth century, Chastellux believed, several great changes occurred in the life of Europe which, in their confluence, directly altered the prospects for

[20] Ibid., 1-8, 18-142, 152-234.   [21] Ibid., II, 1-64.

achieving public happiness in the eighteenth century. Lulled into false fiscal security by the bullion of the New World, the monarchs of Europe embarked upon increasingly costly military adventures, in a state of mutual mistrust and terror, at precisely the time when superstition began to lose the power and intensity of its hold on men's minds.[22] Rulers could not afford war by the eighteenth century, because the expenditures were so enormous (due to modern technology, among other reasons); but to avoid war they had to remain militarily strong, a goal now beyond their normal means. So urgent was their immediate need for funds that, increasingly, monarchs had to *borrow* monies from their progressively less superstitious subjects, coaxing it from them on terms increasingly favorable to the latter, and concerning themselves with the prosperity of their peoples, on whom their own well-being depended. Superstition and the desire for martial glory had led Europeans to the New World, led them into continental wars, and inadvertently had produced a combination of exhausted peoples unable to pay more of their time and work to their officialdoms, and desperate rulers, seeking funds to maintain themselves in the international wars and balances of power which they had initiated in the intoxication of their own myths. At this juncture, men now were forced to analyze the true sources of wealth and the true nature of expropriation, in a critical attempt to understand their dilemma and to discover new sources of raising monies. This last phenomenon—the need to analyze without superstition and myth—Chastellux labeled "the progress of philosophy," and it coincided with and further contributed to a weakening of Christian fanaticism. "Remember always," Chastellux reminded his readers, "that I mean by 'the philosophic spirit' that which in applying itself to politics and morality concerns itself particularly with the happiness of men."[23]

Turning to eighteenth-century France, Chastellux now articulated the conclusion of his historical inquiry. Removing the superfluous rhetoric from his second volume, one sees the following argument unfold. The occasional and generally unwanted commercial wars of the eighteenth century, added to the debts inherited from the wars of the seventeenth, have created the staggering burden of taxation under which the nation now finds itself. This burden cannot be reduced, for the only assurance of peace lies in

[22] Ibid., 65-78. [23] Ibid., 67, 74-75.

the armed balance of power in Europe. Those who are paying this tax burden are the peasants, the artisans and the workers of France, and this appropriated work deprives them of either subsistence or pleasure. Since these deprivations are inflicted upon the great majority of the population, this unequal taxation, like the work appropriated to build the Egyptian pyramids or to fight the Roman wars, is a direct attack upon "public happiness."[24]

In addition to the expropriation of work by the State, however, there has been, over a long period of time up to and including the present day, an expropriation of the people's work by the monasteries, which have accumulated luxury from society as a whole. Religion and superstition are no longer the causes of war, but their appropriated luxury in the hands of the monasteries is a major cause of the unequal tax burden. The power of superstition being at its lowest point in modern history ("Religious fanaticism? It no longer exists. . . ."), the time has come (in France) to despoil the monasteries as the first step toward solving the present dilemma of the monarchy, and toward equalizing the tax burden in accord with the concept of "public happiness."[25] While for political reasons the secular luxury of the privileged, also expropriated from the public, cannot be seized by the State, the judicious use of the public debt, requiring from them forced long-term loans, can shift more of the tax burden upon them.[26] The alternatives are a desperate war of conquest, and/or revolution, and/or anarchic chaos.[27] In the long run France must pursue a policy of "public happiness" at home, requiring a policy of peace and cooperation abroad.[28] In the interim, however, she must immediately despoil the Church, for this is now possible, and every man is "an heir despoiled by Ecclesiastics."[29]

From the highest perspective, for Chastellux, the future of genuine public happiness in France depended upon the advance of the "philosophic spirit." In the short term, however, there was a certain modest answer to the question of the means of social amelioration: France can avoid an increase of public unhappiness in her current crisis by understanding the historical position of the Church (as expropriator and as dethroned sovereign authority), and by acting accordingly. In one sense, therefore, Chastel-

<hr>

[24] Ibid., 74-76, 171-172, 175-180.
[26] Ibid., 186-200.
[28] Ibid., 149-165.

[25] Ibid., 202-208.
[27] Ibid., 166-168, 207-208.
[29] Ibid., 203-205.

133

lux's history is a word to the sage; in another, it is simply a word to the wise.

* * *

For Charles-Georges Le Roy, a natural historian of animal life, most historical (and philosophical) inquiries into the history of the human species had been falsified by a lack of scientific rigor and an overabundance of wish and imagination. His "Letters on Man" were appended to his animal studies, and they reflected his general scientific assumptions. In particular, they began from the premise that physiology determines the essential patterns of behavior. Thus, for example, in his first two "Letters on Man," published in 1768, Le Roy argued that it was pure fancy to explain the origins of society in human history by virtue of an alleged social compact, a rational decision to abandon a state of nature. Social organization for Le Roy arose from the sexual bond created by the absence of a limited, particular season for sexual relations among humans; from the need for nurture in the long period of infant dependency; from the physical inability of men in certain conditions to raise food without group cooperation; and from the physical vulnerability of man to the elements, creating a need for "first necessities" (such as clothing and shelter), which could only be satisfied by means of certain "arts" requiring social organization.[30]

The organization of human beings into societies created a pattern of behavior which Le Roy believed to be unlike that of any other species. In short, the history of these human societies presented a cycle of action and reaction, of the rise and fall of civilizations, of the simple becoming complex, and the complex breaking down into the simple. To explain this basic structure of human history, Le Roy again referred to the interaction between the particular physical organism and the general conditions of life.

For Le Roy all life sustains itself by means of an instinct to seek well-being. All animals have certain basic needs. These needs give rise to a demand for satisfaction, and each creature both uses its reason (which all animals possess) and expends its energy to the extent necessary to satisfy these needs. This satisfaction is the experience of well-being. Its needs satisfied, each creature enjoys a brief period of contentment and laziness until the cycle begins

[30] Le Roy, "Lettres . . . sur l'homme," in *Lettres sur les animaux*, 175-178, 183-190.

again. Thus, the history of animal life is one of simple repetition, except in the face of changing conditions.[31]

For man the crucial change of conditions was presented by the great success of social organization itself, for it ended his perpetual preoccupation with these basic needs. The motor of life, however, the drive to experience well-being, remains. It is not satisfied by the simple and easy achievement of basic life-needs in society, for nature has insured the survival of species by insisting that experience be "strong" in order to be pleasurable and, hence, a cause of action. Normally in animal life this presents few problems: when a need for the basic life-requirements is constant and pressing, the satisfaction in obtaining them is strong. Yet in society man finds his basic needs satisfied as a matter of course. To experience strong sensations, he must go beyond them. To give an example, which Le Roy does not do, let us imagine a man in isolation for whom the hunt is a matter of life or death. Starving, he stalks and kills his prey, and the mere eating, after uncertainty and effort, is great reward. For the man in society, a meal in and of itself is not a "strong" experience, and to derive pleasure from a meal he requires increasingly exotic foods. Thus continuity without effort weakens sensations, and man in society finds "a new torment" of "involuntary anxiety [and] . . . vague desire," which create "an instability . . . a progression of desires which, always annulled by satisfaction . . . climb toward infinity . . . the torment of the leisured and civilized man. . . ."[32]

The effect of this anxious "progression of desires" is the creation of "synthetic needs" of increasing diversity and complexity (for power, recognition, and wealth), and a dynamic of change for the sake of change. Given this social need, there are no goals which are inherently "right" or "rational" for men. The pattern of human history is thus neither the natural development of social institutions to make life easier, nor the pursuit of thoughtfully conceived and chosen goals. By the fact of its existence, whatever is established must be abolished, for the satisfactions it offers are secondary to the need for different sensations. From Le Roy's point of view, history is a series of socially, politically, intellectually and artistically purposeless cycles. "This penchant [for change]," he concluded, "is manifested also in the totality of the great events which have stirred the earth": randomly, the "best

[31] Ibid., 190-219.   [32] Ibid.

governments . . . the most solidly established" will undergo irra-
tional alterations leading to their disfigurement; randomly, the
mores and science of all nations will prove impermanent; randomly, taste in the arts will fluctuate; randomly, in the world of
thought, a love of clarity more than briefly indulged will be replaced by a love of obscurity. In no other species does this irreg-
ularity assert itself, human society being the agent whereby "men,
with the same [basic] needs and the same means at their disposal,
can be different, and even essentially different, from one century
to another as from one nation to another."[33] For Le Roy this
"blind desire for well-being" always would dominate mankind,
with a few individual exceptions, and no reform of institutions
could be permanent, no rational secular goals could be enduring
guides. In the light of such knowledge the student of human history could only "be moved to an extreme indulgence for the entire species."[34]

Between 1768 and 1781, however, when he published another
"Letter on Man," the problem of accounting for the survival and
at least the minimal coherence of societies in the face of such
random chaos led Le Roy into a new model of the history of
social life. Historians, he noted, have made the behavior of men
in the midst of great passion their object of study—men in pursuit of power, status and recognition. Shifting the entire emphasis
of his "Letter" of 1768, Le Roy now argued that "the history of
the passions is only one part of the history of man." In society
the passionate expression of the instinct for well-being expressed
itself as vanity, and from vanity there flowed what Le Roy saw
as the chaotic events of "public" history. There was a "private"
history as well, however, largely unrecorded, and historians had
to understand it to understand the social bond, the cement of
society. For in addition to vanity, there was compassion, the instinct of "feeling together" among men, of shared suffering and
affection and support. From compassion came the sense of community, the idea of reciprocity, the concept of justice, and the
principles of social morality. From vanity came avarice, ambition,
selfishness and abusive exercise of power. Among the common
people the bonds of society were forged in relationships between
husband and wife, friend and friend, where, beyond the historian's
gaze, the daily acts of private kindness perpetuated the fabric of

[33] Ibid., 197-230.   [34] Ibid., 204-230.

human community. Above them, those people impelled by vanity were led by their ambition to satisfy their needs by seeking and exercising power and influence. There were thus two accounts of society to be written, the one recording the purposeless, cyclic course of public affairs, the second recording the relationships by which men have succeeded in living the social life.[35]

In the last years of his life Le Roy attempted once more to fathom the history of this strangest of all species and wrote two additional "Letters on Man," which were published after his death by his friend Roux-Fazillac. In these his sense of the randomness and chaos of human societies, which he had modified in 1781, gave way before a new structuring of social dynamics. Given man's desire for variety of sensation in society, Le Roy reiterated, and his adaptability to diverse climates and food sources, he has achieved, of all the species, "the greatest diversity of actions." Nevertheless, if one examined this diversity, one found that there was indeed "a character of uniformity" in the human race. It was not as striking as that of animals whose conditions were more constant, but it was there in the form of common *patterns* of cultural development.[36]

There is, Le Roy noted, a certain order of progression in the development of skills, tools, language and social organization among diverse cultures at diverse times. Where life-conditions are the same, a similarity of mores among isolated tribes can be perceived: hunting tribes, wherever they are, share certain values with other hunting tribes which distinguish them from the fishing tribes. There are, he observed, apparent laws which guide the development of moral codes, inherent in the needs and relationships of people coming together in certain forms of society. Thus, he explained, both the French and the Hottentots share similar concepts of patrimony and primogeniture with other nations and tribes. Numerous cultures had the same laws concerning incest, adultery and the dependence of women upon men. Indeed, he wrote, some of the most bizarre rites, such as trial by judgment of the gods, are shared by cultures and centuries greatly removed from each other. Above all, he maintained, the religious developments of human societies bear astonishing similarities. Whereas in 1768 Le Roy had been struck by the inevitable relativity and dis-

<hr>

[35] Ibid. (1781 edn.), 324-349.
[36] Le Roy, *Lettres philosophiques*, 290-293.

137

similarity of human development, he now was struck by "the spectacle of this uniformity."[37]

The problem this posed was a new one for Le Roy. In 1768 he had assumed that all development beyond the meeting of basic needs such as hunger and sexual satisfaction was somehow "artificial," random, relating only to the need for variety and conditioned only by the individualistic experience of phenomena by individual constitutions. Now, however, he recognized a "striking uniformity" in the way societies develop. Presumably, he speculated, these patterns arose as means of satisfying uniform needs throughout mankind, conditioned of course by the particular situation of a culture or tribe, such as whether it primarily hunted, fished for, or grew its food. Presumably, he continued, these patterns of behavior and belief met these original needs, since the cultures survived. Why, then, has "progress" stopped? Why do societies persist in actions even after they no longer can identify the needs which engendered them? The explanation, Le Roy asserted, lies in the fact that what was initiated as a reasoned response to certain needs has become a mechanical activity, a routine. Thus, for example, the first tillers of the soil developed patterns of behavior to meet a challenge that called their reason and their emotions into full activity. Their heirs, however, simply continue to do what was done before them.[38]

In short, the distinction Le Roy had arrived at was one between "reasoned" activity and "mechanical" activity. Reflection occurs in the individual who is seeking to satisfy basic needs in his life, Le Roy concluded; when the actions which satisfy these needs become habitual, the individual no longer needs to be aided by thought. This, however, puts an end to progress, unless the individuals whose actions have become "mechanical" are faced with a great and new crisis. The chaos and seeming purposelessness of history, therefore, is due to the fact that men operate according to habits, values and customs which once served, presumably, a useful purpose, but no longer do so. The positive sciences, because of their cumulative nature, progress, but they are the only aspects of civilization which do.[39] Le Roy, without using the modern terms, was in effect asserting that history is the chronicle of functional forms of social life becoming dysfunctional.

In his conclusion Le Roy reaffirmed the central distinction of his

[37] Ibid., 293-323.   [38] Ibid., 287-290.
[39] Ibid., 287-290, 323-324.

essay, that between reason and mechanism, and returned to the themes of the essay of 1768 in an attempt to synthesize the two. Combining his new construct with his earlier concept of man's need to be constantly "agitated," Le Roy now determined that the desire for novelty and the desire for routine both exist in man, and that both of these are "blind." At certain times, however, reflection, or conscious choice, aided man in crises to satisfy certain basic needs. In the combination of these factors Le Roy could now explain what before had seemed so inexplicable and random: that states progress to order, and gradually deteriorate, only to rise again, in constant cycles. Reflection presides at the *creation* of historical developments; mechanical habit both *stabilizes* such developments and *prevents adaptation* to new circumstances; and the passion for novelty is always there to counteract, at any point, both reflection and blind routine. The prognosis of the species is not encouraging, however, for all its new comprehensibility: "History teaches us that the human race, after several centuries of light, has more than one time plunged back into ignorance and barbarism."[40]

It was scarcely a Heavenly City!

The Fruits of Wisdom

For many students of the Enlightenment the philosophes of Paris were too caught up in their causes and purposes, or their wit and frivolity, or their faith and assurances, to be considered philosophers in the ancient sense of men who asked themselves about the elusive meaning or nonmeaning of the human and the sage's endeavor. There were, however, members of the coterie holbachique who intensely considered the question of with what a wise man must content himself, and who came away from their inquiries with an understanding beyond cause, or wit, or assurance.

D'Holbach's vision of the cosmic solitude, vulnerability and ultimate perishability of man, one which saw man as the sole source of his own guidance, was not, for example, an inherently cheering one. Nor did d'Holbach offer it as such. He described man as "a weak being, filled with needs, [who] requires at each moment aid that he cannot give to himself."[41] It was a sobering vision, but one which for d'Holbach was a necessary one. The

[40] Ibid., 324-328.
[41] D'Holbach, *Système social*, I, 210.

universe did not change its nature because man thought it different. Illusion inhibited realism, and only the sobering awareness that the universe was blind would allow man to alter that part of it which was, in fact, capable of his alteration.[42]

In the last analysis d'Holbach's atheism was positive only insofar as he saw it as a prerequisite of any substantial amelioration of the human condition. Essentially it was an attempt to free man from the host of negative qualities that d'Holbach saw as inevitably issuing from any religious belief. D'Holbach was not an optimist. He believed that a maturation from theism to atheism was vital to mankind, that a true understanding of man's unfavored place in nature must occur before the motivation and ability to change the sorry state of things could actualize, but he had little hope that this would come to pass. Man, he wrote, makes it a crime to dissipate his fears, and will continue in his madness and illusion until the unintelligible notion of God is somehow no longer regarded by him as essential to his happiness. It was not by his (d'Holbach's) own philosophic endeavors, he noted, that this would come about. The philosopher, he wrote, must be content to have the approbation of his own mind for his own deeds, and learn to gain his satisfactions from the knowledge that he is trying to do that which is right. Such was his own personal refuge, for his view of his own effectiveness could give him but little satisfaction: "He who combats religion and its phantoms with the arms of reason resembles a man who uses a sword to kill fruit flies: as soon as the blow is struck, the fruit flies and chimeras return to flutter about, and take again, in people's minds, the place from which one believed to have banished them."[43]

For Naigeon as well, atheism was above all a critical tool, one that could liberate man from certain suffering associated with religion, but not one that offered man either a panacea or an inherently comforting view of the universe. The alternative to religion for Naigeon, as for d'Holbach, was a sobering awareness of the absence of absolutes, and of the fragile, exposed abode of the species. Criticizing Bacon's use of the argument from design, Naigeon replied that the spectacle of nature proved absolutely nothing since, to speak precisely, there was nothing inherently "beautiful" or "horrible." For men who "coexist" successfully

[42] For a critique of the deists and their illusion, see d'Holbach, *Bons-sens*, 141.

[43] Ibid., 132; see also *Système de la nature*, II, 98.

with nature, the universe will appear a beautiful example of art; for men who "coexist" painfully with the universe, the very same sequence of eternal causes and effects will appear ugly and most imperfect.[44]

It would be consoling, Naigeon wrote, to think there could be such a thing as a universal and eternal coexistence, but since we have never observed such a phenomenon, there is no reason to believe it a possibility. The spectacle of nature reveals the permanence only of matter per se, and the impermanence of all of its particular forms, of which man (or any species) is only one. The beings who coexist today will pass away, and no one, wrote Naigeon, "whoever he be, can foresee and determine with some appearance of certainty or even of probability what will become of these diverse aggregates and what will be their organization."[45]

Atheism, Naigeon believed, could free man from the immediate "tyranny" of the priests, from the "sad superstition" of religion, and from the "denials of the senses" imposed by churches on man in this world;[46] however, both Naigeon and d'Holbach knew such atheism could offer but few resolutions to the ultimate mysteries, pains, and insecurities of the human condition, realities which they both saw religion as attempting to mask with its illusions. The tragedy of religion for Naigeon was precisely that it did not console; to a world already afflicted with unavoidable suffering, it added the self-inflicted tortures of superstition. Atheism could at least cause man to be easier with himself.[47]

Yet for all the circumscribed good he believed atheism capable of bringing to man, Naigeon in the last analysis was as deeply pessimistic as d'Holbach about the possibilities of "raising" man from his theistic state. In his commentary on Diderot's thought, he discussed in detail the value of Diderot's materialism, as expressed in the *Rêve de d'Alembert*, but added, "One must not dissimulate: the philosophy taught in the two dialogues suits only a very small number of privileged beings." The majority of mankind, he wrote, even those who are among the best educated, have a blind faith and an irremovable credulity: "Being inherent in human nature, and differing always in each individual only by their degree of energy, [faith, credulity, fear, and the love of the

[44] Naigeon, *Philosophie ancienne et moderne*, I, 368-369.
[45] Ibid.
[46] See Naigeon, "Discours préliminaire," in d'Holbach, *Système de la nature* (1770 edn.), I, 14-15.
[47] Ibid., passim. See in particular, I, 15-16.

marvelous] necessarily will submit the weak human race, in all times and in all countries, to the yoke that fanatics want to impose upon them, however absurd be the superstitions which will re-place, in the succession of centuries, those that have already reigned on the earth, and that have covered it with dark shadows and with crimes."[48] This was Naigeon at his most privately philo-sophical; as a philosophe as well as a philosopher, of course, he cared about what he termed those "occasional epochs" when life could be less "painful" and "disastrous,"[49] and he wrote, perhaps, in an attempt to be one of those "particular and momentary causes" of shadows less dark.

Naigeon's and d'Holbach's belief in the relative liberating po-tential of a literal "a-theism," and their pessimism about the pos-sibility of its establishment, were shared by Friedrich-Melchior Grimm, who added to these a vision of the ultimate futility of philosophy in the face of the chaos of the amoral universe. Grimm was well versed in the materialism of his two friends, but he had, we have seen, a constant aversion to systems of any kind, which prevented him from taking the step to a philosophical construc-tion of atheism.

All things are possible, Grimm once wrote, and nature laughs at whatever systems we devise. His "faith" in science was non-existent, and indeed he seemed overly pessimistic; in order to pro-nounce upon the question of whether the species have or have not been immutable, he once wrote, "one would have to be immortal and occupy all the universe at once." Scientists, he added, believed that progress in their domain was inevitable, and all modern men were certain that the invention of printing had rendered the ad-vancement of our knowledge cumulative and inexorable. Grimm would not consent to this: "We are too continually subject to physical and moral revolutions to draw from this circulation dura-ble advantages." The vulnerability of the species would not allow for optimism: "One unfortunate moment, one fire, one hurricane, one earthquake, one powerful and absurd man, a scourge more cruel than all the others, suffices to destroy the fruits of twenty centuries of effort and genius."[50]

[48] Naigeon, *Mémoires . . . sur la vie et les ouvrages de D. Diderot*, 307-308.
[49] Ibid.: "All these dispositions undoubtedly can, in this or that epoch, and by the action of several particular and momentary causes, have less painful and less disastrous effects."
[50] Grimm, *Corr. litt.*, VI, 23-27.

Grimm's *Correspondance littéraire* was permeated by this tone and by these themes. Scarcely a major event or a book hailed by his contemporaries to be the zenith of human genius passed by him without offering to his skepticism, his cynicism, his irony and his depth the occasion to display themselves. On Voltaire's poem on the Lisbon disaster, so widely seen as a profound statement of humanistic realism, Grimm wrote that it was as hopelessly dogmatic and filled with illusion as the viewpoint it attacked.[51] On Rousseau's *Emile* he wrote that Rousseau's initial error, from which all his other errors derived, was to maintain "a fictive model [of man] in his mind." In the place of man as he has revealed himself during the few thousand years "that we have had several notions about the human race," the author of *Emile* has substituted "this ideal and chimerical man that he created for himself." Grimm then offered a critique of this entire school of thought: "The citizen of Geneva is not the first who has tortured himself to establish this chimerical state that the writers of natural and political law call the state of nature. . . . I would prefer just as much to be told that fish had been created originally to live in the air, above the trees, and that they have degraded themselves and lost contact with themselves ever since they plunged into the waters."[52]

While virtually all of "enlightened" European opinion greeted Beccaria's treatise on crimes and punishments as a work of almost incomparable genius, Grimm wrote (with regret, he admitted) that the entire edifice of the work, which he admired for its sanity, its compassion and its assault upon useless suffering, was based upon the weakest of all foundations, the illusion of the social contract. Instead of basing his opinions on "human sensitivity," Beccaria chose "to play with words." If man would only leave his world of illusion, Grimm wrote, and look at the world as it is: "Let us not be infants, let us not be frightened of words. The fact is that there is no other right in the world except the right of the strongest, and that, since it must be said, this is the only legitimacy. . . ." To the retort that this renders the worst despot legitimate in his authority, Grimm replied, "Unfortunately, the world goes like that in times of darkness. . . ."[53]

Man, for Grimm, was a creature incapable of salvation, either earthly or celestial. Individual men, owing to fortuitous circum-

---

[51] Ibid., III, 244-249. [52] Ibid., V, 121-130. [53] Ibid., VI, 427-429.

stances, might find ease and peace and friendship, but the species as a whole was doomed to the cyclical manifestations of its weaknesses and failings, and it was not in the power of philosophy or any other force to alter this scheme. Discussing the injustice and corruption of French magistrates and administrators, Grimm observed, "This misfortune is not peculiar to France, and it takes but little reflection to be persuaded that it is inseparable from the human condition."[54] In 1772 he commented that there were those who blamed man's state on religion, but that to him religion was as much a symptom of man's problem as it was a cause.[55]

Grimm's pessimism and skepticism were constant throughout his life. In the 1750s he presented to his readers in the *Correspondance* a series of arguments that he was having with Diderot, who found his views excessively dark. Grimm was accused by Diderot not only of seeking to isolate himself from mankind, but of coming close to hating it. Diderot advised him "to reflect," to think of the future, to think of the progress that could be made for the benefit of posterity. Grimm replied that reason and reflection deceived man as much as any other of his faculties, and challenged Diderot by asserting that reason was in fact a misfortune for an animal—poisoning sentiment, distracting us from the present, and giving us, alone among the species, knowledge of our impending deaths. Nevertheless, he asserted, the wise man should not let himself be consumed by gloomy speculations on man's fate. The problem, he wrote, is that "we must see ourselves as we are . . . [and] make the best of it."[56]

In the final analysis, to be a philosophe was for Grimm a personal, not a social, phenomenon. It was, above all, to endure with a sense of the futility of seeking to fundamentally alter the human condition. Neither nature, which was neutral, nor man himself, who was a tragicomic biological accident, offered any hope to someone thinking beyond his own immediate sense of being alive and his own ability to find what pleasures he could in this world. It is understandable that Grimm would have deeply enjoyed the chance to speculate at d'Holbach's home; he did not, however, see much of benefit to the race in such speculations. They were private pleasures, he wrote in 1766, indifferent to the happiness of mankind.[57]

[54] Ibid., 80. [55] Ibid., x, 109-110.

[56] Ibid., iii, 256-259.

[57] Ibid., viii, 128-129; see also 368-369; and iii, 327-331.

There was, he wrote, in every society a small number of wise men who rose above the vulgar prejudices and looked honestly at their world, but their number was undoubtedly constant throughout history. "The experience of all the centuries," he insisted, revealed that in spite of the continual revolutions in opinions, and the changing modes of religions and superstitions, "the human race, in general, has always remained the same . . . has become neither better nor more perverse." The eighteenth century has deluded itself, he observed, with "the chimera of progress."[58]

To be wise, then, for Grimm, meant to see quietly to one's own happiness and to that of one's friends, and to avoid disillusionment by avoiding illusions. He was honest with himself, and if his *Correspondance* is any indication of his conversations at d'Holbach's home, he constantly sought to make his friends be honest with themselves as well. The abuse of the term "natural" and of the deistic concept of "providential order" both struck him as essentially dishonest. The concept of the preservation of the species, he wrote in 1759, was often used to support the view that those things which served this end were somehow "natural" and therefore "good"; but nature, he observed, expended as much energy on the destruction of life as it did on reproduction and preservation. Nature was indifferent. Our view of things, he lamented, was so narrow. We know virtually nothing about ourselves or our surroundings, and we seek to discuss the nature of the species: "Millions of centuries seem a long time to us in duration, and they are nothing." If we were to limit ourselves to our own observations, we would not be convinced that nature was beneficent. If men were honest, "they could not deny that a natural and perpetual war exists among the different species; they work endlessly at their reciprocal destruction." Man does not know the principle, the law, or the goal of this war, and does not even realize that he is part of it: "Man is, of all the animals, the most destructive; he wages war against all the others and against his own species. *There* are subjects worthy of a philosophe."[59]

Philosophy, then, and an end to illusion about man's place in nature, left Grimm with no message of hope to share with the world. His credo—not for the many—was a series of "I-conceive-nothing-abouts," "I-understand-nothing-abouts," "I-do-not-knows," and "All-these-things-are-incomprehensibles."[60]

[58] Ibid., IV, 241; see also III, 509-510.   [59] Ibid., IV, 132-134.
[60] Ibid., III, 509-510.

Oddly enough, however, it was Grimm who once wrote in April 1761 that *he* often found the philosophes overly pessimistic. "Our philosophes," he complained, "have a great taste for misanthropy." D'Alembert had just published his *Apologie de l'étude*, and Grimm claimed that it showed man as always unhappy, always struggling against misery and boredom. Maupertuis, he went on, wrote on happiness in a way that made one weep. Rousseau, he continued, depicted civil life so as to make us all shudder. All that was interesting, he wrote, "but let us not forget to weigh in the balance hope and the simple pleasure of existing."[61] Despair was an excess born of too narrow a vision, and to such a thing Grimm never would give consent.

[61] Ibid., IV, 373-374.

PART II

The Members of the Coterie Holbachique and the Society of the Ancien Régime

* * * * *

FIVE · *Origins*

THE dinners and discussions of the coterie holbachique were not the assemblies of a circle of pariahs and outcasts. On the contrary, almost all the men who met regularly at d'Holbach's homes had enjoyed, from the earliest moments of their mutual association, excellent individual prospects in their society. In the course of the decades that followed, most of them rose successfully into important elites within their chosen professions and areas of endeavor, and into positions which granted them almost universally recognized marks of quality in the hierarchical structures of the Ancien Régime. Some of them were born into honored and privileged positions in those structures; most of them achieved their dignities in ways that taught them certainly as much about their society as did their philosophical study of man.

We know the members of the coterie holbachique because they were philosophes, men of letters and scientists; we probably would not study them had they lived the lives their fathers would have chosen for them. The world of thought in eighteenth-century France indeed altered the intellectual dialogue of the West, and we are still living with its consequences; the Enlightenment is rightly studied primarily as a movement of ideas. However, if we wish to study the men and not merely their ideas, we cannot treat these figures as if they were merely their own thoughts and not complex historical persons. The "pure" history of ideas is becoming less and less fashionable in our time, and despite the occasional reductionism and anti-intellectualism of some of its critics, this is undoubtedly a welcome change. If we run the risk of seeming to imply inconsequentially that we know the "causes" of a thinker's particular orientation toward the world outside and the mind within, when we have grounded him in his social place, at least we are removing historical men of thought from the mythic olympian heights where they so often have been depicted. In so doing, we allow for that complexity of life in which intellectual alienation does not always equal social or political alienation, and in which men may express dear and private visions of human pos-

sibilities while still pursuing the traditional remedies and pleasures of a flawed and public human community.

D'Holbach's home on the rue Royale, after all, was not merely
a salon where men could speculate on the structure of thought,
science, history and society; it was as well a place where d'Holbach lived with his family and planned the business of his and
their success in the social and economic system in which they
actually lived. In 1775 Galiani wrote to Mme d'Epinay demanding news of Paris. She replied in terms that made sense to her,
"You ask me for news of the rue Royale. Everything is marvelous
there. The Baron has made his elder son a *conseiller au Parlement*
[of Paris] and the younger son *dragon de Schomberg* [a junior
officer in the regiment of the comte de Schomberg]." In March
1780 Suard wrote to Wilkes in a similar vein with news of the
"club of the rue Royale": "Mlle d'Holbach *aînée* has not done
like Miss Wilkes. She has just married a splendid captain of dra-
goons and now is called the comtesse de Chatenoy. . . . She still
lives with her husband at the Baron's home. . . ." In April 1780
Morellet sent d'Holbach's regards to Lord Shelburne in England,
and added: "M. le duc de Rochefoucauld has just married his [the
Baron's] niece. . . ."[1]

In short, as an atheist among his friends, Baron d'Holbach was
a man indeed deeply alienated in his thought and often his emotions from the Christian and theistic foundations and fabric of the
Ancien Régime. This did not prevent him, however, from proudly
going to the church of Saint-Roch for the weddings of his daughters and niece into the aristocracy, or as a respectable and wealthy
man from retaining a permanent chaplain at Grandval to hold a
mass every Sunday that the family was there.[2] To marry his deceased wife's sister, he had the duc de Choiseul himself obtain a
papal dispensation for him.[3] When he purchased for himself the
ennobling position of *conseiller-secrétaire du roi* for 112,400
livres, he presented to the company of those dignitaries an official deposition of the curé of Saint-Germain-l'Auxerrois attesting
to his faithful Catholicism and his annual Easter communion.[4] Is
this surprising? Perhaps we should not be surprised at all at this

[1] Mme d'Epinay, *Lettere (Gli Ultimi Anni)*, 159; Suard, *Lettres à Wilkes*,
94; Morellet, *Lettres à Shelburne*, 177-178.

[2] Diderot, *Corr.*, III, 181.

[3] *Mémoires du Duc de Choiseul (1719-1785)*, F. Calmettes, ed., 37.

[4] Lough, "Le baron d'Holbach," 529-530.

side of his life; he did what most men tried to do in the Ancien Régime, seeking to advance and to be secure. What is more astonishing is that he ever risked so much by thinking and writing the *Système de la nature*.

* * *

The figures who found their way into the coterie holbachique came there from remarkably diverse social and professional backgrounds. Their families included *noblesse d'epée, noblesse de robe*, urban bourgeoisie, merchants and artisans; their own personal careers included soldiers, professors, doctors, professional men of letters, professional scientists, tutors, a painter, a priest and a taxfarmer. Their own mutual acceptance and social intercourse revealed the striking heterogeneity of that "republic of letters" to which they all came to belong. However, that "republic," we shall later see, was far from an open society.

Three members of the coterie had been born into the glittering world of the court and administration at Versailles and Paris: Helvétius, Le Roy, and Chastellux. Within the "synagogue" the chevalier and later marquis de Chastellux had the most noble lineage of all. Born in Paris in 1734, Chastellux was a member of what his contemporary, the lawyer Barbier, called "one of the best houses of the nobility of the sword."[5] The maison de Chastellux could trace itself back to before the genealogically critical date of 1400, to one Claude de Beauvoir de Chastellux (1386-1453), *maréchal de France*, who had been the *chambellan* of Jean sans Peur, duc de Bourgogne, and who in 1418 had led the duke's armies in the expulsion of the Armagnacs from Paris.[6]

The branch of the family to which François-Jean de Chastellux belonged was one of the most distinguished military families of France. Founded in the sixteenth century, its sons had served as *gouverneurs* of Cravant, *chambellans* of the prince de Condé, and *maréchaux de camp* in the royal army; in 1621 its lands were

[5] Barbier, *Journal*, I, 185-190.
[6] On the "maison de Chastellux," see P. Lavisse, *Grand dictionnaire universel du XIXᵉ siècle* (Paris, 1867), III, 1,062-1,063; and the article on "Chastellux" in Bayle's *Dictionnaire*. There are two full-length and scholarly studies of Chastellux published in the twentieth century: Fanny Varnum, *Un philosophe cosmopolite du XVIIIᵉ siècle, le Chevalier de Chastellux*, and George Barr Carson, Jr., *The Chevalier de Chastellux, Soldier and Philosophe*. Both are published dissertations, and both are inadequate in their analyses of Chastellux's thought.

151

raised to the status of a *comté*. François-Jean's father, Guillaume-Antoine, marquis de Chastellux, added yet more official prestige to the house by marrying the daughter of Henri-François d'Aguesseau, the chancellor of France. According to the lawyer Barbier, Guillaume-Antoine had an annual income of 40,000 *livres* and a most striking sense of his feudal prerogatives.[7]

Guillaume-Antoine died when his son was only eight, and François-Jean de Chastellux was raised by his mother in the home of her father, the chancellor of France, on the place Vendôme. His grandfather provided him with an excellent private education, an advantage but by no means a necessity for success in his chosen military career. Of the highest nobility, a second son in a family with a grand tradition of martial service to the king, Chastellux enjoyed a status that almost assured his prospects in the military. Entering the army in 1749 in the *regiment d'Auvergne* commanded by his brother, his name, intelligence and talents earned him rapid promotions. By 1754, at the age of twenty, he was a captain. In 1755 he replaced his advancing brother as colonel of the family *regiment de Chastellux*, and distinguished himself in the Seven Years' War. In 1757 he was appointed to the post of *aide-major-général* (the equivalent of an aide to a chief of staff), and in 1759 named colonel of the prestigious *regiment de la Marche*. In 1760 he was decorated with the *Croix de Saint-Louis*. It was shortly after this that he returned to Paris and began his associations with the coterie holbachique.[8]

Charles-Georges Le Roy was born in Paris in 1723, the son of a noble father with a most noble charge, that of royal *lieutenant des chasses* at Versailles, with formal authority not only over the royal hunts on these lands, but over the administration of the woods and parks of Versailles and Marly insofar as that related to the hunt. Charles-Georges inherited this post from his father as a young man and held it all his life. This position enabled Le Roy to make his studies of animal life, almost all his data being limited to deer and other game animals. According to his friend Roux-Fazillac, Le Roy's position also placed him in close contact with the king and royal entourage, which allowed him later to write personal portraits of Louis XV and Mme de Pompadour. Le Roy's father sent him to the prestigious (but Jansenist) col-

---

[7] Barbier, loc. cit.

[8] On the military career of Chastellux, see, in particular, Carson, op. cit., and Alfred de Chastellux, *Notice sur le marquis de Chastellux*.

lège d'Harcourt, after which Charles-Georges vigorously pursued his education autodidactically. His reputation for learning (and undoubtedly his position) secured him a place as a founding member of the Paris Société royale d'Agriculture in 1763, whose twenty-person governing bureau was almost uniquely composed of eminent and prestigious figures of the two first orders of France.[9]

Le Roy was a close friend of Helvétius from his youth (although Helvétius was eight years older), and they met frequently as young men at the home of a mutual friend, the marquis de Vassé. It was Le Roy who in 1757-1758 encouraged Helvétius to publish *De l'esprit*, according to a manuscript account of the affair prepared by P. M. Hennin, a relative of Le Roy, who was an officer in the ministry of foreign affairs. Hennin asserted that Le Roy's role was known at court, and that the *dévots* insisted that the king remove him from his place at Versailles. The king refused, a gesture probably having more to do with Le Roy's status or abilities in administration relating to Louis XV's beloved hunt than any other factors, since the less-favored Tercier was dismissed from his post.[10]

Le Roy's work gave him an abundance of leisure time, much of which he devoted to his studies of animal behavior. By the time he met Diderot, d'Holbach and Suard in the late 1740s or early 1750s, he had developed a certain expertise in rural economy, political economy, and the ways of administration, which he combined with an interest in philosophy. He began to write articles on these subjects for the *Encyclopédie* and to be drawn increasingly into the Parisian world of letters. On the whole, however, he limited his salon activities outside of aristocratic circles to the gatherings at d'Holbach's dinners.

Helvétius was born in January 1715, in favored surroundings. His father and grandfather had both enjoyed a king's grant of personal nobility, and the family's status lay in that confused border area of "quality" where the newly ennobled, the more es-

---

[9] Roux-Fazillac, in Le Roy, *Lettres philosophiques*, v-xiv; Le Roy, *Portraits historiques de Louis XV et de Madame de Pompadour; Almanach royal* (1763), 498-500.

[10] Bibliothèque de l'Institut, MS 1223, folios 82-87 (Hennin manuscript); Archives des Affaires Etrangères, MS *Personnel*, 1ere Série, LXV, 323-338 (Tercier letter). See also D. Ozanam, *La disgrace d'un Premier Commis: Tercier et l'affaire De l'esprit*; D. W. Smith, *Helvétius*; and Grimm, *Corr. litt.*, IV, 29-31, 80-82.

tablished *noblesse de robe* and the upper bourgeoisie of royal service eyed each other with often differing senses of their respective social places. Helvétius' grandfather, Jean-Adrien Helvétius (1661-1727) had been the most favored medical doctor at the court of Louis XIV. After curing the dauphin of what was thought to be a hopeless case of dysentery, Jean-Adrien had been ennobled, honored with high posts and sinecures, and transformed into a man of great personal wealth and prestige. For his son Jean-Claude-Adrien (Claude-Adrien's father), he purchased a position of "doctor of the king," but Jean-Claude-Adrien's own medical talents soon earned him greater rewards. After curing the young Louis XV of a serious illness, he was invited to reside at Versailles, given an initial pension of 10,000 *livres*, elected to the Académie des Sciences, and awarded a series of prestigious and ennobling posts (including that of *conseiller d'Etat*), culminating in his appointment as the personal physician of the queen, Marie Leczinska. He soon became her personal friend as well.[11]

Claude-Adrien Helvétius thus grew up with all the advantages that a father in royal favor could bestow. Educated at the prestigious collège de Louis-le-Grand, he was then sent to stay with a maternal uncle, director of the tax-farm in Caen, to learn the techniques of finance. In 1738 by means of one action by the queen, the young Helvétius entered the highest echelons of personal wealth in France; Marie Leczinska, as a gesture to his father, secured him a vacancy in the directorship of the tax-farm. At the age of twenty-three he found himself a *fermier-général*, with an annual income of 100,000 *écus* (300,000 *livres*). To achieve such an income as a *rentier*, a man would have had to invest six million *livres*. With such wealth, Helvétius established himself grandly in the France of the Ancien Régime. He bought increasingly extensive amounts of land in the Perche and became a celebrated patron of the arts, supporting, among others, Marivaux with a pension of 2,000 *livres* per year and the playwright Saurin, one of his close friends, with a pension of 3,000 *livres* per year. In

[11] On the family and life of Helvétius, see Chastellux, *Eloge de M. Helvétius*; J.-F. Saint-Lambert, *Histoire de la vie et des ouvrages de M. Helvétius*; the remarkably well-documented Albert Keim, *Helvétius, sa vie et son oeuvre d'après ses ouvrages, des écrits divers et des documents inédits*; B. d'Andlau, *Helvétius, Seigneur de Voré*; and D. W. Smith, *Helvétius*. D'Andlau's work is based upon the archives of Helvétius' estate at Voré. See also, Grimm, *Corr. litt.*, IX, 417-424.

1749 he purchased for 370,000 *livres* the noble fief of Voré, also in the Perche, which made him the vicomte de Rémalard. To furnish the chateau of Voré, he purchased an initial 34,087 *livres'* worth of furniture; he employed, at the chateau alone, a *régisseur*, a bailiff, a chaplain, a gardener, five guards, a *concièrge*, a carter, a poultry-yard attendant and six or seven domestic servants.[12]

Increasingly, however, Helvétius was dissatisfied with his life as a *fermier-général*. According to his friends he became progressively appalled at the inequities which the tax system was producing in France, and depressed by his role in this and, in the last years of his tenure, continually embroiled in fruitless debates with his colleagues. Perhaps, however, he simply desired to live a life of a different style. Increasingly attracted to the literary world of Paris and the development of the "new philosophy," he had become the friend of numerous men of letters, including Montesquieu, Buffon, Saurin, Voltaire, Dumarsais, and the aged Fontenelle. He began to write philosophical verses and to dream of making a serious contribution to the world of letters and thought. When he became engaged to the bright and intellectual Mlle de Ligneville, the daughter of an important Lorraine nobleman, he decided to leave the tax-farms. Thus in 1751, to the consternation of all observers save his closest friends, he abandoned his position of *fermier-général*, invested his money in additional lands, and withdrew with his bride to his estate at Voré.[13]

For the next six years Helvétius spent by far the greater part of each year in isolation with his wife at Voré, managing his estates directly and working on his philosophical offering, *De l'esprit*. He spent approximately four months each year in Paris, where he also owned a home, entertaining and spending time with his friends in the world of letters. It is during this period of time that he was drawn into the orbit of the coterie holbachique.

Two devotees of the rue Royale inherited substantial opportunities for advancement from their families, Saint-Lambert and Baron d'Holbach himself, the former by the fact of respectable noble birth in a milieu in which he could shine, and the latter

[12] In addition to the works mentioned above, n. 11, see Bibliothèque de l'Arsenal, MS *Bastille*, 10,250, folio 7 *(Notes de Meusnier, Fermiers-Généraux)*, item 51. On the estate and chateau of Voré during this period of Helvétius' life, see d'Andlau, op. cit., 17-77.

[13] Collé, *Journal et mémoires*, I, 328-330; see also Chastellux, *Eloge de M. Helvétius*, and Saint-Lambert, *Histoire de M. Helvétius*.

by virtue of the great fortune of an uncle who treated him like a son.

Saint-Lambert was born in Nancy in 1716, the heir of a noble, military family with firm and honored roots in Lorraine. He himself was somewhat uncommunicative about his origins, for he was a *poseur* of sorts, passing himself off rather successfully in Paris as a marquis, which he was not. In fact, his father was one Charles de Saint-Lambert, an uneducated chevalier, lord of the small *seigneurie* of Orgement, and a *lieutenant des grenadiers* in a *regiment des gardes* of the king. The paternal family into which Jean-François was born was poor, but of a long-established nobility whose earlier representatives had seen far better days. The Saint-Lamberts traced themselves back to Gille and Gillet de Saint-Lambert, two brothers who in the thirteenth century served as knights attached to Thibaut IV, comte de Champagne and roi de Navarre. François-Jean's great-grandfather, African-Charles de Saint-Lambert, had been one of the great military figures of the early seventeenth century, maintaining in this what was already considered to be the family tradition; serving the duc de Lorraine, he had acquired substantial lands and wealth. It was, alas, François-Jean's grandfather, Charles-Philippe de Saint-Lambert, who caused the family to sink into relative poverty. Lord of extensive domains, and a *lieutenant-commandant* in the army of his liege lord, Henri de Lorraine, comte d'Harcourt, Charles-Philippe gambled and squandered away much of his fortune, then joined his protector in a ruinous struggle against the crown of France. In July 1666 most of his land was confiscated by the king. François-Jean's father, Charles, inherited one-fifth of what little remained, but he added to this somewhat by a good marriage and the early deaths of several brothers.[14]

A gifted child, apparently, and son of an ancient family whose mark of treason undoubtedly no longer weighed heavily against it, François-Jean de Saint-Lambert attended the collège de Pont-à-Mousson, one of the twelve collèges of the *école royale militaire*, requiring a nobility of four degrees for entry. There he became the constant and closest companion of his boyhood

[14] On the family of Saint-Lambert, see the local monographic study of Georges Mangeot, *Autour d'un foyer lorrain: La famille de Saint-Lambert (1596-1795)*. An excellent recent study of Saint-Lambert, focusing primarily upon his poetry, is Luigi di Nardis, *Saint-Lambert, Scienza e paesaggio nella poesia del Settecento* (Rome, 1961).

friend, Charles-Juste, prince de Beauvau, a peer of France, who later became a *maréchal de France* and *gouverneur* of Provence; they remained devoted to each other until Beauvau's death during the Revolution.[15]

In 1739, still following his father's wishes, Jean-François began his military service in Lorraine, and like Chastellux his advancement was steady. He was raised to the posts of lieutenant in the *regiment des Gardes-Lorraines* (1740), captain (1744), captain of the cavalry (1755), *aide-major-général* of the infantry (1756), and *maître de camp* of the cavalry (1758). Serving actively in major campaigns, he proved to be a distinguished professional soldier, and he was decorated as a *chevalier de Saint-Louis* on July 23, 1756, the same year in which he arranged for the clandestine publication of his recently acquired friend d'Holbach's *Christianisme dévoilé*.[16]

A dashing figure with an important boon companion, Saint-Lambert was invited into the circle of the exiled king of Poland's court at Lunéville in the 1740s, where Beauvau was an honored guest, and given the sinecure of captain of the royal bodyguard. The Polish court at Lunéville attracted many men and women of letters, and it was there that Saint-Lambert began to write increasingly celebrated society verse, and there as well that he met Mme de Châtelet and fathered the child whose birth would cost Voltaire's beloved friend her life. Soon after her death in 1750 Saint-Lambert arrived in Paris, eager to gain a literary reputation in the capital. He quickly became the friend of Rousseau, Grimm, Diderot and d'Holbach, and spent as much time in Paris as the annual spring campaigns of the war would allow. Through Mme d'Epinay he met Mme d'Houdetot, Rousseau's model for Héloïse, and became her lover and companion in a relationship which flourished for over fifty years. Introduced by the prince de Beauvau and by his new literary friends into the finest salons of Paris, admired for his poetry, and beloved by (if we are to believe Rousseau) one of the most remarkable women of France, it is

[15] On the early life of Saint-Lambert, see Mangeot, op. cit.; Grimm, *Corr. litt.*, VIII, 277-279; for a concise discussion of the requirements for entry into the system of *écoles royales militaires*, see P. du Puy de Clinchamps, *La Noblesse* (Paris, 1962), 44-45.

[16] Mangeot, op. cit., 88-89, has published the records relative to Saint-Lambert's military career from the archives of the ministry of war. On Saint-Lambert's role in the publication of the first edition of the *Christianisme dévoilé*, see Barbier, *Dictionnaire des anonymes*, I, 594-596.

small wonder that Saint-Lambert chose in the late 1750s to remain in the capital almost permanently, and to devote himself to literature and his friends.[17]

D'Holbach, like the "marquis" de Saint-Lambert, also apparently sought at times to inflate his origins. When seeking approval of his purchase of the position of *conseiller-secrétaire du roi* in 1756, he submitted a dossier which included the claim that both of his parents were noble.[18] In fact he was born Paul Henry Thiry, only son of Johann Jakob Thiry and Katherina Jakobea Holbach, landowners of some local importance in Edesheim, in the Palatinate, but without any titles of nobility. As a very young boy he was sent by his parents to live in Paris with his mother's brother, François-Adam Holbach, who recently had amassed a fortune through speculation in Law's fiscal régime and secured for himself noble lands and titles. It was from his uncle that the host of the coterie holbachique was to acquire his name, his title, his fiefs in the Low Countries and in Germany, and his wealth.[19]

We know nothing of Paul Henry Thiry d'Holbach's early education. During the War of the Austrian Succession he lived on his uncle's estate at Heese (which included a large chateau), and in 1744 he entered the Faculty of Law at the University of Leyden, accompanied by a servant. It was at this juncture that he adopted the nobler "d' " Holbach, matriculating as "Paulus von Holbach." He remained at Leyden until 1749, when he returned to Paris and was naturalized a French citizen.[20]

The family structure into which d'Holbach was twice to marry was a somewhat complex one whose intricacy, it would seem logical to suppose, was related in some way to an effort to avoid dissipation of the vast fortune of his uncle. François-Adam and Paul Henry Thiry's mother had a sister, Margareta, who in 1705 married one Christian Westerbourg, a cobbler. Their daughter (our Baron d'Holbach's first cousin), Suzanne Westerbourg, fared much better in the status of her groom, however, undoubtedly

[17] On this period of Saint-Lambert's life, see Mme d'Epinay, *Mémoires*, passim; Rousseau, *Confessions*, 511-576; Rousseau, *Corr.* (Leigh), III, 304-306; Grimm, *Corr. litt.*, v, 465-468; Collé, *Journal et mémoires*, I, 58-60, 68-69.

[18] Lough, "Le baron d'Holbach," 530.

[19] Naville, *Paul Thiry d'Holbach* (1967 edn.), 457-461; Lough, loc. cit.; and H. Lüthy, "Les Mississipiens de Steckbar et la fortune des barons d'Holbach," *Schweizer Beiträge zur allgemeinen Geschichte* (1955), 143-163.

[20] Lough, op. cit., 525.

due to her uncle's newly acquired fortune. In the 1720s she married Nicolas d'Aine, son of a high functionary, and saw her husband ennobled, then accepted as a *conseiller-secrétaire du roi* in 1728, the latter title giving to its holder a nobility equivalent to four degrees. Nicolas and Suzanne d'Aine had three daughters and a son, all second-cousins to our Baron and all of them much doted upon by François-Adam, who was equally generous to Suzanne. In the course of the 1750s our philosophical host was to marry two of those second cousins, an arrangement with significant economic benefits to himself and the family.[21]

With his personal share of the vast fortune he helped oversee for the d'Holbach–d'Aine family, and which included complicated arrangements to insure the wealth of all their immediate descendants, Baron d'Holbach invested heavily in *rentes* and in positions which would grant him important social standing. In 1756 diverse heirs of Nicolas d'Aine agreed to sell to him the family position of *conseiller-secrétaire du roi* for 112,400 *livres*, but which in fact actually cost him far less, for his own wife and his children by his first marriage (of whose share of Nicolas' estate he was guardian) were among the beneficiaries. This position was a sinecure that gave him French nobility, the right of entry to the court and, as he was to discover to his later regret, a liability to forced loans in times of fiscal crisis. In 1757 or 1758 he purchased the home on the rue Royale so associated with his name for 56,000 *livres*. By the 1750s the host of the coterie was the head of a family of immense wealth in land and *rentes*. He entertained as befitted that wealth, and nobles such as Sartine, Montamy, Croismare and Margency were among his earliest guests, all of them being official witnesses as well at diverse family occasions such as baptisms, weddings and burials. By 1757, when the parish of Saint-Germain-l'Auxerrois recorded the birth of his second son, d'Holbach already was involved in the publication of various scientific and philosophical works and translations, but he did not refer to himself as a "man of letters." He was, "*Messire Paul Thiry d'Holbach, baron d'Heeze, Leende, Seigneur de Walperg et autres lieux, Conseiller-secrétaire du Roi, maison couronne*

[21] Lüthy, op. cit.; Lough, op. cit., 526-527; see also Naville, loc. cit.; and the documents published in C. Nauroy, *Révolutionnaires*, 270 ff. On Mme d'Aine, see Diderot, *Corr.*, II-VIII, passim; in particular, on life at Grandval, the d'Aine estate, during this early period, see ibid., II, 239-286, and III, 86-207.

de France et de ses finances, associé externe de l'Académie royale des sciences et belles lettres de Prusse."[22] In terms of his quotidian concerns, the sequence of titles reflected not only his society's, but to a great extent his own sense of the necessary order of things.

Most members of the coterie did not have such inherited or simple routes to positions of social and/or financial promise. Two of them, however, Darcet and Raynal, were born into comfortable and respectable families and appeared destined, during a period of their youths, to pursue successful careers quite removed from the choices they ultimately made. Darcet, had he followed his father's urgent wishes, would have been a local magistrate; Raynal, had he remained true to his own original choice, would have been a Jesuit professor in a Faculté de Théologie. Life in the eighteenth century, however, for better or worse, was no more predictable than it is today.

Jean Darcet was born in September 1724 in Douazit, not far from Bordeaux.[23] The family whose name he bore belonged to the local *petite noblesse*, which enjoyed what a regional historian has termed "an efficacious prestige" in the region, then as now. Jean's grandfather had fathered two sons. The eldest, Marc-Antoine d'Arcet, entered the king's armies, became a colonel and *chevalier de Saint-Louis*, and was known in the region as the seigneur de Bellegarde; the second son, Jean's father, François d'Arcet, was a local magistrate, presiding in Douazit, and rose to become *lieutenant-général* of the *baillage* of Gascogne. According to Jean Darcet's friend Dizé, the judge's great local prestige derived partially from the fact that not one of his decisions ever had been overturned by the parlement de Bordeaux. He married twice, both of his brides also being members of the local *petite noblesse*. His first wife, Jean's mother, brought her modest but locally important wealth to the family, and after her death, while still a young man Darcet received the revenues from her small but successful farms in the area.

Darcet's first known studies were at the ecclesiastical collège d'Aire, several miles from Douazit, which the local historian Cuzacq called the most prestigious ecclesiastical school in the

[22] Lough, op. cit.; see also Naville, op. cit., 457-468.
[23] On Darcet's life and early career, see Michel Dizé, *Précis sur Darcet*, and the local monograph by Cuzacq, *Darcet*. These works are the sources for this and the next four paragraphs.

region. He was a successful student there and asked his father's permission to continue his studies in Bordeaux. His father had misgivings about Darcet's burgeoning interest in the natural sciences, but consented. That the judge should have had such misgivings is understandable. According to Cuzacq, the traditions of the local *petite noblesse* demanded that younger sons (Jean had an older brother) enter some "useful activity," above all, some office of justice or administration, always in the service of the king. With the eldest son expected to advance the family's status, the father was determined, according to Dizé, that Jean succeed him in the judgeship.

Once at the Faculté de Médecine in Bordeaux, however, Darcet announced his decision to pursue both his studies and a later career in chemistry and medicine. For this his father disowned him, transferring his rights of inheritance to a son by his second marriage, and cutting Jean off from all financial assistance. To survive, Darcet taught Latin to the sons of artisans in Bordeaux.

As in many provincial capitals in eighteenth-century France, local notables in Bordeaux were asserting their desired cosmopolitan and uncommon status by participating in the enthusiastic patronage of local centers of culture and learning, a development that we too often associate only with Paris. The period from 1735 to 1745 was a good time for a poor but respectable young man with manifest intelligence to find support for his ambitions. Darcet's friends at the University, including Augustin Roux, introduced him to eminent figures interested in science in Bordeaux, including the great figure of the city, Montesquieu. The latter, impressed by Darcet, brought him to Paris in 1742 to direct the education of his son, Jean-Baptiste de Secondat. At the time, Darcet was eighteen and his pupil twenty-four.

For the next thirteen years until his patron's death, Darcet remained in Montesquieu's service, aiding him in the accumulation of materials for the *Esprit des Lois* and pursuing with him common researches. It was in the midst of this relationship with Montesquieu, where he appears to have been part family-tutor, part secretary, part intellectual companion, and part son, that Darcet began to attend the dinners at d'Holbach's home. Cut off from his own family and original options, he had no choice but to attempt to succeed in the scientific community in Paris.

What Raynal's family expected of him we do not know, but he was born into a family with proud traditions, and he made an initial choice of career that was a most traditional means of advancement in the world. Raynal was born in 1713 in the village of Lapanouze, in what is now the department of Aveyron.[24] His family was a prestigious one locally. On his father's side the Raynals traced their position as one of the leading bourgeois families back to the fifteenth century; for hundreds of years they had served as "patriarchs" of the village, a title given to the three men most prominent in village affairs. Raynal's father, Guillaume Raynal, was a merchant. He must have been a successful one, for he married the daughter of an important noble family of the region, the Girels, *seigneurs* of la Cassagne, near Ségur, who traced their title back to at least 1453.

Raynal studied at the Jesuit collège de Rodez, and after graduation he took the tonsure and became a Jesuit priest. His rise within the Jesuit order was impressive. In rapid succession he taught the humanities at the collège de Pezenas, was given a post teaching eloquence at the prestigious collège de Clermont, and was made a professor of philosophy at the Faculté de Théologie of the University of Toulouse. Then, early in 1747, for reasons unknown, he suddenly left the Society of Jesus and, an ex-Jesuit but ordained priest, moved from Toulouse to Paris. There are reasons to believe that his parting with the order was not particularly bitter, if at all, for even in the most anticlerical passages of his later writings, he spoke well of the Jesuits and described their mission in the colonies as a civilizing one.[25]

In Paris he found clerical employment as a chapel priest in the parishes of Saint-Sulpice and Saint-Eustace, receiving fifteen *sous* per mass at the former and three *livres* per mass at the latter. For a man who had come to Paris perhaps expecting to make his fortune, this was obviously not adequate remuneration, and very shortly after his arrival he was relieved of his duties, the charge being made that he sold spiritual rewards and buried Protestants in the holy cemetery of Saint-Sulpice for sixty *livres* per funeral. He supported himself briefly by tutoring and by writing sermons which he sold to preachers less talented than himself.

[24] The basic archival research on the family and early life of Raynal has been done by A. Feugère, *Un précurseur de la Révolution, L'Abbé Raynal (1713-1796)*, upon whose research and publication of documents this and the next three paragraphs are based.

[25] This was the only Christian clerical order Raynal spoke well of in the *Histoire philosophique des Deux Indes*.

He was rescued from this life in the spring of 1747 by the abbé d'Aoul, a priest and friend who was a *conseiller* at the parlement de Paris. The abbé d'Aoul, impressed by Raynal's abilities, hired him to draft reports for the parlement. Raynal, whose experience teaching eloquence perhaps served him well here, began to meet and impress leading figures in parlement and the ministries; his talents were in demand, and within a short time after he commenced his ghost-writing, he became the confidant and advisor of the comte de Saint-Séverin, one of Louis XV's foremost councilors, and of the marquis de Puysieux, a leading French diplomat who rose to become secretary of foreign affairs.[26] As a result of his connections and writing abilities, he was in that same year appointed by the court of Saxe-Gotha as its Parisian literary correspondent, and he began to write for them a semimonthly newsletter which he pursued irregularly into the mid-1750s.[27] He began as well to frequent the social and literary salons of Paris, meeting Rousseau in 1748, who described in his *Confessions* how Raynal, already wealthy with impressive pensions and salaries, "offered his purse to me on occasion with an uncommon generosity."[28] In 1750, by which time he was a friend of Grimm, Diderot and d'Holbach, one of Raynal's patrons secured for him the editorship of the *Mercure*, which, despite his less than brilliant management of it, made him an important figure in the world of French letters. He held this post for four years. Participating in the highest levels of public affairs and prominent in literary circles, Raynal at thirty-seven had little to regret about his decision to leave the clergy.

Two members of the coterie holbachique, Grimm and Suard, had well-educated fathers active in dignified matters of local administration. Friedrich-Melchior Grimm, the only Protestant of the group, was born in December 1723 in the free imperial city of Ratisbon (now Regensburg).[29] His father was a superintendent of

[26] Morellet, *Mémoires*, I, 214-215.

[27] Raynal, "Nouvelles littéraires," published by M. Tourneux in Grimm, *Corr. litt.*, I-II, 1-238; see Jeanne R. Monty, "Grimm et les nouvelles littéraires de Raynal," *MLN* (1961), 536-639.

[28] Rousseau, *Confessions*, 437.

[29] On the family and early life of Grimm, see Meister, in Grimm, *Corr. litt.*, I, 2-13, and Tourneux, in ibid., XVI, 249-267, and the most ambitious study of Grimm's life, which incorporated major archival research, André Cazes, *Grimm et les Encyclopédistes*. Although Cazes' work is in need of

the Lutheran churches of the Upper Palatinate, a post that made him an important figure at least among members of his sect, and that surely gave him a respectable status within the imperial bourgeoisie. One of the superintendent's closest friends, in fact, was the noble Graf (count) Schomberg, whose son Gottlieb-Ludwig (1726-1796) we have noted among d'Holbach's guests in the 1760s. Friedrich-Melchior and Gottlieb-Ludwig were childhood friends, a fact that was later to help make possible the former's move to Paris.

Grimm studied at the Gymnasium in Ratisbon, where he became proficient in French and developed a life-long interest in literature. In 1742 he entered the University of Leipzig, pursuing his interests in the classics, writing a French tragedy, but in the end devoting most of his time to the study of public law, completing a thesis on the changes in imperial civil law during the reign of Maximilian I. This made him most useful to his friend. In August 1745, the year before Grimm actually submitted his thesis, he was called upon by Gottlieb-Ludwig, now himself the count of Schomberg, to accompany him as secretary and advisor to the Electoral Diet at Frankfort. When they returned, he remained in his friend's employ as tutor of the count's younger brother.

In 1748 the count of Schomberg moved his residence to Paris, and Grimm accompanied him and his charge, arriving there in February 1749. Through the count he was introduced into the German diplomatic and aristocratic circles of the French capital, where his learning and talent were marketable commodities. The baron Thun, governor of the young prince Frederick of Saxe-Gotha, named him "reader" for Frederick and gave him lodgings in his home. Later that same year he was named to the more responsible post of secretary to the count of Friesen, another German dignitary in Paris, and he became the count's trusted friend, maintaining this position until Friesen's death six years later. Almost all these German nobles had close links with literary society in the capital, and through them Grimm began to establish his own ties. At the home of prince Frederick he met Rousseau, and a mutual interest in music led to a warm association. Rousseau introduced him into the home of the wealthy financier and music

significant revision in the light of recent studies on Diderot and the encyclopédistes, Cazes did the basic research on Grimm's origins and early years.

lover, La Popelinière, and, according to the *Confessions*, to the salon of Baron d'Holbach as well. By the early 1750s, when he published the most successful of the brochures in the "music war" between supporters of French and Italian opera, Grimm was a personality in his own right in Parisian literary circles and a favored protégé of the distinguished German community.[30]

In 1755 after Friesen's death, the duc d'Orléans offered Grimm the post of secretary of his commands, a sinecure which made few demands on his time and provided a remuneration of 2,000 *livres*. This in no way interrupted a situation which Grimm was developing for himself as literary correspondent for (initially) German courts; beginning in 1753 Grimm utilized his Parisian diplomatic contacts to secure subscribers for his own *Correspondance*, who for the sum of 144 *livres* per year received copies of a semimonthly survey of cultural and political events in the capital.[31] In 1754 he replaced Raynal, who by now was on to more important affairs, as the correspondent of the court of Saxe-Gotha. With his reviews he was even able to aid (or begin) the reputation of his friends abroad, as when he wrote in his first year that a writer by the name of "Saint-Lambert is the one of all these poets [at the Parisian salons] who is currently most in vogue and who enjoys the greatest reputation"; that a certain patron by the name of Baron d'Holbach has just purchased a remarkable new painting for "one-hundred pistoles"; that the brilliant *Encyclopédie* is once again available; and that a veritable "handbook for the philosopher," *Pensées sur l'interprétation de la nature*, has just been published by one Denis Diderot.[32]

Suard, who also would serve as a literary correspondent to a German court during a transitional period of his life, was born in late 1732 or early 1733 in Besançon. His father, an educated bourgeois, served as a secretary in the administration of the University of Besançon, and encouraged him in his learning. He initially studied at home with his father where, he later claimed, the

[30] On Grimm's early years in Paris, see Mme d'Epinay, *Mémoires*, passim; Rousseau, *Confessions*, passim; and the sources cited above, n. 29. Grimm's contribution to the music war was *Le petit prophète de Boemischbroda*.

[31] Grimm, *Corr. litt.*, II, 239; on the question of the establishment of Grimm's *Correspondance*, see Jeanne R. Monty, loc. cit.

[32] Grimm, *Corr. litt.*, II, 270-272 (on Saint-Lambert); 283 (on d'Holbach); 298-301 (on the *Encyclopédie* and the contributions of Diderot and d'Holbach); 308 (on Diderot).

finest minds of the university city were frequently present. After continuing at a local collège he entered the university's Faculté de Loi, where he won prizes not only for his scholarship but also for his fencing. The latter interest soon placed him in deep difficulty. As the result of some dueling between bourgeois students at the university and young aristocratic officers stationed with a royal regiment in the city—provoked, Suard claimed, by their objection to the bourgeois carrying swords—an aristocratic officer was wounded (not slain, as Suard was to tell his wife and friends), and Suard, a second, was imprisoned. He told both his wife and Garat that he had been secretly transferred to a military dungeon for a harrowing thirteen months, but a recent researcher has discovered no evidence to cast doubt on the official record indicating an incarceration of three months. Following his release Suard attempted to continue his study of law, but he found that it no longer held his interest. According to his own version of his past, he had been introduced to Bayle's *Dictionnaire* by the commander of the dungeon, who had come to take pity on his depressed and frightened prisoner, and he had developed a love of the letters during his ordeal. After a brief return to his studies, he began to hunger for the literary capital, and with a letter of introduction from his father to a family friend in Paris in his pocket, he left Besançon in 1750.[33]

In Paris his father's friend secured him secretarial employment in the offices of a man named Peyre, a successful financier. Like most newly arrived provincials with a love of the letters, Suard began to frequent the literary cafés, and it was perhaps at the Procope that he met and became the friend of the abbé Raynal. The latter, already a well-connected figure in Paris, found him a more suitable post as the tutor of several wealthy and aristocratic families, including that of the prince of Nassau. It was also on Raynal's invitation that he began to attend the literary salons. In his first few years in Paris he became close to the group around Montesquieu, which included Darcet, Roux, and Helvétius, just before the latter abandoned the tax-farms. By the mid-1750s he was a regular guest at d'Holbach's home. According to many accounts, including what he himself later told his wife and his friend

[33] On the life and early career of Suard, see Mme Suard, *Suard*; Garat, *Suard*; and Alfred C. Hunter, *J.-B.-A. Suard, un introducteur de la littérature anglaise en France*.

Garat, it was d'Holbach and above all Helvétius who undertook to support him during this financially difficult period.[34]

Although not wealthy or even secure, Suard by the mid-1750s nevertheless had prospects by no means discouraging. He had important friends, and through them he was beginning to meet potentially useful people. His major problem appeared to be his lack of any particular talent that might distinguish him from a host of other young men quite like him in the city. His friends, he later recalled, suggested that he learn English since the public was starved for translations of works from that increasingly intriguing land. He learned it rapidly and began his hand at translations from recent literary works and journals. His talent as a translator was to start him on his own successful literary career.[35]

The figures we have treated thus far were all born into markedly favored circumstances, even though in some cases, as in Darcet's, they chose not to take full advantage of them. Leaving aside for the moment the cases of Galiani, for whom French society was merely an interlude in his life, and of Naigeon, whose origins remain obscure, the remaining four members of the coterie— Morellet, Diderot, Marmontel and Roux—emerged from clearly humbler backgrounds, from conditions many traditional Frenchmen in the eighteenth century would have agreed upon as "vile." Within that preponderant demographic entity labelled "vile," however, they were all advantaged, and their circumstances did not leave them without resources for advancement.

Morellet was born in Lyons in 1727, the eldest of fourteen children.[36] He described his father as a man of very limited means,

---

[34] Mme Suard, *Suard*, especially 43-47; Garat, *Suard*, especially I, 207-215; Hunter, op. cit., 1-51.

[35] Mme Suard, loc. cit.; Garat, loc. cit.; Hunter, op. cit., 108-125.

[36] Morellet awaits his serious biographer, but he has provided a remarkably candid portrait of his own life in his *Mémoires*. The *Mémoires* are occasionally self-serving, but on the whole, as we have seen, for example, in our discussion of the problem of atheism at the coterie, Morellet wrote accurately and with a distinguished sense of detail. It is possible that a future biographer will discover errors in Morellet's presentation of his life prior to his coming to public attention in Paris, but given the general accuracy of his reports for the period when it is possible to monitor the *Mémoires*, we shall give the abbé the benefit of belief in his account of his early years. The sole caveat we need observe is his sense of "mediocre" wealth, which was that of a man who, by the time he was writing the *Mémoires*, had enjoyed many years of good fortune. It is apparent from the account he offers of

who could not provide adequately for his family. Being the eldest had its advantages, however, and Morellet was sent to a local Jesuit collège where, he recalled in his *Mémoires*, "the mediocrity of my state" caused him to be neglected during his first two years. In his third year there a young Jesuit took an interest in him and, finding him responsive, encouraged him in his studies. By the time he was fourteen Morellet had won local prizes for his work and was being encouraged to continue his education.

Although he wanted simply to become a Jesuit priest, his father could not afford to send him on to further schooling, and a "sensible" uncle intervened and insisted that Morellet advance himself. In his *Mémoires* Morellet recalled that his uncle was capable of reading the local gazette, which gave him great authority and the nickname "the doctor," and his counsels ultimately prevailed. The uncle knew the family of the superior of the prestigious ecclesiastical séminaire des Trente-trois in Paris, and through them had his promising nephew admitted on pension at the "modest" cost of 300 *livres*. Thus, after a journey by horse, stagecoach, and canal barge, the young scholar arrived in Paris in 1741.

At the seminary, Morellet later noted, most of the students were confident of their future careers and not terribly interested in difficult studies. Struggling to impress his teachers enough to win a scholarship, Morellet must have worked hard, for he was appointed a master, which now gave him free room and board. To allow him to become a bachelor of theology, his father and uncle somehow made "yet another financial effort," and he received his degree.

To advance further, however, and seek his *license* in theology, would have required a sum of money wholly beyond his father's and uncle's means. At this point, however, a cousin of Morellet, studying philosophy at the collège d'Harcourt, inherited a "large" sum of money, and he gave the aspiring theologian 1,000 *livres*. With this Morellet applied to the Sorbonne (the Faculté de Théologie of the University of Paris) and was admitted in 1748 not only to the Faculté, but, after rigorous examinations for the few spaces made available to those "from obscure families," to the "society of the Sorbonne," an elite collège for special students,

---

his education that his family, if not his father himself, had respectable means. For the period from 1727 to 1752, see Morellet, *Mémoires*, I, 1-34, which applies to this and the next four paragraphs.

professors, and eminent clerics. There he received special privileges, room and board, and found himself in the company of two fellow students already destined for importance, Turgot and Loménie de Brienne, with both of whom he became close. Unlike Turgot, who remained at the Sorbonne only two years, Morellet remained until 1752 when he was awarded his *license*.

Morellet later recalled how his classmates in the society were preparing for august clerical careers (de Brienne, he remembered, was certain he would be a bishop and a statesman), while he, in 1752, now found himself unable to get a teaching position in a good collège, unwilling to become a mere parish priest, and uncertain of how to support himself. After applying and being rejected for a position as theological advisor to a Portuguese abbé who was the nephew of the archbishop of Lisbon, Morellet was sought out by his former superior at the séminaire des Trente-trois, the abbé de Sarcey. The former principal, now spiritual advisor to several *dévotes*, among them the mother of the chancellor of the king of Poland in Lorraine, de La Galaizière, secured for Morellet the position of tutor for the ten-year-old son of the chancellor, which not only provided Morellet with basic security, but with generous leisure time.[37]

Continuing "to see and to cultivate" Turgot and de Brienne, Morellet began to study "public economy and government" in a new interest arising from his friendship with them. In 1755 Turgot, by now a *conseiller au parlement* soon to become a *maître des requêtes*, introduced him to de Gournay, an *intendant du commerce*, who introduced him into the milieu of the advocates of a freer economy. In 1757 the elder Trudaine, a member of the *conseil*, engaged Morellet to study and publish a critical report on the restrictions on the free manufacture and use of (cloth) prints in France; his study appeared early in 1758, and the *conseil* voted to end all such restrictions later that same year.[38] By 1759 Morellet was in the frequent employ of Trudaine, "from whom I could expect my humble fortune by occupying myself with matters of administration"; modestly pensioned by the chancellor de Galaizière in return for the successful studies of his charge; a good friend of important figures in the intendancies and *cours*; and introduced by his administrative friends into the literary and

[37] Ibid., I, 24.

[38] Morellet, *Réflexions sur les avantages de la libre fabrication et de l'usage des toiles peintes en France* (Paris, 1758); Morellet, *Mémoires*, I, 42-43.

social salons, including that of Mme Geoffrin.[39] Already in contact with Diderot and d'Alembert in the aftermath of his work on toleration, Morellet was about to become a regular guest of the coterie holbachique at the same time that he was becoming an important researcher and writer for the increasing number of advocates of economic reform stirring within the official bodies of the Ancien Régime.

Like Morellet, Denis Diderot also decided in his youth to be a priest, and like Morellet he became instead an abbé and then a philosophe. Diderot was born in 1713 in Langres (Champagne). His mother was the daughter of a merchant tanner; his father was a master-cutler, with an excellent local reputation and a modest but respectable holding of land. The family on both sides had a history of sons and daughters entering the Church, and of Diderot's four surviving siblings, one became a canon (with whom Denis would be in constant dispute), one became a nun, and one remained a spinster at home. Denis went to Paris to continue his education, and emerged to be perhaps the most remarkable antireligious thinker of the eighteenth century.[40]

Nothing is known of Diderot's earliest education, but at the age of ten he entered the Jesuit collège de Langres, earning notes of merit which are still extant. In 1726 he received the tonsure at the age of only fourteen, in what appears to have been an attempt by his family to secure for him the succession to an uncle's benefice.[41] The plan did not succeed, however, and Diderot continued with his education, sincere enough about his clerical state to consider seriously, according to his daughter's memoir on his life, the possibility of becoming a Jesuit priest.[42] In 1728 or 1729, for reasons wholly unclear, it was decided that he should complete

---

[39] Morellet, *Mémoires*, I, 53-138.

[40] On Diderot's family and early life, see the important contribution and synthesis of A. M. Wilson, *Diderot: The Testing Years*; cf. Mme de Vandeul, "Mémoires pour servir à l'histoire de la vie et les ouvrages de Diderot," in Diderot, *Oeuvres* (A-T), I, xxxix-lxii; Naigeon, *Mémoires . . . sur la vie et les ouvrages de D. Diderot*. See also, Franco Venturi, *La jeunesse de Diderot*; Louis-François Marcel, *Le Frère de Diderot*; Louis-François Marcel, *Un Oncle de Diderot: Antoine-Thomas Diderot et l'Ordre des Frères Prêcheurs*.

[41] Wilson, op. cit., 14-24; cf. Mme de Vandeul, op. cit., lix-lx. See also Marcel, *Le Frère de Diderot*, 25-33.

[42] Mme de Vandeul, op. cit., xxx.

his schooling in Paris, where he largely disappeared from further public records until the 1740s.

There is an as yet unresolved debate over where Diderot studied in Paris, but it seems certain that he continued either at the Jansenist collège d'Harcourt or the Jesuit collège de Louis-le-Grand, or perhaps, as Arthur Wilson has suggested, at both. Whichever it was, he attended classes over a long period of time, receiving a degree at the University of Paris, where he was recorded as a master of arts in 1732.[43]

Between 1732 and the mid-1740s Diderot vacillated among several possible courses of action. His father wished him to be a solicitor, and Diderot spent two years studying the law firsthand while working in the Parisian law office of a man his father had known in Langres. To the disappointment of his father, however, Diderot would not remain on this path, and he appears to have wavered among projected clerical, medical and various other sorts of careers, all the while "borrowing" money from home and taking assorted odd jobs as a tutor and writer.[44] Increasingly alienated from his father, he married without informing his parents, began to write reviews and articles for diverse publications, and took to translating from the English. Drawn to the "new philosophy," he started writing some longer pieces of his own. Some of these rewarded him quite well. His loose translation of Shaftesbury's *Inquiry Concerning Virtue and Merit* earned him 1,200 *livres* from a publisher in 1745, and his own deistic *Pensées philosophiques* was purchased for the same price in the following year. In 1748 he sold his *Bijoux indiscrets* to a publisher for another 1,200 *livres*. In addition, he was collaborating as translator and partial editor of several projects.[45]

What dramatically altered his prospects, however, was his association with the incipient *Encyclopédie*. In 1745 several publishers who already had published material by Diderot became associated with the project of the *Encyclopédie*, and by 1746 Diderot was on its payroll, receiving occasional sums for work rendered.

[43] The debate over Diderot's schooling is summarized in Wilson, op. cit., 25-27.

[44] See his daughter's account of his recollections of this period in Mme de Vandeul, op. cit., xxxiii.

[45] Wilson, op. cit., 37-91, which incorporates the contributions of many important sources to a clarification of these years; see also Jacques Proust, *Diderot et l'Encyclopédie*, 89-92, and Diderot, *Corr.*, 1, passim.

171

Learned in many fields as a result of his long and diverse studies, and "experienced" as a translator from English, he was a natural choice as a collaborator. In October 1747 a change in the editorial direction of the work made Diderot and the already celebrated d'Alembert co-editors, providing Diderot with the first assured income of his life.[46]

By 1751, when he was a well-known if notorious figure in Paris, a new contract with the associated publishers of the *Encyclopédie* granted him a raise of approximately fifteen per cent, to 2,000 *livres* per year. In 1755, with the publicity and furor over the *Encyclopédie* promising the publishers ever-increasing profits, Diderot received a more significant contract, which now assured both him and his growing family of a secure future: he was to receive 2,500 *livres* per volume (which appeared at the rate of one per year approximately), plus a lump sum payment of 20,000 *livres* three months after the publication of the final volume, a settlement transferable to his heirs. This was certainly not a contract that made him a wealthy man by any means, but he moved his family to new quarters on the rue Taranne and hired a maid as a result of it. In 1759, the same year that his father died and left him a significant settlement, including some productive land in Langres, the publishers invested 20,000 *livres* earmarked for Diderot, giving him the proceeds as a *rente*, which would have amounted to about another 1,000 *livres* per year. He was working hard for his money, and in his eyes the publishers were not giving him his due, but he was at this point, after years of irresolution and struggle, a man of letters supporting himself by his chosen labors, and that was a rare accomplishment in the eighteenth century.[47]

Marmontel, who would come to command extraordinary prices as a man of letters, described his own origins, as Morellet had done for his, as obscure and poor. Marmontel was born in Bort, a small village in the Limousin near the border with Auvergne, in 1723. His father, whom he described as a tailor, had a household of fifteen persons, including his wife, children, parents, and in-laws. Marmontel was to claim in his *Mémoires* that the family got by with "order and economy, work and a small commerce," but a recent researcher examining records in Bort has discovered that Marmontel's father owned a house and garden, an animal pen in

[46] See Proust, op. cit., 47-52, 89-93.   [47] Ibid., 89-105.

another part of Bort, and a small farm near the village. Marmontel was taught to read by the nuns of a convent on whose nearby farm his maternal grandfather was the tenant, and received his primary education from a local priest, who did this for no charge. In 1734 the priest convinced Marmontel's family to send him to the collège de Mauriac in Haute-Auvergne, where he studied rhetoric and the humanities. His father wanted him to work in the service of a merchant after he completed his studies at the collège, but after a short period of such work in Clermont, Marmontel entered the city's collège, studying philosophy and earning his means by tutoring other students.[48]

Like so many other members of the coterie, Marmontel considered an ecclesiastical career during this period, claiming in his *Mémoires* that he took the habit in 1739, and studied at a seminary in Toulouse from 1741 to 1744. It is not clear what he did or did not do in this regard in Toulouse, but he did begin to write poetry during this period, and he took the liberty of sending an ode to the already legendary Voltaire, having been deeply disappointed over its critical reception in Toulouse. Voltaire was impressed by it and initiated a correspondence with Marmontel. Voltaire, always searching for young writers to mold, encouraged Marmontel to make his home in Paris, offering him an introduction to Orri, the *contrôleur-général*. Thus assured, Marmontel arrived in Paris in October 1745 with only (he later claimed) fifty *écus* to his name, just as Orri was disgraced by the king.[49]

The early years in Paris were difficult ones for Marmontel, if not as bleakly impoverished as his *Mémoires* describe, but gradually he began to make his mark. Two of his poems were "crowned" by the Académie Française; he published a successful translation of Pope; he wrote for several journals; and through Voltaire he became the protégé of the celebrated Vauvenargues. Late in 1746 he moved into new, if still modest, quarters with a

---

[48] Marmontel, *Mémoires*, I, 1-99; Jacques Sirat, "Eclaircissements sur l'enfance de Marmontel," in J. Ehrard, *Marmontel*, 43-48. See also Morellet, *Eloge de Marmontel*. Marmontel was the subject of a biography by S. Lenel, *Marmontel: Un homme de lettres au XVIIIᵉ siècle, d'après des documents nouveaux et inédits*, which shed important light on the details of Marmontel's life, but which was pedestrian in its analysis of his thought and milieu. Of great importance in re-establishing the eighteenth-century presence of Marmontel is the recently published collection of papers edited by J. Ehrard.

[49] Marmontel, *Mémoires*, I, 99-134; Voltaire, *Corr.*, XIV, 263-264.

writer for the *Journal des savants* and a young abbé soon to cause a grand stir, the abbé de Prades. In the late 1740s the financier la Popelinière, who had aided other members of d'Holbach's group, took a great liking to Marmontel and took him to live in his household. There, Marmontel came into contact with his host's circles of aristocrats, diplomats and men of letters. Within a short period of time he was a guest at d'Holbach's home.[50]

Although he was without personal wealth, Marmontel by 1750 was fully in the center of the social and literary world of Paris. As he unabashedly recalled, he and several other figures from this milieu began to visit Mme de Pompadour at Versailles every Sunday, when she entertained the artists, scientists, and men of letters of Paris soliciting favors, work, and advancement from her. He became a veritable poet-courtier, writing inflatedly flattering verses in her and the king's honor, and in the end his fawning was profitable to him. In 1753 Mme de Pompadour secured for him the sinecure of *secrétaire des bâtiments*, and he was invited to reside at Versailles. He remained there, despite frequent visits to Paris and continued connections with the coterie holbachique, until 1758.[51]

In that year Mme de Pompadour secured for him the editorship of the once vital journal of the world of letters, the *Mercure*. Retaining his sinecure he left Versailles for Paris to occupy this new post. The royal *privilège* of the *Mercure* provided a fund from which pensions for a large number of men of letters were derived, but the journal had been somewhat moribund in the years preceding Marmontel's assumption of this post, and it was earning little money for anyone. Marmontel was its editor from August 1758 until December 1759, and in these sixteen months he wholly transformed the image of the *Mercure*, brought it a far wider circulation (above all in the provinces, whose literary pretenders he knew how to flatter), and left it a prosperous journal handsomely supporting its editor and its pensioners. Among its most popular pieces were its editor's own *contes moraux*, which for

[50] Marmontel, *Mémoires*, I, 121-253; Voltaire, *Corr.*, XV, 74, 118, 234-235; XVI, 9, 19, 79, 93, 95, 111; XVII, 95-96; Diderot, *Corr.*, II, 127; Morellet, *Eloge de Marmontel*.

[51] Marmontel, *Mémoires*, I, 232-325. Collé, *Journal et mémoires*, II, 166-170, wrote of Marmontel performing literary tasks at the bidding of Mme de Pompadour, and commented that he "owed to her his fortune" and that he "could refuse her nothing."

reasons difficult to understand today achieved a success in his life-time that scarcely could be overstated. In addition Marmontel was writing some of the most important literary articles for the *Ency-clopédie*, and was gaining a reputation as a significant critic. These latter successes were almost unnecessary, however, for his trans-formation of the *Mercure* and its income made him an important and appreciated figure in the world of letters. He was yet to ascend to his later and more remarkable fame, but by the end of the first decade of the coterie holbachique's existence, he had indeed earned the reputation which had eluded him in Toulouse.[52]

Like Marmontel's father, Augustin Roux's was an ostensibly poor tailor with too many mouths to feed. Roux was born in January 1726 in Bordeaux, to a family which once had been respectable bourgeois involved in the professional life of Bor-deaux, but had fallen upon hard times. Nevertheless, as the eldest son, carrying the family's hopes for advancement, young Augus-tin attended the Jesuit collège de Guienne. According to his friend Deleyre, Roux's family had retained the professional man's admiration of learning and had encouraged their son to gain an education, after which he was to work with his father as a tailor. His friend Darcet's account seems more probable. According to the latter, who knew him in Bordeaux, Roux's family expected Augustin, as the eldest son, to provide for the family, and insisted that he become a priest; Roux convinced them that going to the collège would be the most auspicious beginning of such a career, and they provided for him to attend.[53]

Both accounts agree on what followed. At the collège Roux excelled in mathematics and philosophy and decided to attend the University of Bordeaux. His father opposed this and sent him to study theology with an uncle who was a curé in Bordeaux; after a short time Roux rebelled and secretly began to study medical texts, encouraged in his efforts by one of his former Jesuit teach-ers. At some point in the mid-1740s he announced his decision to enroll formally in the Faculté de Médecine. His father, as Darcet's had done, cut him off from all family support and hospitality,

[52] Marmontel, *Mémoires*, I, 326-336; Grimm, *Corr. litt.*, IV, 340-341, 349-350; J. Wagner, "Marmontel, journaliste au *Mercure de France*," in J. Ehrard, op. cit., 83-95.

[53] On Roux's family and early life, see Darcet, *Eloge de Roux*; Deleyre, *Eloge de Roux*. See also Naigeon, "Lettre . . . sur Roux," 60-72; Dizé, *Précis sur Darcet*, 6-7.

and Augustin found himself without the means for shelter, food or study in his native city.[54]

As in Darcet's case as well, Roux took advantage of the intellectual ferment of the city. A provincial center such as Bordeaux had only a small but proud and influential community of men of thought and creativity, and they generally managed to discover and to encourage each other. Before long Roux came to their attention. The great Montesquieu befriended him, and above all, Barbot, president of the *cour des aides* and a man of letters, came to his aid. Professor Grégoire, the leading medical doctor at the Faculté, found him a job in a hospital while he continued his education. After several years of intermittent work and study, Roux was received as a *docteur* by the Faculté in 1750, and for a short time joined Grégoire in the latter's medical practice. He also was elected to the Académie de Besançon, in which Barbot had great influence.[55]

That same year, or perhaps in 1751, Roux decided to leave Bordeaux for Paris. According to Darcet, who had left Bordeaux some eight years earlier, Roux appreciated how much he lacked in "knowledge, wisdom and, above all, experience, and decided to come to Paris to continue his studies, to force fortune to be less unfavorable to him." Since fortune had not exactly frowned on Roux in Bordeaux, his sense of his possibilities must have been great. He borrowed 600 *livres* from Barbot and, upon his arrival in Paris, cast his lot in with a group of former students from Bordeaux. Darcet, one of these latter, recalled how they found in each other's company "the means of avoiding the solitude, the boredom and the sickness that is felt by a young man isolated in the midst of an immense city." They were not, however, wholly isolated. Montesquieu, apparently the patron saint of the young men from his city, found Roux a position as the private tutor of the young d'Héricourt, who became in later years a leading *parlementaire*.[56]

The 1750s were busy years for Roux. On the advice of his friends, he also learned English and began the translation of scientific works from that language, and from Latin, into French. Early in that decade he became the friend of Baron d'Holbach, and they combined their talents in a joint effort of scientific dissem-

[54] Darcet, *Eloge de Roux*; Deleyre, *Eloge de Roux*.
[55] Darcet, *Eloge de Roux*; see, in particular, Deleyre, *Eloge de Roux*, 6-12.
[56] Darcet, *Eloge de Roux*; Deleyre, *Eloge de Roux*.

ination, with d'Holbach translating from the German and English under Roux's informal editorship. In addition Roux began to follow the course in chemistry offered by the pre-eminent chemist of the period, Rouelle, and favored by him, began performing, often under royal commission, experiments with liquids and analyses of water sources. In 1755 he was named an editor-translator of the important second volume of the *Collection Académique*, dealing with the philosophical transactions of foreign academies. His success in this led him to be appointed in 1758 as an editor of the ambitious publishing venture, the *Annales typographiques, ou Notice du progrès des connaissances humaines*, whose first volume appeared in 1760. His life in many ways paralleled Darcet's: cut off from his family and favored by his region's great intellectual names, he was on the verge of a significant scientific career in Paris.[57]

Of Naigeon's career prior to his association with the coterie holbachique in the mid-1760s, we unfortunately know almost nothing. He was born in Paris in 1738 or 1739, and had either worked or studied, by the time Diderot met him in 1765, as "a draftsman, painter and sculptor before becoming a *philosophe*."[58] If he were in any way related to the Naigeons who became active during the Revolution, there was a successful Dijon mustard-merchant somewhere in the family, but this is a wholly conjectural connection. Assuming that he *studied* to be a "draftsman, painter and sculptor," we can also assume that his family probably had at least a moderately respectable station in life. This hypothesis is further strengthened by Naigeon's younger brother's having revealed himself to A.-A. Barbier, and having informed him of his role in d'Holbach's and the elder Naigeon's publications, including the information that he was a *contrôleur des vivres* at Sedan, a post "which gave me nothing to do."[59] Let us tentatively assign the mysterious Naigeon a bourgeois family living above mediocrity, therefore, and make no further use of his case.

Galiani, another special case, brought an eminently distinguished

---

[57] See Roux, *Recherches historiques et critiques*; Roux (trans.), Robert Whytt, *Essai sur les vertus de l'eau de chaux*. . . . (Paris, 1757); Roux, ed., trans., *Collection académique*, vol. II: *Transactions philosophiques*; Roux, ed., *Annales typographiques, ou Notice du progrès des connaissances humaines*.

[58] Diderot, *Oeuvres* (A-T), III, 9-14, 346; see also Rudolf Brummer, *J.-A. Naigeon*.

[59] A.-A. Barbier, *Dictionnaire des anonymes*, I, xlii, n. 1 ff.

past with him to the coterie holbachique. Born in Naples in 1728 he was favored by his uncle, Celestin Galiani, the archbishop of Thessalonica, who was prefect of higher studies at the University of Naples and first chaplain of Charles VII. A child prodigy, Galiani had published a successful treatise on money at the age of sixteen, and was the toast of the Academy in his home city. After studying at a leading monastery, he was attached to his uncle the archbishop's service for eleven years, and in 1759 sent to Paris on an important diplomatic mission by the king, as secretary to the ambassador.[60] It was a group of men with strikingly auspicious prospects whom he met at d'Holbach's home, soon after arriving in Paris.

* * *

What in the backgrounds and early experiences of these men prepared them for their eventual audacious belief that, as philosophes, they had the right to talk with and preach to and teach their social superiors and their leaders? What provided them with the remarkable self-confidence of thinkers who would instruct, invited or not, the highest-born, most powerful and wealthiest figures of their age? What in their society had taught them their remarkable sense of their rightful place? What did they learn enroute to manhood about their possibilities?

In reference to the most early favored among them, Chastellux, Helvétius, Le Roy, and perhaps even d'Holbach and Saint-Lambert, the questions are less pressing. They were accustomed, from young ages, to titles, honors, rewards and a sense of their own high worth. D'Holbach and Saint-Lambert indeed felt the need to inflate their own origins, d'Holbach giving the appearance of early nobility and Saint-Lambert adopting the title of marquis, but all of them grew up with varying amounts of the right to command others, of power, of security about their futures. If Helvétius and d'Holbach did not have French titles, they had the means to purchase them, which they did, Helvétius buying a noble *terre* and d'Holbach the post of *conseiller-secrétaire du roi.* All of their interests in the letters and the new philosophy attest strikingly to the growing prestige of literary and intellectual pursuits, and when they moved into the philosophic circles of Paris, it is not surprising that they did so with ease and self-confidence.

[60] On Galiani's early life, see Luigi Magnotti, *L'Abbé Ferdinand Galiani,* 7-16.

They were all accustomed to deference and respect, if not from all elements of *haute société*, at least from enough of them. If anything, their singular self-confidence was more than a sense of reality ought to have allowed, as when Helvétius and Le Roy pressed on with the grossly miscalculated publication of *De l'esprit*, and d'Holbach, with such astonishing aplomb, began to publish the atheism of his various *Systèmes*.

What of the others, however, none of whom, with the exception of the disowned Darcet, was nobly born? Traditionally, we seem to explain the phenomenon with answers applicable to the broadest groups, perhaps necessary as bases, but woefully inadequate to the task of limiting the variables and allowing us to predict individuals who will behave one way and individuals who will behave another. Thus, we read often of the rising confidence and self-assertion of the bourgeoisie, and of the adjustment of *criticism* and *perspective* which must follow the *economic* changes of a society. Yet few in number, after all, were the bourgeois who sought the intellectual attention of sovereigns, dukes and duchesses, and who preached to their nation the duties and proper science of man. By the end of the 1750s Raynal, Diderot, Marmontel, Grimm, Darcet, Roux, Morellet, and Suard, to list them by age, all expected to be heard and to make strong marks on their society. Can we distinguish, perhaps, *some of the contributing factors* to such a chosen role? It is not enough, one suspects, to cite the rising prestige of the sciences and the letters, and their devotees' perception of their historic role; self-confidence, we know, rarely flows from pure intellectual cognition. There is in the lives of all men a social learning that begins from the very first day.

Where, after all, did a man learn his "place" in the society of eighteenth-century France? Surely he did not learn it at Versailles if he were born in Lapanouze, Langres, Bort, Ratisbon, Douazit, Bordeaux, Lyons or Besançon, and what seemed "humble" looked back upon from success in Parisian society might not have taught one humility in those original milieus. Darcet is the easiest to observe in this light, son of a noble and successful magistrate in a small rural town. But were the others born as obscurely as their memoirs and later comments recalled? Raynal was the son of a "patriarch" merchant who had married a daughter of the local nobility. Diderot's and Marmontel's fathers were not only artisans, but respectable landowners in small towns. Diderot's uncle was an important canon; Marmontel was singled out as the only male to be educated in his town by the local convent, a favor to his family.[61] Grimm's and Suard's fathers held important, respectable, and in certain ways influential positions in their respective cities; they may not have seemed such growing up in Versailles or Paris, but in Besançon it was important to be secretary of the University, and in Ratisbon important to be superintendent of all the Lutheran churches of the Upper Palatinate. Roux and Morellet indeed were born more obscurely, and in large cities at that, but both were first and favored sons, and both of their families managed to send them to a collège, although Morellet indeed recalled feeling insecure and ignored in his early years there. That he *was* there, however, proved significant, and it is worthwhile to recall that every individual among this group of eight went to a collège. The period which covers their childhoods, roughly from 1720 to 1740, with most of them being born between 1723 and 1727, was not a time of great prosperity in the provinces, and few were the families in France which could send their sons to an excellent education, if indeed to any education at all.

Often when we look at the formal education of the philosophes, it is only to stress that the Jesuits introduced them to literature, or to comment upon their rebellion against the philosophies and theologies they were taught. Yet formal education is a social education and an education of the ego as well. In case after case, among the members of the coterie, we find them receiving honors, being singled out for special attentions, and encouraged to continue in their work. Even after all the years of success, when he was a member of the Académie and a friend of the titled and the great, Morellet could not help but recall, writing his *Mémoires*, the thrill of winning prizes in competition against all those wealthy and noble schoolmates he encountered. In the collèges they met the heirs of all that was prestigious in their towns or regions, and they had the opportunity to measure themselves against those others. They often had staked their futures on their educations, and they pursued them passionately, not one of them stopping after his first experience at a collège. They learned to speak well and to write well. It is a remarkable fact: of the eight men born to less than glittering social places, seven spent time at universities, and most of these received their university degrees. We do not

[61] Marcel, *Le Frère de Diderot*, 30-33; Sirat, "Eclaircissements."

often think of the Enlightenment as born or nourished on the benches of the eighteenth-century universities. Yet there they are: Grimm at Leipzig, Darcet and Roux at the Faculté de Médecine at Bordeaux, Diderot receiving his master-of-arts from the University of Paris, Morellet at the Sorbonne, Suard at Besançon, and Raynal teaching in the Faculté de Théologie at the University of Toulouse. Marmontel did not attend the university, but he did go on to a seminary after his collège, tutoring his fellow students to earn his keep.

What did they learn of a personal nature at these universities and seminaries? Once again, they learned that they were more intelligent and more gifted than their superiors and peers, by winning the honors, completing the degrees, being favored by their teachers, tutoring those who could pay them for such aid. They learned as well, no doubt, a good deal about how to behave in the presence of society, how to address people of rank, make friends with the great, and how to maintain the forms of deference around the substance of self-assertion. In pursuing their studies, these young men spent the better portion of their youths and adolescences in socially diverse environments where learning, science and letters were respected and valued, environments in which they succeeded and received the dignities attendant to that success. *That* was a lesson which created an expectation they were never to lose.

Such a lesson was reinforced by their personal experience of the response of their society to the fact of their educational and intellectual accomplishments. What they could do with their minds indeed mattered. Darcet and Roux, promising scientists, were aided and accepted by the learned and socially prestigious academicians and officials of Bordeaux. Grimm, a student of public law, was taken by the count of Schomberg to the Diet of Frankfort and to Paris. Morellet was made a member of the elite société de Sorbonne and later the tutor of a powerful family; when he turned his mind to economics and administration, he was hired by important officials to think and write for them. Raynal was named a professor of theology, and when he later began thinking and writing for other men, he was hired by powerful magistrates and future ministers. Marmontel's verse was praised and encouraged by none other than the master Voltaire, and then by Mme de Pompadour. Diderot found his talents rewarded with the position of coeditor of an ambitious new project with the already redoubtable d'Alembert. They learned something positive, and they continued in the paths that so rewarded them.

Perhaps because the two most celebrated philosophes, Voltaire and Rousseau, never attended a university, we have not looked at that institution as an important part of the formal and informal education of a philosophe, but Voltaire and Rousseau, after all, were not typical of the population of the Parisian salons. In addition to its providing formal and social learning, however, a university was also a corporate body of the Ancien Régime, and its graduates acquired a formal dignity that added to their social place. In 1610, we should recall, Loiseau had listed the *docteurs*, *licenciés*, and *bacheliers* of the facultés of theology, law, medicine and arts as the first rank of the Third Estate, and if no one accepted such an ordering in practice, respect for such qualities and their traditions was by no means minimal. The nobles did not need a university education to begin their advancements in society; of those born aristocrats—Saint-Lambert, Le Roy, Chastellux and Darcet—only Darcet attended a faculté, rebelling against his father's choice of a career. Helvétius, whose father enjoyed personal nobility, went directly from his collège into his worldly training as a financier; d'Holbach, born more humble, attended the University of Leyden.

A second lesson that arose from these years, more subtle than at first it might sound, was the nature of important connections. Almost every member of the coterie holbachique, with the possible initial exceptions of Chastellux, Le Roy, Diderot and d'Holbach, saw his career significantly advanced by a person of important rank or dignity in the structures of his society. For Darcet and Roux, it was Barbot and Montesquieu; for Marmontel, Mme de Pompadour and La Popelinière; for Saint-Lambert, the prince de Beauvau and the king of Poland; for Morellet, Turgot, Trudaine and Gournay; for Helvétius, the queen, Marie Leczinska; for Raynal, Puysieux and Saint-Sévérin; for Grimm, the duc d'Orléans; for Suard, the friends of Raynal, and indeed the tax-farmer turned gentleman, Helvétius himself. They discovered several things from this. First, of course, they learned that one could succeed by being well thought of by the powerful, an obvious fact in the abstract, but one they lived: they were to seek and cultivate such favorable judgments continually. Second, they learned that their society and circumstances were indeed mobile, that persistence would not go unanswered, that a man could change his fortune and his prospects in a moment's time; it would keep them ebullient and confident at the darkest times. Third, despite what they would write of their civilization and despite what they thought they believed, they learned, correctly or incorrectly, that their society rewarded merit, that their nation had the ability to offer men their just deserts. Their talents were being recognized. From the multitude of ambitious and competing young men in Paris, they were already singled out, or were being so, for honors and success. They could never quite rid themselves of the belief that they had deserved it. As a result, virtually none of those among them who lived long enough to see the end of that society could quite believe the men of 1789 and beyond.

SIX · *Ascent*

LET us cast one last backward glance at the members of the coterie holbachique before we examine their careers and standing within the structures of the Ancien Régime. Leaving aside Galiani, for whom France was only a temporary home, we have fourteen men of relatively diverse origins and early careers. Of the fourteen, ten were born in the provinces or foreign countries, and four were born in or near Paris.

If we divide the coterie holbachique into those born to great station and wealth, and those who had to earn for themselves a place in the sun, a striking configuration emerges. Of the former, including Chastellux, Le Roy, Helvétius, d'Holbach, and Saint-Lambert (whose advantages were possibly fewer), four were either born or raised in Paris, while only Saint-Lambert was a provincial. Of the nine remaining members of the coterie, including the disowned Darcet, eight were born in the provinces, and only Naigeon was of reportedly Parisian origins. The only "social categories" in which the demographic study of Daumard and Furet found any percentage of "immigration" to the capital anywhere approaching that of our less favored members of the coterie were "domestics" and "unskilled laborers," undoubtedly forced by sheer economic necessity into Paris from neighboring regions. For the group closest in terms of social background and education to these nine men, Daumard's and Furet's "*professions libérales*"— including lawyers, medical doctors, surgeons, university professors, etc.—marriage contracts reveal that a full third to two-fifths of such grooms were originally from Paris, a figure above the average for Parisian grooms of 1749 as a whole.[1]

Despite the smallness of the sample, the remarkably disproportionate provincial origins of the well-educated scientists and men of letters in the coterie holbachique perhaps suggest something of significance. These were men who chose not to remain in the

---

[1] A. Daumard and F. Furet, *Structures et relations sociales à Paris au XVIIIe siècle*, 59-65.

184

milieus of their origins, either geographically or professionally, but who chose to enter the distant literary and scientific world of Paris. This choice would appear to reflect their operational belief, acquired at some point in their youths or educations, that advancement was indeed possible in their society and that a man, through risk, wit and work, might earn a better place in the world. They did not see their situations as even relatively static; they did not resign themselves fatalistically to their given stations. For almost all the members of the coterie holbachique destined to advance by their intellectual qualities, the move to Paris and away from their fathers' lives was one of deliberate choice. In the end it was a choice that advanced the fortunes of their own successions more in one lifetime than the fortunes of most ambitious but relatively humbly born French families could be advanced in two, three, or even four generations.

* * *

The professional and social careers of most of the members of the coterie holbachique did not in fact reveal an unbroken progress toward security, recognition and increased status. There were indeed fluctuations in many of their fortunes, moments of doubt and insecurity in many of their situations, and grave crises in many of their lives. Almost all of them, however, evidenced a mastery over the forces which controlled their destinies in the Ancien Régime, and rose into important elites within their chosen fields of endeavor, themselves coming to control the fate of those who came after them. The mechanisms, nuances and occasional cycles of this phenomenon will prove revealing of the social climate in which they struggled to succeed, but for the moment let us establish the fact of their success.

Among the least secure when we left them in the 1750s were the scientists Darcet and Roux. Both, however, began to study with the eminent chemist Rouelle in the 1750s, and from this scientifically important connection they were launched upon their careers. In the mid-1750s the wealthy comte de Lauraguais asked Rouelle to recommend to him a chemist to direct his practical research on the art of manufacturing porcelain, a luxury industry in France in which there was a fortune to be made. Rouelle chose Darcet, and thus in 1757 the latter began to direct his attention to a descriptive chemical analysis of that material.

Darcet's work led him to devise a method of pyrolytic analysis which produced an important breakthrough in the production of superior types of porcelains.[2]

This success not only secured him continued patronage from Lauraguais, but brought him an increasing reputation within the scientific community. In 1766, 1768 and 1770 he read memoirs on pyrolytic chemical analysis to the Académie des sciences, the cumulative effects of which brought him to prominence. This work also provided him the means to pursue his "official" education and secure his official credentials. Although he was not actively pursuing a medical career (despite his degree from the University of Bordeaux), he was in 1771 received as a *docteur-régent* of the Faculté de Médecine of the University of Paris, and almost immediately he was appointed to a series of its important commissions. In 1772, for example, he served on its committee dealing with the testing and circulation of new medicines in Paris. In 1774 he was awarded the first chair in experimental chemistry at the collège de France, where he caused a sensation by delivering his inaugural address in French rather than Latin and by appearing in ordinary clothing, instead of in his doctoral robe. Such iconoclasm, however, in no manner impeded his career. In 1777 he was appointed a member of the Société de correspondance royale, a court-supported association of celebrated medical doctors involved in policing and regulating the medical profession, and in 1784 he was rewarded with membership in the most prestigious scientific body in France, the Académie des sciences itself.[3]

Darcet continued to work at his chosen field of applied chemistry, but his admission to the Académie des sciences secured his fortune and his fame. The Ancien Régime rewarded its "official" scientists handsomely. In addition to commissioned scientific work, favored scientists received their share of more enduring patronage. Between 1784 and 1789 Darcet was placed in charge of research at the royal porcelain works at Sèvres, appointed *inspecteur-général des essais des monnaies* at the royal mint, and named *inspecteur* of the dye-ateliers of the royal tapestry-works of Gobelin. In 1785 he was appointed by the *contrôleur-général* to the Comité d'Administration de l'Agriculture, and in 1788 to

[2] Dizé, *Précis sur Darcet*, 9-13.

[3] Ibid., 11-14; Cuzacq, *Darcet*, 16-19; P. Delauney, *Le monde médical Parisien au dix-huitième siècle*, 44, 302-303, 310-323, 337, 344-347, 355-366, 387.

the prestigious Société royale d'Agriculture. By 1789 he was one of the most privileged members of the scientific community of France.[4]

Roux did not live so long as Darcet, and thus did not attain such full marks of recognition, but his career was a successful one and indeed in some ways ahead of Darcet's rate of advancement when ended by his death in 1776. Roux also began his scientific career in Paris under Rouelle's tutelage, and secured, by the 1750s, royally commissioned scientific work. Without a patron, however, such as Darcet's Lauraguais, his initial advancement was somewhat of a financial burden. He had to borrow the 6,000 *livres* necessary to seek acceptance first as a *licencié* then as a *docteur-régent* of the Faculté de Médecine of the University of Paris. But he telescoped several years of work into one, finishing first among the concurrents, and received both degrees in 1760. He began to practice medicine in Paris to support himself and to furnish a small private laboratory. His abilities, however, were now known in the capital.[5]

In 1762 the scientist Vandermonde, the editor of the most successful medical journal in eighteenth-century France, passed away, and a search for his successor began. Because of his prior experience in scientific journalism, and perhaps because of his brilliant showing at the Faculté, Roux was chosen for this prestigious post. From 1762 until his death in 1776, Roux edited and managed the *Journal de médecine, chirurgie et pharmacie*, a post which allowed him to influence both the directions and the reputations of his professional community. In his hands, the journal became a thoughtfully assembled collection of reviews of current medical literature; extracts from important new works; case histories; letters from Paris, the provinces and abroad on medical, surgical and pharmaceutical matters; warnings about the prevalence and movements of epidemics and diseases; anatomical and surgical charts and diagrams; obituaries; and announcements of courses, degrees and prizes. It was the most vital clearinghouse of such information, a widely read journal that earned Roux great prominence in professional circles. To the best of his ability, Roux sought to

[4] *Almanach royal* (1784-1789); Delaunay, loc. cit.; Delauney, *La vie médicale au XVIe, XVIIe et XVIIIe siècles*, 473-475; Bachaumont, *Mémoires secrets*, XII, 140; Cuzacq, *Darcet*; Dizé, op. cit., 13 *ff*.

[5] Deleyre, *Eloge de Roux*, 25-31; Darcet, *Eloge de Roux*, 8-14.

keep Parisian and provincial doctors, surgeons and pharmacists well-informed and wary of charlatanism. It was an ideal post for a medical philosophe.[6]

It was not, however, a post lucrative enough to allow him to add to his private laboratory as he wished and, according to both of his eulogists, it was now Baron d'Holbach who came to his aid. In the mid-1760s the royal glassworks of Saint-Gobain were undergoing a difficult period financially and, as Darcet recalled, "the administrators felt that they were susceptible of improvement. Baron d'Holbach was consulted, and he determined their choice in favor of M. Roux, whom he loved and esteemed infinitely."[7] For his experiments and advice at Saint-Gobain, Roux received enough reward to terminate his medical practice (serving henceforth only on charity cases and for several of his close friends) and to devote himself to his journalism and private experimentation.[8]

Other honors began to accumulate for Roux. In addition to serving on various influential committees of the *docteurs-régents* of the Faculté, Roux was appointed to the Société royale d'Agriculture in its first year of 1763, and in 1770 he was named by acclamation to the first chair of chemistry at the Faculté de Médecine. The latter position may not have been vigorously pursued by many of his colleagues, for there was no honorarium attached to it. To be a professor was a dignity, however, with many official benefits. Roux accepted it, teaching there until his death, in respect for which his colleagues struck a medal in his honor. Dying as he did at the age of fifty, his certain greater successes and rewards were unrealized.[9]

Equal and often greater successes awaited the members of the coterie holbachique who chose more purely literary careers as the arena of their professional ambitions. Their achievements in this pursuit were often inextricable from social and indeed political successes as well, and the demarcation between recognition for their literary efforts and social favor is often difficult, if not impossible, to establish. Nevertheless, they were men who cared

[6] *Journal de médecine, chirurgie et pharmacie, etc.*, A. Roux, ed., July 1762–July 1776.

[7] Darcet, *Eloge de Roux*, 12-15; see also Deleyre, *Eloge de Roux*, 32-35.

[8] Darcet, *Eloge de Roux*, 15-17; Deleyre, *Eloge de Roux*, 32-36.

[9] Darcet, *Eloge de Roux*, 15-17; Deleyre, *Eloge de Roux*, 32-36; Delauney, *Le monde médical Parisien*, passim; *Almanach royal* (1763), 499.

about the letters, so let us first attempt to delineate their accomplishments in the exercise of their talents.

Marmontel, after losing his editorship of the *Mercure* in December 1759, experienced a brief setback to his literary ambitions, but his *contes moraux* and his articles for the *Encyclopédie*, later reprinted as his *Eléments de littérature*, had made him an already celebrated figure in Paris, and from the early 1760s on, his life was an almost uninterrupted rise in reputation and rewards.

In the 1760s and 1770s Marmontel found his medium as a playwright of sorts (after some early failures as a tragedian) by writing almost all of the librettos for the comic-operas of Piccini, whose staunchest defender he became in the "musical war" against the partisans of Gluck. He enjoyed popularity, wealth, and critical recognition from these works, and fought desperately for his reputation when the attack from the "Gluckistes" came. In 1767 his most controversial work, the novel *Bélisaire*, raised a temporarily dangerous furor, but in the end, as we have seen, he triumphed with the help of his philosophic friends, of Voltaire and Turgot, and of Catherine the Great and several other foreign princes, and he was hailed throughout the continent. His novel *Les Incas* (1772), another attack upon intolerance, was greeted with great enthusiasm, and this time the Church did not attempt to challenge him.

In 1763 he was elected to the Académie Française, and as an academician he received from the court new sinecures (and pensions), for which his only duties appeared to be the writing of flattering verses for special royal occasions.[10] In 1772 he was appointed royal *historiographe de France*, which gave him another handsome pension, a residence at royal expense, and entry to all of the festivals at Versailles.[11] Among the academic "immortals," he made a great name for himself, delivering orations and reading from his works on almost every special occasion. His apparent grand style and assiduity rewarded him. On the death of d'Alembert in 1783, he attained perhaps the highest position attainable in

[10] Most of such verses were published in Bachaumont, *Mémoires secrets*, passim; and Grimm, *Corr. litt.*, passim, with disobliging comments; in 1773, however, Bachaumont, op. cit., VI, 257-258, was pleased to report that Marmontel was donating the proceeds from the sale of his *Epître* on the fire at the Hôtel-Dieu to the hospital itself.

[11] Bachaumont, op. cit., VI, 121, much admired "les agrémens" that such a post procured for Marmontel.

189

the world of letters of the Ancien Régime, being elected *secré-taire-perpétuel* of the Académie Française.[12]

With his growing reputation, his official positions, and perhaps with the memory of his embroilment of 1767 in everyone's mind, Marmontel commanded an extraordinarily high price on a literary market which did not generally favor the writer. The publishers of *Les Incas*, expecting perhaps another storm such as that over *Bélisaire*, which had netted its publishers a fortune, paid Marmontel 30,000 *livres* for rights to it in 1772; the sum astounded Meister, who claimed it was Marmontel's name, not the merits of the book, which brought forth such a scarcely conceivable fee.[13] His fame, it appeared to some contemporaries, was even transferable. When in 1785, Morellet, who had written almost nothing of literary merit, was voted a member of the Académie Française, the distraught authors of the *Mémoires secrets* could only explain, "His great title is to be the uncle of Mme Marmontel."[14]

Suard's rise within the literary world was scarcely less striking than Marmontel's. He had been far from well-launched upon a career in the 1750s, but his mastery of English provided him with the means to success. As a translator he soon became associated with the abbé Arnaud, a collaboration which lasted a lifetime, and throughout the 1750s they published editions of translations from English literature and literary journals. Such work coincided with and contributed to a rising anglophilia in Paris and brought them to the attention of higher society and the public. One of Arnaud's protectresses, the comtesse de Tesse, and one of Suard's, the princesse de Beauvau, Saint-Lambert's close friend, prevailed upon the duc de Choiseul to grant them the editorship of the *Journal étranger*, which was under his jurisdiction at the ministry of foreign affairs. They edited this review from 1760 to 1762. In 1764 Choiseul established them as editors of the *Gazette littéraire*, also under his jurisdiction, and ordered French embassies all over Europe to supply them with literary news. The ministry abandoned this publication in 1764, but Suard and Arnaud were then given the direction of its *Gazette de France*. Mme Suard later wrote that it was

[12] No one else addressed the Académie so frequently, nor read so many verses and excerpts of his works to it. See Institut de France, *Les Registres de l'Académie Française 1672-1793*, III, 174-534.

[13] Meister, in Grimm, *Corr. litt.*, XI, 454-456.

[14] Bachaumont, *Mémoires secrets*, XXVIII, 325.

190

as editor of this gazette that her husband advanced from "medioc-rity" to "wealth."[15]

Throughout this period, and throughout the years that fol-lowed, Suard's reputation as a translator earned him important recognition. Hume chose him as his translator in France, as did Robertson, whose *History of Charles V* earned Suard his greatest literary fame. These translations alone, according to his friend Garat, gave Suard "a bit of *aisance*." The eminent Gibbon solicited him as his translator, but Suard was by this point secure enough to decline the honor. When Walpole asked the well-placed Mme du Deffand to recommend a translator, she chose Suard.[16]

Although the disgrace of his benefactor Choiseul brought about a few years of relative obscurity for Suard, his star was soon again on the ascendant. In 1774 he was received as a member of the Académie Française, and the usual (perhaps, in his case, a dispro-portionately great) amount of official literary honors, sinecures and rewards soon followed. He was given a well-pensioned sine-cure at the *Almanach royal*, appointed as censor to the *Journal de Paris* and, with no manifest musical abilities (but an ardent "Gluckiste," which would have pleased the queen) named a cen-sor at the Opéra.[17] These appointments culminated in his being named by 1780 the censor of all published or performed dramatic works in Paris, a post from which he tyrannized the literary com-munity. It was Suard, most students of the eighteenth century will recall, who censored and sought the suppression of Beaumar-chais' *Mariage de Figaro*. His prestige, nevertheless, was real; in the election of 1783 to the post of *secrétaire-perpétuel* of the Académie, Suard finished second in the voting to Marmontel.[18]

Less dramatic, but also less vital to their over-all stations in life, were the literary careers of Chastellux and Saint-Lambert; both of these soldiers nevertheless found their efforts in the letters recog-nized and rewarded by their society. Chastellux saw his verse well-

---

[15] Mme Suard, *Suard*, 92 ff; Hunter, *Suard*, 88-107.

[16] Garat, *Suard*, I, 343-363; Gibbon, *Letters*, II, 121-124; *Lettres de la marquise du Deffand à Horace Walpole*, P. Toynbee, ed., I, 385, 393, 396; Suard, *Mémoires et correspondances*, 103-110.

[17] Mme Suard, *Suard*, 132-133; Bachaumont, *Mémoires secrets*, XXI, 97-99, 163-164.

[18] On Suard's judgments as censor, see, for example, Suard, *Mémoires et correspondances*, 160-210; Grimm, *Corr. litt.*, XIV, 91-93, 116-119. On the election at the Académie Française, see Grimm, *Corr. litt.*, XIII, 401-402.

received in salons, and his plays, primarily society comedies, performed at Chantilly, the estate of the prince de Condé.[19] In 1775 he was elected to the Académie Française although, as Meister observed at the time, it was not certain whether he had been elected as "a man of letters or a man of quality."[20]

This involvement with the world of letters in no way detracted from Chastellux's military career. When he solicited the ministry of war for a post in the American campaigns, in which he served from 1780 to 1783, he was recommissioned as a *maréchal de camp*, second in rank only to Rochambeau himself. Because of his fluency in English, Chastellux served as liaison officer between the French and American commands. He travelled throughout the United States, and in the course of his activities became an intimate friend of George Washington, James Madison and Gouverneur Morris, with all of whom he corresponded on the warmest terms after his return to France. Upon that return he was rewarded with the important posts of *inspecteur de l'infanterie* and *gouverneur* of Longwy.[21]

Saint-Lambert's distinguished military career never attained the glitter of Chastellux's, but it was not an insignificant one. After a brief retirement from the military in 1758, he was recalled in 1759 to serve as an *aide-major-général* in the expeditionary corps assembled in Brittany in 1759, and he did not officially resign his commission until 1761. As in the case of Chastellux, his literary pursuits did not diminish his military stature, and in 1776 he was appointed as military *gouverneur* of Joinville, a sinecure.[22]

What truly interested Saint-Lambert, however, was the world of letters, and it was in this realm that he was most avid for glory. He received it. He had enjoyed moderate successes with his "Essai sur le luxe," an article for the *Encyclopédie* which enjoyed a separate printing in 1764, and with his often reprinted *conte, Sara Th—*. In 1769, however, Saint-Lambert achieved one of the most (contemporaneously) heralded literary successes of the eighteenth

[19] Grimm, *Corr. litt.*, passim. His plays were also performed at the private theater of de Magnanville, *garde du trésor royal*, at the latter's chateau at Chevrette (ibid., IX, 297-298).

[20] Ibid., XI, 66-69; see also Bachaumont, *Mémoires secrets*, XXX, 234, "Additions."

[21] See "Letters of Chastellux" discussing his involvement in American campaigns and his appointments upon his return to France, in Carson, *Chastellux*, 142 ff; see also Chastellux, *Voyages dans l'Amérique*.

[22] Mangeot, *Autour d'un Foyer Lorrain*, 88-89.

century, his *Les Saisons*, whose views of nature and the French countryside, and whose contrasts of war and rural peace, charmed the public and earned him fame. He had worked on it, according to his friends, for fifteen to twenty years, and its triumph must have mattered a great deal to him. On the basis of this work he was elected in 1770 to the Académie Française. Collé, one of the few who did not join in the celebration of Saint-Lambert's poem, could scarcely believe his sudden ascent: "M. de Saint-Lambert was in the Army; he has the *croix de Saint-Louis*; they say he spent his youth in Lorraine, at the court of King Stanislaus, whom he stuffed with servile madrigals. . . . He wanted to live with men of the court, and he perpetually praised them in prose and verse: they have become his partisans. He is supported, besides, by a cabal of the Encyclopédistes. . . . Whatever he is, there he is a member of the Académie."[23]

Despite the criticism of Collé, and of Grimm, who also could not understand the enthusiasm for the poem, Saint-Lambert's popularity continued to increase.[24] *Les Saisons* was reprinted continuously throughout the century, and to each new edition Saint-Lambert would add other verses, and even unrelated *contes* and fables, all of which were acclaimed loudly by the literary public. The reputation which he gained, we soon shall see, he was willing to go to great lengths to preserve.

Although Morellet gained an immediate literary reputation upon his election to the Académie Française in 1785, even he felt obliged to justify publicly his inclusion in that august literary body, and in his inaugural discourse he offered a brief eulogy of his predecessor, followed, most unusually, by a description of his own accomplishments. He had rectified, he claimed, the language of commerce during his long period of interest in and writing on commercial affairs. Two speakers followed him that day—Chastellux, who as *directeur* welcomed him effusively, and Marmontel, who as *secrétaire-perpétuel* spoke on the importance of clarity of language. It was a good day for the three friends.[25]

Chastellux, however, committed an indiscretion that day, recalling, in his welcome of Morellet, how Lord Shelburne had se-

---

[23] Collé, *Journal et mémoires*, III, 254-256.

[24] Grimm, *Corr. litt.*, VII, 277-288.

[25] *Registres de l'Académie Française*, III, 556, 558; Morellet, *Mémoires*, I, 277-284; Bachaumont, *Mémoires secrets*, XXVIII, 325; XXIX, 88-94; Marmontel, *Mémoires*, I, 179-180.

cured a secret pension for the new academician from the ministry of foreign affairs as part of the peace settlement of 1783, in return for services rendered in the establishment of that peace. This infuriated the French ministry, who did not want such information made public, but it reminded all listeners of the more important side of Morellet's career, and that part of his life which the academician took the most seriously—his involvement in the affairs of government and administration.[26]

By 1760, we already have seen, Morellet was a ghostwriter and spokesman for important elements within the administration of finances. With his usual disarming candor, he admitted freely in his *Mémoires* how many of his own works were written on the basis of the orders of and often the information provided by others, and how diligently he sought to ingratiate himself with those administrators sympathetic to freer internal and external trade, to secure for himself pensions and rewards. In the 1760s and '70s, reformers within the ruling circles of the administration frequently used Morellet's pen to see that points of view which they favored were expressed without their own overt involvement in the matter. Thus, as Morellet admitted in his *Mémoires*, even his celebrated translation of Beccaria's *Dei Delitti e Delle Pene* was written at the instigation of Malesherbes.[27]

In 1768-1769 Morellet entered the lists against his good friend Necker over the issue of the monopolistic *compagnie des Indes*. D'Invaux, the *contrôleur-général*, "charged me" with the task of writing against the *compagnie*, and Boutin, *conseiller d'état* and *commissaire du roi*, "had all of the documents of the situation communicated to me." Morellet began what proved to be a lengthy series of brochures on the matter.

The memoirs against monopoly led Morellet into an intense period of writing for ministers, *secrétaires* and *intendants*: for Choiseul and Trudaine, his refutation of Galiani's attack on free trade in grains; for Trudaine, his attack upon Linguet; for Sartine and Le Noir, diverse memoirs on the provisioning of Paris. These are the writings which earned Morellet his public recognition. They all represented not a philosophical party's opposition to the government, but one powerful side of an intragovernmental struggle for control over French commercial and fiscal policies. Occasionally his writings were suppressed (by Terray, for example),

[26] Morellet, *Mémoires*, I, 277-284.   [27] Morellet, *Mémoires*, I, 157-158.

only to be published at last under Turgot. This did not represent two different administrative attitudes toward the Enlightenment; Morellet, as a respected and useful thinker and writer, was simply in the employ, and soon an integral part, of an administrative element that was alternately more or less in control of the ministries. Later, in a moment of panic during the Terror, Morellet would attempt to present these works as signs of his having been a fearless and lonely enemy of past tyranny.[28] He did not convince anyone.

The period following the disgrace of Choiseul was not one favorable to Morellet's career, but these were not difficult years for him. Trudaine had introduced him to the powerful Lord Shelburne (it was, perhaps, Morellet who introduced Shelburne to d'Holbach's home), and in 1772 Shelburne invited Morellet to England where he went, on Trudaine's advice and funds, to study English matters of commerce. This connection led Shelburne to use Morellet's good offices in 1782-1783, leading to the latter's secret pension.[29] By then, however, Morellet already was a truly important figure in France, for the ministry of Turgot raised him to an eminence and wealth that would survive the minister's disgrace.

Under Turgot, Morellet served not only as a writer but as a member of Turgot's informal circle of advisors, and he was well-rewarded. He frequently dined with Turgot at Versailles, and according to Galiani, he was "all powerful beside the *contrôleur-général*."[30] He was scarcely that, of course, but the appearance of such power did not harm a man's standing in the world. When Mlle de Lespinasse dined at Versailles, she sat "between the Archbishop of Aix and Morellet."[31] When the ministers assembled at Montigny, Trudaine's estate, to choose a new minister of war in October 1775, Morellet was there.[32] Mme d'Epinay wrote to Galiani that "prosperity suits Panurge [Morellet's nickname] marvelously, and he has changed greatly to his advantage . . . calm . . . polite . . . less opinionated."[33]

In the years following Turgot's fall, Morellet, now indepen-

[28] Ibid., II, 74-76.
[29] Ibid., I, 195-210; see also Morellet, *Lettres à Shelburne*.
[30] Galiani, *Lettres*, II, 189-190.
[31] Mlle de Lespinasse, *Lettres*, E. Asse, ed., 119.
[32] Ibid., 245-249.
[33] Mme d'Epinay, *Lettere (Gli Ultimi Anni)*, 136.

dently wealthy, devoted himself to his family and friends, initiating his own salon, offering occasional (and minor) literary pieces, and moving in the circles of Mme Helvétius, Loménie de Brienne and, despite his economic differences with him, Necker. A member of the Académie and an influential public figure, Morellet was called upon after 1785 to return to the attack against the newly reconstituted *compagnie des Indes*, this time in the name of the maritime cities and their Parisian agents. When Loménie de Brienne succeeded to the ministry, Morellet addressed a series of memoirs to him in the name of the proponents of free trade, and moved once more to influence and guide the actions of the monarchy and its *conseil*. As he later put it so succinctly, such power was no longer his: "But the torrent of civil discords soon carried off our memoirs, and the *compagnie des Indes*, and the monarchy."[34]

Raynal, it will be recalled, had secured his own close connections with the ministries long before Morellet had begun his career, and by the 1750s had already converted his rewards into substantial wealth, largely in the form of *rentes*.[35] This gave him an independence and ease which allowed him to pursue less a career than a life-style of his own choosing. He drew upon his friends and their contacts for the information utilized in his *Histoire philosophique des Deux Indes*, frequented both the "philosophical" and the more worldly salons, and worked on his *Histoire* continuously. Occasionally he would, like Morellet, produce works on behalf of his reform-minded friends in the administration, such as his three-volume *Ecole militaire*, "composed by order of the government" and published in 1762, his *Considérations sur la paix de 1783*, or his critical *Essai sur l'administration de Saint-Domingue* (1785). Morellet, discussing his friend's place in d'Holbach's group, recalled that "The abbé Raynal . . . spoke of almost nothing but politics and commerce. . . . He was priceless to our society, because he knew very well the news of the day, and because of his liaisons with M. de Puysieux and M. de Saint-Severin."[36] His *Histoire philosophique des Deux Indes* went

[34] Morellet, *Mémoires*, I, 236-315. The final quotation is from p. 315.

[35] Raynal also loaned substantial amounts of money to private persons at 4 per cent interest; a list of such loans during an unspecified period prior to the Revolution can be found among his personal papers in the B.N., MS *Fonds français*, 6429, folios 4-5.

[36] Morellet, *Mémoires*, I, 214-215.

through more than forty editions in his own lifetime and made him one of the most widely known and heralded philosophes of France, and perhaps, after the deaths of Rousseau and Voltaire, the most celebrated. Despite, we shall see, the eventual and long-delayed personal difficulties which his *Histoire* caused him, he lived a comfortable and favored life until the Revolution.

Grimm had to work harder at the task than Raynal, but he too succeeded in obtaining the life-style he desired, although for Grimm life-style and career were inseparable. He was, and he hid it from no one, a man who wished to be useful to the titled and the powerful, to be their agent, their confidant, their advisor, and indeed their friend. He utilized his initial German contacts in the capital to establish himself as a valuable Parisian agent for an assortment of German courts, and his rise in international diplomacy and service was surely more than even he initially could have expected. Those who sought his talents included: in the beginning, the municipal leaders of Frankfort, the hereditary prince of Brunswick, the margrave of Baden, the prince and landgrave of Hesse-Darmstadt, the ducal family of Würtemberg, the court of Saxe-Gotha, the electress of Saxony, and the margrave of Brandenburg-Anspach; by the end of the 1760s, the royal family of Sweden, Catherine the Great, the court of Vienna, Frederick the Great, and the prince of Brunswick; by the 1770s, the duke of Weimar, and the king of Poland.[37] From 1759 to 1761 he served as the *chargé d'affaires* of the imperial city of Frankfort at the court of France, but when the French intercepted one of his dispatches and discovered that he had made humorous remarks at the expense of certain French ministers, he lost his place.[38] His German patrons compensated him for his loss, however, and in return for services he was made a baron of the Holy Roman Empire in 1770. In 1769 and 1770 he made a tour of central Europe which developed into a series of diplomatic and personal receptions from court to court. In 1775 he became the *ministre-plénipotentiare* of the duke of Saxe-Gotha to the court of France, and Mme d'Epi-

[37] Meister, "Grimm," in *Corr. litt.*, 1, 5-11; Grimm, "Mémoire historique sur l'origine et les suites de mon attachement pour l'Impératrice Cathérine II," in ibid., 17-63; Grimm, *Lettres à Cathérine II*; Grimm, "Lettres à la Reine-Mère de Suède," V. Bowen, ed., *Revue de littérature comparée* (1958), 565-572; Cazes, *Grimm et les Encyclopédistes*, 365-377.

[38] Meister, "Grimm," 5, wrote that Grimm had referred to the comte de Broglie as "le capitaine Tempesta."

nay could write to Galiani: "M. le baron de Grimm moves about more than ever in high society. I hardly see him. There he is, attached to the diplomatic corps. The duke of Gotha has made him his minister at our court; the duke of Weimar has done as much for him; thus, his fate is fixed. . . . it is a great affair to have here [in Paris] a secure and fixed state."[39]

Grimm indeed had a remarkable way with royalty. In his *Correspondance littéraire*, to which many of his foreign patrons and employers subscribed, he wrote candidly and openly, never disguising his skepticism, his anticlericalism, his close friendships with atheists and, indeed, occasional republicans. He continued to use it as a vehicle for increasing the reputation of his friends abroad, especially of Diderot, although he rarely hesitated to condemn many of their works as second-rate in the light of some rarely attained intellectual and aesthetic ideal. There is, at present, disagreement on the question of exactly who, in fact, subscribed to his literary service, but there is agreement that Catherine the Great, the king of Sweden, the court of Saxe-Gotha and the king of Poland were among those who did, undoubtedly joined by several German courts.[40] By 1770 Grimm was too busy to continue writing this correspondence himself, and he delegated it to Meister, a young Swiss who had come to Paris in circumstances similar to Grimm's earlier situation. Grimm maintained, however, a personal and strikingly familiar and undeferential correspondence with Catherine the Great, and with the queen-mother of Sweden.[41]

It is remarkable to see Grimm at the height of his success, being veritably courted by the crowns of Europe. In 1774 the king of Poland, Stanislaus-Augustus, received Grimm, and wrote enthusiastically to Mme Geoffrin, expressing his hope that Grimm had not merely feigned interest in him. Grimm's singular reception by Catherine created a sensation in Paris, and Mme Geoffrin expressed her wonder that he ever would return to France.[42]

All these foreign connections made Grimm a valuable person ultimately for the French ministry of foreign affairs as well, and

[39] Mme d'Epinay, *Lettere (Gli Ultimi Anni)*, 164; Meister, "Grimm," 5-11; Cazes, op. cit., 367-370, 375-376; Grimm, *Corr. litt.*, VIII, 426; XVI, 451, 463, 467.

[40] The compelling argument in this belongs to Joseph R. Smiley, "The Subscribers of Grimm's *Correspondance littéraire*," *MLN* (1947), 44-46.

[41] See above, n. 37.

[42] Mme Geoffrin, *Corr.*, 472, 481; see also 465-466, 470, 485, 501.

under Vergennes he performed diplomatic services for his adopted nation, serving as an intermediary, for example, between Vergennes' staff and Barbé-Marbois in the United States during the American campaign.[43] Thomas Jefferson called Grimm "the pleasantest and most conversable member of the diplomatic corps."[44] By 1789 he was at the height of his importance.

It was Grimm, through his influence with Catherine, who allowed his friend Diderot to achieve his own most desired professional ambition, which was to have the financial independence to write what he wanted for posterity, free from the need to satisfy the publishers and their demands. Diderot maintained his reasonably profitable relationship with the *Encyclopédie* and the fruits of the *rente* he had acquired in the late 1750s, and to be sure, his editorship of the *Encyclopédie* had made him one of the best-known and most celebrated men of letters in Europe. Yet he was unhappy over the constant demands upon his time and his lack of some greater financial ease. In 1765 Grimm convinced Catherine to become Diderot's benefactress, and the Empress purchased Diderot's library for the grossly inflated price of 15,000 *livres*, granting him not only usufruct during his lifetime, but paying him 1,000 *livres* per year as its guardian; in 1766 she sent him 50,000 *livres* in one lump sum, as his payment for the next fifty years.[45] In return he wrote flattering statements about her and sent her memoirs on politics and administration.[46] In 1773 Grimm made him come along to Saint Petersburg to meet and flatter his benefactress in person, and there Catherine returned the pleasantries in kind. If this relationship indeed allowed Diderot the peace of mind to write the great philosophical works composed after 1765 and left in Naigeon's hands for posthumous publication, it was an excellent bargain.

For the others, Naigeon, Helvétius, Le Roy, and d'Holbach, it is difficult to speak of their "careers" at all. None of them after 1760 sought personal recognition for their written works, Naigeon, Le Roy, and d'Holbach publishing anonymously or pseudonymously, and Helvétius, bullied into silence by the events of 1758-1759, writing for posthumous publication. Naigeon worked closely with d'Holbach, apparently well-supported by him (for

[43] B.N., *Fonds français*, 12,768, folios 272-277.
[44] Quoted in Wilson, *Diderot*, 120.
[45] Diderot, *Corr.*, v, 25-34; vi, 354-361.
[46] Diderot, *Corr.*, vi, 355-358; xiv, 78-86.

it was only after d'Holbach's death that he began publishing almost anything—including editions of Rousseau's works—in an effort to find revenues), and commenting in 1789 that d'Holbach had been a father to him.[47] In 1781 he did receive an indication that his knowledge and erudition might prove rewarding, when the publisher Panckouke, who was Suard's brother-in-law, awarded him the editorship of the four volumes on philosophy in the new *Encyclopédie méthodique*, a prestigious publishing venture.[48] Le Roy, enjoying his days as *lieutenant des chasses* at Versailles, lived a life of leisure, publishing his letters on animals and man when he thought the time right, often in Suard's gazettes, and saving others for publication after his death. For a time he appears to have served as an officer in the administration of the *maison du roi*, in which capacity he became involved in the dispensation of patronage, writing Buffon in 1771 in the name of "M. le duc d'Aumont, with whom I supped yesterday," on the matter of Buffon's charge as *intendant du jardin du roi*.[49] Helvétius lived richly and generously in Voré and Paris, tending to his estates, entertaining his friends, patronizing the letters and arts, and writing the works he hoped would avenge *De l'esprit* after his death. D'Holbach succeeded in making his salon one of the most celebrated in Europe, supported young free-thinkers, managed his wealth, and enjoyed the storms his own works caused. His scientific translations earned him membership in the academies of Mannheim and Saint Petersburg, and that for him was official recognition enough. He was in some ways the member of the coterie least ambitious for fame.

* * *

Participation in what Brissot later was to term derisively "that aristocracy of talent" was profitable for the members of the coterie holbachique.[50] Often they simply were rewarded for services rendered, such as Morellet's and Raynal's acquisition of pensions in return for their services to the ministries and *chambres*. At a more personal level, the duc d'Aiguillon could call upon Marmontel to write an eloquent brief for him in a lawsuit being heard

[47] *Journal de Paris* (1789), 9 February.

[48] Diderot, *Corr.*, xv, 228.

[49] Buffon, *Correspondance inédite du Buffon*, 397, n. 1.

[50] J.-P. Brissot de Warville, *Mémoires . . . sur ses contemporains et la révolution française*, F. de Montrol, ed., i, 75-79. (Brissot was writing in reference to Raynal in this passage.)

by the parlement de Bretagne. When the brief succeeded, d'Aiguillon paid his debt handsomely; as he wrote to Marmontel: "I have just asked the king, Monsieur, for the place of *historiographe de France* for you. . . . His Majesty has granted it. . . . I hasten to announce this to you. Come give thanks to the king."[51] According to Bachaumont, the duc d'Orléans pensioned Marmontel with 800 *livres* per year in return for the author's aiding his reputation in the journals. According to d'Angiviller, Necker gave Suard, d'Angiviller's good friend, 20,000 *livres* to write articles favorable to the Swiss banker and official in the Parisian press.[52]

It is impossible to establish with any precision the wealth of the members of the coterie holbachique, and estimates would in all probability be lower than the actual figures, for undoubtedly many sources of income were, if not covert, at least not openly discussed. Many documents relating to their fortunes are missing or incomplete. Nevertheless, the information that does exist points to a situation very close to *aisance* for most of d'Holbach's initiates.

Those who had acquired wealth by the 1750s appear to have suffered no reverses in the course of the following decades. The initial domain purchased by Helvétius in the Perche had included eighty-nine fiefs divided into eight parishes; ten successful farms; over three square miles of forests; and numerous profitable installations (such as granaries, mills and ovens) and rights (such as high, middle and low justice, tolls and passage charges). He added to his holdings and rights continuously, and by the year of his death possessed the leading domain of the region.[53] He owned a large home in Paris as well, and as Gibbon described him in 1763, the former tax-farmer's life was a good one: "He has a very pretty

[51] Lenel, *Marmontel*, 418-419. See also Grimm, *Corr. litt.*, x, 18.

[52] D'Angiviller, "Episodes de ma Vie," in *Efterladte Papierer fra den Reventlowske Familiekreds I Tidsrummet* 1770-1827, L. Bobé, ed., 198; Bachaumont, *Mémoires secrets*, XXXIV, 100.

[53] D'Andlau, *Helvétius*, passim; on p. 83 d'Andlau, noting Helvétius' manifest efforts to preserve and expand his rights and revenues, concluded, "Helvétius, it is obvious, was very devoted to the maintenance of his seigneurial rights." There is evidence, however, that for all this concern, Helvétius did not punish his peasants for violations of these, and he also worked diligently to free them from impositions such as the maintenance of troops. He encouraged the development of light industry on his domains, and appears to have accepted in his own management of his estates the philosophical dictum that the prosperity of the sovereign was dependent upon the prosperity of his subjects (ibid., 60-66).

wife, a hundred thousand *livres* a year, and one of the best tables in Paris."[54] When he died his estate was valued at "almost four million [*livres*] in possessions."[55] D'Holbach may or may not have been quite so wealthy personally, but he managed the fortunes of a family of extraordinary means. Morellet estimated his annual income from *rentes* alone, independent of the revenues produced by his extensive landholdings, as 60,000 *livres*, but this probably was a low estimate; Morellet termed "a small landholding" a property that d'Holbach sold for 400,000 *livres*.[56] In addition to his expensive offices, and the home on the rue Royale, d'Holbach owned and rented for profit a large house at 24 rue St.-Anne, abutting his own residence.[57] He spent over 60,000 *livres* to secure for his eldest son the post of *conseiller au parlement* in 1775, and in 1781 he provided his youngest daughter with a dowry of 150,000 *livres*, both of these without any apparent loss of his own comfort.[58] He was wealthy and secure enough to face possible drastic losses from fiscal machinations with a certain humor and equanimity. Diderot quoted him as saying to his wife, when he was being subjected to drastic forced "loans" during the Seven Years' War: ". . . if that continues, I'll surrender the equipage, I'll buy you a lovely hat with a handsome parasol, and we will bless for the rest of our lives [the *contrôleur-général*] who will have delivered us from horses, lackeys, coachmen, maids, cooks, great dinners, false friends, boring people and all of the other privileges of opulence."[59] In 1770 he wrote to Galiani that he had shown the wit to lose at least temporarily some 80,000 *livres* under the régime instituted by Terray.[60]

[54] Gibbon, *Letters*, I, 133-134.

[55] Keim, *Helvétius*, 597-599; Bachaumont, *Mémoires secrets*, VI, 196. According to Grimm, *Corr. litt.*, IX, 417-424, Helvétius left 50,000 *livres* per year in *rentes* to each of his two daughters, so that "they will have only the burden of choice in finding husbands." Grimm, in this obituary notice, wrote of d'Holbach and Helvétius as "two men of merit, both of them wealthy, who have both passed their lives with men of letters." On Helvétius' great wealth in general, see d'Andlau, op. cit.

[56] Lough, "Le baron d'Holbach."

[57] *Atlas de la Censive de l'Archevêché dans Paris*, Armand Brette, ed., plate XIV. The existence of this house is the only item of which I am aware that has escaped the attention of Lough, "Le baron d'Holbach."

[58] Lough, "Le baron d'Holbach," 533-534.

[59] Diderot, *Corr.*, II, 318. (Cited also by Lough, "Le baron d'Holbach.")

[60] D'Holbach, "Lettres à Galiani," 31. (Cited also by Lough, "Le baron d'Holbach.")

Raynal was secure enough by 1788 to bestow some 50,000 *livres* upon the royal Académies. One can assume that this represented but an easily expendable portion of the monies he had placed in *rentes*.[61] For Le Roy there are no figures available which indicate his wealth, but he lived *noblement*, aided the Suards during their period of difficulty, refused payment from Diderot for his work for the *Encyclopédie*, and indulged himself with the style, at least, of a man of ease.[62] Diderot described him as going nowhere and doing nothing during "the season of the hunt, which he loves with a passion."[63] Chastellux must have inherited considerable wealth from his family, and there are indications he was a man of great fortune. Mlle de Lespinasse described him in the 1770s as someone "so rich and so generous . . . giving everywhere and to everyone."[64] Such *largesse*, however, apparently did not dissipate his fortune. In 1784 the French officers who joined the American Society of Cincinnatus were assessed in dues a sum "in proportion" to their conditions; Chastellux was charged twice as much as the other *maréchaux de camp* (4,000 *livres* instead of 2,000).[65] This sum was more than compensated for by his succession upon his return to the post of *gouverneur de Longwy*, which carried a *traitement* of 10,000 *livres* per year, independent of all his other military pensions, and even provided a pension of 4,000 *livres* per year for his wife, after his death.[66] It is doubtful, however, that

[61] B.N., MS *Fonds français*, 6429, folios 11-14. The exact total of his gifts was 51,428 *livres*, 10 *sols*. This same memoir includes a list drawn up by Raynal, apparently for his collector Corrange, of interests due to him from loans to relatives and friends; if, as he indicated, they were arranged at 4 per cent, they represented a total of 143,000 *livres*. How much money he had invested in the "*rentes* on the revenues of the king" from which he drew his gifts to the Académies is not indicated, but he did not have a reputation for undue charity, and one must speculate that the 50,000 *livres* were but an unimportant portion of these.

[62] See Garat, *Suard*, 316 *ff*; Diderot, *Corr.*, VII, 158-159; IX, 29-31; and Hennin's manuscript in Bibliothèque de l'Institut, MS 1223, folios 82-87. See also Mme du Deffand, *Lettres à Walpole*, III, 170, 204, where we find Le Roy in the social company of the prince and princesse de Beauvau, Necker, président de Cotte, the bishop of Arras, the comte de Broglio, and the maréchale de Luxembourg.

[63] Diderot, *Corr.*, VII, 157-160.

[64] Lespinasse, *Lettres* (Asse), 140-141.

[65] Bachaumont, *Mémoires secrets*, XXV, 70-71.

[66] *Etat nominatif des pensions sur le trésor royal*, Assemblée Nationale, I, 166, 280, 318 (on the post of *gouverneur de Longwy*); and the *Livre rouge . . . des pensions sur le trésor royal*, 10th Supplement, 44-46, for the pension accorded the wife of Chastellux.

this represented anything important in the total of Chastellux's wealth.

Farthest removed from great prosperity among the members of the coterie holbachique was Roux, whose means were noted as being particularly "modest" by two of his friends, Darcet and Deleyre. It is interesting to note what constituted modesty, however, for both of these men were struck by Roux's ability to live on annual *rentes* of 5,000 *livres* and to support certain of his less fortunate friends and relatives from this sum. It is not clear if that figure included the 3,000 *livres* per year he received from his post at Saint-Gobain, and it did not include whatever he earned from occasionally practicing medicine.[67] Roux's decision to abandon a major medical practice, however, indicates that he found his situation more than sufficient, for as an important *docteur-régent* of the Faculté de Médecine of the University of Paris, he could have earned some six *livres* per visit and twelve *livres* per consultation, sums which a diligent practice could have multiplied into an important income.[68] Darcet, with his patrons, sinecures and official positions at the mint, the porcelain works at Sèvres, and the *manufacture* at Gobelins, probably earned three or four times what Roux had secured.[69]

Grimm's economic position reflected the regal wealth of his patrons and employers. He lived extravagantly, and among the papers seized from his Parisian home were large numbers of bills and receipts from merchants in the luxury trades, including many for an expensive, perfumed "fine powder" for his wigs. By 1771 he was seeking advice on how best to invest some 186,000 *livres* which he had not yet placed in *rentes*. In a detailed memoir to the French government in 1801, he valued the possessions and capital seized from him at 554,894 *livres*.[70] Simply, he was the favorite of rulers who were generous to him and to those whom he recommended to them, and he profited enormously. When he casually

---

[67] Deleyre, *Eloge de Roux*, 56-58; Darcet, *Eloge de Roux*, 15-19. Both men agreed that Roux was able to furnish a fine private laboratory and scientific library with his means.

[68] Delauney, *Le monde médical Parisien*, 34.

[69] This is possibly a low estimate, for many *inspecteurs* in the *manufactures* received considerable incomes from their work; see F. Bacquié, *Les inspecteurs des manufactures sous l'Ancien Régime, 1669-1791*. That he saw Roux's 5,000 *livres* as notably mediocre tells us something about his position.

[70] On 1771, see Diderot, *Corr.*, XI, 86-89; on his alleged fortune by 1789, see A.N., MS F⁷ 5624.

mentioned to Catherine in 1782 that Mme d'Epinay had lost 8,000 *livres* in yearly income under Necker's reforms, the empress sent him 16,000 *livres* to give to his friend. When Grimm wrote to Catherine of the inadequate dowry of his protégé, the comtesse de Belsunce (later the comtesse de Bueil), the empress sent him 12,000 *roubles* for her. He and his friends prospered.[71]

Diderot by 1771 estimated his fortune (in a letter to his sister) at "not far from 200,000 *francs*," predicting that it soon would increase by fifty per cent, and ultimately be double that original amount. From his father's estate, which had prospered greatly in the end, he had inherited the better third of some 200,000 *livres* in capital, properties and goods. In 1772 he could provide a dowry for his Angélique of 30,000 *livres* (as a *rente* of 1,500 *livres* per year), and in 1775 could establish a modest independent income for his wife from an investment of 20,000 *livres*. He lived in comfort.[72] Saint-Lambert's fortune had been assured by his relationship with Mme d'Houdetot and the great success of *Les Saisons*. He owned a home in Paris designed by the celebrated Ledoux and either owned or rented an estate at Eaubonne, near the chateau of Mme d'Houdetot. In addition he received 3,725 *livres* in royal pensions, most of these rewards for his military service, plus the revenues from the lands he inherited from his father.[73]

Naigeon's circumstances remain obscure, but the financial successes of Suard, Morellet and Marmontel were perhaps, given their origins, the most remarkable of all. In 1770-1771 during a period of disgrace, Suard experienced a few months of what his wife termed "poverty" before his friends began to rescue him. What his wife meant by poverty was "only 1,000 *ecus* [3,000 *livres*]

[71] *Lettres de Cathérine II à Grimm*, 225; see also ibid., passim, and Grimm, "Mémoire historique," for similar examples of Catherine's generosity. On Grimm's expenditures on luxury items, see A.N., MS T 319[5] (which was called to my attention by Wilson, *Diderot*, 119-120).

[72] On Diderot's financial status until the mid-1760s, see J. Proust, *Diderot et l'Encyclopédie*, 81-113; on his daughter's dowry, see the documents published in Diderot, *Corr.*, XII, 119-120; on his establishment of a *rente* for his wife, see *Corr.*, XIV, 148-149. The revenues from the family's farm in Langres varied, but in 1777, when it brought Diderot only 796 *livres*, he told his sister not to be at all concerned about this apparently unusually low return (*Corr.*, XV, 73); on Diderot's evaluation of his fortune at 200,000 *francs* in 1771, and his hopes of doubling it, see *Corr.*, XI, 141-142.

[73] On Saint-Lambert's residence and mode of entertaining, see *Censive*, plate III; Mme Suard, *Suard*, 54-72; on his pensions, see *Etat nominatif des pensions*, I, 517-518. See also Mangeot, *Autour d'un foyer lorrain*.

of *rente*."[74] He returned to favor, however, and began a remarkable accumulation of pensioned places and sinecures. By the early 1780s, his wife admitted, despite her tendency to portray them as continually making do with the barest necessities, he had added some 12,000 *livres* in official pensions to those recent *rentes* which he had established with Necker's and Coigny's generous rewards, and the Suards began their period of "a *grande aisance*." Suard bought a home in Paris, a country home at Fontenay-aux-Roses, a cabriolet, and hired the services of coachmen and lackeys.[75] By 1789, not including the returns on his very successful translations, he was receiving over 18,500 *livres* in *rentes*, and was himself entertaining at his own salon in grand style.[76]

Morellet was yet more successful. As an ecclesiastic he was eligible for benefices, and his important friends secured these for him to the extent of 30,000 *livres* annually by 1772, which led the abbé Galiani to write him to cease attacking the Church and to join in the "cause" of Italian music: "It is patently better to reason badly about music, while sipping the champagne of Baron d'Holbach, than to rant against the Church when one receives 30,000 *livres* per year to pray for it."[77]

In addition to these ecclesiastic revenues, Morellet enjoyed important pensions from the *chambres de commerce*, a *rente* of 2,000 *livres* per year left to him by Mme Geoffrin in her will, and diverse remunerations for his services to individual intendants, ministers and cities. He also received an annual retainer by the would-be publishers of that *Dictionnaire du commerce* which he never produced. His description of his life during the last years of the Ancien Régime reveals that he had achieved a position

[74] Mme Suard, *Suard*, 84-88. Diderot, at the time, referred to Suard's pension from the *Gazette de France* as having been "a small fortune," and spoke of "these thousands of *écus* of revenues" enjoyed by his friend (Diderot, *Corr.*, IV, 171, 205).

[75] Mme Suard, *Suard*, 137-138; Suard's house was on the northeast corner of the rue Saint-Honoré and the rue du Four, see *Censive*, plate XXXIV.

[76] Hunter, *Suard*, 144.

[77] Galiani, *Lettres*, II, 308-312. In 1788 Morellet added the priory of Thimer to this, with a country habitation and 15,000 to 16,000 *livres* in annual *rente*. It had, in addition, "seigneurial rights of the hunt, of *cens*, and of honorific *rentes*." According to Morellet, he spent 2,000 *livres* on furniture for his new country home, and hired several skilled artisans to work on it for several weeks (Morellet, *Mémoires*, I, 325-327).

which afforded no small degree of pleasure: "Committed but not obliged to this consequential work [on commerce]; surrounded by my family [having brought a brother and sister to Paris and secured their financial independence]; having a handsome lodging, friends [who were] men of letters, men of the world, artists; frequent good music at my home, and always good conversation [having established a salon at his own home]; also going to dine several times a week at the homes of my friends; regularly spending two or three days at Auteuil, where I had the company of Franklin and all of that of Mme Helvétius; and during the summer and fall, going to the valley of Montmorency, to Montigny, to the home of Trudaine, of Brienne, etc., these five or six years passed deliciously for me."[78]

If Morellet had secured a "delicious" life, Marmontel had secured a banquet. We have seen the vast sums of money he was paid for his literary works, and the number of pensioned sinecures he obtained, to which he added in 1784 that of *historiographe des bâtiments*. He received not only individual pensions of 2,000 *livres* each for his posts as *historiographe*, and 1,200 *livres* as *secrétaire-perpétuel* of the Académie (raised to 3,000 *livres* in 1785), but in addition lodgings at Versailles and the Louvre for these, which he rented to others for over 1,800 *livres*. By 1777, the date of his marriage (which brought him a dowry of 20,000 *livres*), he already had established *rentes* worth 20,000 *livres* annually from the proceeds of his literary and dramatic works, income added to his pensions and continued royalties. In the 1780s he began to buy land outside of Paris, and in about 1783 he purchased a country-home at Grignon, where he spent several months of the year and entertained his Parisian friends. He hired a private tutor for his sons, enticing a teacher from the famous école de Sainte-Barbe to leave his post and live permanently in Marmontel's home.[79] What would he have thought if he had seen again the letter he had written to d'Holbach in 1749 or 1750: ". . . I have no money and I

[78] Morellet, *Mémoires*, I, 262. See also ibid., 236-240, 250-251. Morellet was convinced that Mme Geoffrin had given him the pension in the hope that he would discontinue writing against the Compagnie des Indes, the source of her *rentes*.

[79] Marmontel, *Mémoires*, II, 182-190; Morellet, *Mémoires*, I, 240. According to the latter, Marmontel had hired the tutor, Charpentier, away from the école de Sainte-Barbe.

don't give a damn. I am thus a philosophe . . ."?[80] Definitions and perspectives, to say the least, had changed.

* * *

That perspective which appears to have changed least for the members of the coterie holbachique, and which separated them most from the official values and beliefs of the Ancien Régime, was their deep and intense hostility to Christianity in general, and the Roman Catholic Church in particular. Even in this realm, however, we should recall that a certain anticlericalism, and in some ways a genuine antireligiosity or antisupernaturalism, had been fashionable in many aristocratic and privileged circles since the days of the Regency. Voltaire had been lionized in important quarters before the thinkers of the coterie holbachique had come upon the philosophical and social scene; Montesquieu had been elected to an aristocratic Académie Française for his *Lettres Persanes*, whose barbs against the Church and papacy were scarcely unnoticeable. The devotees of the rue Royale were to intensify the secular and critical trends of the milieus in which they moved, and add significantly to the corpus of arguments and attitudes which supported the increasing respectability of incredulity and heterodox thought. They did not create such trends and circumstances, however, and many of their patrons and admirers had held such views before being influenced by their writings.

The men of the rue Royale were intellectual, not social, rebels against the Church. Any other course of action would have involved sacrifices which clearly they were not prepared to make. They did not marry clandestinely in the deserts and mountains, like the Protestants of the south of France; they did not hide their children from the priests. When they married, they married legally in the Churches, of course, taking communion and Catholic vows. When they had children, their children were of course baptized, and they as parents pledged formally to insure the Catholic upbringing of their heirs, thus giving their children a legal status in their world. The members of the coterie holbachique were respectable men, who wished to live respectable lives and, whatever Diderot's deathbed scenes, wished to be buried respectably in Catholic graves.

An example of this social Catholicism was the behavior of those among them who achieved membership in the Académie Fran-

---

[80] Facsimile in B.N., Imprimés: Ln27. 13,548.

çaise. The Académie's annual mass in the chapel of the Louvre, on the day of Saint-Louis, generally was poorly attended. Indeed the avoidance of this mass by most members of the Académie was something of a scandal. In 1760 only eleven members out of forty had gone to the chapel, and this had produced both a public and an official outcry.[81] From 1760 until 1784 attendance hovered between fifteen and twenty, dropping below fifteen in every year from 1784 to 1789. Despite their deep antipathy to Christianity, the members of the coterie holbachique proved to be above reproach in this context; after their elections, Marmontel, Saint-Lambert, Chastellux, Suard and Morellet were almost always at the official mass on every August 25. They took their status seriously. Marmontel might enjoy scandalizing Mme Geoffrin by not knowing the name of his parish, but he was one of the most assiduous of the academicians to take communion in the company of "the immortals."[82]

The social respectability of unbelievers was not acknowledged in all quarters, but most figures in the strata occupied by the philosophes of d'Holbach's circle continually made distinctions between the person and the thought of any given individual, across a wide spectrum of permutations. When Suard announced his desire to marry the sister of the important publisher Panckouke, the latter at first opposed such a match; his editors at the *Année littéraire* warned him against the "philosophical" connections of his prospective brother-in-law, intimating the "dubious" moral and religious principles of Suard and his circle of friends. Ironically, according to Mme Suard's recollections, the eminently respectable Baron d'Holbach reassured Panckouke on this matter, vouching for Suard's character and convincing the publisher to allow the union.[83]

Those members of the coterie holbachique who possessed by birth, inheritance or early title an inherent prestige did not suffer any social decline as a result of their attachment to the philosophic camp. One measure of this is the marriages they secured for themselves and their children. D'Holbach's two wives were indeed his own second cousins, but the paternal side of their family was one

[81] F. Masson, *L'Académie Française, 1629-1793*, 238-249.

[82] *Registres de l'Académie Française*, III, passim. On Marmontel's real or feigned ignorance of his parish, see Mme Suard, *Suard*, 69-72.

[83] Mme Suard, *Suard*, 51-59. This was in January 1766, before Suard had achieved the eminence that awaited him in the course of the next twenty-three years.

beginning to make its mark in the world. Nicolas d'Aine was a rising functionary, whose son Marius-Jean-Baptiste-Nicolas had a particularly distinguished career, rising to become the *intendant* of Pau and Bayonne (1767), Turgot's successor as *intendant* of Limoges (1774), and the *intendant* of Touraine (1783).[84] D'Holbach's elder daughter married the comte (and later marquis) de Fontenoy-Chatenoy, descended from a family of high noble functionaries which traced its titles back to twelfth-century Lorraine.[85] His younger daughter married the marquis de Nolivos in 1781; the Nolivos were an ancient family of the *noblesse d'épée* whose lineage necessitated the signature of the royal family on the marriage contract.[86] D'Holbach's younger son had risen to the rank of captain in the *regiment de Schomberg* by 1789, and in January 1791 he married the daughter of Dompierre d'Hornoy, *président* of the parlement de Paris. His bride, in these last moments of the afterglow of the Ancien Régime, was attended by Dupleix de Pernau and Thiroux de Gerviller, both *maréchaux de camp* in the royal armies.[87]

Helvétius married a woman destined to become as celebrated as the author of *De l'esprit* himself, Mlle de Ligneville, the daughter of one of the four most eminent and prestigious families of the Lorraine nobility, and the niece of Mme de Graffigny. Helvétius' two daughters themselves married into titles of nobility, the eldest becoming the comtesse de Mun, and the youngest the comtesse d'Andlau.[88] Chastellux, after his return

---

[84] On d'Aine's career, see Lough, "Le baron d'Holbach"; *Almanach royal* (1757-1783).

[85] Naville, *Paul Thiry d'Holbach* (1967 edn.), "Annexes," 466; on the Chatenoy family, see any armorial or dictionary of the nobility.

[86] Lough, "Le baron d'Holbach," 534.

[87] The *acte de mariage*, from the *registre* of the parish of Saint-Roch was printed in Naville, op. cit., 465.

[88] At the time of her marriage, the woman who was to become so famous as Mme Helvétius was already socially famous as Anne-Cathérine, comtesse de Ligneville d'Autricourt. The Ligneville family was one of the four families of the highest Lorraine nobility, the "grands chevaux de Lorraine," the other three being the Soreau, the Rampont and the d'Issembourg; the mother of Mme Helvétius was a Soreau. The paternal aunts of Helvétius' wife were the princesse de Beauvau-Craon and Mme de Choiseul, mother of the duc de Choiseul. Unfortunately for the Ligneville, they were not wealthy, for all their social eminence, and above all they were not wealthy enough to provide adequately for the nineteen brothers and sisters of Anne-Cathérine. It was another aunt, Mme de Graffigny, who saw to the education of

from America, married a young noblewoman of Irish Catholic origins, a certain "demoiselle Plunkett," who, according to the duchesse de Bourbon, sat reading *De la félicité publique* at Spa, where Chastellux was on vacation, recognizing its author as "a good catch." Demoiselle Plunkett had become the good friend of the duchesse d'Orléans at Spa, and the wedding, according to the gossip of the *Mémoires secrets*, was contracted under the auspices of the duchesse. After that event the marquise de Chastellux became attached to the duchesse d'Orléans' court. The groom, unfortunately, was to die within a year, before the birth of his son.[89]

Among the others, the abbés Morellet and Raynal of course could not marry, and Roux, Naigeon, Le Roy, Saint-Lambert and Grimm remained bachelors. The last two, however, enjoyed their celebrated liaisons with Mme d'Houdetot and Mme d'Epinay, two ladies of wealth and social dignity. Morellet appears to have compensated somewhat for his single state by bringing his closest brother and sister to Paris, and seeing to their happiness. Earlier, he had seen his sister married to Louis-René de Montigny; after the latter's death he brought the widow and her daughter, Marie-Adélaide de Lerain de Montigny to his own home. It was this eighteen-year-old niece whom Morellet arranged to give as a bride to the fifty-four-year-old Marmontel in 1777, along with a dowry of 20,000 *livres*. For his own brother Morellet secured a position in the *domaines des finances*, with an income of about 12,000 *livres* per year.[90]

Darcet in 1772 married the daughter of his mentor and early patron, Guillaume-François Rouelle, one year after the death of the great chemist. Whatever the motivation for this union, it tied

---

Anne-Cathérine, and it was in the former's social circle that Helvétius met his future bride. On official documents, Mme Helvétius was always the "très haute et très puissante Dame Cathérine de Ligneville, née comtesse du Saint-Empire" (see Keim, *Helvétius*, 180-189). On the earlier friendship of Anne-Cathérine with Turgot, see Morellet, *Mémoires*, I, 134-136. Both of Helvétius' daughters married shortly after his death, and given the wealth which he left them and their mother's social prominence, it is not surprising that they married into two families of quality.

[89] See the duchesse de Bourbon's letter to the comtesse d'Oberkirch, in Oberkirch, *Mémoires*, II, 390; and Bachaumont, *Mémoires secrets*, XXXVI, 282-283. He did not enjoy a long period as a married man, but he described himself to Governor Morris in January 1788 as "the happiest of men" (Chastellux, "Letters," in Carson, *Chastellux*, 168-169).

[90] Morellet, *Mémoires*, I, 236, 238-241; Marmontel, *Mémoires*, II, 115-127.

Darcet to one of the most scientifically eminent and prestigious families in France. The late Rouelle had taught in the *Jardin du roi* and had been offered the post of *premier-pharmacien du roi* (a post he declined, choosing to serve as *inspecteur-général* of the charitable Hôtel-Dieu), and he was universally acknowledged as the leading chemist of his age; his brother (Darcet's bride's uncle) had succeeded him at the *Jardin*. It is not certain that this family connection aided Darcet's career, although he did follow his late father-in-law into the *monnaies* (where Rouelle had been an important figure), rising to become *essayeur en chef des monnaies*.[91]

Diderot alone had married while young and poor, long before his fortune and reputation were secure. It was an unhappy marriage (it would be to Sophie Volland that he would look "to love . . . and to be loved"),[92] but it produced for him his beloved daughter Angélique, and it was perhaps for her above all that he too began to worry about his estate and to restrain and censor his own philosophical publications. He did not approve of the institution of marriage, as he revealed in a somewhat anguished letter to Grimm at the time of his daughter's engagement, but he wanted Angélique to be happy following her own lights.[93] He moved heaven and earth to secure for his prospective son-in-law a position that would allow the new couple to live near him, in Paris, and in relative comfort. His new in-laws were respectable bourgeois friends of his family in Langres, but it was by the use of his own administrative connections that Diderot raised his son-in-law's station and fortune in the world.[94]

For those members of the coterie who married and raised families, the role of head of a household appears to have been taken

[91] Dizé, *Précis sur Darcet*, 14. On Rouelle, see Delauney, *Le monde médical Parisien*, passim; and C. Secrétan, *Un Aspect de la chimie prélavoisienne (Le Cours de G.-F. Rouelle)*, 219-444.

[92] Diderot, *Corr.*, x, 183: "I have need, more need than ever, to love someone and to be loved by her. I have counted on you all of my life; if you leave me, I will be alone." The letter was written in November 1770. Diderot's relationship with Sophie Volland appears to have been, from his correspondence, the most humanly satisfying relationship of his life. Only to Grimm could he also write with unadorned sentiment, as when in 1772 he wrote to "my tender, my only friend. . . . I feel myself united to you with such a power that I have never separated your actions, good or bad, from my own . . . that whatever you thought, you said, you did, it is I who speaks, who thinks and who does. For twenty years I have believed myself to be someone in two persons" (ibid., xii, 62-63).

[93] Ibid., xi, 84-86.   [94] Ibid., xi-xv, passim.

most seriously, but it did not interfere in most cases with the heady pace of their lives in "society." They continued to dine most of the days of the week not with their families, but with their friends in the salons of Paris, and to spend much time away from their own homes, in stretches at Grandval, for example, or at Mme d'Epinay's estate at La Briche. Some, such as Suard and Marmontel, began to entertain at their own homes, and introduced their wives into their circles of friends, but more often than not they dined without their wives. As their wealth increased they all saw to their families' luxuries, hiring, when possible, tutors for their children and servants to add to the ease of their wives, and in the cases of Suard and Marmontel, buying country homes and carriages and maintaining equipages (as d'Holbach and Helvétius had done) for family outings and seasons away from the capital. The central focal points of their energies, nevertheless, remained the literary and social worlds dominated by select hostesses and hosts, and by established men of letters and admiring aristocrats; they did not abandon these to retire to the hearths and tables of their homes. Marmontel recalled the pleasures of staying at his country home during the season, and driving in his carriage to Paris three times a week for meetings of the Académie and visits with his friends, and on other days visiting the d'Angivillers at Versailles or the de Sezes at their estate at Brevane, then returning to his growing family at Grignon. "[U]ntil the era of the Revolution," he wrote, "I cannot express the delight which I found in life and in society."[95]

[95] Marmontel, *Mémoires*, II, 185-190.

SEVEN · *Privilège*

In some respects, the lives of the members of the coterie holba-chique during the period from 1760 to 1789 appear simply to reflect a continuation of the patterns observable in the 1750s. The real or imagined abilities of these figures as men of letters, scientists, thinkers and writers were valued or found particularly useful by important institutions and public figures, the latter often their friends or flattered patrons, and that recognition led to advancement in their chosen careers and their stations.

There was a point, however, when the quantity, nature and cumulative effects of the honors, sinecures, dignities, positions, pensions and other remunerations obtained by the members of the coterie holbachique in the exercise of their talents and useful connections constituted a significant *qualitative* change in their status in the Ancien Régime. This qualitative change was gradual and self-perpetuating: each new increase of status made a man worthy of certain new rewards and dignities, which in turn qualified him for yet more important positions. Over time most of these philosophes were able to translate their increased status into increased influence and power over other men, in the process often becoming figures of a prestige now virtually independent of the favor of the particular men who originally had conferred it or its preconditions. In the 1750s the members of the coterie holbachique had achieved a certain degree of security and opportunity. In the decades that followed they became not only men of a more substantial financial, social and professional security, but also, on the whole, the usufructuaries of a high and often haughty *privilège*.

* * *

The most salient (if least complex) feature of this pattern was the acquisition by members of the coterie holbachique of "official" positions which conferred upon them, by virtue of title, a formally recognized dignity and elite status in the diverse hierarchies of the Ancien Régime. Membership in an Académie, for example, advanced one's status along many overlapping scales. It altered a man's legal status, making him a member of a royally sponsored

214

corps from which were derived considerable personal privileges and rights. It conferred upon a man a certain impressive social status, making him the equal, in academic matters, of princes of the royal blood and cardinals of the Church, and placing him in a context where he associated undeferentially with the powerful and the great. It provided a man with the foundations for economic advancement, enhancing his reputation and thus the value of his work, in addition to providing a not insignificant remuneration by its system of payments for attendance at meetings. It increased a man's influence and power over his former peers, giving him a vote on future membership of the Académie, and placing him on committees which dispensed prizes, honors and official recognition. It also conferred upon a man a certain intellectual respectability in the eyes of those whose judgments were not formed simply by their independent evaluation of a man's work, thereby stamping the intellectual persons (if not the works) of deists, unbelievers and critics of the Church with an official seal of approval.

The security of an academician underwent a thorough test during the crisis over *Bélisaire*, when the belief was widespread that Marmontel could not possibly be permitted to remain in that favored body after his censure by the Sorbonne and the archbishop of Paris. The court, however, did not move against its academician, and indeed by 1772 Marmontel was the royal *historiographe de France*. This latter position was in fact a sinecure, but it derived an appreciable prestige from the antiquity of its origins (which were placed by the eighteenth-century court in the twelfth century) and from the dignities attendant to it—lodgings in Versailles, and the right to entry to all royal celebrations.[1] Despite the absence of any serious or significant historical contributions on his part, as *historiographe* Marmontel was by title the official historian of France, and such a designation had manifest consequences. When the Lycée de France was organized in 1786, Marmontel was, to the "astonishment" of the writers of the *Mémoires secrets*, listed as its professor of history, gaining thereby a remuneration of 3,000 *livres*. He then simply hired someone competent to teach the subject in his place, paying him with that portion of his pension that rewarded merit rather than title.[2]

The official positions sought and acquired by members of the

[1] B.N., MS *Nouvelles acquisitions françaises*, 3739, folio 46.
[2] Bachaumont, *Mémoires secrets*, XXXI, 10-11; XXXIII, 122-123.

215

coterie holbachique were by no means, in most cases, simply sine-cures, and the motivations for gaining them were undoubtedly varied and complex. Chastellux did not need membership in the Académie Française to rise above his social origins, but as was the case of many aristocrats, he wanted the additional luster of recognition of his talents by celebrated men of letters. Le Roy's place on the illustrious central *bureau* of the Société royale d'Agriculture undoubtedly reflected less his need for recognition of his high status than his genuine interest in rural economy. Nevertheless, it added significantly to the reputation of even the well-born to be recognized as men of learning and culture, and they sought such places avidly. Chastellux persuaded Mlle de Lespinasse to wage a campaign for him among the academicians, with whom her ties were legion, and her comment on this to her friend Guibert demonstrated how seriously the chevalier took this effort: "Speaking of [Chastellux], he is very pleased with me; I inspired his friends, and things are so well arranged that we need only the death of one of the forty for him to be received at the Académie. That is just, no doubt, but it was not without difficulty: the interest, the pleasure, the desire that he staked on his triumph vitalized me. My God! Fontenelle was right: there are toys for every age. . . ."[3]

If the academic role was a "toy" for a man so well-born as Chastellux, and perhaps for a Saint-Lambert, it was a signal dignity for the sons of artisans, merchants and simple bourgeois such as Suard, Morellet and Marmontel. The rule of the Académie Française was one of complete equality among its members, who included, during the last three decades of the Ancien Régime, princes of the royal blood and prestigious nobles such as the comte de Clermont, the prince de Beauvau, the prince-cardinal de Rohan, the duc de Nivernais, the marquis de Paulmi, the maréchal de Belle-Isle, the duc de Villars, the *avocat-général* Seguier, the duc de Duras, the comte de Choiseul, the marquis de Montesquieu, the eminent Malesherbes, and the maréchal de Richelieu. In the period from 1760 to 1789, there were ten cardinals, archbishops and bishops in the Académie. Such notables had paid a deferential personal visit to the home of each member of the Académie upon seeking admission, and they themselves honored new members with flattering *discours* and reverences. All members of the Académie presided over sessions, as *directeur*, by rotation, voted

[3] Lespinasse, *Lettres* (Asse), 129.

as equals on new members, and regardless of rank or estate, sat in the first vacant seat upon their entrance into the meetinghall in the Louvre. Each member of the Académie enjoyed the privilege of settling all litigation affecting him in the parlement de Paris. They all were presented to the king at Versailles upon their respective elections, given specimens of all medals issued by the royal treasury, and granted places at royal spectacles. When foreign rulers and heirs visited France, they often made a pilgrimage to the Louvre to salute the members of the Académie. Upon the death of an academician, a solemn mass was offered for his soul in the chapelle des Cordéliers, and a royal pension was granted to his widow. In 1788 the *gouverneur* of the dauphin and the *premier-président* of the *chambre des comptes* both sought entrance to the Académie, and thus paid solicitous visits to the homes of Marmontel, Morellet, Suard, Chastellux and Saint-Lambert. In May of that year the entire Académie was fêted at a dinner given in its honor by the royal duc de Penthieure, at his estate at Sceaux. It was in this glittering milieu that five members of the coterie spent much of their time, and it was this body which elected Marmontel as its *secrétaire-perpétuel*.[4]

Those philosophes who received formal dignities were the beneficiaries of a system of rewards by virtue of which men engaged in favored activities could be rendered formally worthy of association with their social betters. Favor, in the Ancien Régime, did not necessarily confer, directly and of itself, a rise in the legal or social status of its recipient. If a man were merely rewarded financially by a duke, minister, prince, or, indeed, a king, he was simply wealthier, and not by that alone a more important *personnage*. Wealth, of course, could be utilized to purchase formal dignity, as when d'Holbach bought the ennobling position of *conseiller-secrétaire du roi*, but it was the latter place that increased his status, not his riches alone. The primary means by which favor translated into an advancement of a man's social station was the acquisition

---

[4] *Registres de l'Académie Française*, passim. See also Masson, *L'Académie Française*; G. Boissier, *L'Académie Française sous l'Ancien Régime*; and L. Brunel, *Les philosophes et l'Académie Française au 18ᵉ siècle*. All three of these classic works argue the traditional thesis, implicitly or explicitly, that the philosophes attempted in one way or another to "convert" the Académie to the philosophic cause. There is a certain truth in this, but the "conversion" of the philosophes to the academic cause was in many ways the more substantive of the two.

of official title and dignity. In the seventeenth century Louis XIV had brought to Versailles those men of letters and artists whom he had calculated would help make of his court the cultural as well as political capital of Europe. Such men of talent were rewarded, as payment, with places in the new Académies, formal titles, and honorific sinecures, but these rewards served as well the function of making the recipients socially *digne* of such proximity to the king and court. In the complex etiquette of that court, where social standing and inherited or acquired rank were so often divorced from personal merit or accomplishment, it was the title itself, and not the qualities and talents which may or may not have moved the king to grant the title, which determined the status of a man.

By the mid-eighteenth century, of course, the talents and qualities of men of letters (and scientists) were valued intrinsically much more deeply and broadly than they had been in the seventeenth or early eighteenth century. Voltaire had complained in his *Lettres philosophiques*, early in the century, of the lack of esteem granted to men of letters;[5] by the second half of that century, however, in his article "Hommes de Lettres" in the *Encyclopédie*, he could note approvingly that "The spirit of the century has made most [men of letters] as much at ease in society as in their study. . . . Up to the time of Balzac and Voiture, they were not admitted to society; since then they have become a necessary part of it."[6] This development should not obscure for us that such a trend had by no means wholly transformed the consciousness of formal hierarchy in even the most liberal elements of the court and aristocracy, nor that large segments of "society" continued to make their most important distinctions on the basis of inherited or acquired official dignities. As Diderot noted in 1776, "In spite of all the distinction that I accord to the philosophe and to the man of letters, I nevertheless think that perhaps a man would expose himself to ridicule by parading in society the dignity of this estate. . . ." Diderot qualified this in the cases of those rare individuals whose accomplishments were truly singular, but his general thesis was that formal rank indeed mattered greatly for the man of letters as for the whole of French society: "I find myself placed among citizens distributed in different classes which are elevated the ones above the others, and

5 Voltaire, *Lettres philosophiques*, "Lettre XXIII."
6 *Encyclopédie*, VII, "Hommes de lettres."

decorated with different titles which indicate to me the importance of their functions."[7] Diderot himself was one of the few humbly born members of the coterie holbachique who did not actively and continually pursue such titles, and he may indeed have been one of those rare individuals whose talent alone earned him proximity to the socially eminent. Nevertheless, his place in society was distinguishable from that of other men of letters with formal dignities. Thus in 1784, just before his death, the *Mémoires secrets* could note: "Since [Diderot] . . . belongs to no academy, is attached to no family and has no substance of his own, the clergy proposes to revenge itself on him. . . ." After his death the same authors described the position he had occupied as precarious, since "belonging to no literary *corps* in France, he was an isolated individual, in favor of whom the priests did not fear protests."[8]

In the seventeenth century "the endowments established by Louis XIV," as Voltaire termed them, had been the gifts of the king himself and of his immediate court. As such they could reflect royal approval and royal taste. By the mid-eighteenth century, however, two important developments had come to pass. First, the privilege of assigning men of letters to honorific places and sinecures had been parcelled out, for all practical purposes, to diverse aristocrats and ministers, many of whom did not represent the king's or the court's taste in letters, philosophy or religion. Second, the Académies had become genuinely cooptative, allowing critics of the Church and of certain important aspects of the status quo to rise into their midsts. The honors and places, however, continued to make their recipients worthy of proximity to Versailles and thus to high society, and continued to help set the parameters of respectability in the highest circles. When "philosophic" academicians and *historiographes* clashed with doctors of the Sorbonne, it was a struggle between two established bodies of *clercs*, between two favored groups within the intellectual elites of the Ancien Régime. In theory, of course, society owed its primary intellectual allegiance to its established religion, but it was not the doctors of theology who determined the composition of the Académies or the appointments of *secrétaires du commerce*, *censeurs royaux*, *historiographes* and *docteurs-régents* of the other faculties. If, at the Louvre, princes of the Church sat collegially in the Académie with Marmontel during the crisis over *Bélisaire*,

---

[7] Diderot, *Corr.*, XIV, 223-228.
[8] Bachaumont, *Mémoires secrets*, XXII, 285-286; XXVI, 153-154.

it was difficult for even the most religious citizens to look upon him as a social outcast. When the king and the parlement sought advice on the controversial question of inoculation, they turned to two official bodies—to the Faculté de Théologie of the University of Paris, but also to the Faculté de Médecine, where Darcet and Roux could speak their piece.[9] To be a *docteur-régent* was not only to add a certain official weight to one's opinions, and to help govern the Faculté and the medical profession; it was also to enjoy all of the "rights and privileges" of personal nobility, and to participate in a body which thought highly enough of itself to petition the crown in 1718 and 1770 for recognition of those "rights and privileges" as a full legal and inheritable *noblesse*.[10] Perhaps that is one of the reasons why Darcet, in the struggle between the more privileged Faculté de Médecine and the more intellectually progressive Société royale de Médecine, to both of which he belonged, vigorously favored and supported the cause of the Faculté.[11]

This is not to deny that there was a useful public role embodied in most of the official positions gained by the members of the coterie holbachique, and that these roles may have mattered a great deal to them. Chastellux made active inspection tours as *gouverneur* of Longwy; the academicians worked on committees of their bodies which helped determine the future of their disciplines; Morellet campaigned against monopolies as a *secrétaire du commerce*; Roux and Darcet performed important investigative work as *docteurs-régents* of their Faculté; Grimm was an active diplomat as the accredited *ministre plénipotentiaire* of the court of Saxe-Gotha and others. These were also positions, however, which altered their legal and social statuses, modified the patterns of their social relationships and associations, and added greatly to their personal security and independence.

Another indication of a significant shift in the position of the members of the coterie holbachique during the period from 1760 to 1789 is their own increased ability to aid each other in important ways. In the 1750s d'Holbach had assisted Suard and possibly others financially; by the 1760s, we have seen, his contacts were imposing enough to secure for Roux the post at Saint-Gobain.

[9] Ibid., II, 237.

[10] Du Puy de Clinchamps, *La Noblesse*, 32-33.

[11] Delauney, *Le monde médical Parisien*, 310-323; Bachaumont, *Mémoires secrets*, XII, 140.

Suard himself, as an editor, was able to provide an outlet for Le Roy's "Lettres," and as a censor to secure *permissions tacites* for his friends, including Diderot.[12] Grimm, with his powerful foreign contacts, was able to do far more for his friends, gaining the assistance of foreign crowns for Marmontel during the *Bélisaire* affair, and achieving financial independence for Diderot through his intercession with Catherine the Great. Diderot's own friendship with the *lieutenant-général de police* allowed him to aid his friends as well, for Sartine occasionally would call upon him as a censor, as he did when unsure of how to proceed vis-à-vis works by Galiani and Morellet.[13] Marmontel, of course, from his strong position within the Académie, undoubtedly influenced the decisions which led to the admission of so many of his friends, most obviously in the case of Morellet. As academicians, censors, editors with royal privilege, ministers, *docteurs-régents, gouverneurs*, aides to ministers, and friends of the great in France and of foreign kings and queens, they were in positions to aid themselves and each other continually. They were men of useful importance.

Such a view of these figures contradicts in some fundamental ways the self-image they often projected as philosophes, namely, that they were men persecuted for their ideas and subject to the tyrannies of their powerful enemies. There is a certain truth to that self-image, but it is embodied more in terms of negative than of positive consequences—the books they did not write or did not publish; the self-censoring, self-denials and cautions which they incorporated into their intellectual lives. Their enemies in the Ancien Régime could not prevent them from achieving the places we have seen them occupy in their society; only during the Revolution could those who hated them persecute them effectively and strip them of their ranks and honors.

Their lives were not without moments of extreme *"inconvénients"* prior to 1789, but it is important to determine the nature and nuances of these. The fact of Diderot's imprisonment in 1749 is probably the best-known such incident, but it is by now equally well-known that his incarceration was not a harsh one, and that his friends—above all, the associated publishers of the *Encyclopédie*—carried enough influence to secure his release following a formal apology and promise of good behavior on his part. Diderot had suffered the misfortune of publishing the wrong works at the wrong time, during one of those rare and short-lived periods when

---

[12] Diderot, *Corr.*, xv, 243.   [13] Ibid., 32-35, 72-75.

the *conseil* and the magistrates would decide that it was at last time to impose some "decency" and "order" on the world of letters. He received an administrative slap on the wrist, and he learned from it the need to write, or more accurately, to publish with a certain caution. Observing that caution, he lived well as an avowed atheist in a Catholic nation for the remainder of his life.[14]

Helvétius, of course, had been the victim of a "persecution" in 1758-1759 which had frightened the philosophic camp, but he had signed *De l'esprit* with his own name, deceived a censor, and published it at the least opportune time. Nevertheless, it should help us keep our perspective to recall that for all of the declamations against him by Jesuits, Jansenists, magistrates, courtiers and archbishops, Helvétius suffered no loss of physical freedom, no fines and no exile. He was "humilated" in that he was forced to recant formally and promise his silence on such philosophical subjects, but surely that was small penalty to pay after having so openly defied and embarrassed a government undergoing a difficult period of time. Malesherbes was under intense pressure from Omer Joly de Fleury at the parlement and from the court at Versailles to act vigorously against Helvétius, but he handled the affair deftly, almost serenely, in the author's behalf. With politeness, tact and discretion toward all sides, Malesherbes calmed the most agitated, continuously attempted to reassure Helvétius and his wife, and secured retractions that would assuage the Sorbonne, the parlement and the *conseil*. We should not be misled by the rhetoric of persecution in the Ancien Régime; the execution was almost invariably much weaker than the threats voiced in the laws and *arrêts* of the authorities.[15]

There were incidents of penalties imposed upon members of the coterie holbachique prior to 1789, but these involved less any persecution of them as men in fundamental conflict with their society than it did a punishment for a temporary failure to observe certain social rules and conventions. In fact, the context and resolution of these episodes bear witness more to the ultimate security of these men than to any marginal or precarious position that they occupied in the face of authority.

Marmontel was sent to the Bastille in December 1759 and Morellet in June 1760 for brief and relatively comfortable stays. Both were imprisoned by *lettre de cachet* not because of anything

---

[14] On Diderot's imprisonment, see Wilson, *Diderot*, 103-116.
[15] B.N., MS *Coll. Anisson-Duperron*, cxxxi, folios 27-98.

philosophical or political they had written, but because of their having personally offended important and powerful nobles. Marmontel had spread a parody of *Cinna* in the salons which mocked the duc d'Aumont for his personal arrogance; when he refused to divulge the identity of the author, he was incarcerated, and the editorship of the *Mercure* was taken from him. Morellet had penned a mordant riposte, *La Vision de Charles Palissot*, to the play *Les Philosophes*, and had overstepped himself considerably by maligning Palissot's protectress, the princesse de Robecq; the police investigated, discovered him to be the offending author, and he was seized.[16]

In both cases the king and his ministers had no alternative but to reprimand the young writers for their imprudence; it was a perquisite of high estate to be protected from "libel" and "satire." Everyone knew that. As Diderot himself wrote in 1776, ". . . [T]here is a kind of respect that I owe to [a man's] place; this respect is even consecrated by the laws which deal severely with insult, not according to the man abused, but according to his estate. Knowledge of the considerations attached to different conditions forms an essential part of the propriety and of the common practice of the world."[17]

In the case of Marmontel, he was imprisoned for only some ten or eleven days, allowed to bring his valet to prison with him, and treated as an honored guest by the *gouverneur* of the Bastille, with whom he took his meals. For all the rhetoric of his *Mémoires*, where he reproached the duc d'Aumont for confining him so tyrannically to a dungeon, even Marmontel had to admit that his stay was an easy one and that he was received as a hero by his lettered and aristocratic friends upon his release, especially since he had "protected" a friend by his "suffering."[18] Although he lost the *Mercure*, he retained a royal pension of 3,000 *livres* from its proceeds,[19] and within four years he was being received by the king at Versailles as a newly elected member of the Académie Française. The incident, he admitted, secured his reputation and his fame, and he appears to have enjoyed it. Indeed he wrote to

[16] On Marmontel, see his *Mémoires*, I, 375-404; and his dossier in the Bibliothèque de l'Arsenal, MS *Bastille*, 12,048, folios 218-220, where it was noted explicitly that the offense was one of having "satirized" the duc d'Aumont. On Morellet, see his *Mémoires*, I, 86-96; and his dossier in Arsenal, MS *Bastille*, 12,086, folios 203-205.

[17] Diderot, *Corr.*, XIV, 224. [18] Marmontel, *Mémoires*, I, 375-404.

[19] Ibid., and Bibliothèque de l'Arsenal, MS *Bastille*, 12,048, folios 218-220.

Diderot a warm and humorous letter from the Bastille, which he termed "the French Parnassus," and included in it a facetious article "for the *Encyclopédie*":

> BASTILLE: State Prison, transformed by the munificence of the *lieutenants de Police* into a place of pleasure in which one locks up men of letters from time to time. The ignorant common-people obstinately continue to look upon it as a prison, but enlightened men know that it is a place of distinction . . . which suits men who have much work to do. . . .[20]

Morellet spent a longer time in the Bastille, from mid-June until late July of 1760, but he himself understood the reasons perfectly. As he wrote in his *Mémoires*: "M. de Choiseul loved or had loved Mme de Robecq. She was dying. Palissot had sent to her . . . the joke in which she was involved. . . . She demanded vengeance from M. de Choiseul. . . . The *colporteur* betrayed me."[21] This account corresponds entirely to the report on the affair sent by police inspector d'Hémery to Malesherbes.[22]

Morellet already had gained a reputation as an economist, and had made important friends at court and in the government. At the instigation of his protectors and friends, such eminent persons as the maréchal de Noailles, Malesherbes, Chastellux and the maréchale de Luxembourg were all active in his behalf.[23] Like Marmontel, Morellet was quite well-treated in the Bastille, and he received reading matter directly from Malesherbes himself.[24] In June the latter wrote to Sartine, *lieutenant-général de police*, advising him that "I know [Morellet] very well; . . . he is not one to be treated rigorously." He added that "several considerable persons" were upset that Morellet was being punished, since the abbé was a man of great use to commerce and industry.[25] D'Hémery wrote to Sartine at almost the same time, underscoring that Morellet "is known to the *contrôleur-général*, and to several persons of great position who speak rather highly of him."[26] That same June the well-placed Barbier described Morellet as "a man of superior genius" and noted that "they say that he is extremely

[20] Diderot, *Corr.*, IV, 21-25.   [21] Morellet, *Mémoires*, I, 86-96.
[22] B.N., MS *Nouv. acq.*, 1214, folios 306-308.
[23] Morellet, *Mémoires*, I, 86-96; B.N. MS *Coll. A.-D.*, CXXXI, folios 163-172.
[24] Morellet, *Mémoires*, I, 86-96.
[25] B.N., MS *Coll. A.-D.*, CXXXI, folios 169-172.
[26] See above, this chapter, n. 22.

knowledgeable in commerce, and is being sought after by the ministry, and by *Messieurs les intendants de commerce* as a very useful man; they are counting on his not remaining long in the Bastille."[27] What detained him was the princesse de Robecq's death at the end of July, "which did not fail to raise against me all of the sensitive women and men of the court," Morellet recalled, "who repeated that I had given her the *coup de la mort*, and that an example should be made." A few weeks after her death he was released, politely asked to stay out of Paris for a few months, and upon his return was greeted as a hero in the important literary and social salons of Paris. As he admitted, his period in the Bastille was "an excellent recommendation" to "the men of letters that I had avenged" and "the members of society who loved satire"; the real fruits of his brief imprisonment had been the chance to dine daily on "a bottle of rather good wine, a pound of excellent bread . . . a soup, beef, an entrée, and dessert . . . some roast and some salad . . . ," and to discover how important and respected he in fact was.[28]

To place these incarcerations in the proper perspective, one should understand that the same attitudes of mutual indulgence among courtiers, ministers and the king which allowed a d'Aumont or Robecq to secure the reprimand of their "assailants" also allowed a Beauvau, a d'Aiguillon, a Turgot, a Nivernais or a Pompadour to secure for these same men their sinecures and pensions. In the course of the following decades, Marmontel and Morellet learned to employ such a system of privileges quite profitably in their own interests.

The loss of favor might be frightening, but it was remediable. In 1771 the duc de Choiseul was disgraced, and not atypically, most of those whom he had appointed or favored were caught in the resultant maelstrom; Suard and Arnaud were thus removed as editors of the *Gazette de France*. Suard's financial situation fell drastically. His wife later described the change that this had entailed in their lives, and inadvertently revealed as well the attitude toward "work" not uncharacteristic of many members of the coterie: "He was going to lose a free and an easy circumstance [*aisance*] which had made him independent. He cultivated the letters only for their intrinsic pleasure, [and now] he was going to be

---

[27] E. F. Barbier, *Chronique de la régence et du règne de Louis XV (1718-1763), ou Journal de Barbier*, VII, 256-258, 266.

[28] Morellet, *Mémoires*, I, 86-96.

obliged henceforth to work for his wife and for himself. What a sad difference!"[29]

His friends, however, more than helped him to ward off poverty. Immediately following his loss, the prince de Beauvau, the chevalier de Chastellux and Charles-Georges Le Roy sent to the Suards abundant quantities of deer and other game killed at their hunts. Through the intercession of the duc de Nivernais (apparently at the urging of d'Alembert), Suard and Arnaud were given a pension of 2,500 *livres* from the revenues of the *Gazette de France*, in compensation for their past services. Necker gave to Suard an annual *rente* of 800 *livres*, the equivalent of a gift of 16,000 *livres*. The duc de Coigny, one of his protectors, bought a part of Suard's collection of English books for the extremely inflated price of 12,000 *livres*, books that Suard had received free while editor of the *Gazette* and other journals. By 1772 he was also the literary correspondent of the margrave of Bayreuth (nephew of Frederick the Great), whom he had met at d'Holbach's home during the margrave's visit to Paris. With such connections, Suard was not about to starve.[30]

On May 7, 1772, Suard and the abbé Delille were elected members of the Académie Française. Exercising a rarely employed prerogative, Louis XV on May 9 annulled both elections.[31] It was assumed in some hopeful quarters that this was due to Suard's association with the philosophes, but given the composition of the Académie, this assertion was a dubious one unless one assumed a sudden and dramatic change of heart on the part of the king. Well over half of the men elected and admitted to the Académie during the immediately preceding years were philosophes or figures closely associated with them: Marmontel, Thomas, Condillac, Saint-Lambert, Gaillard and Arnaud. Furthermore, eleven days after crushing Suard's election, the king appointed the philosophe and encyclopédiste Marmontel as *historiographe de France*. What then explains the royal action? First of all there is evidence of an intrigue on the part of the maréchal de Richelieu; he was an enemy of the philosophes, and it was he who, by chance, occupied at that point the rotating position of *directeur* of the Académie, which obliged him to inform the king of the elections. The registers of the Académie Française recorded that on May 16, Richelieu was challenged at a seance of the Académie and denounced

---

[29] Mme Suard, *Suard*, 108-113.   [30] Ibid., 84-88, 114-120.
[31] *Registres de l'Académie Française*, III, 308-310.

for (1) having falsely accused the two men of actions which would displease the king, and (2) having charged to the king that the election of the two men on the same day was contrary to the regulations of the Académie (after having suggested to the Académie that it proceed in that fashion).[32] The latter argument, incidentally, was used by the court as justification for its action and explains why Delille had to share Suard's fate. Furthermore, the political circumstances at this time would explain why the king should have been open to Richelieu's alleged urgings. The election of Suard occurred only one year after the popular Choiseul's disgrace. Suard's name was associated in court circles with that of Choiseul, who had appointed him to his official posts, and his election may have been presented to the king as a show of support for the fallen minister, and thus as an insult to the king who had removed Choiseul and Suard from their places. Bachaumont, for example, recorded in the *Mémoires secrets* that at Versailles it was believed that the king found the election of Suard unacceptable because of his "having been removed from the *Gazette* at the displeasure of the Court."[33]

This view of Suard's exclusion is supported by the acts which followed it. The Académie proceeded to elect two new members, according to royal orders, but then voted *unanimously* to petition the king formally to reconsider his action. The king's cousin, the duc de Nivernais, was chosen by the Académie to present its case to the throne. A friend of Suard by this time, Nivernais both wrote and privately spoke to Louis, urging him to seek true information about the lives of the two men. There was no way to change the facts about Suard's association with the philosophes, but it could be demonstrated that Suard had not been a direct supporter or favorite of Choiseul, but had risen through other protectors. Thus on June 30, 1772, Louis XV's response to Nivernais was read to the Académie Française, and recorded in its minutes: "My dear cousin, I have enlightened myself . . . on the age [Delille's youth had been cited as a pretext for his exclusion] the principles and the morals of these two subjects . . . and as the report on them which was given to me is favorable, I charge you to announce to the Académie that I shall find it good that the Académie proposes them to me as soon as places are vacant."[34] Accordingly, the next two vacancies in the Académie

---

[32] Ibid., 310; see also Bachaumont, *Mémoires secrets*, VI, 131-135.
[33] Bachaumont, loc. cit.
[34] *Registres de l'Académie Française*, III, 311-314.

were filled by Delille and Suard, the latter being received as the successor to the bishop of Tricome on August 4, 1774. Suard's fall from grace in 1771-1772 was a political affair, and a temporary one. We have seen how rapidly his fortunes rose from this time.

The exile of Raynal from Paris (and initially from all of France) in 1781 was a more serious matter, but it is important to understand the nature of his "crime." Raynal's *Histoire philosophique des Deux Indes* had been published in 1770, and so for ten years its author had remained wholly at liberty despite the condemnations of the book by the *conseil d'état*, the parlement de Paris, and the Sorbonne. It was known by everyone that Raynal was the author of the *Histoire*, but he wisely denied it *pro forma*. Despite the fact that the *conseil d'état* even referred to the book in 1777 as "by the abbé Raynal,"[35] this formal denial of authorship sufficed to preserve Raynal from all legal action, while he continued to bask in the salons and among his high-placed friends as "the author of the *Histoire philosophique*." The authorities were perfectly content to condemn the work and police its circulation, without moving against the person of its universally recognized but formally unavowed author. The main effect of official persecution of those who sold the book was to drive up its price drastically, and rumor even had it that seized copies were being sold by government officials.[36]

For eight years this combination of strident condemnation, legal suppression in form, and tacit toleration in practice continued in France. Raynal became overconfident. In 1780 he published in Geneva, under his own supervision, a revised edition of the work which not only bore his name, but his portrait as well.[37] This was both a provocation and an insult to the government, parlement, and the Church, and on May 25, 1781, the parlement de Paris decreed that since the author had named himself, he be

[35] B.N., MS *Coll. A.-D.*, cxix, folio 211.

[36] On the police's treatment of the *Histoire philosophique des Deux Indes*, and their obvious difficulties, see B.N., MS *Coll. A.-D.*, xciv, folios 108, 138, 147; and cxx, folio 64. These documents indicate that a serious but unsuccessful effort to suppress the circulation of Raynal's *Histoire* was made by the inspectors of the police; they did succeed to make the book expensive. The condemnation of the book by the *conseil d'état* on December 19, 1772, is found in A.N., MS AD[III], 27.

[37] This is known as the third edition of Raynal's work. Although many new editions had appeared between 1770 and 1781, this represented the second major revision of the work.

228

"bodily apprehended, and in case of contumacy, his goods be seized and sequestered, until he presents himself before the court for interrogation."[38]

Actually, Raynal was given ample warning to leave France before his seizure, and he began his exile from France, which lasted until 1784. He travelled to the Low Countries, to England, to Germany and to Switzerland, visiting friends and various dignitaries. In 1784 he was allowed to return to France, but an edict of the *conseil* specifically forbade him to return to the capital. Accordingly, he settled in Provence, spending most of his time in Marseilles.[39]

His goods were never seized, and his well-placed friends remained such during his "ordeal." In 1788 in fact, Raynal endowed both the Académie royale des inscriptions et belles-lettres and the Académie royale des sciences with 25,714 *livres* apiece. This was to be used as a perpetual prize of 1,285 *livres* to be paid yearly by each Académie to some deserving aspirant, from "*Rentes* on the revenues of the king . . . in conformity with the intention of M. Guillaume Thomas Raynal, priest, who furnished the principal of the above-mentioned *rentes*."[40]

Raynal was not an outcast from society after his disgrace: the *dévots* had indeed triumphed against him, but only after he had left the authorities with no other choice. Clearly, Raynal's indiscretion forced the government to act against him, not the eight-year-clamor against his book by orthodox courtiers, magistrates and theologians. By the end of May 1781 Raynal was in Liège, where he was fêted by the prince-bishop of Liège, de Velbruck, who had allowed the publication of the *Histoire* in his own domains. He stayed at the home of Sabatier de Cabre, the king of France's *ministre-plénipotentiaire* in Liège, and was received by the leading notables of the city and the resident diplomatic corps. The Church in Liège was outraged by this reception, and after Raynal's departure in late June, when he followed the social elite of Europe to Spa, the local clerics succeeded in forcing their prince-bishop to suppress the *Histoire* locally.[41]

[38] The *arrêt* of the parlement de Paris also is found in A.N., MS AD^III, 27.

[39] On the circumstances of Raynal's departure from France, see G. de Froidcourt, *L'Abbé Raynal au pays de Liège*.

[40] B.N., MS *Fonds français*, 6429, folios 11-14.

[41] Froidcourt, op. cit.

229

When Gibbon met Raynal in Lausanne in 1783, he described the latter's conversation as being "intolerably . . . insolent," adding that "you would imagine that he alone was the Monarch and legislator of the world." Such a tone, however, apparently did not offend the company Raynal kept in Lausanne, for a month later Gibbon wrote to Lady Sheffield: "I was walking on our Terrace, with Mr. Tissot, the celebrated physician, Mr. Mercier . . . the abbé Raynal, M., Mme and Mlle Necker, the abbé de Bourbon—a natural son of Lewis the Fifteenth—the Hereditary prince of Brunswick, Prince Henry of Prussia, and a dozen counts, barons, and extraordinary persons among whom was a natural son of the Empress of Russia—Are you satisfied with this list which I could enlarge and embellish without departing from the truth . . . ?"[42] Wealthy and lionized, Raynal enjoyed his exile, and indeed chose to stay in Marseilles during 1789 and 1790 while the capital clamored for his return.

* * *

In theory, the police and administrators of the *librairie* were committed to the vigorous suppression of all books casting doubt upon the divine establishment of the crown or the Catholic Church, or the wisdom of the fundamental policies of crown and altar. In theory, following the edicts and laws, the authors of such works should have been in great peril.[43] Throughout the period from 1760 to 1789, works by Diderot, d'Holbach, Naigeon, Le Roy, Marmontel, Morellet, Suard, and Raynal were denounced as dangerous to the faith, the government, the social order, and public morals. In addition, works by Chastellux, Roux, and Saint-

[42] Gibbon, *Letters* (Norton), III, 9-10; see also ibid., II, 373, 381; III, 2.

[43] A royal declaration of 1728 condemned all authors found guilty of writing, "without permission," books that raised religious "disputes" (or touched upon those already raised), that "disturbed the tranquillity of the State," or "that corrupted morals" (all of them charges frequently raised against the philosophes), to banishment from the area of jurisdiction of the court which tried them, for a first offense, and to banishment from France in case of a second offense (B.N., MS *Coll. A.-D.*, VII, folio 190). In 1757 the *conseil d'état* raised the penalty for publishing, selling or distributing such works, including now any which "tend to attack religion," to death, even for a first offense, but it was not clear that this edict was directed in any way against authors who merely submitted manuscripts to a publisher (ibid., XXXIII, folio 142). Always present, of course, in theory, was the danger of being found guilty of "lèse-majesté humaine et divine." At any rate, not even the clergy expected such laws as that of 1757 to be utilized.

Lambert teemed with scarcely veiled anticlerical, anti-Christian, and often politically abrasive passages and themes. Why, in almost every case, did the authors go unpunished? Why were the members of the coterie holbachique so secure in their society despite their participation in a movement of thought specifically identified by the Church and its defenders as contrary to the established religion and values of France?

There are several general reasons for this, factors which were reflected in and in some ways magnified by the mechanism of policing the world of ideas and letters. First, and somewhat ironically, the very fact that France was an officially Catholic nation militated against any effective suppression of philosophical work. In nations with an established Church, in which large numbers of active citizens take religious questions seriously and in which the national Church is rent by divisions, two basic avenues are open to those seeking to prevent religious disputation from becoming dangerous political opposition. One is that of favoring one segment of the Church wholly and unequivocally, and of imposing with an iron hand the settlement agreed upon. The other is to allow a broad and comprehensive latitude in private belief, and to seek merely formal acquiescence to the public signs of the faith. In the first system, sustained polemics and bitter dispute are inevitable; the authorities are willing to pay that price, counting on the emergence of their favored side with the vigorous support of the law and of the forces of order. In the latter system, sustained polemics and bitter dispute are precisely what the authorities are attempting at all times to avoid. They know that certain writers are being covertly heretical, but they would prefer that no one notices; if a formal statement of vague orthodoxy is appended to a cleverly polemical work, they appreciate that the potentially explosive issues involved are not being brought to a clear focus. Eighteenth-century France followed the latter course, and Le Roy, Marmontel, Morellet, Suard, Chastellux, Roux, and Saint-Lambert all were perfectly willing to make that profession, however obvious it might be in the *Lettres sur les animaux*, *Bélisaire* and *Les Incas*, the treatises on toleration, the pages of the *Journal étranger* and the *Gazette de France*, *De la félicité publique*, the *Encyclopédie portative*, and the articles and *contes* of Saint-Lambert where their true sentiments toward the Church lay. The nation declared they were Catholics, and they themselves formally maintained that this was indeed the truth. The authorities did *not* want to begin asking the question of who truly was an "orthodox" Catholic by conviction and belief: they knew that such a query was both a religious and a political Pandora's box. That is part of the reason why, however frequently these formally "obedient" philosophes might be denounced, the government refrained from moving against them. Far more dangerous were the Jansenists, the authors of the *Nouvelles ecclésiastiques*, who wanted that fundamental question raised and wanted the ecclesiastical and political upheavals that might flow from it. It is not surprising, thus, that the files of the police and the administrators of the *librairie* reveal far more concern for the suppression of Jansenist propaganda than for the persecution of those members of the philosophical camp of Paris who were willing to make formal protestations, in print, of the innocence of their intentions. If the actual letters and notebooks of police inspector d'Hémery, the letters of Sartine, and the memoranda of Malesherbes in the exercise of their official duties indicate the real concerns of the authorities, then even the works of Diderot, d'Holbach, and Naigeon were perceived as less of a menace to the religious, political and social order than the polemics of Jansenists and Jesuits.[44] Atheism, after all, scarcely had a threatening political base in the France of the Ancien Régime, and it was hardly a vehicle for ecclesiastical opposition to the crown's or parlement's definitions of the Church's duties and rights. The first obligation of the police was to preserve order and respect for royal law. Jansenists, Jesuits, and a remonstrating Assemblée du Clergé constituted potential dangers in this regard, not the atheists of the salons. Scarcely anyone (outside the institutional Church) *truly* believed that the latter were a clear and present threat to the régime until the Revolution and the exile. The police, so long as they could report that only a few copies of the atheistic works were circulating, and at high prices, were not overly disturbed.[45]

[44] The letters of d'Hémery are found in B.N., MS *Nouv. acq.*, 1214; the notebooks of d'Hémery, his *Journal de la Librairie*, in B.N., MS *Coll. A.-D.*, xcvi-cv; the orders of Sartine in B.N., MS *Coll. A.-D.*, xciii-xciv; the memoranda of Malesherbes in B.N., MS *Nouv. acq.*, 3344-3348.

[45] Wholly typical was the response to the second volume of d'Holbach's *Théologie portative* in 1776. Denounced by the clergy and by diverse parlementaires and counselors at the Châtelet, it was pursued in the parlement de Paris by Séguier, the *avocat-général*, who termed it "a criminal project" that had moved from ridicule of religion to an attempt to destroy all foundations of religion; on February 17, 1776, it was condemned by the parle-

Second, in a society so divided by political questions and jurisdictional disputes, there was no way to achieve a unified and
concerted effort to impose intellectual order. The same parlement
that Joly de Fleury or Séguier could move to condemn a philosophical work was itself at odds with a police administration under
royal authority that sought to suppress the circulation of the
parlement's own remonstrances. The same Assemblée du Clergé
that demanded censure of and vigorous enforcement against books
impugning the dignity of the Church would itself contest the

ment (B.N., *Nouv. acq.*, 463, dossier 5619, folios 237, 242, which includes
Séguier's speech to the parlement), and an order was given for the arrest
of the authors listed on the title page of d'Holbach's book, one "abbé
Bernier" and his "disciple" (ibid., folio 239). The police administration
promised to the parlement the arrest of the authors (as well as of all those
involved in its production and distribution), "if it is possible to discover
them" (ibid., folio 237). On February 26, the *procureur-général* wrote a
memorandum to the *lieutenant-général de police*, reminding him of the call
for an investigation and the arrest of the authors, and asking "if you cannot indicate to me several witnesses . . . as well as the domicile of the
so-called abbé Bernier and his alleged disciple . . . ?" (ibid., folio 247). On
February 29, he received a reply, which informed him that "I have given
orders for the search for the abbé Bernier, who appears to be the author
of the work entitled the *Théologie portative*, as well as for the someone
named there as his disciple. As soon as I have information, I should be
honored to share it with you; but I cannot conceal from you, Monsieur,
that in all likelihood it is a name made up by the true author" (ibid., folio
246). With this formality out of the way, the authorities now moved to
the task which they indeed took seriously—to harass the colporteurs and
booksellers, and to attempt to minimize the number of copies circulating,
thereby affecting the price. As Bachaumont reported, that February, in an
effort to assuage the clergy, the customs posts were ordered to open all
packages entering France from abroad, and to do so with more regularity
than was customary; they still limited their searches to "those judged suspect," and the head of the *poste*, Bachaumont declared, was "forming a
library inexpensively . . ." (Bachaumont, *Mémoires secrets*, IX, 35-36).
D'Hémery truly attempted to mobilize his agents only when politically
relevant and thus threatening works were circulating. Faced with the condemned works of d'Holbach and Naigeon, he would note time and time
again, "from Rey [in Amsterdam, d'Holbach's publisher] . . . several copies
have arrived by the *poste*" (see, for example, B.N., MS *Coll. A.-D.*, CV,
folios 61, 63, 73, 96). It was expected that people of quality would read
these; the effort was to prevent them from being read too widely. Thus,
although *L'Antiquité dévoilée* had been condemned in the strongest terms,
d'Hémery could note that he knew to which seller Rey had sent copies, but
that "the magistrate has permitted [him] to sell several copies of this work"
(ibid., CIV, folio 7).

233

authority of a parlement it viewed as sympathetic to the Jansenists. The crown, at odds with both, did not appreciate interference with its jurisdictions in any area, including that of defense of the faith in the realms of police and administration of the *librairie*.[46] In the end, thus, the task of implementing the laws concerning books and authors was given to the royal bureaucracy alone, an intellectually diverse body of men who thrived on protection, patronage, formal (if insincere) statements of obedience, and informal, mutual accommodations among respectable persons—all modes of operation advantageous to the philosophes.

Two examples should suffice to indicate the benefits of such a system to the members of the coterie holbachique. In the mid-1760s Suard's and Arnaud's editorship of the *Gazette littéraire* came under attack from several theologians and the archbishop of Paris, for whom the unorthodox nature of the editors' articles was an outrage. A formal denunciation was presented to the duc de Praslin, who in turn gave it to Suard and Arnaud, who in turn showed it to Morellet, who printed a brochure in the editors' defense, attacking the Church for interfering in a civil matter of this sort. The Church had not even printed its critique. We know the denouement: by early 1766 the ministry of foreign affairs suppressed the *Gazette littéraire* (which was in financial difficulties) and immediately established Suard and Arnaud as editors of the *Gazette de France*, whose content would be philosophically indistinguishable from the former journal. The Church had been taught a lesson for its meddling.[47] The second example is equally revealing. In 1782 the king himself was offended by elements of Diderot's *Essai sur les règnes de Claude et de Néron* (according to Le Noir, Sartine's successor as *lieutenant-général de police*) and instructed Miromesnil, the *garde des sceaux*, "to punish this philosophe enemy of religion." Both Miromesnil and Le Noir, however, were admirers of Diderot, and as Le Noir described the scene of their encounter, which occurred in Miromesnil's office, Diderot genuflected and simply declared his "repentance." Le Noir later attested that "the philosophe was discharged with a severe reprimand." Soon afterward, Diderot

[46] On the policies and jurisdictional disputes of formal censorship, see Nicole Hermann-Mascard, *La censure des livres à Paris à la fin de l'Ancien Régime*, particularly 41-58.

[47] Morellet, *Mémoires*, I, 145-147; Morellet, *Observations sur une dénonciation de la Gazette littéraire*.

wrote to him: "The more I consider your régime, the more I see
. . . that we have in it the guarantee of our persons and properties.
When I was young, I lived on the 4th floor, I wrote nonsense,
and I was imprisoned in the dungeon of Vincennes for my *Bijoux
indiscrets*. Having acquired fortune and celebrity, I came down
from the 1st floor where I live, where I confess to having written
works yet more dangerous. I have been given a good and gentle
lesson; I am reformed [*corrigé*] for the rest of my life."[48]

Typically, one speaks of the "collusion" of men such as Malesherbes with the philosophes, as if those in the administration and
policing of the book trade somehow betrayed their duties out of
sympathy to the philosophic camp. It was not that. In more ways
than not, the police and the administration of the *librairie* served
precisely the role expected of them: to maximize order and calm
and to minimize affairs menacing to royal authority and the public order. Despite the formal duty of these officers to insure the
Catholic monopoly of truth, they were not the servants of the
Church or any of its elements. They were the servants of the king,
and they acted accordingly. As early as 1749, upon Diderot's arrest, the lawyer Barbier understood that the philosophe was not
in any danger. He wrote in his diary: "With regard to those writings which have no other crime than that of *esprit* and regulation
of *moeurs*, since such are read only by a few persons, credit and
protection will be able to save those sorts of [writers]; but for the
authors of verses reviling the king, there should not be any pardon,
and they should be punished severely."[49]

If we make of Barbier's category of "verses reviling the king"
a metaphor representing all attacks upon the authority and dignity
of the king and his court, then we have, within certain limits, the
policy pursued by the police and administrators of the *librairie*
during the period from 1760 to 1789. If one examines the archives
of these two offices, it becomes obvious that it was not the *Recueil
philosophique* of 1770 which truly disturbed them, but the *Recueil
des remonstrances et arrêtés du parlement de Bretagne en 1769 et
1770, concernant l'affaire des six magistrats*. Insults to God did not
send their agents scurrying into shops and *dépôts* to ferret out
offending books so much as insults to the king and queen, to noble
courtiers, to royal ministers and officials. In terms of their priori-

[48] All of the relevant documents relating to this small affair are found in
Diderot, *Corr.*, XV, 300-303.
[49] Barbier, *Journal*, IV, 337-338.

ties and their expenditures of effort, the royal authorities worried
far less about what circulated in the literary salons of Paris than
they did about what latest claim against royal prerogative was being read by the officials and *avocats* in the courtyard and environs
of the *Palais royal*. For some historians, perhaps, the danger to the
Ancien Régime came from the pens of the philosophes; to the
police, the danger to the régime was seen in the works of Jansenists, parlementaires and libelous satirists.[50]

This is not to say that the police or the administration of the
librairie ignored the philosophes, but simply that there was a vast
difference between the antiphilosophic denunciations and tocsins
of the parlement de Paris or the Assemblée du Clergé, on the one
hand, and the apparent quotidian concerns of royal agents dealing
with the book trade, on the other. The philosophes had their enemies, men who detested them for their unbelief, who begrudged
them their social successes, and who saw nothing fashionable or
wise in their works. At the parlement de Paris, Omer Joly de
Fleury and Séguier railed against them and worked hard to out-
law their writings; at the Assemblée du Clergé, leading ecclesiastics such as Lefranc de Pompignan implored the government to
intensify its efforts against impiety and bring offending authors to
account; at the Sorbonne, outraged doctors of theology attempted
time and time again to regain some control over the direction of
the nation's intellectual life; at the court, the party of the *dévots*
and, publicly at least, officials such as the duc de La Vrillière denounced the Parisian free-thinkers and deplored the decline in
respect for the Church and its established values. If one believed
Joly de Fleury, then the absolute first duty of the authorities dealing with the book trade was to protect France from "things which
work to the detriment of religion." He warned against "the philosophes . . . who favor independence in all things, [who] tend in
the most striking manner to downgrade religion, the authority of
the prince and the principles of good morals, from which the
bonds of society inevitably are broken."[51] If one believed Séguier,

[50] See the efforts of d'Hémery to suppress the circulation of the parlement de Bretagne's *Recueil*, for example, during precisely the most intensive
period of d'Holbach's and Naigeon's publications: the *Recueil* received
constant and pressing attention; the works of the latter two men received
the most sporadic and often only the most *pro forma* attention (B.N., MS
Coll. A.-D., xl, passim).

[51] B.N., MS *Nouv. acq.*, 2192, folio 195.

then d'Holbach and Naigeon (whom he listed simply as "the authors" of their books) were "guilty of the crime of divine and human *lèse Majesté*," a crime punishable by death.[52] If one believed the Assemblée du Clergé, then France was a "society doubly threatened by a multitude of audacious writers [who] trample underfoot divine and human laws . . . [respecting] nothing in the civil or in the spiritual order."[53]

During the period from 1765 to 1775, when d'Holbach and Naigeon were exploding what Diderot had termed their "bombs in the house of the lord," denunciations and demands for action against the books and their authors were communicated *ad infinitum* to the police, from the Clergé, the Sorbonne, the parlement, the Châtelet, and important private citizens.[54] Two factors, however, stand out in the police response to this general excitation. One, that when impelled to move vigorously, it was against the colporteurs and middlemen of the trade of these illicit books that they acted, spending almost no time in an effort to establish the identities of the authors. Two, that even under such intense pressure, the impulse to minimize scandal and preserve a system of gentlemanly accommodations still dominated their concerns. Repeated raids were made against merchants and peddlers, but remarkably, the same malefactors continually were simply fined or arrested for brief periods, then set free time and again to pursue the same illicit trade after promising they would not. The colporteur Lefèvre, for example, who was supplying such works as *Bélisaire*, *l'Antiquité dévoilée* and the *Système de la nature* to courtiers at Fontainebleau, was arrested at increasingly briefer intervals from 1766 to 1770. On October 4, 1767, a police raid caught him with contraband, and d'Hémery commented that "he is a bad subject who already has been recaptured several times and who certainly deserves to be chased from the court."[55] Yet ten days later he was rearrested, and d'Hémery, who admitted that his visit to Lefèvre's shop had given other vendors the time to hide their own illicit trade, once more noted that "as he is a bad citizen, I think that the Minister must exile him immediately from the court."[56] Only in August 1770 could d'Hémery at last note that

[52] Ibid., 460, dossier 5572, 124-124[1].
[53] *Procès-verbaux de l'Assemblée générale du Clergé de 1765*, 199.
[54] See, in particular, B.N., MS *Coll. A.-D.*, XL, 103-151.
[55] B.N., MS *Nouv. acq.*, 1214, folios 505-506.
[56] Ibid., folios 506-507.

Lefèvre had been imprisoned, after two years "of being given little fines whose costs [Lefèvre and several other frequently arrested sellers] threw off on the buyers."[57]

Occasionally the system could be vitalized for brief periods to
function efficaciously and imperiously against those engaged in
the circulation of "dangerous and impious books" in the capital
and its environs. The summer of 1770 was such a period. D'Holbach's *Système de la nature* had served as the final straw of impiety
in some quarters, and the agencies of the police and *librairie*
bestirred themselves. Everyone knew, the records reveal, that such
works were coming in from abroad in the trunks or under the
seals of officials, aristocrats, and figures at the court, but no one
was prepared to violate the tacit privilege of such notables to be
free from inspection at customs barriers.[58] As always, therefore,
the brunt of police efforts was felt by the peddlers. Even in this
instance, however, by September those officials opposed to harsh
measures could begin to make their influence felt. Thus, in July
1770 a colporteur by the name of Albois was arrested for distributing condemned philosophical works "in Paris and as far as
Rambouillet," and the police moved vigorously to assemble the
evidence of their case against him, including confessions by other
peddlers who had done business with him.[59] On August 30 the
procureur-général of the parlement de Paris wrote to Sartine, asking if Albois had sold works specifically listed as "criminal" by

[57] Ibid., folios 602-605.

[58] We have noted the apparent exception of 1776, although once again
it was left to the customs officials to decide what was "suspect," and important and titled figures passed such barriers with ease. Another device employed, as noted in the communication of d'Holbach's manuscripts to Holland (see infra, Chapter Two), was simply to send books and manuscripts
across frontiers or provinces under the official seals of functionaries whose
mail was free from inspection. When the abbé Coger or the syndic of the
Sorbonne, Riballier, wished to read the latest atheistic works of d'Holbach
and Naigeon, they knew exactly what to do: they wrote directly and politely to Marc-Michel Rey in Amsterdam, and ordered their purchases to
be sent to Sartine himself. Indeed Coger ordered (for himself and Riballier)
some forty books from Rey, well over twenty of which were either written
or edited by d'Holbach and/or Naigeon. Coger even wrote to Rey com-
plaining that his copy of the *Système de la nature* had arrived in damaged
condition. See J. T. de Booy, "L'Abbé Coger, dit *Coge Pecus*, lecteur de
Voltaire et de d'Holbach," in Besterman, *Studies on Voltaire and the Eighteenth Century* XVII (1961), 183-196.

[59] Albois was captured in the same raid as Lefèvre; see above, n. 57.

the parlement on August 18, which was in fact the case, and which necessitated stern punishment according to that edict.[60] In mid-September, however, the duc de Noailles wrote to the *procureur-général* about Albois, informing him that "several persons who know [Albois] personally, and in whom I take an interest, beg me to solicit your mercy in favor of this unfortunate," concluding that "I have no doubt that he will obtain his liberty from you, and I would be infinitely obliged to you if you would indeed accord it to him."[61] That same week, the duc de Chevreuse wrote to the *procureur-général* with a similar request, informing him that "this unfortunate" had a wife and five children now "reduced to mendicity by their father's imprisonment," that "I know your compassionate heart too well, Monsieur, to believe that you would want to allow an entire family to perish from misery," that "this desolated family" had "no other resource but the commerce of this person when he had his liberty." The letter concluded with the formulary request for the "grace" which would free him.[62] Chevreuse received a positive reply, expressing how "flattered" the official was "to be able to concur in what you desire."[63] In short, once dangerous works were confiscated, those involved in such a trade, even the lowly colporteurs, could benefit from the personal and intellectual sympathies of important figures. Even confiscated books, in fact, could be rescued. In January 1768, for example, when hundreds of seized copies of d'Holbach's and Naigeon's works were being stored in the Bastille, d'Hémery informed Sartine that he would have to send him "one copy in two volumes of *Le despotisme oriental*, which was seized at the bookseller Marin's last December 23, to be returned to Mme de Polignac, to whom this book belongs, and who has charged me to ask for its return from the magistrate."[64]

The laxity of the police toward the philosophes was not always the fruit of ignorance. In May 1768 inspector d'Hémery was perfectly aware that Marmontel was personally supervising the publication of new printings of the forbidden *Bélisaire*, and was receiving 600 *livres* per one thousand books printed. Through an informer, he learned that the printer Gaubry currently was involved in such production. D'Hémery saw such information *not*

---

[60] B.N., MS *Nouv. acq.*, 460, dossier, 5572, folios 130-131.
[61] Ibid., folio 129.   [62] Ibid., folio 127.
[63] Ibid., folio 126.   [64] Ibid., 1214, folio 523.

as a means to act against Marmontel and Gaubry, but as a means to seize prohibited books in Gaubry's shop.[65]

In dealing with respectable persons, the police clearly felt obligated to honor the most correct procedure, not acting until they possessed clear and irrefutable *proof* of their charges, even if such charges could have been formulated on the basis of knowledge provided by their informers. For example, in October 1767 d'Hémery and Sartine were certain they knew which friends of Marmontel, including d'Alembert and Morellet, were overseeing the publication and distribution of a work in support of *Bélisaire*. They several times sent agents to attempt to purchase the work from these philosophes. When the philosophes refused to fall into their trap, however, the police simply admitted defeat.[66] Such a convention helps explain why Raynal was not acted against until he himself provided the demonstration of his authorship of the *Histoire philosophique des Deux Indes*.

On the whole, then, the philosophes of the coterie holbachique had little to fear from the police. Grimm initially had been worried about Diderot's possible persecution for the sins of the *Encyclopédie*, but by 1764 he seemed to understand that it was not the doctors of theology who controlled the fate of the Parisian thinkers. Upon the appearance in Paris of some verses urging the Sorbonne to employ its "thunder" against infidelity, Grimm observed, "It's a shame that the thunder of the Sorbonne resembles the thunder of the Opéra, which no longer frightens anyone, not even children."[67] As clear as this might seem in retrospect, it was by no means obvious to all of them at the time, and the fear of both scandal and persecution could cause them genuine concern. The danger that was perceived perhaps arose from the inconsistencies of administration, including those of police enforcement, in the Ancien Régime. At times, especially after the appearance of particularly outrageous works, the pressures from the Church and parlement must have seemed simply too great to ignore. It must have seemed sometimes as if the political necessities of particular situations demanded that the government move vigorously against impious authors, as in 1770 when the Assemblée du Clergé appeared to demand such action as the price of its *don gratuit*. Diderot feared for d'Holbach and Naigeon from 1767 to 1769 in the

[65] Ibid., folios 536-538.
[66] B.N., MS *Coll. A.-D.*, CIV, folio 87.
[67] Grimm, *Corr. litt.*, v, 444.

240

face of official denunciations; Galiani feared for d'Holbach in 1770, when the Clergé issued its demands.[68] At other times, however, Marmontel could defy the Sorbonne with eventual impunity, and Diderot could receive the slightest reprimand for a book offensive to the king himself. What might have befallen d'Holbach had his identity as author of the *Système de la nature* been discovered by the authorities? Perhaps a terrible example would have been made of him. It is more likely, however, that without formal proof, he simply would have issued a vigorous denial of the charges and ceased his philosophical endeavors. If somehow formal proof of his guilt existed, parlement would probably have ordered his arrest a day or two after his well-placed friends had advised him of the need to leave France. The *conseil* would have exiled him, and he would have established himself—perhaps in London, perhaps in Germany—among his friends. The affair, however, would have been a terrible scandal, compromising his guests, including leading diplomats and even the abbé Bergier. The unmistakable conclusion one must draw from the records of the police and the *librairie* is that it was precisely scandal that they most diligently sought to avoid.

The most effective act of suppression of the printed word in that summer and fall of 1770 was achieved not at d'Holbach's and Naigeon's expense, but rather at that of Séguier, whose *réquisitoire* to the parlement de Paris against the flood of atheistic and impious works was itself ultimately banned by the royal government and, under pressure, by the parlement as well. Séguier apparently had decided that the time was at hand to warn the nation against such incredulity in the strongest possible language. The *avocat-général* had denounced seven works, six of which, in fact, were written, edited or translated by d'Holbach and Naigeon. In

---

[68] See infra, Chapter Two. The harsh punishment of the colporteur Lécuyer and his associates in 1768, which involved deportation to the galleys and imprisonment for several years, horrified the philosophes (Diderot, *Corr.*, VIII, 185-188), but Lécuyer had been arrested and set free scores of times between 1760 and 1768, not only for the sale of condemned philosophic works, but for political brochures as well, and his final arrest involved the sale of libels, and defenses of parlementaire rights, as well as of works by d'Holbach and Naigeon. See B.N., MS *Nouv. acq.*, 1214, passim (beginning with folio 323). See also Bachaumont, *Mémoires secrets*, IV, 113. The case of Lécuyer, with his constant recidivism, reveals the laxity of the administration, and the danger, above all, of the occasional overconfidence which this produced. In its conclusion, nevertheless, Lécuyer's case was a dramatic exception.

his *réquisitoire*, which normally would have been printed at the head of the parlement's *arrêt*, he painted the darkest picture of the scourge of disbelief, extensively quoting from or paraphrasing the condemned books to demonstrate their criminal content. He then denounced the general sympathy and tolerance of men of letters for such thoughts and opinions. Both of these aspects of his *réquisitoire* were considered a scandal, the first for disseminating the very words whose circulation the *arrêt* was attempting to prevent, the second for offending a large body of respectable citizens. The philosophes had the pleasure of seeing their implacable enemy Séguier humiliated by the odd title of this condemnation, "*Arrêt du parlement*, printed without the *réquisitoire* of M. Séguier, on the basis of which it was rendered. . . ."[69]

In the midst of the scandal caused by Séguier's *réquisitoire*, an incident developed at the Académie Française of precisely the sort that the royal government was seeking to avoid by its suppression of Séguier's earnest attack upon the world of letters. The details of this incident bring into sharp relief some of the anomalies of intellectual, social and political life in the milieu of the philosophes. On September 6, 1770, the archbishop of Toulouse, Loménie de Brienne, was received as a member of the Académie Française. At the seance in his honor, Marmontel read a long section from his work *Les Incas*, a bitter attack upon Catholic intolerance. The philosophe Thomas officially welcomed de Brienne to the Académie that day, and his welcoming speech to the archbishop was a stern rebuke of Séguier for his antiphilosophic *réquisitoire*. Séguier, a member of the Académie since 1757, rushed from the meeting to see the chancellor, Maupeou, who forbade the publication of Thomas's *discours*. At the next seance of the Académie, Saint-Lambert, a member only since June 23 of that year, denounced Séguier publicly for his censorship of Thomas and proposed the dismissal of the *avocat-général* from that body, accusing him of "treason." The philosophe Duclos argued against the motion, apparently fearing its consequences, and dissuaded Saint-Lambert from pursuing his effort. That this member of the coterie holbachique felt secure enough by 1770 to so assault the dignity of the king's advocate, however, is significant, as is the ability of

[69] For Séguier's *réquisitoire*, see B.N., MS *Nouv. acq.*, 460, dossier 5572, folios 147-151; for the crown's intervention against the parlement's inclusion of the *réquisitoire*, see ibid., folios 119, 140-141, 146; for the *Arrêt* "printed without the *réquisitoire*," see ibid., folio 117.

a fellow devotee of the rue Royale, Marmontel, to describe to the archbishop of Toulouse, from an official platform, the horrors of forced Catholic conversion.[70]

As we have seen in the cases of Marmontel's and Morellet's imprisonments, to be protected from libel and satire by the authorities was the right of those of high rank or official favor. In 1757 a work ridiculing Diderot and his associates had been allowed to circulate in Paris; d'Hémery had commented that it was "a very strong satire against the encyclopédistes, who do not appear too much in favor at the present."[71] In 1770, however, when *L'homme dangereux*, an attack upon Diderot and the philosophes, was submitted to the authorities, Sartine wrote to Diderot, sending him the manuscript and asking him if the book should be tolerated or suppressed. Diderot thanked the *lieutenant-général* for letting "the philosophical camp" see it, assured him that its insults were risible and would do the most harm to their author, and advised him that no one would overreact to such a work.[72] After Marmontel's rise to fame, Malesherbes threatened with total suppression a journal which had criticized the eminent literary figure harshly, and informed the offending journalist that "the intention of *M. le chancelier* is to prohibit absolutely this periodical if a piece of this nature appears again."[73] In 1772, when the Sorbonne decided not to move against Marmontel's *Les Incas* despite their syndic's desire to do so, Bachaumont recorded that Marmontel himself made much of that fact: "the Academician today takes pride in that silence, and claims that the doctors [of theology] did not dare to attack him."[74] In 1773 Helvétius enjoyed a posthumous triumph which demonstrated quite well the helplessness of those who did not admire the works of the philosophes, but who accepted the social conventions of their age. As the marquis de Noailles wrote to the duc d'Aiguillon from The Hague: "I believed, M. le duc, that the ecstasy of the philosophes had achieved its summit; but I have just come to realize that there is always some [new] path to be travelled. . . . A posthumous work by Helvétius [*De l'homme*] appeared not long ago. . . . This new

---

[70] *Registres de l'Académie Française*, III, 279; Collé, *Journal et mémoires*, III, 268-275.

[71] B.N., MS *Coll. A.-D.*, c, folio 67.

[72] Diderot, *Corr.*, X, 72-75. See also Grimm, *Corr. litt.*, IX, 50-55.

[73] B.N., MS *Nouv. acq.*, 3531, folio 183.

[74] Bachaumont, *Mémoires secrets*, X, 67.

243

work . . . is dedicated to the empress of Russia. M. le prince Galitzine, her minister at the Hague, has circulated the maximum number of copies that he possibly could. He even forced me to accept one of them. . . ."[75] Most of the members of the coterie holbachique, however, fully enjoyed the fruits of favor and rank while still alive.

* * *

Unless they wantonly ignored those proprieties and social conventions which so served their ascent, the philosophes of the rue Royale enjoyed a security befitting their inherited or achieved status and the influence of their friends and protectors. Increasingly from 1760 to 1789 they enjoyed the pleasures of fame as well, even in the midst of those who detested their beliefs. The Baronne d'Oberkirch was shocked and horrified by Raynal's *Histoire philosophique des Deux Indes*, but she received and entertained him at Montbéliard because he was "a famous personage" with "a great reputation": "we welcome all celebrities," she wrote, ". . . except that we don't [feign] to approve of opinions that we do not share."[76] So many persons of noble and high estate admired the work and abilities of these philosophes, or simply approved of them as social companions, that the men of the coterie could pass most of the time they spent in the company of notables being flattered and truly courted. Even their minor difficulties with the authorities could not dampen this. As the comte de Ségur recalled, "Public opinion became a force of opposition which triumphed over all obstacles. The condemnation of a book was a title of consideration for the author."[77] Ségur was born in 1753 and came to manhood at a time when most of the members of the coterie holbachique occupied places of prestige in the literary, scientific and philosophic worlds. In his *Mémoires* he attempted to describe the attitude held by his generation of "liberal" aristocrats toward the philosophes of his day. The *dévots* of Versailles might look upon the Parisian intellectual community with dismay, he concluded, but they simply did not represent the current tastes and values: "The court alone preserved its habitual superiority; but as the *courtiers* in France are much more the servants of fashion than the servants of the prince, they found it good for the sake of

[75] Published in Diderot, *Corr.*, XIII, 56.
[76] Baronne d'Oberkirch, *Mémoires*, I, 123-125.
[77] Comte de Ségur, *Mémoires et Anecdotes*, II, 11.

appearance to descend from their rank, and to come pay their court to Marmontel, to d'Alembert, to Raynal, in the hope of raising themselves, by this proximity, in public opinion."[78]

D'Holbach and his devotees could flatter the courtiers with equal assiduity, and there are letters, verses and dedicatory epistles which they themselves scarcely could have taken seriously. In the final analysis, however, they rose far above dependence and servility and were men of genuine importance and respectability. At the most general level, it is tempting to say that they offered to "enlightened" men born to privilege a chance to demonstrate to themselves and society their liberality. They allowed the privileged to incorporate into their self-images their associations with and support of men who seemed to be the enemies of arbitrary authority in literary, scientific, philosophical, ethical and even, in theory, political realms, at the same time that they all continued to benefit socially and economically from the arbitrary conventions of the Ancien Régime. The ultimate fruit of such associations for even such relatively humbly born figures as Marmontel, Suard, Grimm, Roux and Diderot was an elevation into positions of arbitrary authority and influence themselves. In 1782, for example, the authors of the *Mémoires secrets* complained of Suard's unmerited appointment to the governing board of the Opéra: "He persuaded the minister of Paris that he would be very useful at the Opéra, and . . . he had himself initiated into the committee which passes judgment on the works to be presented. . . . For that he received 2,400 *livres* in pension from the treasury of this theater."[79] Two months later Suard was being ignored by the authors at the Opéra. He complained to the minister, who strengthened his position and insisted that he be obeyed. "The authors," the *Mémoires secrets* added, "are still murmuring against it."[80] In a very real sense, the Revolution struggled not only against the privileged or delegated powers of men such as Chastellux, Saint-Lambert, Le Roy, d'Holbach and Grimm—men who were able to gain positions and sinecures for themselves and their friends—but also against precisely the sort of arbitrary authority granted to men such as Suard. The revolutionary campaign against the Académies, the Facultés, the boards of royal censors, and the editors of privileged journals was an attempt to overcome

---

[78] Ibid., 53.
[79] Bachaumont, *Mémoires secrets*, xxi, 97-99.
[80] Ibid., 163-164.

that intellectual elite of the Ancien Régime in which the members of the coterie holbachique were so enmeshed.

* * *

Whatever their private reservations and whatever the shape of things they desired for posterity, most of the members of the coterie holbachique reflected, in the way they lived their lives, the fundamental values and attitudes of the milieus in which they had succeeded. They vied for formal positions and dignities, often irrespective of the emoluments attached to them, and served willingly as agents of the authorities in their respective fields. They accepted the legitimacy of the institutions of privilege into which they rose, and defended the prerogatives of these. They not only tolerated, but actively sought, the benefits of favoritism offered them by social or political notables.

For some, such as Diderot, such profit may have necessitated basic changes in their own manners of thinking, but perhaps if we knew them better in the 1740s and their early years in Paris, when the public records of their thoughts and actions were few, we should find nothing to cause surprise concerning their later lives. Nevertheless, it is interesting to note some of the apparent adjustments of attitudes. In 1753 Grimm wrote to a noble German friend: "I beg of you never to give me either quality or title; the one and the other are ridiculous in this country, where one finds that an honorable man can bear nothing more honorable than his name alone."[81] In 1770 he was ennobled by the Empire, and he clearly insisted on being known as the "baron de Grimm." His affectations became manifold, and while a haughty aristocrat such as Tilly could accept hospitality in Grimm's private *loge* at the Feydeau, he could not restrain himself from remarking privately on Grimm's social pretensions, his lack of any social modesty.[82] Among Grimm's friends, only the always cynical Galiani appears truly to have teased the new baron, and even Diderot began referring to him by his title in his letters. In 1771 Galiani wrote a newsy letter addressed, indeed, to "Monsieur le baron de Grimm," in which he asked his friend to "tell these miracles to the real baron [d'Holbach]."[83] The next year he wrote to Mme d'Epinay

[81] Quoted in Cazes, *Grimm et les Encyclopédistes*, 12.
[82] Comte A. de Tilly, *Mémoires . . . pour servir à l'histoire des moeurs de la fin du 18ᵉ siècle*, II, 293-294.
[83] Galiani, *Lettres* (Asse), I, 257-258.

with news for "the baron (I mean the baron de Grimm), for whom we must find a name to distinguish him from the veritable baron, for the true Amphitryon is the one who wines and dines, and the baron de Grimm does not give dinners. . . ."[84] Although Galiani was being less than serious when he described the role of host as critical to true regality, or in this case gentility, it is not without interest that as soon as they had adequate means, Grimm, Morellet, Marmontel and Suard began their individual salons, as Helvétius and d'Holbach had done.

We have alluded to Darcet's loyalty to the Faculté de Médecine when its place as the premier medical body in the institutions of the Ancien Régime was challenged by the Société royale de médecine in the late 1770s. In his youth Darcet had defied his father and sacrificed his position to pursue his apparent love, the study of chemistry and medicine. Ultimately this earned for him a prominent place within an official body, the Faculté, which, despite its honors to Darcet and its provision of opportunities to him and its handful of competent *docteurs-régents* to perform useful public services, was an intellectually narrow and moribund scientific institution. The Faculté de Médecine, for example, had been the center of opposition to the introduction of inoculation in France, a cause in whose behalf Roux, Chastellux, Morellet, Diderot, Marmontel, and Grimm had taken active roles, and which Darcet, who generally was among the most progressive elements of the Faculté, undoubtedly supported.[85] The doctors who had come together in the Société de médecine, which soon received royal recognition, had done so to provide a voice and public role to less tradition-bound and antique medical and scientific figures than the *docteurs-régents* of the Faculté, and Darcet was one of those few of the latter who joined them. When the Société and the *docteurs* came into jurisdictional conflicts, however, Darcet was one of the first to leave and condemn it, and to denounce in particular the "ingratitude" of those who had "betrayed" their

---

[84] Ibid., 343.

[85] Bachaumont's description of the doctors of the Faculté de Médecine who came *en masse* to the crucial vote against lifting a ban on inoculation is worth quoting: "The anti's . . . had gathered up all the old men, the ill, the gouty, the most obscure doctors, in a word, the dregs of their confrères, and had come in a formidable force." On the Faculté de Médecine and the question of inoculation, see Bachaumont, *Mémoires secrets*, II, 89, 98, 106-107, 170-171, 261-262; III, 293-294; IV, 60-62, 74-75, 96-97; and Grimm, *Corr. litt.*, VI, 248-252, 300-301; VII, 319-321.

official *corps*.[86] In short, the man who earlier had gambled everything for his intellectual attachment to medical science now valued less the progress of his discipline than the preservation of the singular position of a privileged and often despotic medical ruling elite from which he derived so much of his patronage and status.

Such loyalty was by no means atypical. We have seen Saint-Lambert's effort to oust Séguier from the Académie as traitor to the *corps*. In 1782 Suard, as royal censor, banned a play parodying an academician for "attacking the glory of a member of the Académie Française."[87] In 1786 Marmontel, as *secrétaire-perpétuel*, suppressed the publication of the inaugural discourse of the newly elected Sedaine, censuring it as injurious to many members of the Académie; Sedaine had attacked the pretensions of contemporary men of letters.[88] In the final analysis, perhaps even the attendance of the members of the coterie holbachique at the mass of the Académie was an act of loyalty, of *esprit de corps*.

They were all men who quite naturally accepted the benefits of their privileges and positions. When Roux, as editor of the *Annales typographiques* and, later, of the *Journal de médecine*, found himself in conflict with other journalists concerning the scope of his exclusive *privilège royal*, Malesherbes intervened decisively on his behalf.[89] When a publisher in Toulouse counterfeited Marmontel's *Contes moraux* in 1781, in an age when writers were notoriously unprotected from such abuses, he pursued a case against them, and the *conseil d'état* itself, the highest court in the land, condemned the publisher to a fine of 6,000 *livres*, one-third of which went directly to Marmontel.[90]

Many of them either accepted the validity of their society's distinction between the free expression of ideas and libel (or satire) against important persons or were guilty of a great inconsistency. Once they themselves had risen into positions of dignity, they often were willing to use their status in the world of letters and in society to secure their reputations and to protect themselves from critics less favored than they. In 1771 a writer by the name of Clément published a study critical of several leading fig-

---

[86] Bachaumont, *Mémoires secrets*, XII, 140; see also Delauney, *Le monde médical Parisien*, 310-323.

[87] Bachaumont, *Mémoires secrets*, XX, 19.

[88] Grimm, *Corr. litt.*, XIV, 300, 304.

[89] B.N., MS *Coll. A.-D.*, LXXV, folios 171-179; ibid., LXXXI, folio 93.

[90] Bachaumont, *Mémoires secrets*, XVII, 198.

ures in the letters and arts; he took Saint-Lambert to task, allowing himself several disparaging personal allusions, much as Marmontel and Morellet imprudently had allowed themselves in 1759-1760. As Grimm's *Correspondance littéraire* related the affair, the figures criticized in Clément's piece sought the intervention of the authorities, and among them, "M. de Saint-Lambert, more determined than anyone to have the authorities act successfully, is the one who took the steps to halt the publication of the work." Clément, told of Saint-Lambert's actions, sent him a note "which the latter found impudent, and M. Clément, as a result, was imprisoned in Fort-l'Evêque. . . ."[91] It is not clear if Clément remained there for one or for three days, but it demonstrated strikingly to unprotected writers the dangers of considering successful philosophes as targets for attack. Several years later, when another critic dared write against Saint-Lambert, Bachaumont could record that once again the outraged poet "used his credit to have this book suppressed."[92]

Even Diderot, when he informed Sartine that he personally had no objections to allowing the publication and performance of *L'homme dangereux*, had qualified his recommendation somewhat by warning Sartine against being associated with the granting of permission to a work that posterity would hold in opprobrium.[93] Suard, however, as a royal censor, relieved Sartine of that choice: he banned the work as "a libel, not a comedy," and advised the police that "this genre must be proscribed."[94] Ultimately, the author who had dared satirize the philosophic camp had to publish his work clandestinely in Geneva. Clearly there were members of the coterie holbachique who distinguished quite sharply between their own freedoms and those of others, when certain conventions were at stake. Even an ardent defender of religious and philosophical toleration such as Marmontel could write to Malesherbes demanding "justice" after a personal criticism of his poetic judgment had appeared in a journal.[95]

Brissot recalled in his *Mémoires* that he had been so outraged by affairs such as these, and in general by the "egoism and arrogance . . . [and] despotism" of the established Parisian philosophes,

[91] Grimm, *Corr. litt.*, IX, 241-243.
[92] Bachaumont, *Mémoires secrets*, V, 203.
[93] Diderot, *Corr.*, X, 74-75.
[94] Suard, *Mémoires et correspondances* (Nisard), 160-210 (which includes many of Suard's judgments as censor).
[95] B.N., MS *Nouv. acq.*, 3531, folios 129-130.

that he had been tempted to write for an antiphilosophic journal alongside of Clément and Palissot; only his aversion to men who were also "the enemies of Voltaire and Rousseau," he maintained, restrained him. Brissot recalled as well that when he had sought to publish letters critical of Chastellux's analysis of slavery, the editors of the *Journal de Paris* (where Suard was then *directeur*) refused to print them. The reason, he was certain, was that Chastellux was "powerful," while he (Brissot) was merely "an isolated *politique*, without worshippers." If we are to believe Brissot, Morellet and Suard were among a group of pensioned figures who dissuaded him from printing a paradoxical dissertation on property and theft. Given Suard's role in attempting to suppress *Figaro* as contrary to decent order, the charge is not improbable.[96]

It would be a mistake, undoubtedly, to generalize such behavior to include all members of the coterie holbachique, but such incidents do illustrate the authority and proximity to power found within a group that Becker could term "beyond the social pale" and Gay could see as "indefatigable radicals."[97] Even a relatively unassuming person such as Darcet experienced that authority, sitting on royal committees which determined the legal status of "mesmerism" or the electrotherapy of Ledru and Marat.[98] Even Roux could decide to publish articles supporting inoculation and to suppress those opposed to it, excerpting the work of his medically unqualified friend Chastellux for the medical community of France.[99]

They also could use their influence and authority for the benefit of others, and this was for them an important part of their lives. When the writers of the *Journal de Paris* found themselves in difficulty in 1786, the *Mémoires secrets* could speak of Suard as "their protector at this time" and of how they were "supported by his credit and his intrigues."[100] When a liberal aristocrat undertook a study of accidental deaths and working conditions among the building-trade workers of Paris, he could write to Suard: "As M. Suard has the greatest credit with the police, I beg of him to obtain for me the following answers."[101] In 1768 and 1771 Diderot and Marmontel could intercede successfully at court with the comte

---

[96] Brissot, *Mémoires*, I, 87-88, 137-138; IV, 18, 22, 44.
[97] See infra, Introduction.
[98] Delauney, *Le monde médical Parisien*, 356-366.
[99] *Journal de médecine*, XIX-XXI (1763-1764), passim.
[100] Bachaumont, *Mémoires secrets*, XXXII, 282-283.
[101] B.N., MS *Nouv. acq.*, 23,639, folio 19.

de Saint-Florentin to gain assistance for "two . . . unfortunate women."[102] Indeed in 1771 Diderot could advise a supplicant that when one needed help at court, "visit Marmontel."[103] When Necker wanted d'Angiviller to seek the ministry of finance, he solicited the "strong urgings" of Raynal.[104] When the comte de Ségur aspired to the post of *ministre-plénipotentiaire* of the king of France at the Russian court, Grimm secured Catherine's approval.[105] In 1778, when Buffon wished to secure a privilege from the court, specifically from Maurepas, it was to Le Roy, among others, that he turned.[106]

D'Holbach's influence, whatever the philosophy he openly espoused among his friends and important visitors, was significant, as befitted the brother-in-law of a *maître des requêtes* and *intendant*. On August 13, 1763, d'Holbach's friend the banker Foley came to him in desperation, the victim of a false rumor started by a postal agent named Blatry to the effect that Foley was on the verge of bankruptcy. D'Holbach forwarded Foley's written complaint against Blatry to Sartine himself, with the following note: ". . . M. Foley, English banker residing in this city, knowing your benevolence towards me, believed that you would indeed consider favorably the contents of the enclosed petition. I thus dare to beg of you, Monsieur, to secure for him the just satisfaction that he demands. . . . I have no doubts that your friendship for me will engage you to satisfy so equitable a request."[107] Sartine forwarded the note to an inspector that same day, with instructions "to verify [this] very promptly, to arrest this agent if the facts are correct, [and] to report to me on it immediately." Before the day was over, Blatry was a prisoner in the Bastille.[108]

[102] Diderot, *Corr.*, VIII, 95-96; XI, 219-221.

[103] Ibid., XI, 221.

[104] Comte d'Angiviller, *Mémoires de Charles Claude Flahaut Comte de la Billarderie d'Angiviller. Notes sur les Mémoires de Marmontel*, L. Bobé, ed., 69.

[105] *Recueil des instructions données aux ambassadeurs et ministres de France*, IX, 385-386; Grimm also involved Helvétius, at the behest of d'Argental and Praslin, in a high-level diplomatic effort to secure an alliance between Frederick the Great and France. Helvétius, coached by Grimm and the French ministry, played the role of intermediary and advocate. See the archival material published by Keim, *Helvétius*, Appendix I, 701-713.

[106] Buffon, *Corr.*, II, 397-398.

[107] Bibliothèque de l'Arsenal, MS 12,176, folios 22-23. Lough, "Le baron d'Holbach," has printed this, but he did not indicate Sartine's note in response to it, which follows.

[108] Bibliothèque de l'Arsenal, MS, 12,176, folio 23.

We already have seen how d'Holbach was able to intervene with the comte de Bissie at Versailles, to secure a passport for Lawrence Sterne during a period when France and England were at war. When Diderot was embroiled with his publisher in 1764, he threatened Le Breton with the Baron's name: "How the Baron d'Holbach would send you to pasture, you and your plates, if I said one word to him." Indeed, Diderot threatened him with the entire coterie, telling Le Breton that his messenger had arrived just as he was leaving for d'Holbach's salon, and that if he chose to denounce the publisher there, "your work would be discredited and lost."[109] He would not have written such a letter if the names involved did not carry a certain weight. The Baron was a man of importance. When Hume came to Paris with the English ambassador, he wrote to Robertson about the great reception of the *History* there, "whose success has given me the Occasion to promise your Acquaintance to several Persons of Distinction, the Duc de Nivernais, the Marquis de Puysieulx, President Hainaut [*sic*], Baron d' Holbac [*sic*], etc."[110]

D'Holbach employed his great wealth effectively, utilizing it, as he once told Naigeon, "to effect the good more efficaciously. . . ."[111] He supported young writers and patronized artists and musicians; according to Diderot, he even loaned the *Encyclopédie* a large sum of money for three years without interest during one of its difficult periods.[112] In 1772 Diderot described a more intriguing use of the Baron's fortune: "The Baron has a kind of policy which will make you smile. When some religious work in a foreign language appears, he quickly calls upon some imbecilic tartar whom he has in his pay, who translates this work, who translates it glumly and strikes it dead."[113]

If, on the whole, d'Holbach acted out of the public eye, other members of the coterie holbachique preferred to see their reputations ever enhanced by their actions. In 1784 when the University of Pennsylvania wrote a grandiloquent letter to Chastellux, praising him for having obtained from the king (actually through the intercession of Vergennes) a large number of books from the royal library for their own collection, it was reported that "M. le marquis de Chastellux justly glories in such a correspondence,

---

109 Diderot, *Corr.*, IV, 300-306.
110 Hume, *Letters* (Grieg), I, 495-496.
111 *Journal de Paris* (1789), 9 Feb., 177.
112 Diderot, *Corr.*, IX, 29-31.   113 Ibid., XII, 45.

and shows it to whomever wants to read it, and has even had fragments of it inserted in the *Mercure*."[114] Saint-Lambert did much the same when he was named an honorary citizen of New Haven for his devotion to American liberty.[115] Marmontel, of course, had published every letter in Paris that he had received from foreign crowns during the *Bélisaire* affair, but he could act in a similar manner for a less exalted cause. In 1786 he not only shocked everyone by competing for a literary prize that many felt should have been reserved for less laureled brows, but "took himself to Versailles to read the piece to M. le comte d'Artois," and "had it sent to the German courts, in the same hope of obtaining some more solid gift" and obtaining public praise from the eminent.[116] It was important to demonstrate one's influence. In 1779, when Grimm wrote to Catherine the Great asking her to show kindness to a relative of Baron d'Holbach visiting Russia, a Mlle d'Audet, he added that "without counting that she deserves it, it is that if she ever boasts of having spoken to the empress, it will be looked upon in part as my work, and that will do me an infinite honor."[117]

* * *

Two members of the coterie holbachique, Diderot and Naigeon, openly dissociated themselves from the pursuit of privileges, honors and contemporary acclaim. Commenting derisively on Grimm's behavior, in a passage written after the Revolution, Naigeon described himself as a man "who did not have for titles, dignities and cordons that servile and almost religious respect by which Grimm above all distinguished himself, be it in Paris or in foreign lands." Unlike Grimm, Naigeon added, he was someone "who neither desires, hopes for nor fears anything from kings, from the great, from the priests."[118] Diderot, writing to Grimm in 1769, was more indulgent, telling his friend that if it indeed made him happy, he should continue his ways: "Gallop, my friend; cover the world; frequent palaces and cottages."[119] In 1748 Diderot had written that "one is a good geometrician, man of letters, savant, [and] antiquarian, without being a member of any academy."[120] He argued twenty years later that the patronage of kings meant nothing to the philosophes, that royalty did not truly care

[114] Bachaumont, *Mémoires secrets*, XXVII, 94-95.
[115] Ibid., XXXIII, 126.   [116] Ibid., 19-20.
[117] Grimm, *Lettres à Cathérine II*, 69-70.
[118] Naigeon, in Diderot, *Oeuvres* (N), XIII, "Avertissement," iii-iv.
[119] Diderot, *Corr.*, IX, 88-90.   [120] Ibid., I, 70.

for men of thought.[121] When Grimm's friend and patron, the prince of Saxe-Gotha, wished to meet Diderot, the latter refused, and Grimm had to disguise the ruler as a "M. Erlich," a young Swiss visitor to Paris, and send him to Diderot's apartment in ordinary clothes, where the two talked literature and philosophy. According to Grimm, Diderot entered the Baron d'Holbach's a few days later, saw "M. Erlich," and to the consternation of all the guests ran up to him, threw his arms around him and kissed him on the cheek, saying, "Well, who would have looked for you in the synagogue?"[122] Diderot, however, wrote to Sophie Volland that someone had forewarned him, and that he knew the identity of "M. Erlich" all along.[123] There is, nevertheless, something intriguing about a prince in street clothes knocking on the door of Diderot.

There is also something revealing about the incident, for Diderot could not, if he had chosen, avoid the fame and honors that came to him. Despite his aversion to "academies," he was elected in the course of his life to the Prussian Royal Academy of Science, the Academy of Berlin, the Imperial Academy of the Arts (in Saint Petersburg), and the Society of the Antiquaries of Scotland.[124] At official ceremonies, such as standing witness at marriages and baptisms in the d'Holbach family, he used his titles on the documents.[125] D'Holbach might have to argue Diderot into going to a dinner at the Hôtel de York given by the visiting king of Denmark in 1768, in honor of eighteen men of letters, but Diderot went, joining d'Holbach, Morellet, Grimm, Helvétius and Marmontel.[126] In 1781 the *conseil municipal* of Langres wrote to inform him that his bust had been installed in the town hall, alongside the *Encyclopédie*, in a ceremony attended by all the important local, provincial and royal officials of the city.[127] He did not solicit any of these recognitions, but they all added to his stature in the public eye.

Diderot's acceptance of Catherine's patronage, above all, made him something of a courtier, however involuntary the language and style, and after 1765 he both flattered and ran artistic and intellectual errands for the Russian imperial court, family and aris-

[121] Ibid., VIII, 233-234.
[122] Grimm, *Corr. litt.*, VIII, 221-222.
[123] Diderot, *Corr.*, VIII, 233-234.
[124] Ibid., I, 113; VII, 27; XV, 258-259.
[125] Lough, "Le baron d'Holbach."
[126] Grimm, *Corr. litt.*, VIII, 213-214.
[127] Diderot, *Corr.*, XV, 183-189, 228-236.

tocracy. He knew the conventions necessitated by this role, and however frankly or altruistically he could write to Catherine on politics and education, he understood how one truly thanked a crowned head. He could express his gratitude appropriately in 1766 upon receipt of his 50,000 *livres*: "Great Princess, I prostrate myself at your feet, I extend my two arms toward you; I would speak, but my soul is rent, my head is confused, my ideas flounder, I am moved like a child, and the true expressions which fill me expire on the edges of my lips. . . . Oh Catherine! Know for certain that you do not reign more powerfully over hearts in Petersburg than in Paris."[128]

Diderot was neither unaware of nor loath to use his influence in his own and in his family's behalf. When Sartine replaced Saint-Florentin at court, Diderot wrote: "Judge how that will facilitate my work, if it were subject to difficulties."[129] Soon after Sartine entered the *conseil*, Diderot wrote him to solicit a royal monopoly for his daughter and son-in-law, reminding Sartine of their friendship and of Sartine's "affability" toward Angélique, "which she has not forgotten and will never forget," and admitting that "despite my former ties with the minister of finance [Turgot] and my intimacy with his *premier commis* [Devaines], my [own] poor small fortune remains the same." He stated his goal to Sartine quite openly, that concerning "my children . . . although I believe wealth more opposed to happiness than mediocrity . . . I want them [to be] rich; yes, Monsieur, very rich!"[130] He also solicited d'Angiviller for privileges for his daughter, so assiduously and deferentially, in fact, that d'Angiviller remembered the incident long afterward with distaste, for Diderot wished this particular monopoly denied to a family with better claims of merit and service than the Vandeuls.[131] In December 1776 Diderot at last could write to his sister that the "children" had succeeded: "Masters of the forges of Monsieur [the duc d'Orléans], they have become masters of the forges of M. le comte d'Artois." In addition they had been for several years beneficiaries of several revenues in the domains, of the *inspection* of the duché de Nevers, and masters of the forges of Senoche and of Châteauroux. After describing their poverty to ministers and courtiers for several

[128] Ibid., VI, 355-358.   [129] Ibid., 42-43.
[130] Ibid., 150-152.
[131] Ibid., 167-169; d'Angiviller, *Mémoires*, 47.

years, Diderot finally could admit that "this is not bad for young people just beginning."[132] In the abstract Diderot might believe in fiscal reform, but when Necker suppressed "interests" in the king's domains, Diderot wrote him directly, reminding him of Necker's prior assistance to his (Diderot's) daughter, and insisting that "it is not [a man such as] you that one must tell to respect your own acts of benefaction."[133] The philosophe was only fulfilling a promise he had made to his daughter's future mother-in-law back in 1771, when he assured her that he would employ "all of my protectors, great and small" in order "to procure for [your son] an honorable estate."[134]

A man who could write with no small measure of success to Turgot, Necker, the marquis d'Angiviller, the duc d'Aiguillon, Devaines and Trudaine on behalf of his family, securing for them a fine and largely unmerited fortune (to which he added a dowry made possible by an empress's gift), was not a man unaware of his influence and of how to use it.[135] His style in "society" may have been different from that of most of his friends, but he did not occupy a different world.

Nor, for all his rhetoric, did Naigeon! We know so little about d'Holbach's and Diderot's good friend, but there are glimpses of his life which reveal that it would be an error to see him as isolated from all the glitter around him. By the mid-1760s (and perhaps earlier), he had secured for himself the post of an officer in the *garde-magasin du roi*, living henceforth in free royal quarters at the *menuisier du roi*, on the rue Champfleury. It was at that address and in that capacity that he was listed when he served with Grimm as a "collector" for subscriptions to aid the Calas family, a capacity which must have placed him in contact with many important people in the capital.[136] He apparently was close to Mme de Maux and her daughter, Mme de Prunevaux; the latter referred to him repeatedly as "my little brother" in a warm, informal letter of September 1770, and insisted that he write to her and to Mme de Maux, concluding either flirtatiously or indeed as a "sister" that "It is mama who says all that [about writing], and I who do not doubt your attentions, providing that the pres-

---

[132] Diderot, *Corr.*, xv, 33-35.   [133] Ibid., 45-47.

[134] Ibid., xi, 13-14.

[135] In addition to the passages cited above, see ibid., x, 209-211; xi, 199-200; xii, 119-121.

[136] Grimm, *Corr. litt.*, xvi, 357, n. 1.

ent must be judged somewhat by the past."[137] In June 1771 we find Naigeon present at a ball at Versailles given by the Russian ambassador, where he went in the company of Diderot's wife and daughter, and surely by invitation. They perhaps were out of place there, for Angélique wrote to Langres that finding themselves faced by a table with endless varieties of ice cream, she took eleven servings at once, while "M. Naigeon also took sixteen." At Versailles, Naigeon was surrounded by the *grands*, and he did not leave, according to Angélique, until seven in the morning. If he danced, in general, to the beat of a different minuet, on that night he did not.[138] In 1781, as we have noted, Panckouke chose Naigeon to edit the three volumes on philosophy in the prestigious *Encyclopédie méthodique* (for which, ironically, the abbé Bergier was chosen to edit those on theology), and Diderot formally authorized him to utilize all the relevant articles of the original *Encyclopédie*.[139] In that same year, despite his later recollection that he avoided all "dignities," he secured by unknown means a pension of 2,000 *livres* from the royal treasury for his position of *garde-magasin*, now listed as "*garde-magasin des utensiles de la Maison-Bouche du Roi.*"[140] Possessor of his first royal *privilège* to publish and his first significant pension, Naigeon in his forties may well have been moving toward the successes of his *confrères*. It is true that of all those members of the coterie holbachique still alive in 1789, he had the least to lose from a major upheaval in the life of France. That is comparing him, however, to a group of men who stood to lose a world they had mastered.

[137] Published in Diderot, *Corr.*, x, 120-122.
[138] Published in ibid., xi, 55-57.   [139] Ibid., xv, 228.
[140] Assemblée Nationale, *Etat nominatif des pensions*, ii, 131.

PART III

The Members of the Coterie Holbachique
and the French Revolution

* * * * *

EIGHT · *The Remnant*

ON January 21, 1789, Baron d'Holbach died. He was buried in his parish of Saint-Roch, in the presence of his titled daughters and sons-in-law, members of the noble and powerful d'Aine family, and his two successful sons, the elder now the baron d'Holbach in his turn.[1] Although on February 9 the *Journal de Paris* devoted its first three pages to a letter from Naigeon in praise of the Baron's life and works, the news of his death did not cause a great stir. The Baron had been in ill health for several years, and his salon, rent by deaths and departures, had not assembled regularly during most of the past five years. In the last *Almanach royal* to be published before the fall of the Bastille, d'Holbach still was listed as *conseiller-secrétaire du roi*. Perhaps, looking through that directory of the Ancien Régime to see if their own names had been spelled correctly, or reading Naigeon's eulogy, Le Roy, Darcet, Grimm, Morellet, Marmontel, and Suard saw the name of their late friend and had a moment of regret. We do not know how or when Raynal heard the news in Marseilles. These eight men were all who remained of the coterie.[2]

We know nothing about the Baron's attitude toward the calling of the *Etats-généraux*. D'Holbach had been a member of the *Salon des Arts*, a society of men of letters and the arts founded in 1784, which met above the Café du Caveau, in a new section of the Palais Royal, to discuss politics and affairs of state. In 1786, however, he formally resigned from the group for reasons unknown.[3] Those of his former guests who were still alive moved in the opposite direction in these last years of the Ancien Régime, joining in the national debate on the crisis of France.

When it had appeared that the king was in the process of seeking the advice of his people, before the word "revolution" was on any person's lips, the academicians among the remnant of

---

[1] *Acte de décès* of the Baron d'Holbach (from the *régistres* of the parish of Saint-Roch), published in Mme d'Epinay, *Mémoires*, II, 496-497.

[2] *Almanach royal* (1789).

[3] Lough, "Le baron d'Holbach," 536.

d'Holbach's circle had sought to play a part they took most seriously, that of enlightened advisors of the nation and the monarchy. In 1788 Morellet wrote three pamphlets in favor of the demands of the Third Estate for an equal voice in the *Etats*. In one of these, a *Projet de réponse du roi*, written in opposition to the *Mémoire des princes* and its concept of noble dominance, Morellet asserted that the Third Estate had called not for "a gift of grace," but for "justice."[4] In December 1788, one hundred and eight "inhabitants of Paris" addressed a "Mémoire et Consultation" to the king, opposing the Hôtel de Ville's alleged customary right to choose the Parisian deputies to the *Etats-généraux*, and calling instead for "the free expression of the will of all citizens"; among its signatories were Suard, Morellet, and Saint-Lambert.[5]

Well-known and widely respected, these figures were important personages in their local electoral assemblies and logical choices as their sections' electors in the Parisian assembly to select deputies to the *Etats*. In the section of Les Feuillants, Marmontel was chosen as an elector by his 210 fellow bourgeois, and as one of seven men charged with drawing up the *cahier de doléance*.[6] According to Bailly, one of the seven, Marmontel was chosen by the group as its principal writer.[7] In the district of Les Petits Augustins, Darcet was one of a vociferous assembly of 318 men which refused to accept a presiding officer appointed by the Hôtel de Ville. Darcet probably had spoken out, for in the defiant election of a chairman which followed, he finished second with 117 votes to 165 for d'Hermand de Cléry. He was chosen, quite naturally, as an elector.[8] In the section of Les Jacobins Saint-Honoré, Suard was selected both as one of five representatives to the provisional commune of Paris, and as an elector of the

---

[4] Morellet, *Projet de réponse du roi à un mémoire répandu sous le titre de mémoire des princes*; see also Morellet, *Observations sur le projet de former une assemblée nationale sur le modèle des états généraux de 1614*; and *Nouvelle discussion des motifs des douze notables du bureau de MONSIEUR contre l'avis des treize*.

[5] Cited in *Les élections et les cahiers de Paris en 1789*, C.-L. Chassin, ed., I, 79-83. All three signed themselves "de l'Académie Française." A second *Mémoire*, supporting that first one of "the 108 inhabitants," appeared shortly after, signed by twenty-one persons, including Suard (ibid., 94-99).

[6] Ibid., II, 306-307, 325-331; Marmontel, *Mémoires*, II, 280 ff.

[7] J.-S. Bailly, *Mémoires*, S.-A. Berville and J. F. Barrière, eds., 11-13.

[8] Chassin, op. cit., II, 303-304, 325-331.

Third Estate.[9] In Marseilles the electoral assembly of the Third Estate, meeting in advance of that of Paris, offered Raynal a place as one of its deputies to Versailles, despite his formal membership in the First Estate.[10] On April 27, Darcet, Marmontel, and Suard attended the meeting of the 407 electors of the Third Estate of Paris, where the last two were among the thirty-six men chosen to write the assembly's *cahier*.[11] On May 5, Suard was appointed to a deputation of nine electors sent to the assembly of the Second Estate to call for a single sitting of the *Etats*.[12] In that spring of 1789, therefore, the remnant of the coterie holbachique included men very much in the forefront of events.

* * *

We know almost nothing about Le Roy's activities during this period, but the company he kept at the court at Versailles was scarcely conducive to support of the Third Estate at any point. The salon of his friend Vaudreuil was a center for the most intransigent opponents of the political bourgeoisie, and the society of his closest friend, d'Angiviller, was a center for the publication of the ultra-royalist and ultra-aristocratic *Actes des Apôtres*.[13] If we assume any basis in fact whatsoever for his "confession" among the courtiers, it is not unlikely that he indeed bemoaned the growing disorders of France. He was to die in the fall of 1789 without having played any important public role in political events, but by then many of his former associates of d'Holbach's group were as well bemoaning the course of affairs.

The political successes of the members of the coterie holbachique in 1789 did not prove to be enduring. When the electors and deputies of the Third Estate began to discover the bolder voices in their midst and their self-confidence, and when the violence that was simmering throughout France erupted in the streets

[9] Ibid., 325-331; *Actes de la commune de Paris pendant la Révolution*, S. La Croix and R. Fargue, eds., Ière Série, II, 510-516, 678-679.

[10] See Raynal's reply in *L'Abbé Raynal aux Etats Généraux*. In the Bibliography I provide the B.N. listing to distinguish Raynal's publications during the period of the Revolution from others of similar titles, written by individuals hoping to gain attention for their words by using the name of the celebrated author of the *Histoire philosophique des Deux Indes*.

[11] Chassin, op. cit., III, 31-32; Bailly, *Mémoires*, 26-27.

[12] Chassin, loc. cit., 154.

[13] A. Challamel, *Les clubs contre-révolutionnaires*, 554-555; see also infra, Chapter Two.

of Paris, those members of the coterie holbachique who had participated so actively in the direction of events began to draw back in a reflex of distrust, contempt and fear. In addition, men who at first had looked to them as leaders and spokesmen now began to see them with a more knowing eye. Ultimately, the rejection was to be mutual between these philosophes and the Revolution; initially, however, it was Marmontel, Morellet, Suard and Raynal who took the first steps back. They saw, before it became apparent to all, the conflict between themselves and the men of 1789.

Marmontel claimed in his *Mémoires* that he first became aware of the "dangerous fanaticism" of certain leaders of the Third Estate when he found himself among the many lawyers in the Parisian electoral assembly. In his section, he noted, the spirit of the participants was "reasonable and moderate." In the Parisian assembly, however, "quibbling lawyers," all competing for prominence and oratorical glories, stood ready to incite and serve as leaders of factions, some even preaching overt republicanism. Schooled in the eloquence of the bar, he continued, they dominated the minds of other men. Until the Parisian assembly, Marmontel recalled, he believed the nation was sincerely assembling to advise the king. In April, however, he discovered there was a new body of men who wished to become "almost the sole legislators of France," and he was frightened. The more he discussed affairs with other electors, the more he realized how unpopular were his own moderate views. He had gone to this assembly expecting to be named a deputy, but he had revealed himself to be too opposed to the "extravagant" demands of the Parisian bourgeois: "My principles were well-known: I had made no secret of them, and care was taken to spread the rumor that I was the friend of ministers, and was loaded with favors from the king. The elections took place, I was not chosen; the abbé Sieyès was preferred."[14]

According to Bailly, an active participant at this assembly and later the mayor of Paris, what cost Marmontel his expected place as an elector was not the extravagance of the assembly, but an act of defiance on Marmontel's part, his opposition to a measure that had the unanimous approval of the electors. On May 7, following Bailly's account, the *conseil d'état* had suppressed Mirabeau's *Journal des états-généraux*; on the following day the Parisian

---

[14] Marmontel, *Mémoires*, II, 280-290.

assembly moved to condemn this action, since the king and the *conseil* on December 27, 1788, had agreed to allow the *Etats-généraux* to resolve for itself the matter of the free reporting of its deliberations. In order to avoid a conflict with the king, the Parisian assembly decided to treat the suppression as an *acte* rather than an *arrêt* of the *conseil*, the latter having the character of an expression of the king's will. There was no apparent opposition to the motion to condemn the *conseil's* "acte," and the matter was put to a vote. Bailly described what followed: "It is said in the decree [of the Parisian assembly] that it was passed unanimously. That is true, with the exception of a single member. When it was voted upon, I noticed indeed that one person alone, M. Marmontel, did not rise. He was in the second row, and as a consequence hidden by those who were standing. I said nothing; but despite the apparent unanimity, someone, no doubt out of malice, called for the opposing vote, which was not always called for at such times. The president was obliged to obey, and M. Marmontel had the courage to stand alone. Although I was not of his opinion, I admired his resoluteness, which did him honor in that respect; but the discontentment over the substance of his opinion made me foresee that he would not be a deputy."[15]

If the "immoderation" of the bourgeoisie of Paris in early May was enough to separate Marmontel from the spirit of his fellow electors, the "spirit of licence, faction and anarchy" spreading throughout "the multitude," as he phrased it, was enough to cause him to believe by early July that the forces of repression should be used vigorously. The raids on arms-shops, and the attacks upon the Invalides and the monastery of St. Lazare, frightened him dreadfully, he recalled, as did the "weakness" of the king in response to these. The fall of the Bastille and the deaths of de Launay and Berthier were the point of no return. Although he claimed that he approved of the resolutions of August 4, by the end of summer 1789, Marmontel was already on the path of counter-revolution.[16]

[15] Bailly, *Mémoires*, 38-43. Bailly also was somewhat surprised, as Marmontel had been, that "the lawyers" at the Parisian assembly emerged so strong and so confident, and spoke of "a rivalry" between them and "the men of letters." Bailly, and of course Marmontel, believed that "The men of letters nevertheless are the most enlightened men." Bailly noted, however, that the latter "were not of sufficient number" to stand against the dominance of "the lawyers and the merchants" (ibid., 50).

[16] Marmontel, *Mémoires*, II, 310-402.

At the end of 1789 Panckouke gave to Marmontel, La Harpe and Chamfort the direction of the literary pages of the *Mercure*; while the last two wrote favorably of the events of the day, Marmontel's abiding hostility to the Assemblée Nationale and the activities of its leaders and partisans became increasingly manifest in his pages. Although he was appointed in the spring of 1790 by the representatives of the commune of Paris to a committee to choose a new director for the *établissement des sourds-muets*,[17] his popularity wholly had dissipated. In an election that spring for a *secrétaire-greffier adjoint* of the *conseil-général* of the commune, he was nominated and received 1 vote out of 110.[18] If we believe his *Mémoires*, he sensed the danger of his isolation, but he could not restrain himself. His articles increasingly stressed the rights of the royal prerogative, the security of property and rights whose title depended upon established privileges (such as those, he explicitly noted, of the Académie Française), and the need to suppress disorder.[19] On April 20, 1791, he was denounced in print by Marat for his antipopular journalism, and in early August he fled Paris and Grignon for Normandy, finally settling in a small cottage in Abloville, where he remained in obscurity and silence until 1797.[20]

Suard was undergoing the same process of disaffection in May 1789. On May 5 he still was popular enough to be chosen to serve on the deputation of the Third Estate of Paris to the Second, but on May 23 he signaled his opposition to his assembly and earned notoriety by being one of the twenty-three (of 407) electors who refused to sign the *cahier* which, in theory, he had helped to write.[21] By February 5, 1790, he was one of thirty-one (of some 300) representatives in the assembly of the commune of Paris who

[17] *Actes de la commune de Paris*, Ière Série, v, 11-16.
[18] Ibid., IIème Série, I, 119.
[19] *Mercure de France* (1789-1791), passim.
[20] *L'Ami du peuple* (1791), 20 April; see also ibid., 21 Sept., when Marmontel's articles were once again denounced; Marmontel, *Mémoires*, II, 414-422. There is a concise and factual article on Marmontel's behavior during the Revolution by Simone Locher, "Marmontel et la Révolution," in J. Ehrard, *Marmontel*, 71-80. Locher was somewhat surprised to find Marmontel in his hostile role, and believed that his early disaffection set him noticeably apart from even his most moderate philosophic friends. As we shall see, there was nothing unique in Marmontel's opposition in the spring and summer of 1789.
[21] Chassin, op. cit., III, 299.

had to be called upon by name to swear the *serment civique*.[22]
By the fall of that year he was among a group of seventy-nine
communal representatives who refused to recognize the authority
of their *conseil de ville* to direct them to affirm publicly their
acceptance of an oath of good behavior in office.[23] It must have
come as no surprise to Suard, thus, when in the fall elections of
representatives to the *conseil* of the newly organized *municipalité*
of Paris, he was among a group of only some twenty to thirty
well-known former representatives who were not re-elected.[24] As
in Marmontel's case, Suard too could not veil his antipathy to the
events and mood of the day in his continued articles in moderate
royalist journals such as *Les Indépendants*. In 1790 he wrote frequent lines brimming with anger and contempt. "We hear it repeated every moment that we have conquered liberty," he
opined, "we have still only conquered the Bastille." Such sentiments might be considered ambiguous, but that rapidly became
less possible. "Hearing the cry of liberty from every mouth, one
could believe oneself for a moment to be transported to Athens,"
he wrote that same year, "but by reading all of these disgusting
pamphlets in which the holy name of liberty is soiled by so many
horrors and absurdities, one can only believe oneself to be in the
caves of Boeotia." By 1791 he was explicit in his contempt for the
work of official legislation as well: "We have destroyed everything with a barbarous precipitation, and when we wanted to reconstruct, we brought to light a ridiculous ignorance of all the
means of rebuilding. We didn't know how to put either men or
things in working order; we wanted to begin a new edifice by the
roof, without thinking to establish the foundations. Enormous
scaffolds have been necessary to make works which will collapse
at the moment when they are believed to be completed."[25]

According to his friend Garat, whose politics differed strikingly
from Suard's, the latter feared from the earliest days of the Assemblée that the Third Estate was going too far, and that it posed

[22] *Actes de la commune de Paris*, Ière Série, IV, 1.

[23] Ibid., VII, 328-342. The issue in this affair, as stated explicitly by the
conseil de ville on September 27, 1790 (ibid., 302-303), was not whether
any improprieties had been committed by any representatives, but whether
the latter would recognize the right of the *conseil* to direct them to take an
oath.

[24] Ibid., IIème Série, I, xxxii.

[25] Published in Suard, *Mémoires et correspondances* (Nisard), 110 *ff*; see
also *Journal de Paris* (1790-1791), passim.

a grave threat to the sovereignty of the monarch.[26] The salon of Suard and his wife assembled men who shared that fear, such as the *fermier-général* Boulogne, Dupont de Nemours, Lavoisier and Morellet.[27] They could use the language of "patriots," but the devotion of *Les Indépendants* to "constitutional monarchy" was above all else a devotion to what they perceived to be the cause of the king.

Raynal in the spring of 1789 revealed his lack of enthusiasm as well. Offered the post of deputy to the *Etats-généraux* by the Third Estate of Marseilles, he declined the opportunity to return to the center of things, pleading ill health and fatigue. He suggested as his replacement "M. Bertrand, *directeur-principal* of the Compagnie d'Afrique," and offered, as "my *cahiers*," a collection of some of the most moderate thoughts from his *Histoire philosophique des Deux Indes*, stressing the need to eliminate the influence of "courtiers" but upholding the need for a strong, sovereign and secure king on the throne.[28] He remained in Marseilles, associated with moderate royalist circles, and watched with a jaundiced eye the course of events. In 1790 the Assemblée Nationale, still courting him, as a gesture formally repealed the royal order banning him from Paris. Touched or embarrassed by this attention, he returned to the capital, but in the spring of 1791 he shocked France by sending to the Assemblée a fiery *Adresse*, read at the session of May 31, in which he attacked the ignorance of the political clubs, the seduction of the people into violence and disorder, and the violation of the rights of property: "What do I see around me? Religious troubles, civil dissensions, the consternation of some, the audacity and uncontrollable fury of others, a government that is the slave of popular tyranny, the sanctuary of the laws surrounded by unruly men, who alternately want to dictate or disobey them; soldiers without discipline, leaders without authority, magistrates without courage, ministers without means, a king, the foremost friend of his people, plunged into bitterness, outraged, threatened, despoiled of all authority, and the public power no longer existing except in the clubs, where gross and

[26] Garat's account of Suard's revolutionary role can be found in Garat, *Suard*, II, 307-451; Mme Suard's account stresses somewhat more the emotional nature of his royalism, in Mme Suard, *Suard*, 134 ff.

[27] Challamel, *Les clubs contre-révolutionnaires*, 557.

[28] Raynal, *Aux Etats Généraux* (see above, n. 10).

ignorant men dare to make pronouncements on all political questions."[29]

The most prestigious of the living philosophes at last had spoken, and revolutionary France did not appreciate his words. Chénier and Sinéty immediately rushed forward to refute him, for as Sinéty observed, "the name alone of Guillaume-Thomas Raynal today provides the greatest importance of this [*Adresse*]."[30] According to Sinéty, Raynal had wanted "to establish the sect of the philosophes upon the ruins of religion," and could not accept that the thinkers who had dominated France under the Ancien Régime were being displaced during the Revolution.[31] While Raynal came under increasing attack in the clubs, the printer Volland quickly published a false edition of Raynal's *Adresse* in an effort to discredit the abbé. This edition altered certain phrases and sentences to make Raynal appear senile, arrogant and corrupted. Where Raynal had objected to "civil dissensions," Volland's edition made the author the enemy of "civil discussions"; where Raynal had spoken with the voice of "posterity," he now spoke with that of "prosperity"; what Raynal had been incapable of "foreseeing [*prévoir*]," he now was incapable of "proving [*prouver*]."[32] His position compromised, Raynal, by

[29] Raynal, *Adresse de Guillaume-Thomas Raynal*. The quotation is from pp. 5-6. See also *Archives parlementaires*, xxvi, 650-655.

[30] A.-L.-E. de Sinéty, *Réflexions importantes sur l'adresse . . . par . . . Raynal*, 1-2; Sinéty added in this passage that because of Raynal's prestige, his *Adresse* "has created impressions which could be dangerous." See also André Chénier, "A Guillaume-Thomas Raynal," in the *Moniteur* (1791), 5 June.

[31] Sinéty, op. cit., 10-12. Sinéty also asked why Raynal had not come to Paris when first invited, if his disaffection were truly so recent.

[32] Volland's edition bore the same title, and the B.N. catalogued it before the genuine edition, in B.N., Imprimés: Lb39.4971. As a result, most people in all probability have read Volland's altered version after requesting Raynal's *Adresse*. I have counted over thirty-five major (and many minor) alterations, in the forms of deletions, additions and word changes. The examples I have given in the text may be seen by comparing pp. 5-11 in Raynal's text to pp. 3-7 in Volland's. Many of Volland's "minor" changes altered Raynal's "nous" to "vous" when the abbé addressed "the people," establishing a Raynal more aloof than that which the rhetoric of the actual *Adresse* attempted to project. Typical changes were from "inquisition" to "institution," "dream" of liberty to "vow" of liberty, and from "corruptible" to "corrupted." This was not the first time that Volland had altered a text.

now an old man approaching eighty, dropped out of sight and attempted to live out his days in quiet.

In 1788 Morellet had been an ardent partisan of the "rights" of the Third Estate, but by June 1789 he was writing to a friend in England that the demands of that group were "extravagant" and on a par with the "levellers."[33] Two factors above all seem to have altered his perception of affairs—the growing violence in Paris, and the designs of the Assemblée Nationale upon the wealth of the Church, from which he derived so much of his own great fortune. In the spring of 1789 Morellet's close friend Réveillon, the paper manufacturer, had called in royal troops for assistance against his unruly workers, in the course of which many of his employees were killed. Réveillon, widely denounced, and fearing for his life, placed himself in the Bastille for his own protection. Morellet, at no small risk to himself, visited Réveillon frequently, and spoke in his favor among his own acquaintances.[34]

More significantly perhaps, Morellet discovered to his dismay that the Assemblée contained loud and well-received voices speaking in favor of a suppression of ecclesiastical benefices and tithes. In 1788 Morellet had obtained possession of the priory of Thimer, including a benefice of 16,000 *livres* and "a charming habitation" some twenty-four leagues from Paris.[35] This, added to his previous benefices, made him a person whose financial security depended upon the tithes of the Church and the system of ecclesiastical property. Whatever his opposition to the intellectual Church, he now found himself threatened with ruin by the Assemblée's apparent opposition to the fiscal Church. Thus in December 1789 he published a brochure, in his own name, on "The Way to Dispose

---

In May 1790 Volland had changed the title and language of a publication from the electors of Les Petits Augustins, embarrassing them by the violence which he added (see *Actes de la commune de Paris*, Ière Série, v, 340). In Marseilles a bust of Raynal was moved from the Jacobin club to the *hôpital des fous*, which pleased the Parisian Jacobins no end. Raynal was vilified in the Parisian Jacobin club, and the phrase "to reason like the abbé Raynal" was used as a term of abuse (see F.-A. Aulard, *La société des Jacobins. Recueil de documents pour l'histoire du Club des Jacobins de Paris*, II, 387, 492, 501, 510).

[33] Morellet, *Lettres à Lord Shelburne*, 275-276.

[34] Chassin, *Élections et cahiers en 1789*, 50-63; see also Morellet, *Mémoires*, II, 1-4.

[35] Morellet, *Mémoires*, I, 325-327.

of Ecclesiastical Property in a Manner Useful to the Nation." He had seen the handwriting on the wall, but he wished to salvage what he could. As he had written to Shelburne in September, "The agitation of [the nation's] spirits and the danger of our situation are at their height, and I will not hide from you that I absolutely do not know how we will extricate ourselves." No one's legitimate fortune was secure, for "we have come to create the most dangerous of all wars: that of the poor against the rich, while placing, at the same time, force on the side of need and weakness on the side of all those who have something to lose."[36]

In his brochure Morellet revealed, in his particular argument and in his general tone, how isolated a figure he was destined to become. He declared that it was both "impossible" and "unjust" to abolish the ecclesiastical tithes, for such an action would leave the Church with "only sixty million *livres*, . . . manifestly insufficient to satisfy the needs of the cult alone." It would deny to the holders of benefices "the most modest return that justice and humanity demand. . . ." Morellet's own plan urged that holders of benefices valued at more than 1,200 *livres* (in the countryside) or more than 1,800 *livres* (in the cities) should pay one-third of these revenues as a tax to the public treasury of the administrative region in which the benefice lay, the whole fiscal program to be administered by the secular government. A "harsher plan," he added, would lead to disorder, dislocations and unnecessary suffering. "Is it not time," he asked, "to dispose of these biases, these hatreds, this partisan spirit which alters the soundest ideas and soils the purest intentions?" The abolition of tithes, he continued, would be "a sentence of death or poverty" against several thousand citizens, who would be "uncertain of their future . . . attempting, often without success, work to which they are not accustomed." The true means of regenerating a nation, he concluded, "never can be unjust toward a considerable segment of society, and still less can they be violent and sudden in their action."[37] In February 1790 he wrote to Shelburne that while he was willing to sacrifice one-third of his property to the nation, he would consider himself fortunate to escape with one-half.[38]

Morellet decried, throughout the period from 1790 to 1792, the

---

[36] Morellet, *Lettres à Lord Shelburne*, 279-280.

[37] Morellet, *Moyen de disposer utilement, pour la nation, des biens ecclésiastiques*.

[38] Morellet, *Lettres à Lord Shelburne*, 291-293.

"public and private misfortunes" of the Revolution, in articles in the *Journal de Paris* and *Les Indépendants*, in diverse brochures, and in letters to his friends.[39] After he had lost most of his wealth, he wrote to Shelburne in July 1791 of "the injustice that I have experienced": "I was chased from the home [at Thimer] that I had embellished, from the garden that I had planted, from the *domaine* that I had improved. I have lost about a thousand pounds-sterling [24,000 *livres*] that I had placed in my benefice. My property, with the improvements I have made in it, is being sold under my eyes without my being given a *sou* for it."[40]

He claimed, in this letter, to have lost two-thirds of all of his income through this despoliation and the reduction of his pensions, and identified himself with "the majority of ecclesiastics" whose estates had been equally destroyed. He also expressed his political sentiments in language more forceful than that which he allowed himself in his articles: "I love liberty, and I have given proofs of that, but [until] I am proven wrong by the success of the great experiment that we are conducting, I will not believe that so numerous, so ignorant, so gross, [and] so giddy a people, [and one] so violent in its fluctuations, can govern itself completely and safely following forms so democratic as those adopted by the Assemblée, and above all without any repressive and coercive power [*pouvoir*] that is indivisible and independent."[41]

In 1792, the same year he published a critique of Brissot's concept of property, he came to the conclusion that all was lost. Of the new Republic he wrote to Shelburne that he only saw "the destruction of all government, a complete anarchy, an established and organized anarchy: the legal violation of all properties; the absolute domination of the armed poor over the oppressed and disarmed rich." He predicted that the worst was yet to come.[42]

Darcet, while avoiding any publication of his atttitudes and per-

---

[39] In addition to the works that will be discussed below in this chapter, see his *Réflexions du lendemain*; the *Mercure* (1789-1791), passim; and the *Journal de Paris* (1789-1792), passim. See also *Lettres à Lord Shelburne*, 279-305; and *Mémoires*, II, 1-46. Morellet, in these latter pages, expressed great admiration for the "courage" of his friend Suard throughout the revolutionary period.

[40] Morellet, *Lettres à Lord Shelburne*, 302-303.

[41] Ibid.

[42] Ibid., 305. Morellet's critique of Brissot, which Suard published in the *Journal de Paris* in May 1792, was reprinted in Morellet, *Mélanges de littérature et de philosophie du dix-huitième siècle*, III, 194-208.

ceptions, also was falling from a state of early grace. There are no records of his formal utterances, but either through his own moderation or the appearance of newer and more popular men, his position of eminence in his section was being lost. In 1789 he had been a strong second in the votes of his district assembly; in the elections of 1790, however, the 318 voting citizens of his section had increased to 2,100 "active citizens," and he was elected nineteenth out of the twenty-one new electors chosen.[43] It was the last time he was selected to represent his fellow citizens until Napoléon appointed him to the *Sénat conservateur*. His friend Dizé reported that Darcet always remained faithful to the "principles" of 1789, but recalled that Darcet was increasingly disturbed by what he saw as the "anarchy" and "public misfortunes" which soon transpired.[44] Darcet was one of the most privileged and well-rewarded scientists of the Ancien Régime, still serving in 1790 as *docteur-régent* of the Faculté, *professeur royal* of the collège de France, a member of the increasingly reviled Académie des sciences, a member of the aristocratic Société royale d'Agriculture, and a commissioner and inspector of the royal monopoly at the *manufacture* of porcelain.[45] Such positions could not have endeared him to an increasingly revolutionary Third Estate. According to Dizé, Darcet's friendships with the duc d'Orléans and with the emigré d'Angiviller were well-known, and began to cause him difficulties as the Revolution moved toward ever narrower definitions of its friends.[46]

The "marquis" de Saint-Lambert, closely tied to the prince de Beauvau and to the aristocratic salons of Paris, and ostensibly the military *gouverneur* of Joinville, took fright early in the Revolution and retired to his country home at Eaubonne, near his mistress Mme d'Houdetot. Damiron recalled (from information provided by friends of Saint-Lambert) that the marquis "remained faithful to the party of the aristocracy," and that "he had the fortune to make himself forgotten" in his retreat, where he worked on his *Catéchisme universel* for almost a decade. Damiron detested Saint-Lambert's "incredulity" and "philosophic" morality, but he admitted that Saint-Lambert could not be associated with any of the anarchic forces in France. He described Saint-Lambert

[43] *Assemblée Electorale de Paris, 18 novembre 1790–15 juin 1791*, E. Charavay, ed., 59-61.

[44] Dizé, *Précis sur Darcet*, 21.   [45] *Almanach royal* (1791).

[46] Dizé, op. cit., 23.

as increasingly weighed down by "sadness" and "discouragement" as the old order collapsed, and careful to avoid any public role.[47] In fact, Saint-Lambert did allow himself the defiant statement of loyalty to the old institutions contained in his frequent visits to the seances of the Académie Française during the years from 1790 to 1793.[48] After that, he simply disappeared from the political or literary life of France until the publication of his work in 1797.

Grimm, at the height of his wealth and success in 1789, did not enjoy one moment of benevolence toward the movement of reform. As he later recalled, "My happiness disappeared with that of France."[49] A diplomat who loved the life of a courtier, and whose ties were to the established order of Europe, he dissociated himself from the "French" aspect of his life and became a "German" diplomat in full. Early in 1790 he left Paris for Bourbonne and then Frankfort, staying with Nicolas Romanzoff, and after attending the coronation of Leopold as emperor, he spent several months at the court in Gotha. He returned to Paris briefly late in 1790, but after the sacking of the hôtel de Castries, he once again left the capital for the courts of the German princes to whom he was attached, stopping in Frankfort, Aix-la-Chapelle and Coblentz. In October 1791 he returned to Paris on Catherine's behalf, to remove from France the official and personal letters written to him by the empress since the 1770s. Catherine already understood that he could not remain there, having written earlier in the year that "you were very happy in Frankfort, . . . because you were beyond the brawl [*bagarre*] of Paris . . . surrounded by the corral of German princes. . . ." In February 1792, after the departure of the Russian ambassador, Grimm left Paris, never to return, traveling just ahead of the French army to Aix-la-Cha-

---

[47] P. Damiron, *Mémoires pour servir à l'histoire de la philosophie au XVIIIe siècle*, II, 179-180. Damiron received his doctorate shortly after the Restoration, and devoted his research to the philosophes of the eighteenth century, interviewing all those he could find who knew them or participated in their lives before and after the Revolution. One suspects, reading his "Mémoires" on the individual philosophes, that he would have preferred them to have been genuine revolutionaries, for he saw the direction of their impiety as leading precisely to such a role; he faithfully reported his findings concerning Saint-Lambert, however. In the final analysis he found Saint-Lambert "*galant*," someone "who lived and thought a bit too much like people lived and thought in his time."

[48] *Registres de l'Académie Française*, III, 635-662.

[49] Grimm, "Mémoire historique," in *Corr. litt.*, I, 28-29.

pelle, and then at last to Gotha, where he remained among the community of French emigrés protected by his patron, the duke of Saxe-Gotha. Grimm lived with the family of the emigrée comtesse de Bueil, whom he earlier had helped in her rise in aristocratic society, both of them now generously supported by Catherine. An agent of the enemies of the new order in France, he began to reconstruct his life.[50]

Only Naigeon, of all the survivors of the coterie holbachique, wrote in exuberant support of the assault upon crown and privilege. In his *Adresse à l'Assemblée Nationale*, published late in 1790, he specifically attacked two articles by Morellet which had appeared in the *Mercure*, in which the abbé had urged the Assemblée Constituante to adopt "the British constitution," by which he meant a strong monarch, a wealthy and moderating upper chamber, an efficacious concern for public order, and a rigorous censorship of "libels" and "satires" which inflamed "the people" against important figures and estates.[51] For Naigeon, however, the king's executive power was "the most dangerous of all . . . the most in need of being ceaselessly under surveillance." According to the *Adresse*, the deputies in Versailles were the nation assembled, and in their presence the king was a mere citizen. The Assemblée had the duty to limit the powers of the monarch in any way it saw as conducive to the implementation of its "Declaration of the Rights of Man."[52]

After "twelve-hundred years of oppression," the people were attempting to conquer freedom from the "ministerial tyranny" of those who with impunity had opposed "the liberty, honor and life of the citizens." Such a conquest, he was willing to accept, "necessarily is marked by troubles, dissensions and storms, [which are] more or less long and/or destructive." Among the rights being demanded by the people was the full liberty to think and to publish their opinions, and only the supporters of tyranny would condemn and suppress, "under the generic term seditious libels," all works which have as their objects the execution of the Assemblée's laws, the rights of the people, and "the desire and enthusi-

[50] Ibid., 29 *ff*; *Correspondance inédite du Baron Grimm au Comte de Findlater*, André Cazes, ed., 11-17.

[51] Morellet's articles appeared in the *Mercure de France* (1790), 25 July and 31 Aug. See Naigeon, *Adresse à l'Assemblée Nationale, sur la liberté des opinions, sur celle de la presse, etc.*, 77-78.

[52] Naigeon, *Adresse*, 85, 110-140.

asm for liberty." "In no case whatsoever," Naigeon urged, could the state legitimately censor the works of its citizens. Indeed, a wholly free press might increase temporarily the volume of false libels and even incite individuals to violence, but these were prices that had to be paid. "The laws of the freest nations," Naigeon urged, "like those of the most enslaved, all have been engraved with the point of the sword."[53]

On the question of a religious settlement in France, Naigeon was opposed in theory to what he viewed as the prior actions and probable course of the Assemblée. He could not accept the mention of "the Divinity" in the statement of the Rights of Man, and he implored the deputies to proscribe theological concerns from affairs of natural and civil law. Furthermore, he vigorously opposed the continued establishment of the Catholic Church. Citing the actions of the state of Virginia, he argued that only voluntary contributions and voluntary religious associations befitted a free people. Condemning the priests as "ferocious beasts" motivated almost solely by greed, he insisted that the Assemblée create conditions in which "no one have any interest in believing or chanting such and such a thing," and in which "he who believes nothing, and consequently has nothing to chant, is not obliged to pay the ministers and costs of worship of a religion that he does not accept."[54]

Naigeon's *Adresse* outraged Morellet, who published a harsh and often personal refutation of it early in 1791. The central concern of the abbé's *Préservatif* was the consequence of eliminating religious education among "the common people" and "the lowest classes of society," and of allowing "fanatics" to preach their contempt and hatred for the ecclesiastical state on every "street corner." According to Morellet, whatever one believed philosophically, it was empirically true that "a gross and uneducated people, degraded by the poverty and ignorance inseparable from its state, loses all morality the moment it is not restrained by the bridle of religion." France was daily slipping further into violence and disorder, and "the sole restraint" that remained was "the ministers of religion" and their message of "an avenging God." Any citizen who truly cared about preserving the monarchy and the social fabric now had to realize that "the ancient foundations" of these were the poorer classes' belief in and obedience to the lessons of their priests, and such a citizen would work to secure the ecclesi-

[53] Ibid., 60-88.   [54] Ibid., 13-32, 55-60.

astical *corps* from the vilification to which it was currently subjected. The very fact that a coward such as Naigeon, Morellet
urged, who for so long had published with the greatest caution
and in strict pseudonymity, now felt that he could address such
thoughts to the Assemblée revealed the danger in which the nation found itself. In his *Mémoires* Morellet recalled the "alarm"
that seeing Naigeon's pamphlet had caused him.[55] His *Préservatif*
indeed read like the work of a man afraid. The days of pleasant
debates on the rue Royale were past.

There were two aspects of Naigeon's *Adresse* which Morellet
did not focus upon, and which revealed a certain moderation in
their author, and indeed a certain self-declared distance from the
most strident anti-Catholic and anticlerical voices being heard.
First, Naigeon admitted, in a lengthy and important digression,
that his own vision of a people without religion was "chimerical
and impossible" in the current state of affairs in France. The majority of the nation was indeed "ignorant," "credulous," and
"superstitious," and the Assemblée would have to deal with
that fact. The deputies, however, in Naigeon's view, appeared
to be attaching importance to these religious questions, instead
of simply correcting prior abuses while still allowing the people to have their cult. The Assemblée, Naigeon urged, should
concern itself with eliminating the profit motive for joining the
ecclesiastical state, thus ending the attraction of a clerical career
for that "vast majority"of the priests who were insincere in their
sacerdotal role. It should break the power of the hierarchy by
making a clerical career open to all by their choice, "as in all
métiers," a circumstance that combined with drastically reduced
remuneration would produce, at the least, priests who were not
consciously enemies of the people and, at best, the natural and
uncoerced ruin of the Church. In short, Naigeon was calling for
a drastic reduction of the Church's wealth and the power of the
bishops, but he was asking as well for the Assemblée to see its role
as one of merely removing the conditions which allowed for clerical "tyranny," and not as one of directing the religious life of
France.[56]

---

[55] Morellet, *Préservatif contre un écrit intitulé: "Adresse à l'assemblée
nationale, sur la liberté des opinions"*; Morellet, *Mémoires*, II, 27-29. Morellet
recalled, in this passage of the *Mémoires*, that "I had with [the author], in
the society of Baron d'Holbach, frequent and lively disputes in which I
fought against his dogmatic atheism. I had not converted him."

[56] Naigeon, *Adresse*, 32-50.

The reverse side of this, and the second aspect of the *Adresse* ignored by Morellet, was Naigeon's warning against both the persecution of the Catholic Church and the creation of an official revolutionary creed to take its place. The state simply ought not to interfere in any manner whatsoever in the religious life of its citizens, once it annulled the favored and privileged position of the Catholic hierarchy. He warned those who were preaching a crusade against the Catholic faith that Tertullian had been correct in asserting that Christianity grew from the blood of its martyrs: "Proscribe tomorrow the Christian religion, whose certitude, already so shaken, continues to weaken every day, [and] punish by death those who preach it: and you will soon have martyrs, even among those who would not have given a fingernail or a hair from their head to establish or propagate it, if they could have done so freely and without risking their lives."[57]

What France required, both as its right and as a means to a better future, was not the outlawing of the Catholic Church for which some now called, but rather "the most unlimited religious liberty." The members of the Assemblée had no right to weigh the truth or falsity of religious systems, for "all opinions, true or false, religious or impious . . . must have a full and complete liberty to show themselves." The Assemblée under no circumstance should place a "restriction" upon thought and its expression, including the right of the superstitious citizen to worship as he would. Thus, according to the most strident atheist of d'Holbach's circle: "All religions, all sects, all of the different manners of serving and offering a cult to God must be equally permitted, authorized, protected by the Law and received in the State. . . . All the Temples must be open, and each sect, without exception, must have the freedom to practice in peace, under the protection of Law, *and in the places destined for such use*, the cult that it has chosen according to its lights. . . ."[58]

Naigeon's vision of a state without censorship and a secular government unconcerned with the religious beliefs of its citizens was in many ways a structurally radical scheme in 1790, calling

[57] Ibid., 51-60.

[58] Ibid., 48-50; the emphasis is added, signaling Naigeon's antipathy to those who would "convert" the churches into civic buildings. Naigeon added that people should be free to persevere in the religion in which they "find themselves engaged by education," and in whatever cult they "believe the most pleasing to God."

as it did for full disestablishment of the Church and for complete freedom of the press for even the most incendiary publications. It was also a curiously irrelevant vision in its consistency, however, allowing as it did for a full criticism of any revolutionary regime and opposing as it did any official campaign against the Catholic faith. Naigeon sensed this, one suspects, for he withdrew from his attempt to influence the Assemblée after this publication, and devoted himself increasingly to the production of his atheistic *Philosophie ancienne et moderne*. He was, at his most inflammatory, a philosophe, and not a statesman or a *politique*. His ultimate goal, he admitted in the *Adresse*, was religious "indifference," and he believed that noninterference by the state in religious matters was the quickest route to such a circumstance. He truly believed that most priests were such for the wealth involved, and he hoped that forcing the faithful alone to support their ministers would end the influence of the clerical party in France. When, as he had predicted, the blood of martyrs began to rekindle the religious ardor of the nation, he could not have been surprised by the consequences. The cult of the Supreme Being would appall him, but the one line of the *Adresse* that Morellet had quoted approvingly was Naigeon's observation that if Christianity were persecuted and suppressed, it would be "replaced by some new monstrosity."[59] A sound and enduring change of opinions, Naigeon believed, was only possible in the full competition of ideas, without political rewards or penalties attached to beliefs. The Revolution did not provide such an arena, and Naigeon was soon disillusioned. An anecdote concerning Naigeon's mood during the reign of Robespierre conveyed his isolation: "One day, at the height of the terror, friends who saw him [Naigeon] believed his life to be in danger, given his troubled and shaken air, and asked him if he were on the list of victims: 'It's worse than that,' he cried. 'What then?' 'This monster Robespierre has just decreed the Supreme Being.' "[60]

Unlike Morellet, Naigeon appears to have wanted at least a genuine and fundamental political and ecclesiastical revolution in the life of France. But as he himself noted, that which he most desired, a nation of free-thinking men, was "chimerical and im-

---

[59] Morellet, *Préservatif*. Naigeon had written this sentence as an argument for the *futility* of persecution; Morellet, on the last page of the *Préservatif*, quoted it as if it had been the hoped-for prophecy of his former friend.

[60] Damiron, *Histoire de la philosophie au XVIIIᵉ siècle*, ii, 417.

possible," and he was to retire from the actual Revolution into the privacy of his scholarship and his books. He wanted the Assemblée to free the pens and the minds of the populace, totally and without restriction. At the time, to expound such a doctrine made him a public figure. Damiron, who hated the atheism of Naigeon, understood nevertheless that he was a man with a passionate commitment to ideas, a man "self-condemned to solitude" and too independent to participate actively in revolutionary affairs. He was, as Damiron described him, "the monk of atheism," and for Naigeon the society of the Revolution was at least as lonely intellectually as an Ancien Régime without Diderot and d'Holbach would have been.[61]

* * *

Morellet separated not only from Naigeon in the course of the early years of the Revolution, but from many of his former Parisian friends. In his *Mémoires* he recalled with sadness how his own pessimism and hostility to the armed population of Paris began to strain his relations with his long-term and close friends in Mme Helvétius' circle at Auteuil. Most of them were filled with enthusiasm and hope at the turn of events, but by June 1789 Morellet "no longer could share my fears with the abbé de Laroche and with Cabanis." After he was dispossessed of his priory in the early spring of 1790, Morellet was given lodging at Auteuil by Mme Helvétius, but the "divergences" of his thought from most of his associates there made his place uncomfortable. In the summer of 1790 Morellet wrote a brochure in support of a delegation from Bas-Limousin who had come to Versailles to solicit the aid of the Assemblée in suppressing the "violence and brigandage" allegedly being fomented by the political clubs of that region. Two days after this *Mémoire* appeared, he returned to Auteuil from a brief trip, and his friends, upset that he had written this pamphlet without telling them of his plans, "did not greet me, did not answer when I spoke to them, and departing quickly, left me alone with Mme Helvétius." He left Auteuil and never returned.[62]

He found friends who shared his attitudes among the handful of academicians who continued to attend the séances of the Académie after the spring of 1789. The Académie had members who

61 Ibid., 407-409.
62 Morellet, *Mémoires*, I, 7-17; Morellet, *Mémoire des députés de la ville de Tulles*.

initially revealed enthusiasm for the events that so appalled Morellet—men such as Condorcet, Chamfort, Bailly, La Harpe, Target, Ducis, Chabanon and even Sedaine. Most of these figures were to recant this early support, and some were to die in the maelstrom, but Morellet recalled that there were bitter arguments that spring between these men and the ultramoderates such as Marmontel, Suard, Saint-Lambert, Delille, Beauvau, Morellet himself, and others.[63] The Académie as an institution came under violent attack in the press of 1789 and 1790, when writers who perhaps long had resented its privilege, arrogance, and domination of the world of letters emerged to denounce its inconsistency with a society of merit. Chamfort himself led a campaign for its suppression.[64] After March 1789 the Académie did not attempt to fill any vacancies which occurred, and the vast majority of its members, whatever their private attitudes, cautiously avoided its séances in the Louvre. Throughout the period from 1790 to the spring of 1793, attendance at its meetings was down to eight members, instead of the usual twenty to thirty before 1789. It was generally the same eight who were there; among them, with constancy, were Suard, Morellet, Saint-Lambert, and until his departure from Paris, the *secrétaire-perpétuel*, Marmontel.[65]

It was an oddly defiant, courageous and senseless act of loyalty to the Ancien Régime, this attendance at a purely ceremonial Académie now deserted by its members, unable to work, vilified daily in the press, and denounced with increasing violence in the Assemblée and then the Convention as a vestige of the aristocracy and of royal privilege. At the solemn mass for Saint-Louis on August 25, 1790, held almost clandestinely in the chapel of the Louvre, only eight members dared to attend, including Marmontel, Suard and Morellet.[66] In 1791 Morellet agreed to serve as acting *secrétaire-perpétuel* in Marmontel's absence, and he defended

[63] Morellet, *Mémoires*, II, 52-53 (mispaginated 52-33).

[64] Chamfort's attack was published in *Registres de l'Académie Française*, IV, 171-184. There is an acrimonious but interesting discussion of Chamfort's curious relationship with the Académie whose destruction he worked so hard to bring about, in Boissier, *L'Académie Française sous l'Ancien Régime*, 185-257.

[65] *Registres de l'Académie Française*, III, 622-659. The exception to attendance out of devotion was the frequent presence of Chamfort, presumably there to keep an eye on his confrères.

[66] Ibid., 635.

the Académie in print against Chamfort.[67] After the execution of the king, when continued attendance at the royally tainted institution constituted a serious danger, and no one could deceive himself about its fate, the number of those who persisted in assembling dropped from eight to seven, then to five, among whom were always Morellet, usually Suard, and frequently, until the spring of 1793, Saint-Lambert. By August 1793, when the suppression of the Académies was decreed, Morellet alone would agree to act in the name of the literary body. Ordered to deliver all its papers to the Republic, he committed his one final act of devotion: at the risk of his life, by deceiving the agents of the Convention, he withheld those papers which he believed necessary to the re-establishment of the Académie in better times.[68]

* * *

The days of the Terror were the most trying times of all for the remnant of the coterie holbachique, even for Grimm in his exile. When Grimm had fled Paris after the departure of the Russian ambassador, he had done so in haste, leaving behind, in the care of his secretary and servants, his real and capital wealth. He believed that these were secure, given his status as a foreign minister, and that one day it would be safe to reclaim his fortune. On February 2, 1793, however, he was officially declared an emigré, and on April 25, despite the efforts of his secretary, his property was sequestered by the Republic.[69] Grimm quickly protested in a note to the *comité de salut publique*, and on May 13 the *conseil exécutif provisoire* accepted his argument that he was a neutral foreign diplomat and ordered the seals removed from his apartment.[70] To save his wealth, however, Grimm apparently would have had to return to Paris to establish the fact of his residence. He chose to sacrifice his purse instead, and in November he once more was inscribed on the list of emigrés, and his possessions were

[67] Morellet, *De l'Académie française* (Paris, 1791); this was also printed in *Registres de l'Académie Française*, IV, 184-226.

[68] *Registres de l'Académie Française*, III, 656-663.

[69] Grimm, "Mémoire historique," in *Corr. litt.*, I, 32 ff; Meister, "Grimm," in ibid., 9; Grimm, *Corr. au comte de Findlater*, 17-18.

[70] *Recueil des actes du comité de salut publique*, Aulard and Mautouchet, eds., IV, 143-144. (This has escaped the attention of Cazes, the editor of Grimm's correspondence with Findlater, who declared, on p. 18 of that work, that Grimm's first appeal to the *comité* was on May 25, 1793, and that he received no reply from them.)

catalogued by the nation. All the financial independence he had secured in his lifetime now was gone forever, and he henceforth would be wholly dependent upon the gifts of Catherine and his German patrons. As he wrote: "I had spent forty-five years of my life in France; I had invested all of my fortune there in good faith; I did not have an *écu* elsewhere. My capital, my *rentes*, all of my revenue have been seized, to the profit of the Republic."[71]

For the others, these were years of attempted obscurity and hiding. Marmontel moved briefly to a neighboring town in Normandy with his wife and children, but the mayor asked him to leave, and he returned to Abloville, where he devoted himself to writing works on literature, philosophy and morality, volumes that would not be published until after his death.[72] Suard, severely compromised by his outspoken royalism in *Les nouvelles politiques* (1792), left Paris for his country home in Fontenay-aux-Roses after the fall of the monarchy, and remained in seclusion until Thermidor. When his formerly close friend Condorcet knocked on his door seeking refuge, only a few days before the police located the proscribed girondin, Suard gave him food and tobacco and, pleading that he could not endanger Mme Suard, sent him on his way.[73] Saint-Lambert stayed silently in Eaubonne, writing his philosophical works and not attempting to publish a word.[74] Raynal, his fortune eliminated and his silver confiscated,

[71] Grimm, "Mémoire historique," in *Corr. litt.*, I, 42; Meister, "Grimm," loc. cit.; *Procès-verbaux de la commission temporaire des arts*, Louis Tuetey, ed., I, 259 ("Inventaire des livres trouvés dans la maison de Grimm et Beuil, émigrés . . . 27 prairial, an II), and 331 (a report on musical instruments found "chez l'émigré Grimm . . ."). The inventory was published by Maurice Tourneux, *La bibliothèque et les papiers de Grimm pendant et après la Révolution*.

[72] Marmontel, *Mémoires*, II, 414-430; see also Locher, "Marmontel et la Révolution," in Ehrard, *Marmontel*.

[73] Garat, *Suard*, II, 307-451; Mme Suard, *Suard*, 134 *ff*. Condorcet's widow wrote a long letter to the *Publiciste* in 1802, defending Suard's role in the final days of her husband's life (see *Le Publiciste*, 29 Oct. 1802). Morellet also attempted to defend Suard, claiming that the latter had tried to secure a safe-conduct pass from Garat in Paris, and was unable to locate Condorcet upon returning to Fontenay-aux-Roses (see Morellet, *Mémoires*, II, 100-107); this particular fact, however, was only a repetition of an assertion made by Mme Suard.

[74] Damiron, op. cit., II, 179-180. Saint-Lambert had ceased attending the Académie Française in about April, 1793 (see *Registres de l'Académie Française*, III, 656-662).

moved from commune to commune in the Seine-et-Oise, receiving "certificates of residence valid for three months," and settled
at last in Montherry, poor and forgotten.[75] These men survived
by silence.

Darcet's lot proved to be more precarious. In mid-September
1793 he was dismissed from his post at Sèvres, and on September
26, in connection with his case, the *commission temporaire des arts*
declared ominously that "all of the workers of the national *manufactures* are perhaps influenced by foreigners and . . . it would
be of interest to warn the *comité de salut publique* of this."[76]
Sensing his own danger, Darcet, who still was in possession of
important documents from Sèvres, sought to withdraw from all
attention, and wrote to the commission in late October, begging
to be "discharged of the papers . . . of which he was possessor."
The commission wrote back that "Citizen Darcet" must continue
to serve as "depository" of the papers "until he is otherwise ordered."[77] According to his friend Dizé, Darcet was indeed denounced at the *comité*: his friendships with proscribed aristocrats,
especially with the duc d'Orléans (whom he had tutored in chemistry), were offered as proof of his sentiments, and he was placed
on a list of suspects. He was saved, still following Dizé's testimony,
only by the active intervention of his friend Fourcroy, who as a
member of the Convention heard of the denunciation and defended
Darcet personally to Robespierre.[78] There is some evidence that
Darcet retired to a family farm in Prouilh shortly after his experience of danger,[79] but by March 1794 he was called upon to evaluate work being done in the refining of saltpeter, which he continued to do throughout the spring and summer.[80]

Morellet, in Paris throughout the Terror, had lived true to his
principles through the summer of 1793, serving his Académie at
no small peril to himself. What frightened him into ignobility, he
admitted in his *Mémoires*, was the decree of September 18, 1793,
rendering "suspects" subject to arrest. Just prior to that decree, in
order to be able to draw a republican pension as a man of letters
deprived of his former royal pensions, he had initiated action to
obtain a *certificat de civisme*. He was a pathetic figure throughout

[75] B.N., MS *Fonds français*, 6429, folios 7-9.
[76] *Commission temporaire des arts*, I, 7-8, 10.
[77] Ibid., I, 15. [78] Dizé, *Précis sur Darcet*, 21-26.
[79] Cuzacq, *Darcet*, 24-29.
[80] *Actes du comité de salut publique*, XII, 172, 186; see also Dizé, loc. cit.

this attempt, as he himself recognized, justifying to his friends his inclusion of this narrative in his *Mémoires* by its usefulness to future historians. By the time his case was heard, he knew that a failure to obtain his certificate automatically would make of him a "suspect." At his first hearing, a member of the *conseil* questioned his *civisme*, and accused him of favoring despotism.[81] Morellet had known how to talk to archbishops and royal ministers in the Ancien Régime; he was at a loss over how to talk to the "men of the people" upon whom his fate would now depend.

Morellet sought out each of the men who would hear his case, desperately attempting to win their favor. When they attacked the Académie which he had earlier defended, he answered by praising the early revolutionary fervor of Target, La Harpe and Chamfort, whom in fact he detested for their betrayal. When they alleged his close ties with the royal ministries, he denied them, citing only his close association with Turgot, whom he hoped they might admire. To the *conseil* itself, his one remaining servant dragged along a sack of his books, the ones he thought might aid his case: the *Manuel des inquisiteurs*, the translation of Beccaria, the many brochures against monopoly, and the *Refléxions sur la liberté d'écrire et d'imprimer*, despite the fact that he effectively had renounced the views of the first and last of these from 1789 to 1792. When they spoke of the favors he had received, he brought up his imprisonment in the Bastille and presented it as if it had been punishment for his philosophy and his devotion to the cause of Voltaire. When he visited a member of the *conseil* or went to his frequently delayed hearings, he left his good clothes (and even, when it rained, his umbrella) at home, wearing instead "a sorry frock-coat to gain the goodwill of my judges." He was being judged by common people, including "a ladies' hairdresser . . . [which] would have made me laugh in any other circumstance," and he saw with growing desperation that nothing he was saying to them was making any impression. They wanted to know about his place in the Ancien Régime, and about his obvious antipathy to the events of the past few years. He pleaded "humbly" for "a fraternal correction" instead of "an accusation," and promised to learn to be "civic" from them. At last, in a reform of procedure, it was decreed that before cases could be judged by the commune, local sections should first pass on the *civisme* of those seeking cer-

---

[81] Morellet, *Mémoires*, II, 62-70.

tificates, and Morellet, relieved, abandoned his effort and attempted to fade into obscurity. His sense of security only returned some six weeks later, however, when a friend of his told him that Hébert, prosecutor of the commune of Paris in his case, had said in reference to Morellet that "all these old priests no longer can harm us . . . they would not be annoyed to be imprisoned and fed at the nation's expense, but we won't give them that satisfaction."[82]

By his own admission Morellet spent almost the entire next year, until the ninth of Thermidor, in a state of depression, fear and cowardice, as friends of his from former times went to the prisons and scaffolds of the Republic. He wrote, for himself, sardonic and (he later declared) "horrible" pages in moments of "fury," in one of which he urged the Republic to feed the bodies of those who were guillotined to the poor. He did what he could to allay suspicions against him, hiring as his laundress, for example, the most "revolutionary" of the women in his neighborhood, who terrorized him by calling him "an aristocrat." In mid-July 1794 he was denounced at his local *comité*, and ordered to a hearing. The main charges against him seemed to be his possession of favors under the old regime, and his lack of enthusiasm for or participation in any of the "grand days" of the Revolution. He answered the first charge by citing, once again, his association with Turgot, and this time his local *comité* responded favorably to that name. He answered the second by citing his age, and swearing his submission to the present authorities. He was acquitted. In the course of his interrogation, however, as Morellet reported it, he was asked a question which indeed summed up the heart of the matter: " 'Why,' someone asked me, 'were you happy before August 10, and why have you been sad ever since?' " The only mistake the interrogator made was in the date: Morellet had been sad since the spring of 1789. To save himself, he denied it.[83]

Just as Naigeon had been alone among his former friends of the rue Royale in welcoming the Revolution in its early years, now he was alone in a certain principled defiance of its course. At the height of the Terror and the cult of the Supreme Being, he published the third volume of his atheistic *Philosophie ancienne et moderne*, and in his own name he declared his dissociation from both the deism of Robespierre and the "unphilosophical" atheism of the Hébertistes. Declaring that "there cannot be a middle way"

[82] Ibid., 70-99.   [83] Ibid., 108-127.

between "atheism" and "the baptism of the Churches," he never-theless condemned the new atheism of the streets. "[A]ll these little philosophers, these *minuti philosophi* . . . all these atheists by their own word," he wrote, were certain to prove themselves to be like a man he knew, who by "four arguments from a sophist . . . was converted in one quarter-hour, and believed the next day, as firmly, everything most ridiculous and most absurd that super-stition could imagine." In this he might have seemed to ally him-self with the doctrine of Robespierre himself, who also had con-tempt for the atheists of Paris. For Naigeon, however, the new deistic cult was above all others to be damned: ". . . of all religious opinions, more or less absurd, for which men destroy each other with fury from one pole to the other, deism is necessarily the most intolerant. Indeed, the deist, once attacked, . . . in this last asylum of the religious man, has nowhere to rest his head. . . . He thus must hate, persecute, [and] even exterminate, if he can, the de-stroyer of the phantom of his exalted imagination, the enemy of the god of which he was the inventor."[84]

To term deism more intolerant than Christianity during the Terror was courageous, but there is no evidence that any author-ity moved in any manner against Naigeon. Most likely, he was safe during this period for the same reason that abstract philos-ophers on the whole were safe during the Ancien Régime: it was not the authors of metaphysical tomes whom the authorities feared, but those authors of pamphlets, brochures, critical journals and satires who were men with followings. It was not Naigeon who went to the guillotine, but the author of *Père Duchesne*.

However precariously, the remnant of the coterie holbachique survived, and before judging that they were men who could not adapt successfully to the new world that opened to them in 1789 and beyond, one perhaps should ponder the curious irony of ends: that it was Chamfort who perished, not Morellet; Bailly, not Marmontel; André Chénier, not Raynal; Lavoisier, not Dar-cet; Condorcet, and not Suard. There was, it would seem, a cer-tain fortuitous security in their antipathy to the Revolution, for it occurred early enough to remove them from the perilous cen-ter of events.

* * *

The Thermidorians and the *Directoire* attempted to make peace with the surviving scientists and men of letters of the Ancien

[84] Naigeon, *Philosophie ancienne et moderne*, III, 660-661.

Régime, and for some of the remnant of the *coterie holbachique*, this meant a return to more ordered, comfortable and publicly useful lives. In late December 1794 Darcet was reimbursed for the work he had performed for the *comité de salut publique*, and he resumed the full exercise of his duties at the collège de France and at the mint. By the end of 1795 he was living once more at the *maison de la Monnaie*, where he was again *inspecteur-général*, and was serving, in addition, as a *commissaire ordonnateur des guerres*.[85]

Raynal was less fortunate, in that he still bore the stigma of his bitter outburst of 1791, and as late as January 1796 his commune had to issue him a form emphasizing "that he did not emigrate and he is not being detained." He lived on no other income than a pension of 2,787 *livres*, according to his commune, and had engaged in no actions that would cast doubt upon his patriotism.[86] In March 1796, however, the *Directoire exécutif* decided to add the aged Raynal to the list of those important cultural figures from the old regime whom it had decided to favor, and as its third order of business on March 2, it decided to "accord to the author of the *Histoire . . . des Deux Indes* the bread, meat and wood necessary to his personal use, and a sum of 600 *livres* per month."[87] Raynal asked if the government might aid him to produce a new edition of the *Histoire philosophique des Deux Indes*, and the *Directoire* ordered its ambassadors to send him any information he requested.[88] On March 6 the *directeurs* named him to the new *Institut National des sciences et des arts*, but his rescue was short-lived, and within twenty-four hours he died of natural causes.[89] Had he lived to attend the opening meetings of the new Institut, he would have joined Darcet, who was placed in the section of mineralogy with a pension of at least 4,000 *livres*, and Naigeon, placed in the section of moral philosophy, with a pension

[85] *Actes du comité de salut publique*, XVIII, 626-627; XX, 16; XXVII, 29; *Recueil des actes du Directoire exécutif*, A. Debidour, ed., I, 150; *Almanach national* (1795-1797).

[86] B.N., MS *Fonds français*, 6429, folio 9.

[87] *Actes du Directoire exécutif*, I, 712. This must have been a somewhat extraordinary procedure, for almost seven months later, the *directeurs* decided to aid a former diplomat, and instructed the minister of the interior to proceed "as that was done with regard to Raynal" (ibid., III, 715).

[88] *Gazette française* (1796), 11 March.

[89] *Actes du Directoire exécutif*, I, 712, n. 1; *Gazette française* (1796), 11 March.

of at least 2,000 *livres*.[90] For some, life was returning to normalcy.

In Grimm's case the new attitudes of the regime in France produced but few benefits. Late in 1795 the *Directoire* reversed the prior judgment against him and removed his name from the list of emigrés. Most of his possessions already had been sold, however, so he was reimbursed in *assignats* at their par value, which meant, in effect, that he was not reimbursed at all. What little that did remain of his once great fortune was sent to him in Gotha: three lace cuffs and several pieces of muslin. As he wrote sardonically to the count of Findlater, France valued the pieces of fabric, apparently, at some 20,000 to 30,000 *livres* each. His only "happiness, the first since the Revolution," he wrote in August 1795, was that he was able "to rescue" his favorite servant from France, after one year of effort, and she was coming to join him in Gotha. Catherine continued to support him, but his letters revealed a certain bitterness about his loss of all hope of restoring his past condition. He was now actively utilizing his connections to aid the most *ultra* of the emigrés to find security and comfort, and he was wholly unreconciled to the *Directoire*. The French successes in Italy in the spring of 1796 were "a new mortal blow which plunges me into cruel sleepless nights." He became enthusiastic over word of Burke's opposition to "a regicide peace," and wrote Findlater to send him copies of Burke's *Letters* so that he might translate them into French and German, and influence the thought of the Empire.[91]

Darcet and Naigeon seemed best to adjust to the regime of the *Directoire*, and they began to reconstruct their careers. Darcet devoted himself to his scientific work, and advanced within the new governmental scientific hierarchy as a useful and dedicated scientist and administrator. He may have been somewhat insecure in his own mind, however, for he had himself inscribed again among the *corps* of practicing medical doctors and, as well, among the *société libre* of pharmacists.[92] Naigeon entered a period of calm, during which he began to acquire the reputation he would have at the end of his life, that of a bibliophile and pedant. He

[90] *Almanach national* (1796), 443-451.

[91] Grimm, *Corr. à Findlater*, passim, and in particular, 19-23, 111-116, 125-129, 148-153, 185-189; see also Grimm, "Mémoire historique," in *Corr. litt.*; Meister, "Grimm," in *Corr. litt.*; Cathérine II, *Lettres à Grimm*; Grimm, *Lettres à Cathérine II*.

[92] *Almanach national* (1797), 130, 143, 378, 389, 398, 412-413.

engaged in extensive literary and philosophical editing, including among his publications works far removed from his own atheism. As a member of the Institut, he had achieved a respectability which previously had eluded him, and he did not seek to jeopardize that.[93]

Marmontel and Saint-Lambert, more royalist in their thought and more wary in their perception of the state of France, remained in their rural retreats until 1797. The *Directoire* was not courting aristocrats, and Saint-Lambert was not offered a place in the Institut; still in Eaubonne, he continued to work on his *Catéchisme universel*. Marmontel was being courted, but he chose to refuse the honors. Named a member of the Institut in 1796, he decided upon "nonresident" status and moved with his family to Gaillon, near Rouen.[94] Invited several times to assume teaching and administrative functions in his locality, he declined to occupy any public post.[95] In his *Mémoires* (written after 1797), he recalled that for him the clash between "the Jacobins" and "the republicans" of the *Directoire* was a clash between two evils, "anarchy" and "despotism," and that the *Directoire* represented "a despotism absolute and tyrannical beyond any former example."[96]

For Morellet and Suard, Thermidor produced a revival of courage, and both men recommenced their critique of the course of public events. In 1795 Suard revived *Le Publiciste*, and its manifest royalist sympathies soon placed him in great difficulty. In December of that year, Suard was denounced by the *jury d'accusation* of Paris along with the royalist editor Richer-Sérizy, and, ironically, Camille Babeuf. Warned by Necker's daughter, Mme de Staël, Suard appears to have fled for the first time to the Neck-

[93] Part of this, of course, is that he had completed his *Philosophie ancienne et moderne*, but he did not produce another "atheistic" work until 1800, when he published his edition of Diderot's works. At the same time, however, he was working on an edition of Rousseau's works. He did not attempt to publish his openly atheistic *Mémoires* on the life and work of Diderot during his lifetime, and they appeared posthumously. At this time of his life he began to acquire the reputation of a bibliophile, so that Damiron, who truly found Naigeon's words those of a violent man, knew of him by reputation as someone who loved his books "before" his atheism. In the end the Revolution turned a polemicist into a scholarly figure in the Institut. See Damiron, op. cit., II, 407. According to Damiron, however, Naigeon still enjoyed arguing his atheism with the philosophers among his confrères.

[94] *Almanach national* (1797), 403-404.

[95] Locher, "Marmontel et la Révolution," in Ehrard, *Marmontel*, 75-76.

[96] Marmontel, *Mémoires*, II, 423-431.

ers' home in Coppet, Switzerland.[97] In January 1796, however, the *Directoire exécutif* crushed the case against him due to "irregularities in procedure," and, at liberty, he returned to Paris, once again becoming involved in royalist agitation.[98]

Morellet, meanwhile, had thrown himself with great enthusiasm into a new cause, that of the families of the emigrés from and the victims of the Revolution, whom he defended against the laws which penalized them for the alleged "crimes" of their relations. From December 1794 to March 1796 he published at least ten brochures on behalf of the children and parents of emigrés and victims, most of them general in nature, but at least one directed to the particular case of the survivors left by his friend Trudaine. In several of these he specifically attacked representatives calling for strict maintenance and execution of the laws.[99] Now that he was an active opponent of the regime, he even wrote again on behalf of the freedom of the press.[100] He compared unfavorably the government's unwillingness to reverse the decision of its courts to the attitude toward the rectification of justice that had prevailed under the Ancien Régime: "The judgments against Calas and Sirven had been rendered with as much solemnity as those of the revolutionary tribunals, and no one would dare say that this solemnity should have prevented them from being revised."[101] In pamphlets increasingly passionate and bitter, the old man of seventy castigated those who seemed not to understand that a concerned relative would not have attempted to prevent a loved one from leaving a France in which no one's life was safe.

[97] Garat, *Suard*, II, 307-451; Mme Suard, *Suard*, 134 *ff*; *Actes du Directoire exécutif*, I, 353-354.

[98] *Actes du Directoire exécutif*, I, 353-354; *Nouvelles politiques, nationales et étrangères* (1797), passim.

[99] Morellet, *Le cri des familles* (Paris, Dec. 1794), in which he attacked several deputies; *La cause des pères* (Paris, March 1795); *Observations sur un article du Journal de Paris . . . et réponse aux reproches du représentant Chazal* (Paris, May 1795); *Supplément à la cause des pères* (Paris, July 1795); *Nouvelles réclamations pour les pères et mères d'émigrés* (Paris, Dec. 1796); *Mémoire pour les citoyennes Trudaine, veuve Micault, Micault, veuve Trudaine, et le citoyen vivant Micault Courbeton* (Paris, 1797); *Dernière défense des pères et mères, aïeuls et aïeules d'émigrés* (Paris, Jan. 1797); *Appel à l'opinion publique du jugement du conseil des cinq cents* (Paris, Feb. 1797); *Discussion du rapport de P.-J. Audouin sur les pères et mères d'émigrés* (Paris, March 1797).

[100] Morellet, *Pensées libres sur la liberté de la presse.*

[101] Morellet, *Le cri des familles.*

In effect, he called upon the current authorities to declare almost the entire past of the Revolution unjust. Such publications did not win him favor. In January 1796 the police denounced a journal as suspicious on the grounds that one of its articles "made the greatest *éloge* of a new work by citizen Morellet in favor of the fathers and mothers of emigrés."[102] In April of that year, a journal called the *Patriotes de 89* denounced Morellet's "solicitude for the emigrés."[103] Had the "patriots" known his true sentiments, they would have found things far more grave to condemn. In February the abbé had written to Shelburne in England that the government could never establish itself with any security or legitimacy, and that "in any case, the people no longer will be able to be contained except by military despotism, which in its own way will complete the ruin of our country."[104]

* * *

Whatever their distrust of "the people," Suard, Marmontel and Morellet all perceived, throughout the years from 1795 to 1797, a growing royalist sentiment among the bourgeoisie, and this perception encouraged them to attempt once more to effect more directly the political future of France. Once more, the Revolution would do what the Ancien Régime never had been able to accomplish: it would frighten and silence them, sending Suard into exile, Marmontel into his final retreat, and Morellet into quiet literary pursuits.

Suard participated actively in the resurgence of the constitutional monarchists in 1796, closely associated with Benjamin Constant and Mme de Staël. He also had ties to the more absolutist royalist camp around Brottier, the representative of the pretender in Paris. In the revived *Les nouvelles politiques*, he polemicized against the regicide *perpétuels*, and by the summer of 1797 he was openly sympathetic to the disgraced Cochon, the only minister whom he had supported. The *Amis des Lois* referred contemptuously to him as one of "the king's journalists," and his safety soon was again in peril.[105] Warned once more by Mme de Staël, he fled to Switzerland only a few days before the *Directoire* included him

---

[102] *Paris pendant la réaction Thermidorienne et sous le Directoire*, F.-A. Aulard, ed., II, 672.

[103] Ibid., III, 122.

[104] Morellet, *Lettres à Lord Shelburne*, 317.

[105] Aulard, *Paris . . . sous le Directoire*, IV, 219. See also *Nouvelles politiques* (1796-1797); Garat, loc. cit.; Mme Suard, loc. cit.

among those condemned on 18 Fructidor, when he was charged with "conspiracy against the internal and external security of the Republic, and especially with provocation of the re-establishment of the monarchy and the dissolution of the republican government."[106] In Switzerland the situation for French emigrés soon deteriorated, and he fled to Anspach in Germany, where he was well-received by the aristocratic emigré community. When his possessions were sold by the Republic, his friends in Paris purchased most of his property and gave to his wife adequate money for the family's exile. Mme Suard soon joined him in Anspach, where they lived a life of balls and entertainments which she described as identical to the style of their life in the final years of the Ancien Régime.[107]

Marmontel also was encouraged, after the suppression of the Babouvistes, with the rise in royalist sentiment, and in April 1797 he participated in the elections of his region. On April 12 the royalist and strongly Catholic voters of Louviers elected him, with 303 out of 329 votes cast, to the *Conseil des Anciens*, and in his acceptance speech on the 13th, he "expressed his love for the country and his regret over not having been able to be useful during the time of troubles when truth could not make itself heard."[108] At the age of 74, thus, Marmontel returned to the capital, where he was elected *premier-secrétaire* of the *Conseil*. There he identified himself with the royalist faction, speaking on behalf of the emigrés and against the *directeurs'* calling of troops to the vicinity of Paris, and the *Amis des Lois* soon accused him of being in league with the suspect Portalis.[109] Marmontel, in fact, was

[106] "Arrêté du Directoire sur les journaux et les journalistes," in Aulard, *Paris . . . sous le Directoire*, IV, 317, listing him as "Suard, auteur des *Nouvelles politiques*." On the next day, September 5, Suard was included among those condemned to arrest, deportation and seizure of property and goods, all without benefit of trial, by the "Loi du 19 fructidor," a law directed against those men whom the regime truly believed to be active, royalist conspirators. The law of 19 Fructidor proscribed forty-two members of the *Conseil des Cinq Cents, des Anciens*, and twelve other individuals. Suard found himself in eminent company: Carnot, *directeur*; Barthélemy, *directeur*; Brottier, the archconspirator himself; Cochon, ex-minister of police; Miranda, a *général*; Morgan, a *général*; Mailhe, the ex-*conventionnel*; Ramel, the *commandant des grenadiers du corps législatif*; and three other "lesser" conspirators (ibid., 317-323).

[107] Mme Suard, loc. cit.

[108] Locher, "Marmontel et la Révolution," in Ehrard, *Marmontel*, 76-77.

[109] *Paris . . . sous le Directoire*, IV, 120; see also Locher, op. cit., 78.

working, above all, on his speech against the Revolution's persecution of the Catholic Church, in which he was to call for a dramatic reversal of the religious policy of France since 1789.[110] He never was able to deliver it, however. The coup of 18 Fructidor which sent Suard into exile crushed the election of Marmontel, although he was spared the deportation ordered against many members of the *Conseil des Cinq Cents*.[111] His cause defeated, Marmontel retired to Normandy to write his *Mémoires*, a work passionate in its defense of the king and its condemnation of both the men of 1789 and the republicans. In February 1798 a journal entitled *La poste du jour* reported Marmontel's arrest, but this was a false rumor.[112] He was left in peace, and he died unreconciled in 1799.

Morellet was invited in 1795 to accept a post as professor of political economy at the *écoles centrales*, in what he termed a frank letter from the executive committee of public instruction which expressed some of their own uncertainties about him. In his *Mémoires* he wrote that he chose to remain "in my obscurity," and declined the offer so that he might continue to plead the cause of the families of the emigrés without the embarrassment of occupying a public post. In October 1795, however, despite his fear that any involvement with the present government of France might make him "seem to participate in the crimes they had committed and the injustices they still supported," he joined in the royalist agitation and elections of his section, the Elysée, where the propertied and moderate voters chose him as an elector. At this point, it was believed that the Assemblée was to be wholly renewed, and the *Directoire's* decision to impose a retention of two-thirds of those currently sitting raised a storm in Paris. Morellet wrote that he was frightened of provoking the government in the streets, and the *Directoire's* use of force against the royalists appears to have effectively dampened his desire to oppose the regicides in so active a manner.[113] He continued to write vigor-

---

[110] Published in Marmontel, *Mémoires*, II, 435-463.

[111] *Paris . . . sous le Directoire*, IV, 318; see also *Almanach national* (1798), 43bis-46bis, 47, 51.

[112] *Paris . . . sous le Directoire*, IV, 548.

[113] Morellet, *Mémoires*, II, 146-159. Morellet wrote that he had the chance, after the resignation of several elected deputies, to serve in the *Conseil des Cinq Cents*, but that he declined to do so because of his "reputation as an aristocrat," which meant that he would be "booed and hissed" by the galleries. After the government acted against the royalist demonstrators, Morellet recalled, he hid for ten days, afraid to sleep at his own home.

ously on behalf of royalist causes, but 18 Fructidor was to change that as well. After the *coup d'état* he ceased all political activity and devoted himself to translations of literature, history and travelogues from the English.[114] In his *Mémoires* he described his new circumspection as arising from economic need, but more likely he was determined not to follow Suard's example.[115] Fructidor had struck heavily at royalist journalists, and he understood the consequences of further opposition.

* * *

The *coup d'état* of 18 Brumaire which established the *Consulat* and brought Napoléon to power created, or indeed re-created, in France conditions in which the remnant of the coterie holbachique could feel secure and could regain at least their ceremonial eminence in the world of letters and thought. As first consul and emperor, Bonaparte sought to reconcile diverse political and literary factions to his rule, and he flattered the former literary and scientific elites of the Ancien Régime into a public acceptance of the new order. The style of his regime's relations with the remnant of the coterie recalled circumstances which the latter had known before 1789, and they adapted well to the reappearance of a system of ceremony, inflated modes of address, formal indications of loyalty, patronage, personal favors among gentlemen, and honorary sinecures.

Morellet, in the summer of 1799, had broken his discreet silence by writing against the laws concerning hostages, and he was the most relieved by the coup against the *Directoire*.[116] His opposition to the *directeurs* earned him favor under the *Consulat*, and he appears to have used this to aid in the securing of Suard's return.[117] In the reorganization of the Institut National under Bonaparte, former members of the Académie Française were favored, and Mo-

114 *L'Italian . . . par Anne Radcliffe*, A. Morellet, trans. (Paris, 1797); *Clermont, par . . . Regine-Maria Roche*, A. Morellet, trans. (Paris, 1798); *Constantinople ancienne et moderne . . . par J. Dallaway*, A. Morellet, trans. (Paris, 1797); *Phéodora . . . par M. Charlton*, A. Morellet, trans. (Paris, 1797); *Voyages de Vancouver*, vol. III, A. Morellet, trans. (Paris, 1797).

115 Morellet, *Mémoires*, II, 167, 172-175. On p. 168, Morellet noted that "the loss of all liberty for the press, since the epoch of 18 Fructidor, left me no possibility to publish any of my works relative to public affairs. . . ." This had not prevented him from publishing during the Ancien Régime.

116 Ibid., 176-178; Morellet, *Observations sur la loi des otages*.

117 Morellet, *Mémoires*, II, 179; Mme Suard, loc. cit.; Suard, *Mémoires et correspondances* (Nisard), 277-288.

rellet, Suard and Saint-Lambert joined Darcet and Naigeon among the new immortals.[118]

Morellet, Suard and Saint-Lambert led a campaign to convince the first consul to re-establish the Académie Française upon its former footing, and although the reorganized Institut National represented a compromise with their requests, they were influential in selecting the membership of the new literary members, and were given at least the public appearance of particular favor from the consuls. In return they nominated the consuls to membership in the Institut, as the members of the Académie Française had chosen ministers of state, bishops and princes of the royal blood to join their *corps*.[119] At last they were once again in a world they could understand.

Darcet must have given his own dramatic signs of loyalty to the new regime, for in 1800 he was named to the *Sénat conservateur*, where he served until his fatal illness in December 1801.[120] His family enjoyed a certain respectability in the circles of the new regime, and one of his daughters married Joachim Le Breton, a member of the Tribunat and of the Institut, while the other married Philippe Grouvelle, a member of the *Corps législatif*, of the Institut, and a former ambassador to Denmark.[121]

Naigeon also aspired to the *Sénat* or the *Corps législatif*, but his past was to deny him an expected place in these. Naigeon attempted under the *Consulat* to shed his reputation as a fiery atheist, and appeared to have achieved some success in this. In May 1800 the *Amis des Lois* attacked Naigeon for his licentious thought, and two days after this article appeared, the journal was suppressed for its attacks upon members of the Institut.[122] In September of that year the police moved against the *Revue littéraire* for its criticism of several members of the Institut, including Naigeon.[123] By May 1801 Naigeon was a respectable enough member of the Institut to be named to a committee of six which presented to the first consul a petition requesting permission to

[118] *Gazette de France* (1800), 3 July; Morellet, *Mémoires*, II, 179-217; *Almanach national* (1803); Garat, *Suard*, 445-450; Suard, *Mémoires et correspondances* (Nisard), 277-312.

[119] Morellet, *Mémoires*, II, 179-217; Garat, loc. cit.; Suard, *Mémoires et correspondances* (Nisard), 277-312.

[120] *Almanach national* (1800), 617-625; Dizé, *Précis sur Darcet*, 22.

[121] Dizé, *Précis sur Darcet*, 26-27.

[122] *Paris sous le consulat*, A. Aulard, ed., I, 363-365, and 365, n. 1.

[123] Ibid., 675-677.

296

resume the work of the Académie Française on the *Dictionnaire*; he was invited by Napoléon to be among several members of that body attending the consul's audience for foreign ambassadors.[124] The scandal caused by the appearance of Maréchal's *Dictionnaire des athées*, however, which devoted much of its attention to Naigeon's atheism and his associations with other atheists in the Ancien Régime, made it impossible for Naigeon to be named to higher positions; he spent the last few years of his life participating in the Institut and editing literary and philosophical works.[125]

For Saint-Lambert the re-establishment of order and the decline of anti-aristocratic sentiment under Bonaparte provided one final return to the public eminence he had sought so assiduously under the Ancien Régime. Only after 18 Brumaire did he return to Paris, to occupy himself with the plan to restore the Académie Française and with his new position in the Institut.[126] In the summer of 1800 he participated in a meeting of the former members of the Académie Française held under the auspices of Lucien Bonaparte, and caused a sensation when he produced a letter sent to him by the minister of the interior that referred to the Institut as "the Académie Française."[127] In 1800 Lucien Bonaparte accorded him a pension of 2,400 *livres*, which was confirmed by Chaptal when he assumed the ministry of the interior.[128] Saint-Lambert had lived just long enough to end his days in the sun. When he died in February 1803, he was buried with ceremony at a solemn mass held in the church of Saint-Philippe-du-Roule, attended by a deputation from the Institut and by "a great number of distinguished persons." His *éloge*, pronounced extemporaneously at the cemetery of Montmartre, was read by "his former colleague . . . [and] friend," the new *secrétaire-perpétuel* of their *classe* at the Institut, Suard.[129]

Suard's return to favor was not without its ambiguities, for he remained loyal to the monarchy, but he reached an accommodation with the *Consulat* and Empire, and he prospered. Upon his return to Paris, he re-established the royalist *Le Publiciste* and was again identified as a potential enemy of a "revolutionary" regime.

---

[124] *Journal de Paris* (1801), 22 May.

[125] Damiron, *Histoire de la philosophie au XVIIIe siècle*, II, 440-441.

[126] Morellet, *Mémoires*, II, 185-187.

[127] *Gazette de France* (1800), 3 July.

[128] Aulard, *Paris sous le consulat*, II, 4-5. Morellet received a pension of 2,000 *livres* in the same action.

[129] Ibid., III, 656.

As in the Ancien Régime, however, a formal profession of loyalty, which he always offered, seemed to suffice, and his social connections with men of influence in the government secured his safety. Throughout these early years of the *Consulat*, despite his royalist sentiments, he was both host and guest of ministers and officials, and retained a favored place in the Institut. In February 1800, for example, he was invited to a fête and ball given by the minister of foreign affairs, where Napoléon himself was in attendance.[130] In December of that year a police report charged that "The journalist Suard, deported on the 18 Fructidor, is, they say, the author of several brochures which appeared abroad against the first consul."[131] His loyalty challenged, Suard wrote directly to Napoléon and stated matters rather honestly. "I like any government which offers me tranquillity and security," he wrote the first consul; "The true friends . . . of your government . . . are those who, like me, . . . want only a just government, protector of the people and property."[132]

Moving in the circle of Mme de Staël and Benjamin Constant, Suard found himself in the center of those curious social circles of the Empire which combined the old society of the Ancien Régime with the new figures of the Napoléonic world. At his own re-established salon, Suard entertained Mme de Flahaut, Mlle de la Tour du Pin, the duchesse de Villeroy, Mme de Vergennes, Mme Lavoisier, Ducis and Morellet, but also Guizot, Constant, Garat and even, on occasion, Talleyrand. Once a week he went to visit Mme d'Angiviller, who remained in Versailles. Through his friendship with Talleyrand, he was invited to discuss literary matters with the emperor, and he rose to eminence in the new literary hierarchy, becoming, as we have seen, a *secrétaire-perpétuel* at the Institut, and receiving, from the government, a pension of 6,000 *livres*. As his wife later wrote, they once again could "*vivre noblement.*"[133]

Upon the re-establishment of the monarchy in 1815, Suard had hoped to see the Bourbons accept a constitutional form of government, and according to Constant, the home of the Suards was

---

[130] Ibid., I, 180.   [131] Ibid., II, 74.

[132] Suard, *Mémoires et correspondances* (Nisard), 33-35; Suard wrote several letters to the *premier consul* attempting to explain the "écarts" of *Le Publiciste* (see ibid., 31-44).

[133] Mme Suard, *Suard*, 134 ff; Benjamin Constant, *Journaux intimes*, A. Roulin and C. Roth, eds., passim.

a center for liberal and constitutional monarchists disappointed by the terms of the Restoration.[134] If he objected to the forms adopted by his king, however, he nevertheless held his peace, and was rewarded by the sovereign for whom he had labored through so many difficult years with new pensions, sinecures and honors. He saw the Académie Française established upon its former royally privileged terms, and served as its *doyen* until his death in 1817. When he died, he was succeeded in this by Morellet.[135]

For Morellet the *Consulat* and Empire inaugurated a striking return to favor. His new status, as in the case of Saint-Lambert, derived more from the pretensions of Lucien Bonaparte to the status of literary patron and to intellectual respectability than from any real concern on the part of Napoléon himself, but through Lucien, Morellet was invited to converse with the first consul,[136] and under the Empire was showered with honors. Named the literary correspondent of Joseph Bonaparte, Morellet was awarded the *légion d'honneur* in 1806, and in 1807 was elected by the *Sénat* to a place in the *Corps législatif*, where he served until 1815.[137] With Suard he led the "party of the Académie" in the Institut, attempting to proscribe from its ranks those who had betrayed it from 1790 to 1793 (insisting, according to a police report concerned with the scandal this created, upon the use of "Monsieur" instead of "citoyen" as the form of address at its meetings), and opposing "the party of the government" within the Institut by always referring to their "*classe*" as their "Académie."[138]

Despite such formal acts of loyalty to the France of the Ancien Régime, Morellet prospered under the favor of Lucien Bonaparte. Most of his former pensions were restored, albeit in reduced forms, and new pensions, such as 3,000 *livres* for being named "president of the commission of the *Dictionnaire de la langue française*," began to accumulate.[139] He re-established his salon, where, according to Brifaut, who visited there, he assembled the most important figures from the literary, philosophical, and diplo-

[134] Constant, *Journaux intimes*, 407.
[135] *Almanach royal* (1817-1818); Hunter, *Suard*, 139 ff.
[136] Morellet, *Mémoires*, II, 218-222.
[137] Ibid., 223-233; *Dictionnaire des parlementaires français*, IV, 431-432.
[138] *Paris sous le consulat*, III, 682; Morellet, *Mémoires*, II, 179-203.
[139] J. Delort, *Histoire de la détention des philosophes et des gens de lettres* . . . , II, 353-354, published a list of the pensions which Morellet received under Bonaparte.

matic worlds, to which he added visiting foreign dignitaries and ministers. Brifaut was struck by the breadth and honesty of conversations there, which touched upon all areas of "social utility, political economy, administration, government, finances, morality, [and] literature. . . ." His home, according to this account, was one of "magnificence" and "wealth," and his dinners were "luxurious," even during Lent, when the abbé served turkeys, exquisite pâtés and fine wines, "in contravention of the commandments of the Church." Morellet used his influence with the government to aid his friends, and for his great-nephew he secured the position of subprefect of Provins. He was, Brifaut declared, "the Nestor of philosophy."[140] After all the years of hardship, Morellet had re-created the rue Royale.

[140] *Oeuvres de M. Charles Brifaut*, M. Rives and A. Bignan, eds., I, 310-313.

NINE · *Mastery and Order*

IN the writings of the members of the coterie holbachique there are visions of worlds removed by many steps from the society of eighteenth-century France. There are angry declamations against the abuses of authority in the monarchical, aristocratic and clerical regime under which they lived. If one searches diligently, one can find the apostrophes, the tocsins, the outrage, the marks of an unyielding hostility toward the powers that be—in short, the passionate criticism that created in so many nineteenth-century minds a link between the philosophes of d'Holbach's circle and the Revolution which had riven France.

In 1780 Raynal placed a stirring apostrophe to Louis XVI in his *Histoire philosophique des Deux Indes*, implying in some respects that the monarch had one final chance to alter the course of French history.[1] In that same edition, he warned his fellow citizens that when men lived under despotism, the "slaves" were as much to blame as the "tyrants," for if the latter had "the insolence to encroach upon liberty," the former revealed "the imbecility of those who do not know to defend liberty."[2] Like many members of the coterie holbachique, Raynal did not hide his admiration for the few republican governments in the world, and in the edition of 1780 he expressed his fear of "a secret conspiracy among all of the monarchies to destroy . . . the free states." In the face of this "conspiracy," he boldly expressed his determination and optimism, in a passage which well might seem to have presaged and invited the event that was to come in just eight years: "But liberty will emerge from the womb of oppression. It is in all hearts: it will pass from public written works to enlightened souls; and from tyranny to the soul of the people. All men at last will perceive, and the day of awakening is not distant, that liberty is the foremost gift of heaven, as it is the first seed of virtue. The agents of despotism will become its destroyers; and the enemies of humanity [the armies], those who today seem to be armed only in order to exterminate it, one day will fight in its defense."[3]

[1] Raynal, *Histoire philosophique des Deux Indes*, 3rd edn. II, 260-268.
[2] Ibid., x, 25.
[3] Ibid., 112.

When Charles-Georges Le Roy sketched for his readers "the best possible form of government," in a "Lettre sur l'homme" of 1768, it differed in almost every detail from the regime under which he lived. There would be no extremes of poverty and opulence, he wrote; there would be reward for all publicly useful work. In such a state, the rulers would accept as their duty the achievement of "the greatest happiness of which weak humanity is susceptible." For Le Roy the natural function of social organization was "the happiness of all," and he lamented that in the contemporary world "this happiness of all . . . does not seem to be the object of the particular constitutions of society, ordinarily established by violence, usurpation, or chance, and founded on the interests of the smallest number."[4] The logical conclusion of such knowledge would appear to be the illegitimacy of the established regimes, and indeed Le Roy elsewhere had warned against confusing sovereignty with "the individual prince."[5]

The language of extreme disaffection from the European status quo came easily to the pens of the coterie holbachique, and in particular instances—above all in contexts relating to the Church —such language could cause the authors to appear to be men awaiting some day of ultimate contest and decision. Upon reading Morellet's translation of Eymeric's inquisitorial manual, Grimm could exclaim that there could be no cooperation between those who supported the philosophes and those who supported the Church, "for as their Christ used to say, what bond can there be between the children of light and the children of darkness?"[6] When Suard wrote to John Wilkes in 1768 to inform him that "All the rue Royale toasts Wilkes and Liberty," he added that Grimm was the most enthused of all over Wilkes' success: "You know that what he hates the most after God is the Kings, and he regards you as a hero of political atheism."[7]

Such rhetorical violence and such indignation was not infrequent in the writings of the members of the coterie holbachique. Diderot did write "a dithyrambic fury" in which the last king was strangled in the bowels of the last priest, although he did borrow the thought from Meslier for the express purpose of composing an

[4] Le Roy, "Lettre sur l'homme," in *Lettres sur les animaux*, 210-212.
[5] Le Roy, *Examen des critiques*, 223 *ff*.
[6] Grimm, *Corr. litt.*, III, 310-311.
[7] Suard, *Lettres à Wilkes*, 26-27, 36-38.

example of poetic hyperbole.[8] D'Holbach himself, in his *Essai sur les préjugés* (1770), had so taken the kings of Europe to task that Frederick the Great was moved to write a refutation and to term the author of the *Essai* a "mad dog."[9] According to d'Holbach, the political and religious prejudices of Europe had corrupted both sovereigns and subjects. By means of royal and ecclesiastical censorship, "the priests and the tyrants" sought to eternalize man's ignorance, lest he ever perceive the horror of his condition. The truth for d'Holbach was that in the eighteenth-century, for all its pretensions to progress, religion was oppressive, the laws were unjust, and the courts were venal and in the control of arbitrary, particular privilege. Some philosophes remained silent in the face of these facts, d'Holbach observed, since they were fearful of the crowned tyrants. "But if philosophy finds the ears of the sovereigns closed to its counsels," he urged, "let her address herself to the people." The philosophe, in his view, owed his obligations not to crowns, but to humanity: "[T]he friend of the human race cannot flatter those who oppress it: he who knows the truth must attack error; he must speak; his silence would make him the accomplice of the imposters whose lies and cajoleries cover the earth with unfortunates."[10]

[8] It is at last time to deal with the context of Diderot's celebrated verse about strangling kings in the bowels of priests. The phrase was not table-talk at d'Holbach's dinners. It occurred in an avowedly hyperbolic poem, "Les Eleuthéromanes, ou les furieux de la liberté." As Diderot explained in a prefatory aesthetic "Argument," the poem was an attempt to imitate a classical dithyramb, "the most fiery [*fougueux*] genre of poetry, . . . in which the poet would show himself full of audacity in the choice of his subject and in the manner of treating it." The device adopted for this poem, Diderot elaborated, was the following: "Entirely liberated from the rules of regular composition, and given over to the total delirium of his enthusiasm, [the poet] advanced without submitting himself to any restraint, piling up verses of every kind. . . . It is a poem of this nature that I have attempted." Furthermore, Diderot added, the circumstances of the composition of the dithyramb were "frivolous" (Diderot, *Oeuvres* (A-T), IX, 9-17). Diderot did not invent the phrase, but borrowed it from Meslier (see Meslier, *Le Testament de Jean Meslier*, R. Charles, ed., I, 18-19). Meslier cited Bayle as his source for the phrase, and according to Dommanget, *Le Curé Meslier*, 302-304, Bayle had taken it from a classical poet of antiquity. Naigeon did cite the passage approvingly in his article on Meslier in the *Philosophie ancienne et moderne*, III, 239, but this was in 1794, when the king was already dead and the violence already accomplished.

[9] Frederick II, *Oeuvres posthumes*, VI, 39-76.

[10] D'Holbach, *Essai sur les préjugés*, 124-151.

In the abstract, in the context of other times and nations, or in response to some hypothetical situation in some hypothetical world, the thinkers of the coterie holbachique all seemed to agree that the people had a right to resist when authority acted to deny the fundamental right of all men to self-preservation and happiness. At times, such considerations spilled over into their commentaries upon the structures and patterns of contemporary France. Could not the very assertion of that right in a society theoretically committed to the divine nature of its monarchy be viewed as a call for such resistance in the flesh and blood, especially when coupled as it was with a constant critique of the status quo? Men had a right to happiness, and no one had the right to deny this to them. Men were not happy in their current lot. Was this not an invitation to resistance and, if need be, to a revolution that would establish the liberty to seek happiness and the freedom to speak the truth?

What, after all, were the common motifs of their political theory? In his article on "Autorité publique" in the *Encyclopédie*, Diderot had written what they almost all believed: that government and social institutions existed to support the well-being of their subjects, deriving the legitimacy of their authority from that and that alone.[11] Twenty years after the appearance of that article, Diderot referred to the government of France as one composed of "tyrants" and warned that "there is only a moment, oh beautiful nation," before all options for a freer world would be lost. The future of France under such tyrants would be a state of "imbecilic sheep who believe themselves born for all time to be torn apart," ruled by "tigers who believe themselves born for all time to tear apart [such sheep]."[12] With the well-being of the nation thus not only opposed by the current government, but threatened for all time, surely for Diderot (one might suppose), the people now had the right to restore the purpose of the social compact. As Diderot himself had written in his *Réfutation* of Helvétius' *De l'homme*, "Under any form of government whatsoever, nature has posed limits to the misery of the people. Beyond these limits it is either death, or escape, or revolt."[13]

[11] Diderot, *Oeuvres politiques*, P. Vernière, ed. (Paris, 1963), 9-20. Vernière has assembled most of Diderot's political writings in one well-annotated volume, and where necessary has corrected the texts published in Assézat-Tourneux.

[12] Ibid., 241.   [13] Ibid., 466.

Was this abstract theory and empirical prediction, or was it indeed an incitement to that revolt? Was Helvétius being abstract when he had argued that the human race had two fundamental groups of enemies—on the one hand, tyrannical fanatics, and on the other, "demi-politiques," men who were fearful of dramatic change and lazy in their acceptance of the status quo?[14] Was Morellet merely predicting, when, for example, in a defense of the free circulation of grain, he answered Galiani's fear—that hoarders and speculators would mock such freedom and drive the people to starvation—with the following reference to *taxation populaire* and beyond? He wrote: "A defender of liberty will answer [Galiani]: Necessity has no law. Pillage the storehouses of the merchants, stop the transports, set fires, even commit murder: I have no law to prescribe to you in this moment of horrible extremity."[15]

Chastellux, after all, had ended his *De la félicité publique* with the very concrete call for the public despoliation of the wealth of the monasteries, the same position that Morellet would rush to refute only after the events of 1789. The marquis did not live to see this suggestion acted upon by a government of France, but if he had, could he have opposed it in the context of the Revolution without a fundamental contradiction of his position of 1772? Indeed Chastellux had praised Rome for more than once having saved the empire from "despotism," and he could appear to be speaking to the Paris of his own age when he explained that Rome could do this "because a large number of men is always to be feared . . . when deprived of representatives and protectors. . . ."[16] In a chapter on modern France, Chastellux had expressed a vision of the future that the men of 1789 might well have recognized as their own: "The time is no more when the statesman, more pedant than citizen, refers all of the principles of government to old usages. *Feudal, fiscal* and *domainal* ideas must abandon the tribunals, and the words of *property, agriculture, commerce* and *liberty* will be substituted for the barbarous vocabulary of the schools. . . . Men of letters will become patriots, and savants will become citizens. . . . Whoever makes himself useful . . . will be

[14] Helvétius, *Oeuvres complètes*, I, 293-298.

[15] Morellet, *Réfutation du livre qui a pour titre Dialogues sur le commerce des blés* (written in 1770, but published under the ministry of Turgot in 1774), 277.

[16] Chastellux, *De la félicité publique*, I, 233-234.

inscribed in the registers of beneficence; and every worker who polishes a wheel or a spoke will have at least an idea of the great machine to which his work must be related."[17]

The more clearly that one could envisage a saner world, of course, the more angry one became with the unnecessary evils of one's own society. Thus Chastellux, in a pamphlet on inoculation published in 1763, decried the fact that the current legislation, allowing inoculation only on private estates far from populated areas, favored his own aristocratic class uniquely. Such a law, he asserted, insured the life and expansion of that group of citizens which produced nothing and strained the public treasury to maintain their luxury, while it stood as a death sentence upon "the people," who alone produced the soldiers, workers, cultivators and productive agents of society. The problem, he concluded, was that the aristocrats, who had gained such legislation for themselves, cared more about "the reproduction and preservation of game animals" than they did about that of the general populace.[18] Thus Roux, commenting upon those who equated the fundamental laws of France with the preservation of privileged interests, could condemn in 1761 what he saw as "this barbarous patriotism which tramples underfoot the most sacred rights of humanity" for the benefit of "a handful of ferocious and bloodthirsty men."[19]

In 1789 the representatives of the people of France assembled in Versailles and chose to speak for "the most sacred rights of humanity" in the face of opponents whom they soon would identify as "a handful of ferocious and bloodthirsty men" indeed. Several times throughout the eighteenth century, Diderot had written favorably on the idea of summoning the *Etats-généraux* into session.[20] Once constituted, he wrote, and if assembled in the public interest, the representatives of the people must not allow the king to dismiss them or to impose his will upon them. Fifteen years before such an assemblage was called into being in France, Diderot had expressed his sense of the stakes involved if a body that genuinely spoke for the public interest should find itself in peril: "If this body is well composed, if its members are good, honest and brave citizens, zealous patriots, just and enlightened men, then

17 Ibid., II, 74-75.

18 Chastellux, *Réponse à une des principales objections qu'on oppose maintenant aux partisans de l'inoculation de la petite vérole*, 15-16.

19 Roux, *Nouvelle Encyclopédie*, vii-ix.

20 See, for example, Diderot, *Oeuvres politiques*, 40-54 ("Représentants").

what a beautiful thing it is! A nation ought to let itself be completely butchered rather than suffer its abolition."[21]

* * *

The problem, however, is not whether such sentiments were expressed in the works of members of the coterie holbachique, but rather what to make of them. The philosophes loved to write with fire—to shock, to warn, to predict, to exercise their rhetoric, and indeed, to move without transition from the concrete to the abstract, from the commonplace to the heights of the mind's ability to structure the human experience. What Turgot perceived in Raynal's *Histoire philosophique des Deux Indes* often was equally or partially true of the works of most, if not all, of the abbé's friends from the rue Royale when they turned to political affairs. As Turgot wrote to Condorcet: "While admiring the ease and the brilliant energy of the author's style, I submit to you that I am a bit fatigued by the repeated excursions and by the incoherent paradoxes that he assembles from all the corners of the horizon; he piles up those of all the moral, immoral, libertine and romanesque systems; everything is equally adorned by the colors of his eloquence, and supported with the same heat: also, nothing is resolved by his book."[22]

If one assumes simply that the rhetoric and social-political critique of the members of the coterie holbachique ought somehow to have led the remnant still alive in 1789 to support, at least intellectually, the voices of revolution, an explanation of their inconsistency of course lies at hand. Successful, wealthy, and privileged men by that date, the survivors of the coterie holbachique (with the exception of Naigeon) could be looked upon as men engaged in a reflex of behavior and rationalization designed to protect the continuation of their favored status, despite the logical consequences of their formal thought. If they were sheer opportunists during the Revolution, however, they were particularly blind and self-defeating opportunists, for they took often senseless risks in affirming their loyalty to a departed order, and they often per-

[21] Ibid., 235.

[22] *Correspondance inédite de Condorcet et Turgot 1770-1779*, C. Henry, ed., 93; Suard, *Corr. litt.* (Bonno), 187, was drawn to the form of daring writing in Raynal's *Histoire*: "It is a very well-written and strongly thought piece. Perhaps its views are too general and the results too vague, but one finds in it beauties of every genre, above all of the bold genre [*du genre hardi*]."

sisted in their opposition long after there was anything they conceivably could have hoped to gain by such intransigence. The Revolution certainly appears to have offended their diverse sensibilities as intensely as it threatened their estates. More significantly, however, such an explanation assumes a curious separation of their behavior from their mentalities during the course of their lives in the Ancien Régime. If their opposition to the Revolution is seen solely as a consequence of their acquired stations in the society which it threatened—an action wholly dissonant with what they believed and wrote before 1789—we must accept that they were men of ideas who for a generation or more had led lives that were in flagrant and fundamental disharmony with their own perceptions and thoughts, and that, unlike most men, they did not reduce such dissonance by altering either their cognitions or the practices of their lives.

If we, confronted with anger, indignation and impatience in the thought of the coterie holbachique, are to distinguish between literary and political styles, and if, confronted in their works with visions of a world radically different from that of the Ancien Régime, we are to distinguish between their hopes for a distant future and their sense of the potentials of the century in which they lived, then we must attempt first to delineate a general and political mentality whose components alone could provide us with insight into how to weigh such words. It simply is not enough, one suspects, to assemble quotations. At the risk of blurring certain ambiguities and certain distinctions among individual men, we must reconstruct the core conceptions of the thinkers of the rue Royale, those beliefs which stood as the foundations of their political thought. If we do so, we shall find no inconsistency in their response to the events of 1789 and beyond. The remnant of the coterie holbachique, with the somewhat ambiguous exception of Naigeon, perceived early in the Revolution a threat not only to their stations, but to the possibility of enduring progress as they conceived of it. Given their conceptions of the means of viable and lasting societal change, and their attendant self-images as critics of their own society and civilization, they were correct in that perception. Their thoughts and experiences in their society had prepared them for their hostilely neutral to counterrevolutionary responses. Their opposition to the Revolution was consonant with what they had believed prior to 1789.

The sensationalist epistemology of the thinkers of the coterie holbachique, their broadly Baconian sense of man's relationship to nature, and their naturalistic utilitarianism all led to the same conclusion: to survive, to progress, to leave behind the nightmare of most recorded history, mankind must be able to predict, to control, and, where control proved impossible, to adapt consequentially to events. Their lives in the Ancien Régime taught them essentially the same lesson: to influence the course of affairs, a man must learn to predict, to control and to adapt to the elements of his environment. The Revolution, as almost all the survivors of the coterie perceived it, threatened the order necessary for prediction, control and successful adaptation both in the political life of France and in their own personal lives and roles. They knew, long before 1789, that the disorder and consequent unpredictability of popular revolution were the enemies of the hopes and lives of men such as themselves.

By selective quotation—isolating the menacing predictions, the imprecations and the anger of the thinkers of the coterie holbachique—a portrait of men who seemed not adverse to a violent and fundamental upheaval in their society indeed could be drawn. In context, however, and in the light of the whole of their authors' political and social thought, such passages invariably prove to be a function more of form than of intellectual or political substance, devices calculated to distinguish a work by its daring, to gain the attention of a reader and, above all, to impress upon him the gravity and possible consequences of the matter at hand. The intellectual impatience of the coterie holbachique with the inherited "prejudice" and "injustice" of the Ancien Régime, and with "arbitrary" authority that refused to be converted into "useful" authority, was genuine. They could envisage man in a different set of relationships with himself, with his fellow beings, and with nature. They could extrapolate from their sense of the human potential, considered in the abstract, a world with far more happiness and far less suffering than existed in the world they knew. The achievement of such a world, however, was to be the work not of angry revolution, but of gradual, controlled and maximally predictable reform. Constant in their work were a fear of the forces unleashed by revolution and an elitist mistrust, either in general or in particular reference to their own century, of broad participation in the means of societal change.

309

The examples of d'Holbach and Raynal, two of the most rhetorically violent writers of the coterie holbachique, are particularly illustrative of this circumstance. Throughout his work, d'Holbach stressed that government existed solely to secure the happiness of the greatest number of its subjects, that the moment a sovereign acted in his own particular interest his rule was despotic and thus illegitimate, and that the people had the right to resist any despotic violation of that compact for happiness which alone justified authority. Such arguments led Bergier to denounce d'Holbach's words as "the furies of a madman," and to warn that "history furnishes us no examples of a throne overturned without the people having been crushed beneath its fall."[23] They led Frederick the Great to assert that the consequences of d'Holbach's urgings would be endless civil wars or, at best, a series of exhausted Polands in Europe.[24] D'Holbach, however, agreed with both Bergier and Frederick on the dire and disastrous consequences of popular resistance to despotism, and of the people's violent deposition of a king. The right to resistance was simply a natural phenomenon for d'Holbach, one that emerged from the very nature of man as a creature seeking his self-preservation and happiness; it was simply an unavoidable human reflex which necessarily would occur at the moment that enough men understood their right to happiness and the proper function of government. Because resistance was a natural right and because its consequences would be in fact so nefarious, d'Holbach was imploring the rulers of Europe to act in the interests of their subjects in order to avoid such a catastrophe. It is not enough to cite his discussion of the right to revolution, as Bergier and Frederick did, without citing as well his sense of its results. Thus, in his major political work, *La politique naturelle* (1773), d'Holbach explained why revolutions must be inhibited by reform, and why they were greater evils than any abuses they sought to remedy: "In revolutions, men, guided by fury, never consult reason; their exalted imagination causes them to carry everything to excess, and to envisage only the moment. Blinded by ambitious men, by fanatics, or by political charlatans, the masses, in order to cure a slight evil that reason would have shown them to be a necessary one, or that time would have made disappear easily, often inflict upon themselves deep

[23] Bergier, *Examen du matérialisme*, I, 452.
[24] *Posthumous Works of Frederick II*, T. Holcroft, trans., V, 165-175.

wounds which end by entailing the ruin of the Body Politic, or by weakening it fruitlessly."[25]

In his introduction to *La politique naturelle*, d'Holbach indeed denounced the passions and imaginary interests of "the princes" as the major cause of a *politique* of unhappiness, along with the political influence of metaphysical theology and the "shadowy procedures" of the courtiers, but he asked "the good man" to be undiscouraged by misgovernment and to patiently attempt reform. The patriot, for d'Holbach, should "think upon the misfortunes of his country not in order to augment them by disturbances, but in order to seek their causes and to indicate their reasonable remedies." What was necessary "to reform a State," he urged, was "reason, calm, enlightenment and time," for "passion, always imprudent, destroys without ameliorating a thing." Revolution was always dangerous to happiness, d'Holbach warned, and "nations should bear with longanimity suffering that they cannot remove without becoming more miserable." Friends of humanity must accept a schedule of reform that would extend far beyond their own lifetimes, for "the improvement of politics can only be the slow fruit of the experience of centuries; little by little, it will mature institutions and men, will make them wiser, and from that time on, even happier." The role of the philosophe was simply to help initiate and to participate in the first stages of such a process: "Let the good citizen thus communicate his ideas to his country; let him console it in its present evils by the hope of a kinder future; let him offer glimpses in that future of princes tired of their sad follies and of peoples freed from the yoke of slavery: in a word, let him hope that one day the sovereigns and the subjects, tired of letting themselves be guided by chance, will have recourse to reflection, to reason and to equity, which suffice to put an end to the calamities from which they suffer equally."[26]

Such themes formed the core of d'Holbach's attitudes toward societal change, whatever the political themes of his ultimate visions. In fact, his hopes for mankind rested upon moral and not political transformations, meaning for d'Holbach upon man's ultimate perception that his self-interest was best served by benevolent and altruistic relationships with his fellow man. After reviewing all possible forms of government in *La politique naturelle*,

[25] D'Holbach, *La politique naturelle*, 112-114.
[26] Ibid., v-vi.

311

d'Holbach concluded that almost all except democracy would be workable if man were morally wise, and that none would work while man preserved his current mentality. "The permanent felicity of a people," he concluded, "can be solidly based only upon enlightened reason, the sincere love of the public good, sound morals, and virtue." Without these, neither constitutions, nor the participation of the governed, nor resistance to despotism would alter a thing for the good, for "Men without enlightenment and without morals are destined sooner or later to become slaves." Theorists will continue to speculate about the best forms of government, he concluded, but "let us hope for everything from time and from the progress of enlightenment. . . ."[27]

Frank Manuel indeed might be correct that d'Holbach bequeathed to the Revolution an atheistic political philosophy,[28] but the Baron would not have wanted it that way at all. As he wrote in his *Système social*, "liberty is not acquired by disorder. . . ." After cataloguing the "wounds" of the nation, he warned: "No, it is not by dangerous convulsions, it is not by combats, by regicides, by useless crimes that the wounds of nations will heal. These violent remedies are always more cruel than the evils that one wants to make disappear. It is by the aid of truth that one can make Astraea descend among the inhabitants of the earth. The voice of reason is neither seditious nor sanguinary. The reforms that it proposes, for being slow, are by that only better concerted. By enlightening themselves, men become milder; they know the worth of peace; they learn to tolerate abuses that one cannot eliminate at once without danger to the State."[29]

Raynal held precisely the same views on the proper means and the schedule of political and social change. For all his denunciations of despotism and all his depictions of a future world in which free men would defend their liberty, he consistently warned in the *Histoire philosophique des Deux Indes* against the illusory expedient of revolution. Condemning the government of Portugal as vicious and corrupt, he nevertheless observed that any government "embraces so great a number of concerns . . . that its dissolution, brought about either by the imbecility of its ruler or by the impatience of its subjects can only have the most frightening consequences. If the impatience of the subjects succeeds in

[27] Ibid., 50-85.
[28] Frank Manuel, *The Eighteenth Century Confronts the Gods*, 241.
[29] D'Holbach, *Système social*, II, 33-34.

breaking a yoke under which they are tired of groaning, a nation advances more or less rapidly to anarchy, across waves of blood."[30]

Two or three reigns of enlightened reform, Raynal warned in 1781, would be wholly insufficient to effect any enduring change in the political and social condition of man. After so many centuries of ignorance and prejudice, "the work of circumstances" was stronger than "the wisdom of sovereigns," whoever and however wise the latter might be. "The emancipation, or, to say the same thing under a different name, the civilization of an empire," he thus concluded, "is a long and difficult work." Indeed the fundamental reform of a nation would require untold "centuries" before "a manifest effect" would be obtained from it. While awaiting the results of reform, he added, "a complete security of persons and properties is necessary."[31]

The work of reform would have to be experimental and controlled, and the surest means of such an ordered process was by the enlightened agency of the established kings and sovereigns of Europe. What, after all, had Raynal asked of Louis XVI in his audacious apostrophe of 1781? He had asked the king to consult with the best and most virtuous minds of his nation, to take his subjects' interests to heart, and to rid himself of all useless courtiers and flatterers. He had envisaged for the king the possible good to be accomplished, and he had described a more ideal world.[32] As Raynal informed the Assemblée in 1791, however, his idealizations of 1780 had "presented only the seduction of a consoling

[30] Raynal, *Histoire philosophique des Deux Indes*, I, 184.

[31] Ibid., X, 27-29.

[32] Ibid., II, 260-268. Diderot understood this, and in reply to Grimm's charge that Raynal had gone beyond the bounds of discretion and propriety in so addressing his king, he wrote to Grimm: "I read the apostrophe to Louis XVI; it is simple, *pathétique*, respectful and noble. Everything that it is important to teach a young sovereign is found there; it contains nothing too great nor too small. . . . But, you say, most of its ideas are common. Maybe, but they are no less true for that, and one could not repeat them too often to sovereigns, since it is precisely those [ideas] that one hides from them, and that for their glory and the happiness of their subjects it is all the more important for them to know; but the useful man is not always he who says a new thing, and the eloquent man is almost always he who has the talent to lead one, by the force of his discourse, to the practice of the virtues and the love of the truth which are as old as the world. And what can one imagine that is new about the duties of kings? In everything, we are reduced—for quite some time—to the talent of saying [something] well, and that talent is not too common" (Diderot, *Corr.*, XV, 219).

dream." He had demanded above all a strong and enlightened king, surrounded by enlightened public servants, all of them devoted to leading France into a happier age; instead, the Revolution had given him "a king without any authority, a people without any restraint." Yet the Assemblée, he observed, believed that it was acting in accord with his own designs and hopes. He recalled to the Assemblée that in 1781: "No motive impelled me to weigh the difficulties of application, and the terrible disadvantages attached to abstractions, when they are invested with the force which commands men and things, when the resistance of things and the passions of men are elements that necessarily must be taken into account."[33]

This was not a sudden awareness on Raynal's part. A full generation before, while reviewing Morelly's *Code de la nature* in 1755, he had made the same observation: "From Plato up to M. de la Beaumelle, we have had I don't know how many creators of speculative republics; but these legislators almost always have supposed men to be as they are not; they have done as those geometers who prepare the proportions of a machine on paper: when they come to its execution, there is no longer any recognition, [and] their calculations are found to be at fault: they calculated on lines, on surfaces, and they find wood and iron, on which they must make new calculations."[34]

When Suard, Morellet, Raynal, and Marmontel formally condemned the Revolution as precipitous and doomed to create more suffering than it alleviated, they were not, in their fear and pessimism, renouncing the political and social theories which they had heard articulated at the coterie holbachique. They were proclaiming them.

*　*　*

The fear of passionate disorder and the goal of rational and experimental human control of natural (including social) phenomena were nuclear elements of the thought and attitudes of almost all the thinkers of the coterie holbachique. Both were viewed as consistent with the self-justifying norm of man's search for survival and well-being, and both followed necessarily from the vision of man's plight which they articulated in their major works. What sort of world was described in Diderot's philosophical and

[33] Raynal, *Adresse à l'Assemblée Nationale*, 10-11.
[34] Raynal, "Nouvelles littéraires," in Grimm, *Corr. litt.*, II, 218.

314

political works, d'Holbach's *Systèmes*, Roux's *Nouvelle encyclopédie*, Chastellux's *De la félicité publique*, Le Roy's *Lettres sur les animaux et sur l'homme*, Naigeon's prefaces and his *Philosophie ancienne et moderne*, Morellet's works on tolerance, Marmontel's *Les Incas*, Helvétius' *De l'homme*, Grimm's philosophical and historical expositions in the *Correspondance littéraire*—a world discussed for over thirty years, twice weekly, in d'Holbach's home?

It was one in which men, at the dawn of civilization, helpless and afraid before the awesome powers of a natural world upon which their fate depended, had sought to propitiate nature and win its favor. Ignorant of its real relationships, its real chains of causes and effects, men had sought to appeal to some mysterious will above or beyond the natural world, and had given their absolute obedience, the fruits of their labors, the education of their children, and control over their lives and destinies to those among them who claimed to know the secrets of the supernatural world. From fear, helplessness and ignorance, men had allowed a host of self-proclaimed man-gods, divine agents and divinely ordained kings to create their despotic authority. Acquiescence in this despotism by the people initially was an attempt to secure happiness, in the belief that the mysterious will of nature insisted upon such forms of government. It was hastened by the desperation and credulity produced among the populations of the earth by natural disasters such as floods, famines and pestilence, which they knew that they themselves could not control. The rulers of this world, aware consciously or intuitively that their power, wealth and arbitrary privileges depended upon the ignorance and superstition of the multitude, created or supported cadres of priests to reinforce their regimes. These priests deflected the people's innate hopes for happiness to a world to come, taught men self-contempt and self-denial, caused them to doubt the value of human reason and the lessons of the human senses, and satisfied man's curiosity with fable. In all of this, they made the blind and senseless acceptance of a social structure operating only for the happiness of the few a prerequisite for both earthly and eternal propitiation of their arbitrary gods. Thus enslaving mankind, despots and priests divided the spoils. In the visions of the thinkers of the coterie holbachique, mankind had been for millennia deceived and self-deceived in almost every land and every age, and had built the useless pyramids and fought the senseless wars of its oppressors. History was a phantasmagoric index of crime and suffering, all ultimately

315

founded upon man's ignorance of the actual laws of nature. For both atheists and deists, this denatured state of man was at the core of his tragedy—for the former, there was only nature and her laws; for the latter, God effected his Providence through consistent and regular natural means.

In the past few centuries, however, as perceived by almost all the thinkers of the coterie holbachique, two new and hopeful developments had occurred. First, temporal government had begun to see its interests as separate from those of its churches and priesthoods; its genuine and enduring security and prosperity, it was at last discovering, were in fact naturally dependent upon the well-being and prosperity of its people. Second, thinkers unbeholden to the churches had arisen and had begun to study the real relationships and real chains of causes and effects in the natural world. The more such thinkers demonstrated their ability to master the elements of the natural world—to reduce these to law and thus, increasingly, to offer the means of predictability and control—the more they reduced mankind's perceived need of its misleading and parasitic priests, and the more they impressed the temporal authorities. By the eighteenth century, it was believed, such thinkers had understood a fundamental relationship within the natural world that was of paramount importance to sovereign powers capable of understanding its implications: the well-being and prosperity of the people, which increased the security and prosperity of the rulers, was dependent upon a social organization in which useful contributions to the general good of society alone were rewarded, and malevolent actions alone were penalized; in which, through wise legislation, the particular interests of individual citizens were made consonant with the general interests of society. If and when rulers understood the truth of this relationship, it followed, their support of superstition and ignorance would end, they would become the benefactors of their people, and mankind would begin to progress toward enlightenment and the elimination of useless suffering.

Acting blindly from the unreflective passions of the moment, and victims of ignorance and a superstitious education, the people —as conceived of by the coterie—were the last to be capable of understanding this view of things; rather, the ruling strata of temporal society would see most clearly and urgently the option before them and the need to alter the course of human history. It was the role of the philosophe, thus, to teach, impress and gain acceptance from the established powers of the earth. Indeed, it was the *duty* of the philosophe to gain the attention and the confidence of the men who ruled his society. To accomplish this, to act consequentially, one had to learn the laws and the rules of operation of one's society and learn to predict its courses of action; one had to learn to control where one could control, and to adapt where one could not.

Once committed to the goal of public well-being, the rulers and sages of a society had to proceed cooperatively and cautiously in the experimental and monitored restructuring of education and institutions. Since such work depended upon maximally predictable and orderly events, the men engaged in it must disturb existing relationships as little as possible, winning to their side men and institutions whose roles and behavior one could anticipate and count upon. While the goal of controlled reform was the happiness of the people, the recipients of its benefits could not be trusted to think rationally or to act consequentially. All men acted in some sense in their own interests, but Le Roy's distinction between "the blind desire for well-being" and "the enlightened desire for well-being" precisely separated the masses from both the philosophes and the leaders enlisted into the philosophic cause.[35]

Such an outlook, of course, provided the philosophes of the coterie holbachique with a confident self-justification of their own rise to positions of wealth, influence and privilege. The question for them was not one of eliminating such benefits of society, but of awarding them to "useful" men. As long as they saw themselves as contributing to the general good, they could judge their personal gains to be not only licit, but exemplary. To have removed themselves from the centers of influence would have been, in their own eyes, the greatest sin. Indeed, their society's recognition and reward of them must have been for them, in some ways, the most encouraging political sign of all.

* * *

These attitudes permeated the thought of the coterie holbachique, whatever their formal systems and ultimate goals. Diderot could discuss, in the abstract, the right of revolution, but he warned as well that "in popular riots, one would say that each individual is sovereign, and arrogates to himself the right of life

---

[35] Le Roy, "Lettre sur l'homme," in *Lettres sur les animaux* (1768), 225-228.

and death."[36] His hope was that enlightened ministers and sovereigns would be the agents of necessary reform. When Turgot and Sartine attained their positions in the ministries, Diderot was as optimistic for the immediate salvation of France as any member of the coterie holbachique ever was to be. Thus, when Helvétius intimated, in *De l'homme*, that the political situation of France was hopeless (calling not for revolution, but suggesting the possible benefits of foreign invasion and rule), Diderot responded in his *Réfutation* with the assertion that recent events had proven the very opposite, and he concluded "Let the honest men who at present occupy the foremost places of the State preserve them for only ten years, and all our misfortunes will be repaired."[37] What mattered to Diderot was the outlook of those men who occupied the "foremost places" of the state; it was not a question of appealing to "the nation" to reclaim its rights, despite its being the ultimate locus of concern, but rather of informing and enlightening the persons capable of controlling events: ". . . it is almost useless to enlighten the lower orders, if the blindfold remains on the eyes of those ten or twelve privileged individuals who dispose of the earth's happiness. There you have those whom it is important to convert. . . . To whom, thus, will the philosophe address himself strongly, if not to the sovereign?"[38]

Before a nation could act in its interest, it of course had to know that interest, and the particulars of well-being depended upon complex relationships intellectually accessible at this juncture of history to few men. To understand them, men needed to understand sensationalist epistemology, utilitarian moral theory, and the consequences of man's relationship to nature. There was no shortcut to effective reform. As d'Holbach wrote, "The surest way to make men better is to rectify their theory; [for] without a good theory it is impossible to have good practice, that is to say, to make good laws capable of bringing men to virtue, reason, [and] wisdom."[39] In essence, Morellet's defense of a press free to criticize the administration was a call for the controlling and educated elements of eighteenth-century France to come to basic understandings among themselves, to maintain a dialogue and to search together for economic truth. What was required, he wrote, was

---

[36] Diderot, *Oeuvres politiques*, 177.   [37] Ibid., 465.

[38] Ibid., 141-142.

[39] D'Holbach, "De l'intolérance théologique," added to *Examen des prophéties*, d'Holbach, trans. and ed. (Amsterdam, 1768), 204.

"an analytic knowledge of the whole organization of society, and a complete theory of political economy," since on the whole we all still were dependent upon the theories "of our fathers in what we justly call the centuries of ignorance."[40] Helvétius, in *De l'esprit*, had argued that no fundamental reforms could prevail until thinkers chose "to teach to nations the true principles of morality, to teach them that . . . pain and pleasure are the only motors of the moral universe, and that the sentiment of self-love is the only base on which one can build the foundations of a useful morality."[41] Chastellux urged the new American republic not to place its faith in institutional change, but rather in the development of learning, in "the progress of enlightenment."[42]

The "progress of enlightenment" was only valuable, however, if there were clearly identifiable and strong sovereign powers capable of learning from it and exercising their authority to effect its lessons. Sedition, disorder, violence and divided authority were the enemies of such a desired circumstance. Marmontel's *Bélisaire*, which so terrified the clergy, offered nothing but loyalty toward the king. Marmontel did suggest a plenitude of reforms and excoriated the actions of courtiers and corrupt royal agents, but the basic political theme of his work was that such reforms must come through the agency of the monarch himself, advised and encouraged by wise and devoted counselors. He insisted upon total fidelity to the sovereign, even when wronged by him, and upon total obedience to the laws, even when others ignored or misused them to their profit. "There are inevitable evils" under any form of government, he wrote in 1767, "and all that the just man can do is to not deserve his own."[43] To make government more democratic, Marmontel warned, would only make the process of progressive change more difficult, for "to multiply the foundations of the government is to multiply its vices, for each brings his own to it." Thus, he concluded, "It is not without reason that men have preferred the most simple [form of government]." The agents of the monarchy might well be corrupt, Marmontel explained, but this should not discourage the good citizen: "Corruption is never total; there are good men everywhere; and if they

[40] Morellet, *Réflexions sur les avantages de la liberté d'écrire* . . . , 3-21.
[41] Helvétius, *Oeuvres complètes*, I, Discours Second, chap. 24, "Des moyens de perfectionner la morale."
[42] Chastellux, *Voyages dans l'Amérique*, I, 236-237.
[43] Marmontel, *Bélisaire*, 1-150.

are lacking, they can be brought forth; it suffices that a Prince love them, and that he can discern them."[44]

Chastellux communicated his admiration for the newly independent United States, but he warned strongly against any democratization of its regime. When Samuel Adams suggested to him that any and all citizens who paid taxes should have the right to vote, Chastellux recorded in his *Voyages dans l'Amérique* his prediction that such a course would lead to "civil disorders" and "corruption, perhaps both at the same time."[45] He outraged the Société des Amis des Noirs by his calm and analytic description of the nature and function of slavery in Virginia, but he himself had excused his lack of passionate condemnation of the institution by explaining, "I have always thought that eloquence can influence only the resolutions of the moment, and that everything which is not accomplished by time can be accomplished by reason." Reason, however, had to deal with the strict empirical limits to the applicability of its abstractions, and the political speculator should not deceive himself: "States, like individuals, are born with a particular complexion, the bad effects of which administration and customs can anticipate, but which one can never entirely change; thus, legislators, like doctors, must never flatter themselves that they can give at their will a particular temperament to political bodies; rather they must apply themselves to knowing that one which they already have, and to combatting its inconveniences, so as to multiply the advantages which can result from it."[46]

In his *De la félicité publique*, Chastellux, we have seen, urged the crown to take two strong and drastic steps—the despoliation of the monasteries, and the imposition of long-term low-interest loans to the royal treasury upon the privileged classes. What he had attempted to prove in his two volumes of prior analysis, however, was precisely that such actions could *not* alter the particular constitution of the nation, nor produce any unforeseeable or uncontrollable effects. Above all, he urged, they would inhibit the drift towards chaos and violence.[47] What mattered was the calm control of results. In a discourse on the "advantages" of the discovery of America, Chastellux had urged his readers to ignore both motives and abstract political dogmas in assessing the oppor-

[44] Ibid., 150-230.

[45] Chastellux, *Voyages dans l'Amérique*, I, 225-232.

[46] Ibid., II, 135-138, 149.

[47] Chastellux, *De la félicité publique*, II, 166-168, 207-208.

tunities presented to Europe by the increase in commerce and wealth engendered by this discovery, and to focus solely upon the consequences of such developments, so that they might turn them to yet further advantage.[48] In an appendix added to the third edition of *De la félicité publique*, he deplored the use of "imagination" in political thought and assured his readers that no one could know *a priori* what form "the best government" would take. Since there could be no such entity as "a perfect [form of] government," the wise man attempted to know and deal with his own: "Ameliorate rather than overthrow," he concluded, "in order to reconstruct."[49]

The political concern of the coterie holbachique was thus a gradual progress through the cautious translation into reform of an increase of knowledge and understanding on the part of the thinkers and rulers of France. Morellet in his *Réflexions sur la liberté d'écrire* commented that the history of man revealed an alternation between "lights and shadows, reason and extravagance, humanity and barbarism," but he judged that in the final analysis, the improvement of man's powers of comprehension during the past few centuries had begun to make its benefits felt by society. No one but "a misanthrope," he declared, could be discouraged over the prospects of mankind. What was required was continued freedom for thinkers to study the natural world, and patience to await the fruits of such efforts: "Let us thus hope for the amelioration of the fate of man in the course of the progress of the lights and the works of instructed men, and may the errors and injustices of even our century not cause us to lose this consoling hope. . . . Yes, let us agree that men are moving, albeit slowly, towards enlightenment and happiness. Let us allow the operation of this fortunate activity of the human mind, which impels it to disclose, by means of thought, all the paths which lead to this goal, long before the Administration itself becomes involved. Let us wait for some success from its effects; and after all, when we would despair of being its witnesses, let us write and permit others to write for the century which will follow us. . . ."[50]

Before the intransigence of prejudiced kings and ministers, then, the members of the coterie holbachique counseled patience. The

[48] Chastellux, *Discours sur les avantages ou les désavantages qui résultent pour l'Europe de la découverte de l'Amérique*, 19-38.

[49] Chastellux, *De la félicité publique*, 3rd edn., ii, 304-316.

[50] Morellet, *Réflexions sur la liberté d'écrire*, 70-71.

sovereigns of Europe had stood opposed to progress for centuries, and this was nothing new. For the first time, however, the Church and its priests were being displaced by thinkers devoted to the happiness of mankind in the esteem of important and powerful men. As Chastellux had written in his *Voyages dans l'Amérique*: "As for intolerance and persecution . . . I will whisper a word in your ear. . . : *they are no longer in style* . . . [although] they give abbeys of 100,000 *livres* in *rente* to those who favor them. . . ."[51] Not all the laws of reform will be enacted at once, Morellet observed, but law by law, step by step, the particular interests of sovereigns and rulers will yield to the general interest, for thinkers are creating the conditions in which administrators soon will have a private interest in doing good for society.[52] As he wrote in his *Petit écrit*, the theologians of the Church do not speak for the secular interests of the king.[53] Morellet was convinced, however, that the philosophes, in their doctrines, linked the prosperity of the people and that of sovereigns. At some point, he believed, the sovereigns would understand this, and they would understand it long before the mass of subjects whom they ruled.

Almost all the thinkers of the coterie holbachique believed that involvement of broad elements of the population in political affairs would negate the intellectual preconditions of enduring reform: a calm, dispassionate, scientific analysis of probable consequences, and a rational evaluation of results. Both of these would be lost in the disordered outpourings of purposeless rage and the random actions of the people. The masses were as much to be feared under political as under religious inspiration, for it was not inspiration that was germane to the tasks at hand. "It is obvious," Grimm wrote in 1769, "that ecclesiastical tyranny is approaching its end, and that violent and ambitious minds will be obliged to have recourse to another genre of lies if they want to establish their elevation and their wealth upon the stupidity of the multitude."[54]

In 1773 d'Holbach warned that the "chimera of Democracy" which he saw as currently "fashionable" in certain circles, would lead, if adopted, to "a modified anarchy" in which "a sovereign people, flattered by its demagogues, becomes their slave and the instrument of their perverse designs. Turbulent citizens divide in-

---

[51] Chastellux, *Voyages dans l'Amérique*, I, 236-237.

[52] Morellet, *Réflexions sur la liberté d'écrire*, 63-70.

[53] Morellet, *Petit écrit*, 27-38.   [54] Grimm, *Corr. litt.*, VIII, 321-322.

to factions, and discord fans its flames in all minds; civil wars tear apart a society which, blind in its devotion to its hatreds . . . persecutes with bitterness its true friends."[55]

Helvétius put the matter more simply in *De l'esprit*, urging that "men are, in general, more stupid than wicked," and he concluded that ignorance was far more dangerous than ambition.[56] By the 1780s Le Roy had determined that "only one man in a thousand" rose above "uniform prejudices." Progress, in his view, was due to "a handful of individuals," and this still must be the case today.[57] Roux distinguished between "systematic" and "common" minds, and he commented that a common mind could experience the natural world for a lifetime without making one significant observation.[58] The Jacobins might have approved of Roux's articles on tithes and monopolies in the *Dictionnaire doméstique portatif*, but they scarcely would have accepted his definition of the word "artisan" as "the name by which one designates the workers who . . . profess those [mechanical arts] which presuppose or call for the least intelligence."[59]

For d'Holbach the greatest danger of a republic was precisely that "Reason often is obliged to respect the idols of the people," unless, preserving its integrity, it dangerously allows "ambitious men" to present themselves alone as the friends of the people's illusions.[60] The sage, however, wanted a society in which he could seek the useful truth. History as written in the eighteenth century, Marmontel observed, by focusing upon "the natural mechanism of moral and physical causes," truly illuminated the roads and barriers to happiness, but it could only serve the few as a guide: "It is neither for infants, nor for the people that it is written."[61] In time the number of men capable of understanding their lot might increase, but until that time, basic political change was premature. Criticizing Rousseau, Marmontel had written that neither in Geneva nor in Paris could a free enlightened republic exist: "Oh no, Monsieur, we are not yet there. . . . If it is permitted to say it,

[55] D'Holbach, *La politique naturelle*, I, 61-64.

[56] Helvétius, *Oeuvres complètes*, I, 299.

[57] Le Roy, *Lettres philosophiques*, 287-289, 323-324.

[58] Roux, *Recherches historiques et critiques*, 2.

[59] Roux, *Dictionnaire domestique portatif, contenant toutes les connaissances relatives à l'économie domestique et rurale . . .* , I, 110.

[60] D'Holbach, *La politique naturelle*, I, 68-69.

[61] Marmontel, *Elémens de la littérature* (Paris, 1787), art. "Histoire."

323

one would have to take the flower of the human race to form a republic, which would still be not very numerous."[62] In a letter to Phillip Schuyler, Chastellux stated the matter as bluntly as possible: "Let us consult less the rights of men than the interests of men; and if you want them to be all equal in the civil order, let us make them equal in the eyes of reason; for it is up to the sages to govern, and up to the stupid to obey."[63]

Among an elite group of established leaders and recognized sages, thus, the route of gradual reform was to be charted. The first order of business was to convert the leaders of society; the second, to begin the process of genuine societal change. What should concern all thinkers, Grimm had observed in 1755, was less the idea of popular government (which "has disappeared from the earth") and more the education of young princes, who, for better or worse, represented the best hope of humanity.[64] D'Holbach, in *La morale universelle* and in the *Système social*, and Helvétius in *De l'homme*, stressed much the same theme, identifying the religious education of rulers as the greatest cause of political evils and urging the philosophical, secular education of kings as the surest path to progress.[65] Grimm wrote his *Correspondance littéraire* for the crowns and courts of Europe; Diderot sketched his political schemes for Catherine the Great; Helvétius dedicated *De l'homme* to the empress; Marmontel dedicated *Les Incas* to the king of Sweden. In theory, most of the members of the coterie holbachique envisaged some variant of constitutional monarchy as the inevitable destiny of France, but they had little faith in any existing *corps intermédiaires*, and they placed their immediate trust in the king and the royal ministries, not only in France, but on the whole of the continent. Raynal called for the king of France to have the courage to act in the interests of his people in the face of any opposition.[66] Nobility, he urged, should be taken away from anyone who "disguised the truth to the king."[67] Diderot sent to Grimm in 1769 a stinging attack upon the parlement de Paris,

[62] Marmontel, *Réponse à la lettre adressée par M. J.J. Rousseau à M. d'Alembert*, 48.

[63] Chastellux, "Letters," in Carson, *Chastellux*, 158-159.

[64] Grimm, *Corr. litt.*, III, 123-128.

[65] D'Holbach, *Système social*, II, 91-97; d'Holbach, *Morale universelle*, III, 66-68 (see also II, 191-199); Helvétius, *Oeuvres complètes*, III, 408-411, 417-423 (see also II, 212-215).

[66] Raynal, *Histoire philosophique des Deux Indes*, II, 260-268.

[67] Ibid., X, 65.

declaring that its opposition to the king was "never a question of the defense of the people," but only a defense of "its chimerical rights."[68] D'Holbach in that same year wrote to Galiani that the parlement understood nothing of political economy.[69] Morellet in 1776 denounced the parlementaires to Shelburne, certain that his friend would be "astonished to hear that the parlement was offering resistance to the abolition of *corvées* and to other benefits of the king toward his people."[70] Even Chastellux, who desired a nobility that would speak for the interests of the people, but who saw his own class as nevertheless selfish and retrograde, admitted that the people of France correctly perceived that the crown alone offered a force of good order and a recourse against the tyranny of the *grands*.[71] In his correspondence with the margrave of Bayreuth, Suard offered the example of Catherine the Great as a model of "glory" because of what he believed to be her fundamental reform of education and her efforts to create an enlightened and prosperous middle-class. She understood "the art of forming a nation," he wrote, and all Europe should admire her "strong soul and her enlightened, broad, flexible and bold mind."[72] The names of those monarchs who seek to harmonize their own "glory," "power," and "happiness" with those of their subjects, d'Holbach wrote in the final passage of his *Système social*, will be "cherished by the present race, will be pronounced with rapture by the most distant posterity who, while receiving the durable fruits of your benefactions, will bless the memory of the Kings adored by its ancestors."[73]

In the current juncture of history, then, the thinkers of the coterie holbachique saw their task, on the whole, as one of winning over the royal administration to the cause of secular, utilitarian reform. If they could educate, flatter, persuade, shame, frighten or wheedle the political elite of the nation into more enlightened attitudes, the future of civilization would not remain in the "prejudiced" and "arbitrary" directions of the past. If their warnings of popular impatience and their portraits of where the process of reform might lead contributed to the events of 1789 and beyond, this happened against their intentions and their will. Joseph We-

---

[68] Diderot, *Corr.*, IX, 64-66.
[69] D'Holbach, "Lettres à Galiani," 28.
[70] Morellet, *Lettres à Lord Shelburne*, 99-101.
[71] Chastellux, *De la félicité publique*, 3rd edn., II, 310-313.
[72] Suard, *Corr. litt.* (Bonno), 220-223.
[73] D'Holbach, *Système social*, III, 164-166.

ber, writing in 1807, understood this clearly, whatever his hostility to their anti-Christian views: "People have exaggerated in saying that these philosophes proposed the subversion of societies and the overthrow of thrones. Those of that epoch wanted to be not the destroyers, but the preceptors of the kings."[74]

* * *

In the end, they were better received by the sovereigns of foreign nations than by the kings of France, but they had friends and admirers among the loyal servants and agents of their king and an influence in his land of which they were well aware. Above all, their contestation was with the Church, and the stakes, as they defined them, were whether government after the eighteenth century would define its duty in terms of the needs of humanity or the needs of the faith. Even Grimm, so often skeptical of their successes, believed that in this domain the future was theirs. The intellectual developments which have culminated in the party of the philosophes, he wrote in 1763, "presage today the fall of Christianity."[75] This victory, for them, would be the ultimate "education" of the king, however indirect its communication, for in the final analysis most of them saw the ending of the intellectual link between Church and State as a precondition for all future reform. They saw themselves as teaching mastery and adaptation toward the goal of general human happiness, the Church as teaching fatalistic resignation to a general unhappiness on earth, and they thought they had begun to show the crowns and ministers of Europe that the surest foundation of sovereignty was the philosophic and not the Christian view of life. The education of mankind, they believed, would fall to their heirs in a world which they had helped to transform.

Few of them seemed to perceive any ambiguity in the privileges and benefits they received in the course of their active lives in the Ancien Régime. Their ideal state, of course, was one in which the particular and general interests of men would both be served by identical acts. From the 1750s until the 1780s the thinkers of the coterie holbachique lived in two worlds—one a realm of private philosophical speculation, where they discussed among themselves the problems of knowledge, man and history; the second a realm

[74] *Mémoires de Weber concernant Marie Antoinette*, I, 101-110. (This work was first published in London, 1807).
[75] Grimm, *Corr. litt.*, v, 262.

of personal and practical concerns, where they made their way through the confusing but increasingly open corridors of success in their society. Only Diderot and Naigeon appeared to have any doubts about the relationship between their behavior and their thought, and perhaps that was why both of them, the two members of the coterie least comfortable with the demands of their social lives, became so fascinated with the figure of Seneca, the sage who stayed at Nero's side.

For Diderot the alternative to the rule of the tyrant Nero was revolution, but the people of Rome were ignorant, violent and unpredictable. If they had risen against Nero, Rome would be in the hands of men "without views, without principles, without plans." They would be incapable of providing a better successor. In the final analysis, "the death of a despot comes down to leading another despot to the throne."[76] Seneca found himself in particular circumstances, and he did what he had to do in order to survive, to prosper and to exert what influence he could. It is "a difficult problem to resolve," Diderot asserted, the choice of whether "to be a man of all times or a man of one's century."[77] In the end he identified closely with Seneca, and he justified Seneca's life by Seneca's works, irrespective of the place where he produced them and the sources of his wealth.[78]

Naigeon, in his "Discours préliminaire" to the 1782 edition of Seneca's moral thought, defended Seneca for having remained at the center of corruption and despotic power, citing the necessity for the sage to know and understand such phenomena at first hand, lest he conceive only of "the abstract man, the ideal man, but not the one who is in nature and who lives in society."[79]

The core of Naigeon's introduction, however, dealt not with such a question in the abstract, nor in the context of antiquity, but rather in terms of the eighteenth century itself. The spirit of philosophy, he wrote, "the dominant characteristic of our century," and the cause of the rapid progress of the arts and sciences during the past fifty years, finally has come to influence not only

[76] Diderot, *Oeuvres* (A-T), III, 29-33.

[77] Ibid., 148-158, 325.

[78] In a letter to Naigeon that was used as a preface to the essay on Seneca's life, Diderot wrote of "the difficulty and the dignity of his [Seneca's] role," and accepted the task of being his "apologist" before the world (Diderot, *Corr.*, XV, 111-117).

[79] Naigeon, *Discours préliminaire, pour servir d'introduction à La Morale de Sénèque*, 14-16.

327

the men of letters, but "even the men of the world." One can observe, Naigeon noted, how the philosophical spirit has entered their conversations, their speeches and their books. The reason for this, he explained, is that the discoveries and knowledge acquired by the new philosophy have impressed men, and they wish to avoid the humiliation of being "behind" their century. In Naigeon's analysis, the man who simply retains in the eighteenth century "the prejudices, ignorance and blindness of his ancestors" will find himself as "displaced" as the man who is in advance of his own age. From this perspective, Naigeon concluded, Seneca was to be praised for not despairing at the possibilities of educating men, for having understood that virtue can be taught, and for having tried to teach it, even in the tragic age in which he lived.[80]

What Naigeon was implying—and perhaps not without some pain—one year after he had added to his role of clandestine atheist that of pensioned "*Garde-magasin des utensiles de la Maison-Bouche du Roi*," was that the presence and activity of the philosophes in the inner circles of privilege were having a genuine effect, and that men could learn from them to be "virtuous." Virtue, for Naigeon, meant simply to act for the interests of one's fellow man; if such virtue could become a norm among the ruling milieus of a nation, by shame or by education, the course of history could be changed. If the philosophes were altering the boundaries of acceptable attitudes and behavior, their actions, their involvement at the center, would be justified.

In 1762 Suard, in his *Journal étranger*, devoted a lengthy discussion to the effect of the Reformation upon the Church. By the sixteenth century, he explained, the Catholic Church long had been tainted by barbarity, ignorance, crime and superstition. "Wise and enlightened men" within the Church, he continued, understood full well the evils of their ecclesiastical society, but they restrained themselves from raising "the banner of revolt," knowing that "these stains would be erased by the imperceptible progress of philosophy. . . ." Erasmus, Suard insisted, saw this clearly, and with caution, wit and satire, the sixteenth-century sage attacked several of the worst abuses, hoping to effect "a mild and useful reformation" by such means. Others, however, impatient and importunate, were willing to raise that standard of revolution, and just when genuine reform had seemed possible, "the

[80] Ibid., 70-73, 92-120.

fanatic Luther ruined everthing." The result, Suard believed, had been a retardation of religious progress, two centuries of religious wars, and more fanaticism than mankind had ever known. The evils which Luther's Reformation introduced, Suard observed, are still with us; the good that it accomplished would have occurred without its help. Oddly enough, Suard noted, the doctors of the Sorbonne in the sixteenth century could not understand the difference between Erasmus and Luther, and they saw in the former's activities the cause of Luther's behavior, and the reason for Luther's success.[81]

[81] *Journal étranger* (Feb. 1762), 40-44.

Bibliography

I. Manuscript and Archival Material

Bibliothèque Nationale:
  Collection Anisson-Duperron (Fonds français: vols. 22,061-22,193*)*.
  Nouvelles acquisitions françaises (Collection Joly de Fleury): vols.
  3632, 3807, 4045, 4260, 4576, 4853, 4926, 5026, 5203, 5258, 5419, 5441,
  5572, 5619.
Bibliothèque de l'Arsenal:
  Bastille: vols. 10,249-10,250, 10,296-10,305, 12,048, 12,086, 12,176,
  12,500.
Archives Nationales:
  Registres de la Faculté de Théologie: MM 257-259.
  Registres de l'ancien parlement: AD^{III} 21-27.
Bibliothèque de l'Institut:
  Affaires Etrangères: vol. 1223, folios 82-87 (Hennin manuscript).

II. Journals Cited (Ancien Régime and Revolution)

L'Ami du peuple.
L'Année littéraire.
Gazette de France.
Gazette française.
Journal de Paris.
Journal de politique et de littérature.
Journal encyclopédique.
Journal étranger.
Mercure de France.
Moniteur universel.
Nouvelles écclésiastiques.
Nouvelles politiques, nationales et étrangères.
Le Publiciste.

III. Published Documents and Official Publications

Almanach national.
Almanach royal.
Assemblée générale du Clergé de France. *Collection des procès-verbaux*

331

des Assemblées générales du Clergé de France depuis l'année 1560, jusqu' à présent. 8 vols. Paris, 1767-1778.

Assemblée Nationale. *Etat nominatif des pensions sur le trésor royal.* 2 vols. Paris, 1789.

————. *Livre rouge . . . des pensions sur le trésor royal, imprimé par ordre de l'Assemblée Nationale.* Paris, 1790-1791.

F.-A. Aulard, ed. *Paris pendant la réaction Thermidorienne et sous le Directoire: Recueil de documents pour l'histoire de l'esprit public à Paris.* 5 vols. Paris, 1898-1902.

————. *Paris sous le Consulat: Recueil de documents pour l'histoire de l'esprit public à Paris.* 4 vols. Paris, 1903-1909.

————. *La Société des Jacobins. Recueil de documents pour l'histoire du Club des Jacobins de Paris.* 6 vols. Paris, 1889-1897.

———— and Mautouchet, eds. *Recueil des actes du Comité de salut public.* 28 vols. Paris, 1898-1964.

A. Brette, ed. *Atlas de la censive de l'archevêché dans Paris. Reproduction en fac-similé.* Paris, 1906.

E. Charavay, ed. *Assemblée électorale de Paris, 18 novembre 1790–15 juin 1791.* Paris, 1890.

————. *Ibid., 26 août 1791–12 août 1792.* Paris, 1894.

————. *Ibid., 2 septembre 1792–17 frimaire an II.* Paris, 1905.

C.-L. Chassin, ed. *Les élections et les cahiers de Paris en 1789.* 4 vols. Paris, 1888-1889.

A. Debidour, ed. *Recueil des actes du Directoire Exécutif.* 4 vols. Paris, 1910-1917.

A. Douarche, ed. *Les tribunaux civils de Paris pendant la Révolution (1791-1800).* 3 vols. Paris, 1905-1907.

Institut de France. *Les registres de l'Académie Française 1672-1793.* 4 vols. Paris, 1895-1906.

S. La Croix and R. Fargue, eds. *Actes de la commune de Paris pendant la Révolution.* 24 vols. Paris, 1894-1914.

H. Monin, ed. *L'Etat de Paris en 1789.* Paris, 1889.

L. Tuetey, ed. *Procès-verbaux de la commission temporaire des arts.* 2 vols. Paris, 1912-1917.

Ville de Paris. *Sommier des biens nationaux de la ville de Paris conservés aux archives de la Seine.* 2 vols. Paris, 1920.

IV. PRIMARY SOURCES (members of the coterie holbachique)

Chastellux, François-Jean de. *De la félicité publique, ou considérations sur le sort des hommes dans les différentes époques de l'histoire.* 2 vols. Amsterdam, 1772. (3rd edn., aug. Bouillon, 1776).

————. *Discours sur les avantages ou les désavantages qui résultent pour l'Europe de la découverte de l'Amérique.* Paris, 1787.

———. *Eloge de M. Helvétius.* S.l., 1774.

———. *Nouveaux éclaircissemens sur l'inoculation de la petite vérole.* S.l. n.d.

———. "Pensées sur le mouvement," in Bergasse, *Considérations sur le magnétisme animal.* The Hague, 1784.

———. *Réponse à une des principales objections qu'on oppose maintenant aux partisans de l'inoculation de la petite vérole.* S.l., 1763.

———. *Voyages de M. le marquis de Chastellux dans l'Amérique septentrionale dans les années 1780, 1781, et 1782.* 2 vols. Paris, 1786.

———. "Lettres inédites de Chastellux à Wilkes." G. Bonno, ed. *Revue de littérature comparée* III (1932), 619-623.

Darcet, Jean. *Discours en forme de dissertation sur l'état actuel des montagnes des Pyrénées, et sur les causes de leur dégradation.* Paris, 1776.

———. *Eloge de M. Roux.* S.l., 1777.

———. *Mémoire sur l'action d'un feu égal, violent, et continué pendant plusieurs jours sur un grand nombre de terres, de pierres et de chaux métalliques essayées pour la plupart telles qu'elles sortent du sein de la terre.* Paris, 1766.

———. *Second Mémoire sur l'action d'un feu égal, violent, et continué.* . . . Paris, 1771.

Diderot, Denis (see also under Naigeon). *Correspondance.* Georges Roth et al., eds. 12 vols. Paris, 1955-1970.

———. *Oeuvres complètes de Diderot.* J. Assézat and M. Tourneux, eds. 20 vols. Paris, 1875-1877.

———. *Oeuvres de Denis Diderot.* J. L. J. Brière, ed. 11 vols. Paris, 1818-1819.

———. *Oeuvres philosophiques.* P. Vernière, ed. Paris, 1961.

———. *Oeuvres politiques.* P. Vernière, ed. Paris, 1963.

———, ed. *Encyclopédie, ou Dictionnaire raisonné des sciences, des arts, et des métiers.* 35 vols. Paris, 1751-1780.

Galiani, abbé Ferdinando. *Il Pensiero dell'Abate Galiani, antologia de tutti suoi scritti.* F. Nicolini, ed. Bari, 1909.

———. *Amici e corrispondenti Francesi dell'Abate Galiani. Notizie, lettere, documenti.* F. Nicolini, ed. Naples, 1954.

———. *Lettres de l'Abbé Galiani à Madame d'Epinay, Voltaire, Diderot, Grimm, le Baron d'Holbach, Morellet, Suard, d'Alembert, Marmontel, la Vicomtesse de Belsunce, etc.* E. Asse, ed. 2 vols. Paris, 1882.

Grimm, Friedrich-Melchior. *Correspondance littéraire, philosophique et critique.* M. Tourneux, ed. 16 vols. Paris, 1877-1882.

———. *Le petit prophète de Boemischbroda, le correcteur des bouffons et la guerre de l'Opéra.* S.l., 1753.

Grimm, Friedrich-Melchoir. *Correspondance inédite (1794-1801) du Baron Grimm au Comte de Findlater.* A. Cazes, ed. Paris, 1934.

——. *Lettres de Grimm à l'Impératrice Cathérine II.* J. Grot, ed. 2nd edn. St. Petersburg, 1885.

——. "Lettres inédites de Grimm à la Reine-Mère de Suède." V. Bowen, ed. *Revue de littérature comparée,* IV (1958), 565-572.

Helvétius, Claude-Adrien. *Oeuvres complètes.* 4 vols. Liège, 1774.

——. *Notes de la main d'Helvétius, publiés d'après un manuscrit inédit.* A. Keim, ed. Paris, 1907.

d'Holbach, Baron Paul Henri Thiry. *Le Bon-Sens, ou Idées naturelles opposées aux idées surnaturelles.* London (Amsterdam), 1772.

——. *Essai sur les préjugés, ou de l'influence des opinions sur les moeurs et sur le bonheur des hommes.* London (Amsterdam), 1770.

——. *La morale universelle, ou les devoirs de l'homme fondés sur sa nature.* 3 vols. Amsterdam, 1776.

——. *La politique naturelle, ou Discours sur les vrais principes du gouvernement.* London (Amsterdam), 1773.

——. *Système de la nature, ou des loix du monde physique et du monde moral.* 2 vols. London (Amsterdam), 1770. (B.N. Imp.: Rés. D² 5167, with the rare "Discours préliminaire" by Naigeon.)

——. *Ibid.,* 1775.

——. *Système social.* 3 vols. London (Amsterdam), 1773.

——, trans. Thomas Hobbes, *De la nature humaine.* London (Amsterdam), 1772.

——, trans. John Toland, *Lettres philosophiques.* London (Amsterdam), 1768.

——. *Bicentenaire du Système de la nature: textes holbachiens peu connus.* J. Vercruysse, ed. Brussels, 1970.

——. "Deux cas de prosélytisme philosophique au XVIIIᵉ siècle à-propos de deux lettres inédites du Baron d'Holbach." P. Vernière, ed. *Revue d'histoire littéraire,* IV (1955), 495-499.

——. "Lettres inédites du baron et de la baronne d'Holbach à l'abbé Galiani." F. Nicolini, ed. *Etudes Italiennes* I. Nouvelle Série (1931), 20-40.

Le Roy, Charles-Georges. *Examen des critiques du livre intitulé De l'esprit.* London (?), 1760.

——. *Lettres philosophiques sur l'intelligence et la perfectabilité des animaux, avec quelques lettres sur l'homme.* Roux-Fazillac, ed. Paris, 1802.

——. *Lettres sur les animaux.* Nuremberg (?), 1768. (New edn., aug. Paris, 1781.)

——. *Portraits historiques de Louis XV et de Madame de Pompadour.* Roux-Fazillac, ed. Paris, 1802.

——. *Réflexions sur la jalousie, pour servir de commentaire aux derniers ouvrages de M. de Voltaire.* Amsterdam, 1772.

————. "Instinct des animaux," in Naigeon, *Philosophie ancienne et moderne*, III, 5-47.

Marmontel, Jean-François. *Bélisaire*. Paris, 1767. (New edn. Paris, 1767.)

————. *Les Incas, ou La Destruction de l'empire de Pérou*. 2 vols. Paris, 1777.

————. *Mémoires*, Vols. I and II in *Oeuvres complètes de Marmontel*. 19 vols. Paris, 1818-1820.

————. *Oeuvres complettes de M. Marmontel*. 17 vols. Paris, 1787.

————. *Pièces relatives à Bélisaire* (with Turgot and Voltaire et al.). Geneva and Amsterdam, 1767.

————. *Réponse de M. Marmontel à la lettre adressée par M. J. J. Rousseau à M. d'Alembert . . . sur son article Genève. . . .* Geneva, 1759.

————. "Deux lettres inédites de Marmontel à un correspondant Suédois." F. Baldensperger, ed. *Revue du dix-huitième siècle*, I (1917), 197-199.

————. *Fac-Similé d'une lettre de Marmontel*. B.N. Imp.: Ln27.13548.

Morellet, abbé André. *La cause des pères*. Paris, March 1795.

————. *Le cri des familles*. Paris, December 1794.

————. *Eloge de M. Marmontel*. Paris, 1805.

————. *Mélanges de littérature et de philosophie du dix-huitième siècle*. 4 vols. Paris, 1818.

————. *Mémoire des députés de la ville de Tulles*. Paris, 1790.

————. *Mémoires de l'abbé Morellet, de l'Académie Française, sur le dix-huitième siècle et sur la Révolution*. 2 vols. Paris, 1821.

————. *Moyen de disposer utilement, pour la nation, des biens ecclésiastiques*. S.l. (Paris), December 1789.

————. *Nouvelle discussion des motifs des douze notables du bureau de* MONSIEUR *contre l'avis des treize*. Paris, 1788.

————. *Observations sur la loi des otages*. Paris, 1799.

————. *Observations sur le projet de former une assemblée nationale sur le modèle des états généraux de 1614*. Paris, 1788.

————. *Observations sur une dénonciation de la Gazette littéraire*. Paris, 1765.

————. *Pensées libres sur la liberté de la presse*. Paris, 1797.

————. *Petit écrit sur une matière intéressante*. Toulouse (?), 1756.

————. *Préservatif contre un écrit intitulé: "Adresse à l'Assemblée nationale, sur la liberté des opinions, etc."* Paris, s.d.

————. *Projet de réponse du roi à un mémoire répandu sous le titre de mémoire des princes*. Paris, 1788.

————. *Réflexions du lendemain*. Paris, August 1789.

————. *Réflexions sur les avantages de la liberté d'écrire et d'imprimer sur les matières de l'administration, écrites en 1764. . . .* Paris, 1775.

————. *Réfutation du livre qui a pour titre dialogues sur le commerce des blés*. S.l., 1774.

Morellet, abbé André, ed., trans. *Le Manuel des inquisiteurs, à l'usage des Inquisitions d'Espagne et de Portugal, ou abrégé de l'ouvrage intitulé: Directorium Inquisitorum composé vers 1358 par Nicolas Eymeric, Grand Inquisiteur dans le Royaume d'Arragon.* Lisbon (?), 1762.

———, ed. *Recueil des facéties Parisiennes pour les six premiers mois de l'an 1760.* S.l. n.d.

———. *Lettres de l'abbé Morellet de l'Académie Française à Lord Shelburne, depuis marquis de Landsdowne, 1772-1803.* E. Fitzmaurice, ed. Paris, 1898.

Naigeon, Jacques-André. *Adresse à l'Assemblée Nationale, sur la liberté des opinions, sur celle de la presse, etc.* Paris, 1790.

———. *Discours préliminaire, pour servir d'introduction à La Morale de Sénèque.* Paris, 1782.

———. "Lettre sur M. Roux," in Deleyre, *Eloge de M. Roux.* Amsterdam, 1777.

———. *Mémoires historiques et philosophiques sur la vie et les ouvrages de D. Diderot.* Paris, 1821.

———. *Philosophie ancienne et moderne.* 3 vols. Paris, 1791–l'An II.

———, ed. *De la tolérance dans la religion, ou de la liberté de conscience, par Crellius; L'intolérance convaincue de crime et de folie, ouvrage traduit de l'Anglais.* Baron d'Holbach, trans. London (Amsterdam), 1769.

———, ed. *Oeuvres de Denis Diderot.* 15 vols. Paris, An VIII.

———, ed. *Recueil philosophique, ou mélange de pièces sur la religion et la morale.* London (Amsterdam), 1770.

Raynal, abbé Guillaume-Thomas-François. *L'Abbé Raynal aux Etats Généraux.* Marseilles, 1789 (B.N., Imp.: 8⁰ Lb39.1430).

———. *Adresse de Guillaume-Thomas Raynal.* Paris, 1791 (B.N., Imp.: Lb39.4972). See infra, Chapter Eight, n. 32.

———. *Histoire du parlement de l'Angleterre.* London, 1748.

———. *Histoire du Stadthoudérat.* The Hague, 1747.

———. *Histoire philosophique et politique des établissements du commerce des Européens dans les Deux Indes.* 3rd ed. 10 vols. Geneva, 1781: collection of Firestone Library, Princeton Univ.

———. "Nouvelles littéraires," in Grimm, *Corr. litt.,* I and II, 1-238.

Roux, Augustin. *Nouvelle encyclopédie portative, ou Tableau générale des connaissances humaines.* 2 vols. Paris, 1761.

———. *Recherches historiques et critiques, sur les différens moyens qu'on a employés jusqu'à présent pour réfroidir les liqueurs. . . .* S.l., 1758.

———, ed. *Annales typographiques, ou Notice du progrès des connaissances humaines.* 10 vols. Paris, 1760-1763.

———, ed., trans. *Collection académique.* Vol. II: *Transactions philosophiques.* Dijon and Paris, 1755.

————, ed. *Journal de médecine, chirurgie, pharmacie, etc., Dédié à S.A.S. Mgr le comte de Clermont, Prince du Sang.* Vols. XVII-XLVI (July 1762–July 1777).

————, ed., trans. (with Baron d'Holbach). *Recueil des mémoires les plus intéressants de chymie et d'histoire naturelle, contenus dans les actes de l'Académie d'Upsal, et dans les mémoires de l'Académie Royale des Sciences de Stockholm. . . .* 2 vols. Paris, 1764.

———— and Goulin and La Chenaye-Des-Bois. *Dictionnaire domestique portatif, contenant toutes les connaissances relatives à l'économie domestique et rurale. . . .* 3 vols. Paris, 1762-1763.

Saint-Lambert, Jean-François de. *Histoire de la vie et des ouvrages de M. Helvétius.* London (?), 1772.

————. *Principes des moeurs chez toutes les nations, ou Catéchisme universel.* 6 vols. Paris, 1798.

Suard, Joseph-Baptiste-Antoine. "Correspondance littéraire avec le margrave de Bayreuth." G. Bonno, ed. *University of California Publications in Modern Philology* XVIII (1934), 141-234.

————. *Mémoires et correspondances historiques et littéraires.* C. Nisard, ed. Paris, 1858.

————. *Mélanges de littérature, publiés par J.-B.-A. Suard.* 3 vols. Paris, 1803. (*Mélanges de littérature.* 2 vols. Paris, 1804.)

————, trans. *Exposé succinct de la contestation qui s'est élevée entre M. Hume et M. Rousseau, avec les pièces justificatives.* London, 1766.

————. *Lettres inédites de Suard à Wilkes.* G. Bonno, ed. Berkeley, 1932.

————. *Madame de Staël et J.-B.-A. Suard, correspondance inédite (1786-1817).* R. de Luppé, ed. Geneva, 1970.

V. PRIMARY SOURCES (contemporaries of the coterie holbachique)

d'Angiviller, comte. "Episodes de ma vie," in *Efterladte Papierer fra den Reventlowske Familiekreds I Tidsrummet 1770-1827.* L. Bobé, ed. Copenhagen, 1895-1927. Vol. 7: *Udvalgte Breve Og Optegnelser.*

————. *Mémoires de Charles Claude Flahaut Comte de la Billarderie d'Angiviller. Notes sur les mémoires de Marmontel.* L. Bobé, ed. Paris, 1933.

Aubert, F. *Réfutation de Bélisaire et de ses oracles. . . .* Basel (Paris), 1768.

Bachaumont et al. *Mémoires secrets pour servir à l'histoire de la République des lettres en France.* 36 vols. London, 1780-1789. (Volume III is mispaginated, pp. 275-334 being numbered as pp. 265-324; I have maintained the correct sequence in citations.)

Bailly, J.-S. *Mémoires de Bailly.* S.-A. Berville and J. F. Barrière, eds. 3 vols. Paris, 1821-1822.

Barbier, A.-A. *Dictionnaire des ouvrages anonymes et pseudonymes . . . accompagné de notes historiques et critiques.* 2nd edn. 4 vols. Paris, 1822-1827. (3rd edn. 4 vols. Paris, 1872-1879.)

Barbier, E. F. *Chronique de la régence et du règne de Louis XV (1718-1763), ou Journal de Barbier.* Charpentier, ed. 8 vols. Paris, 1866.

Barruel, abbé A. de. *Mémoires pour servir à l'histoire du Jacobinisme.* 4 vols. London, 1797-1798.

Beaumont, Christophe de. *Mandement de Monseigneur l'Archevêque de Paris, portant condemnation d'un livre qui a pour titre:* BELISAIRE, *par M. Marmontel. . . .* Paris, 1768.

Beccaria, C. *Opere.* S. Romagnoli, ed. 2 vols. Florence, 1958.

Bergier, abbé N.-S. *Examen du matérialisme, ou Réfutation du Système de la nature.* 2 vols. Paris, 1771.

———. "Lettres inédites de Bergier." L. Pingaud, ed. *Mémoires de l'Académie des sciences, belles-lettres et arts de Besançon.* Besançon, 1891.

Bonnefonds and Nepveu. *Notice de livres précieux . . . de manuscrits . . . de lettres autographes . . . dont la vente aura lieu les 28, 29, 30 et 31 mars . . . 1832.* Paris, 1832.

Boulanger, N.-A. *Oeuvres de Boullanger* (containing several falsely attributed works among its contents). 10 vols. Paris, 1792.

———. *Recherches sur l'origine du despotisme oriental.* S.l., 1761.

Brifaut, C. *Oeuvres de M. Charles Brifaut.* M. Rives and A. Bignon, eds. 6 vols. Paris, 1858.

Brissot de Warville, J.-P. *Mémoires de Brissot . . . sur ses contemporains et la révolution française.* F. de Montrol, ed. 4 vols. Paris, 1830-1832.

Buffon, G.-L. *Correspondance inédite de Buffon.* 2 vols. Paris, 1860.

Carlyle, A. *The Autobiography of Dr. Alexander Carlyle of Inveresk, 1722-1805.* J. H. Burton, ed. London and Edinburgh, 1910.

Castillon, Johann von. *Observations sur le livre intitulé Système de la nature.* Berlin, 1771.

Catherine II. *Lettres de Cathérine II à Grimm.* St. Petersburg, 1885.

Cérutti, B. "Lettre sur d'Holbach." *Journal de Paris* (1789), Supplement to No. 336, 2 Dec., pp. 1567-1568.

Chastellux, A. *Notice sur le Marquis de Chastellux par M. Alfred de Chastellux, son fils.* Paris, 1822.

Chaudon, L.-M. *Anti-dictionnaire philosophique.* 2 vols. Paris, 1775.

Choiseul, duc de. *Mémoires du Duc de Choiseul (1719-1785).* F. Calmettes, ed. Paris, 1904.

Coger, abbé. *Examen de Bélisaire de M. Marmontel.* New edn. Paris, 1767.

Collé, C. *Journal et mémoires de Charles Collé sur les hommes de lettres, les ouvrages dramatiques et les événements les plus mémora-*

bles du règne de Louis XV. H. Bonhomme, ed. 3 vols. New edn. Paris, 1868.

Condorcet, marquis de. *Correspondance inédite de Condorcet et Turgot, 1770-1779*. C. Henry, ed. Paris, 1883.

———. *Eloges des académiciens de l'Académie Royale des Sciences.* . . . 5 vols. Paris, 1799.

Constant, B. *Journaux intimes*. A. Roulin and C. Roth, eds. Paris, 1952.

Deffand, marquise du. *Lettres de la Marquise du Deffand à Horace Walpole*. P. Toynbee, ed. 3 vols. London, 1912.

Deleyre. *Eloge de M. Roux, docteur-régent et professeur de chymie à la Faculté de Paris*. Amsterdam, 1777.

Dizé, M. J.-J. *Précis historique sur la vie et les travaux de Jean D'Arcet*. Paris, An x.

d'Epinay, Mme. *Gli Ultimi Anni della Signora D'Epinay. Lettere Inedite All'Abate Galiani (1773-1782)*. F. Nicolini, ed. Bari, 1933.

———. *Mémoires de Madame D'Epinay*. P. Boiteau, ed. 2 vols. Paris, 1863.

Favart, C. S. *Mémoires et correspondances littéraires*. 3 vols. Paris, 1808.

Frederick II (King of Prussia). *Oeuvres posthumes de Frédéric II, roi de Prusse*. 15 vols. Berlin, 1788.

———. *Posthumous Works of Frederick II*. T. Holcroft, trans. 13 vols. London, 1789.

Garat, D.-J. *Mémoires historiques sur le XVIIIe siècle et sur M. Suard*. 2nd edn. 2 vols. Paris, 1821.

Garrick, D. *The Diary of David Garrick, being a record of his memorable trip to Paris in 1751*. R. C. Alexander, ed. New York, 1928.

———. *The Letters of David Garrick*. D. M. Little and G. M. Kahrl, eds. 3 vols. Cambridge, Mass., 1963.

Genlis, Mme de. *Les Dîners du Baron d'Holbach*. Paris, 1822.

Geoffrin, Mme. *Correspondance inédite du Roi Stanislaus-Auguste Poniatowski et de Mme Geoffrin (1764-1777)*. C. de Moüy, ed. Paris, 1875.

Gibbon, E. *The Autobiographies of Edward Gibbon*. J. Murray, ed. London, 1896.

———. *The Letters of Edward Gibbon*. J. E. Norton, ed. 3 vols. London, 1956.

Gleichen, baron de. *Souvenirs de Charles-Henri, Baron de Gleichen*. P. Grimblot, ed. Paris, 1868.

Hume, D. *The Letters of David Hume*. J.Y.T. Greig, ed. 2 vols. Oxford, 1932.

———. *Letters of Eminent Persons Addressed to David Hume*. J. H. Burton, ed. Edinburgh, 1849.

———. *New Letters of David Hume*. R. Klibansky and E. C. Mossner, eds. Oxford, 1964.

La Harpe, J.-F. de. *Correspondance inédite de Jean-François de La Harpe.* A. Jovicevich, ed. Paris, 1965.

――――. *Lycée, ou Cours de littérature ancienne et moderne.* 16 vols. Paris, 1799-1805.

de Legge. *Pièces relatives à l'examen de Bélisaire.* Paris, 1768.

Lespinasse, Mlle de. *Lettres de Mlle de Lespinasse.* E. Asse, ed. Paris, 1906.

――――. *Lettres inédites de Mademoiselle de Lespinasse.* C. Henry, ed. Paris, 1887.

Malouet, baron de. *Mémoires.* 2 vols. Paris, 1868.

Maréchal, S. *Dictionnaire des athées anciens et modernes.* Paris, 1800.

Meslier, J. *Le Testament de Jean Meslier.* R. Charles, ed. 3 vols. Amsterdam, 1864.

Métra, F. *Correspondance secrète, politique et littéraire.* 18 vols. London, 1787-1790.

d'Oberkirch, baronne. *Mémoires de la baronne d'Oberkirch.* Comte de Montbrison, ed. 2 vols. Paris, 1853.

Palissot, C. *Mémoires pour servir à l'histoire de notre littérature.* . . . 2nd edn. 2 vols. Paris, 1803.

Roland, Mme. *Lettres de Madame Roland. Nouvelle Série (1767-1780).* C. Perroud, ed. 2 vols. Paris, 1913-1915.

――――. *Mémoires de Madame Roland.* C. Perroud, ed. 2 vols. Paris, 1905.

Romilly, Sir S. *The Life of Sir Samuel Romilly, Written by Himself.* 3rd edn. 2 vols. London, 1842.

Rousseau, J.-J. *Les Confessions.* J. Voisine, ed. Paris, 1964.

――――. *Correspondance complète de Jean-Jacques Rousseau.* R. A. Leigh, ed. Geneva, 1965–.

――――. *Correspondance générale de Jean-Jacques Rousseau.* T. Dufour, ed. 20 vols. Paris, 1924-1934.

Ségur, comte de. *Mémoires et anecdotes.* 2 vols. Paris, 1859.

Sinéty, A.-L.-E. de. *Réflexions importantes sur l'adresse présentée à l'Assemblée nationale, le 31 mai 1791, par Guillaume-Thomas Raynal.* Paris, 1791.

Sterne, L. *Letters of Lawrence Sterne.* Oxford: Shakespeare Head Press, 1927.

――――. *The Works of Lawrence Sterne.* 7 vols. Dublin, 1779.

Suard, Mme. *Essais de Mémoires sur M. Suard.* Paris, 1820.

Tilly, comte A. de. *Mémoires du Comte Alexandre de Tilly, pour servir à l'histoire des moeurs de la fin du 18ᵉ siècle.* 3 vols. Paris, 1828.

Tressan, comte de. *Souvenirs du Comte de Tressan.* Mⁱˢ de Tressan, ed. Versailles, 1897.

Turgot, A.-R. *Les XXXVII vérités opposées aux XXXVII impiétés de Bélisaire, par un Bachelier Ubiquiste.* Paris, 1767.

Université de Paris, Faculté de Théologie. *Censure de la Faculté de Théologie de Paris, contre le livre qui a pour titre, Bélisaire.* Paris, 1767.

———. *Indiculus propositionum excerptarum ex libro cui titulus, Bélisaire.* Paris, 1767.

Verri, P. and A. *Carteggio di Pietro e di Alessandro Verri.* E. Greppi, A. Giulini, and G. Seregni, eds. Milan, 1923–.

Voisenon, abbé de. *Anecdotes littéraires.* P. Lacroix, ed. Paris, 1880.

Voltaire, A. de. *Voltaire's Correspondence.* T. Besterman, ed. 107 vols. Geneva, 1953-1965.

Walpole, H. *The Letters of Horace Walpole, Fourth Earl of Orford.* P. Toynbee, ed. 16 vols. Oxford, 1903-1905.

———. *Supplement to the Letters of Horace Walpole, Fourth Earl of Orford.* P. Toynbee, ed. 2 vols. Oxford, 1918.

Weber, J. *Mémoires de Weber concernant Marie-Antoinette.* St.-A. and J. F. Barrière, eds. 2 vols. Paris, 1822. (First published in London, 1807.)

Wilkes, J. *The Correspondence of the Late John Wilkes with His Friends.* J. Alman, ed. 5 vols. London, 1805.

VI. Secondary Sources

d'Andlau, B. *Helvétius, Seigneur de Voré (avec des documents inédits).* Paris, 1934.

Avezac-Lavigne, C. *Diderot et la Société du Baron d'Holbach.* Paris, 1875.

Bacquié, F. *Les inspecteurs des manufactures sous l'Ancien Régime, 1669-1791.* Toulouse, 1927.

Becker, C. *The Heavenly City of the Eighteenth-Century Philosophers.* New Haven, 1932.

Belin, J.-P. *Le mouvement philosophique de 1748 à 1789: Etude sur la diffusion des idées des philosophes à Paris d'après les documents concernant l'histoire de la librairie.* Paris, 1913.

Besthorn, Rudolf. *Textkritische Studien zum Werk Holbachs.* Berlin, 1969.

Boissier, G. *L'Académie Française sous l'Ancien Régime.* Paris, 1909.

Brummer, R. *Studien zur französischen Aufklärungsliteratur im Anschlusz an J.-A. Naigeon.* Breslau, 1932.

Brunel, L. *Les Philosophes et l'Académie Française au 18e siècle.* Paris, 1884.

Callot, E. *Six philosophes français du XVIIIe siècle.* Annecy, 1963.

———. *La philosophie de la vie au XVIIIe siècle.* Paris, 1965.

Carson, G. B., Jr. *The Chevalier de Chastellux, Soldier and Philosophe.* Chicago, 1944.

Cazes, A. *Grimm et les Encyclopédistes.* Paris, 1933.

341

Challamel, A. *Les Clubs Contre-Révolutionnaires*. Paris, 1895.

Cragg, G. R. *The Church and the Age of Reason (1648-1789)*. Harmondsworth, 1960.

Crocker, L. G. *Diderot the Embattled Philosopher*. New York, 1966.

———. *Jean-Jacques Rousseau*. Vol. I: *The Quest (1712-1758)*. New York, 1968.

Cumming, Ian. *Helvétius*. London, 1955.

Cushing, M. P. *Baron d'Holbach: A Study of 18th Century Radicalism in France*. New York, 1914.

Cuzacq, R. *Un savant chalossais: le chimiste Jean Darcet (1724-1801) et sa famille*. Mont-de-Marsan, 1955.

Damiron, P. *Mémoires pour servir à l'histoire de la philosophie au XVIIIe siècle*. 3 vols. Paris, 1858 (1857)-1864.

Darnton, R. *Mesmerism and the End of the Enlightenment in France*. Cambridge, Mass., 1968.

Daumard, A., and Furet, F. *Structures et relations sociales à Paris au XVIIIe siècle*. Paris, 1961.

Delauney, P. *Le monde médical Parisien au dix-huitième siècle*. 2nd edn. Paris, 1906.

———. *La vie médicale au XVIe, XVIIe et XVIIIe siècles*. Paris, 1935.

Delort, J. *Histoire de la détention des philosophes et des gens de lettres à la Bastille et à Vincennes*. 3 vols. Paris, 1829.

Deschamps, N. *Les sociétés secrètes et la société*. 5th edn. 2 vols. Paris, 1881.

Dieckmann, H. *Inventaire du fonds vandeul et inédits de Diderot*. Geneva, 1951.

Dommanget, M. *Le Curé Meslier*. Paris, 1965.

Du Puy de Clinchamps, P. *La Noblesse*. Paris, 1959.

Ehrard, J., ed. *Jean-François Marmontel (1723-1799)*. Clermont-Ferrand, 1971.

Fellows, O. E. et al. *Diderot Studies*. 17 vols. Geneva, 1949-1973.

Feugère, A. *Un Précurseur de la Révolution, L'Abbé Raynal (1713-1796). Documents inédits*. Angoulême, 1922.

Frankel, C. *The Faith of Reason: The Idea of Progress in the French Enlightenment*. New York, 1948.

Fredman, A. G. *Diderot and Sterne*. New York, 1955.

Froidcourt, G. de. *L'Abbé Raynal au Pays de Liège*. Liège, 1946.

Gaulmier, J. *L'Idéologue Volney (1757-1820)*. Beirut, 1951.

Gay, P. *The Enlightenment: An Interpretation*. Vol. I: *The Rise of Modern Paganism*. New York, 1966.

Hampton, J. *Nicolas-Antoine Boulanger et la science de son temps*. Geneva, 1955.

Hazard, P. *La pensée Européenne au XVIIIe siècle de Montesquieu à Lessing*. 3 vols. Paris, 1946.

Hedgcock, F. A. *David Garrick and His French Friends*. New York, 1912.

Hermann-Mascard, N. *La censure des livres à Paris à la fin de l'Ancien Régime*. Paris, 1968.

Hubert, R. *D'Holbach et ses amis*. Paris, 1928.

Hunter, A. C. *J.-B.-A. Suard, un introducteur de la littérature Anglaise en France*. Paris, 1925.

Keim, A. *Helvétius, sa vie et son oeuvre. d'après ses ouvrages, des écrits divers et des documents inédits*. Paris, 1907 (reprinted, Geneva, 1970).

Krauss, W., and Meyer, W., eds. *Grundpositionen der französischen Aufklärung*. Berlin, 1955.

Lavergne, L. de. *Le Marquis de Chastellux*. Paris, 1864.

Lenel, S. *Marmontel: Un homme de lettres au XVIIIᵉ siècle, d'après des documents nouveaux et inédits*. Paris, 1902.

Lough, J. *The Contributors to the Encyclopédie*. London, 1973.

Magnotti, L. *L'Abbé Ferdinand Galiani, sa philanthropie et ses rapports avec la France*. Naples, 1933.

Mangeot, G. *Autour d'un foyer lorrain: La famille de Saint-Lambert (1596-1795)*. Nancy, 1913.

Manuel, F. E. *The Eighteenth Century Confronts the Gods*. Cambridge, Mass., 1959.

Marcel, L.-F. *Le Frère de Diderot*. Paris, 1913.

Marx, M. *Charles Georges Leroy und seine "Lettres philosophiques." Ein Beitrag zur Geschichte der vergleichenden Psychologie der XVIII Jahrhunderts*. Strasbourg, 1898.

Masson, F. *L'Académie Française, 1629-1793*. Paris, 1912.

Mayer, J. *Diderot homme de science*. Rennes, 1959.

Mellottée, P. *Histoire économique de l'Imprimerie*. Vol. I: *L'Imprimerie sous l'Ancien Régime*. Paris, 1905.

Mossner, E. C. *The Life of David Hume*. Austin, 1954.

Mousnier, R., Labrousse, E., Bouloiseau, M. *Le XVIIIᵉ siècle, l'époque des lumières, 1715-1815*. Paris, 1953.

di Nardis, L. *Saint-Lambert, Scienza e paesaggio nella poesia del Settecento*. Rome, 1961.

Nauroy, C. *Révolutionnaires*. Paris, 1891.

Naville, P. *Paul Thiry d'Holbach et la philosophie scientifique au XVIIIᵉ siècle*. Paris, 1943. (New edn., rev. and aug. Paris, 1967.)

Ozanam, D. *La Disgrace d'un Premier Commis: Tercier et l'affaire de l'esprit*. Paris, 1956.

Palmer, R. R. *Catholics and Unbelievers in Eighteenth Century France*. New York, 1961 (reprint of 1939 edition).

Picard, R. *Les Salons littéraires et la Société Française*. New York, 1943.

Picot, J. *Un philosophe anti-colonialiste: l'Abbé Raynal.* Paris, 1967.

Plékhanov, G. *Essais sur l'histoire du matérialisme, d'Holbach, Helvétius, Marx.* Paris, 1957.

Pomeau, R. *La religion de Voltaire.* Paris, 1956.

Pottinger, D. T. *Censorship in France During the Ancien Régime.* Boston, 1954.

Proust, J. *Diderot et l'Encyclopédie.* Paris, 1967.

Quérard, J. M. *Les supercheries littéraires dévoilées.* 2nd edn. 3 vols. Paris, 1869-1872.

Rae, J. *Life of Adam Smith* (1895), published with J. Viner, *Guide to John Rae's Life of Adam Smith.* New York, 1965.

Robert, A., et al. *Dictionnaire des parlementaires français.* 5 vols. Paris, 1889-1890.

Rossi, J. *The Abbé Galiani in France.* New York, 1930.

Saint-Surin, P. T. *Notice sur Marmontel.* Paris, 1824.

Scott, W. R. *Adam Smith as Student and Professor. With unpublished documents.* . . . Glasgow, 1937.

Secrétan, C. *Un Aspect de la chimie prélavoisienne (Le Cours de G.-F. Rouelle).* Lausanne, 1943.

Shaw, E. P. *Problems and Policies of Malesherbes as Directeur de la Librairie in France (1750-1763).* S.l. (SUNY Press), 1966.

Silvestre de Sacy, J. *Le Comte d'Angiviller, dernier directeur général des bâtiments du roi.* Paris, 1953.

Smart, A. *The Life and Art of Allen Ramsay.* London, 1952.

Smiley, J. R. *Diderot's Relations with Grimm.* Urbana, 1950.

Smith, D. W. *Helvétius: A Study in Persecution.* Oxford, 1965.

Topazio, V. W. *D'Holbach's Moral Philosophy: Its Background and Development.* Geneva, 1956.

Tourneux, M. *La Bibliothèque et les papiers de Grimm pendant et après la Révolution.* Paris, 1882.

Varnum, F. *Un philosophe cosmopolite du XVIIIe siècle, le Chevalier de Chastellux.* Paris, 1936.

Vartanian, A. *Diderot and Descartes: A Study of Scientific Naturalism in the Enlightenment.* Princeton, 1953.

――――. *La Mettrie's l'Homme Machine: A Study in the Origins of an Idea.* Princeton, 1960.

Venturi, F. *La Jeunesse de Diderot, 1713-1753.* J. Bertrand, trans. Paris, 1939.

――――. *Le origini dell'Enciclopedia.* Rome, 1946.

Vercruysse, J. *Bibliographie descriptive des écrits du baron d'Holbach.* Paris, 1971.

Vyverberg, H. *Historical Pessimism in the French Enlightenment.* Cambridge, Mass., 1958.

Wade, I. O. *The Clandestine Organization and Diffusion of Philosophic Ideas in France from 1700-1750.* Princeton, 1938.

Wickwar, W. H. *Baron d'Holbach: A Prelude to the French Revolution*. London, 1935.

Wilson, A. M. *Diderot* (incorporating *Diderot: The Testing Years, 1713-1759*. New York, 1957). New York, 1972.

Wolpe, H. *Raynal et sa Machine de Guerre*. "*L'Histoire des Deux Indes*" *et ses Perfectionnements*. Stanford, 1957.

Zeiler, H. *Les collaborateurs médicaux de l'Encyclopédie de Diderot et d'Alembert*. Paris, 1934.

VII. ARTICLES

Bingham, A. J. "The Abbé Bergier: An Eighteenth-Century Catholic Apologist." *Modern Language Review* III (1959), 337-350.

Boiteux, L. A. "Voltaire et le Ménage Suard," in Besterman, ed., *Studies on Voltaire and the Eighteenth Century* I (1955), 19-109.

de Booy, J. T. "L'Abbé Coger, dit *Coge Pecus*, lecteur de Voltaire et de d'Holbach," in Besterman, ed., *Studies on Voltaire and the Eighteenth Century* XVII (1961), 183-196.

Dieckmann, H. "L'*Encyclopédie* et le Fonds Vandeul." *Revue d'histoire littéraire* III (1951), 318-332.

———. "J.-A. Naigeon's Analysis of Diderot's *Rêve de d'Alembert*." *Modern Language Notes* LIII, no. 7 (1938), 479-486.

———. "The Sixth Volume of Saint-Lambert's Works." *The Romanic Review* XLII, no. 2 (April 1951), 109-121.

Higgins, D. "The Terrorists' Favorite Authors: Some Statistics from Revolutionary Literature." *Modern Language Review* III (1959), 401-404.

Kafker, F. A. "A List of Contributors to Diderot's Encyclopédie." *French Historical Studies* III, no. 1 (Spring 1963), 106-117.

———. "Les Encyclopédistes et la Terreur." *Revue d'histoire moderne et contemporaine* XIV (1967), 284-295.

Kors, A., "The Myth of the Coterie Holbachique." *French Historical Studies* (forthcoming: Fall, 1976).

Kuwabara, T., Turimi, S., and Higuti, K. "Les Collaborateurs de l'Encyclopédie." *Zinbun, Memoir of the Research Institute for Humanistic Studies, Kyoto University*. No. 1 (1957), 1-22.

Lanson, G. "Questions diverses sur l'histoire de l'esprit philosophique en France avant 1750." *Revue d'histoire littéraire* I (1912), 1-29, and II (1912), 293-317.

Leigh, R. A. "Les Amitiés Françaises du Dr. Burney." *Revue de littérature comparée* II (1951), 161-194.

Lough, J. "Le baron d'Holbach. Quelques documents inédits ou peu connus." *Revue d'histoire littéraire* IV (1957), 524-543.

———. "Essai de bibliographie critique des publications du baron d'Holbach." *Revue d'histoire littéraire* II (1939), 215-234; and III (1947), 314-318.

———. "Supplément à la bibliographie des ouvrages du baron d'Holbach." *Revue d'histoire littéraire* II (1936), 287-288 (supplementary to D. Mornet, "Bibliographie d'un certain nombre d'ouvrages philosophiques du XVIIIᵉ siècle et particulièrement de d'Holbach [jusqu'en 1789]." *Revue d'histoire littéraire* II (1933), 259-281).

Lüthy, H. "Les Mississipiens de Steckbar et la fortune des barons d'Holbach." *Schweizer Beiträge zur allgemeinen Geschichte* XIII (1955), 143-163.

Lux, J. "Fréderich Melchior Grimm." *Revue Bleue* (22 June 1912), 799-800.

Marcu, E. "Un encyclopédiste oublié: Formey." *Revue d'histoire littéraire* III (1953), 296-305.

Mertz, R. "Les amitiés françaises de Hume et le mouvement des idées." *Revue de littérature comparée* IV (1929), 644-713.

Monty, J. R. "Grimm et les Nouvelles Littéraires de Raynal." *Modern Language Notes* VI (1961), 536-539.

Pommier, J. "Le Problème Naigeon." *Revue des sciences humaines* I (1949), 2-11.

Renwick, J. "Reconstruction and interpretation of the genesis of the *Bélisaire* affair, with an unpublished letter from Marmontel to Voltaire," in Besterman, ed., *Studies on Voltaire and the Eighteenth Century* LIII (1967).

Smiley, J. R. "A List of Diderot's Articles for Grimm's *Correspondance littéraire*." *Romanic Review* III (1951), 189-197.

———. "The Subscribers of Grimm's *Correspondance littéraire*." *Modern Language Notes* I (1947), 44-46.

Topazio, V. W., "Diderot's Supposed Contributions to Raynal's Work." *Symposium* (Syracuse, N.Y.), vol. XII, nos. 1-2 (Spring–Fall 1958), 102-116.

———. "D'Holbach, Apostle of Atheism." *Modern Language Quarterly* III (1956), 252-260.

Vernière, P. "Le Spinozisme et l'Encyclopédie." *Revue d'histoire littéraire* III (1951), 347-358.

Watts, G. B. "The *Encyclopédie méthodique*." *PMLA* IV (1958), Part One, 348-366.

Index

Library of Congress Cataloging in Publication Data

Kors, Alan C
    D'Holbach's coterie: an enlightenment in Paris.

    Bibliography: p.
    1. Holbach, Paul Henri Thiry, baron d', 1723-1789.
2. Enlightenment. 3. Paris—Intellectual life.
4. Philosophy, French—18th century. I. Title.
B2057.K67   194   75-2995
ISBN 0-691-05224-7